Mapping Ideology in Discourse Studies

Contributions to the Sociology of Language

Edited by
Ofelia García
Francis M. Hult

Founding editor
Joshua A. Fishman

Volume 118

Mapping Ideology in Discourse Studies

Edited by
Simo K. Määttä
Marika K. Hall

DE GRUYTER
MOUTON

ISBN 978-1-5015-2211-6
e-ISBN (PDF) 978-1-5015-1360-2
e-ISBN (EPUB) 978-1-5015-1373-2
ISSN 1861-0676

Library of Congress Control Number: 2022931138

Bibliographic information published by the Deutsche Nationalbibliothek
The Deutsche Nationalbibliothek lists this publication in the Deutsche Nationalbibliografie;
detailed bibliographic data are available on the Internet at http://dnb.dnb.de.

© 2023 Walter de Gruyter Inc., Boston/Berlin
This volume is text- and page-identical with the hardback published in 2022.
Cover image: sculpies/shutterstock
Typesetting: Integra Software Services Pvt. Ltd.
Printing and binding: CPI books GmbH, Leck

www.degruyter.com

Contents

Simo K. Määttä & Marika K. Hall
Chapter 1
Introduction —— 1

Simo K. Määttä
Chapter 2
Discourse and ideology in French thought until Foucault and Pêcheux —— 21

Samuel Vernet
Chapter 3
Teaching French in Acadia: From a discourse of linguistic diversity to a standard ideology —— 45

Mariem Guellouz
Chapter 4
Ideology and emancipation through the prism of performativity: Immolation and mottos of struggle as moments of popular counter-discourse —— 67

Nadia Louar
Chapter 5
Language trouble.s —— 87

Jef Verschueren
Chapter 6
The ideological grounding of the new normal: Anti-discourse meets utopia —— 103

Elizabeth R. Miller
Chapter 7
Hiding in plain sight: Methodological ideologies in discourse research in applied linguistics —— 117

Teun A. van Dijk
Chapter 8
Ideology in cognition and discourse —— 137

Elizabeth Peterson
Chapter 9
Licensing through English —— 157

Jyrki Kalliokoski & Anne Mäntynen
Chapter 10
Language ideologies and the translation of scholarly texts —— 179

Eleanor Lutman-White & Jo Angouri
Chapter 11
Negotiating ideologies and the moral order in child protection social work —— 201

Raquel Lázaro Gutiérrez & Jesús Manuel Tejero González
Chapter 12
Challenging ideologies and fostering intercultural competence: The discourses of healthcare staff about linguistic and cultural barriers, interpreters, and mediators —— 223

Brett A. Diaz & Marika K. Hall
Chapter 13
Taking a corpus-based approach to investigating discourse and ideology in the language sciences —— 247

Christina Higgins
Chapter 14
Afterword —— 273

Index —— 285

Simo K. Määttä & Marika K. Hall
Chapter 1
Introduction
Ideology and discourse: Convergent and divergent developments

Keywords: discourse, ideology, discourse studies, critical theory, epistemology

1 Introduction

For those of us who study language and social practices, the concepts of discourse and ideology provide a means to examine social structures – the what, how, and why of communication. As such, discourse and ideology are quintessential, albeit contested, concepts in many critically and functionally oriented branches of the study of language, such as linguistic anthropology, critical discourse studies, sociolinguistics, and sociology of language. Throughout this introductory chapter, we broadly refer to "discourse studies" as an umbrella term for various approaches that incorporate the social aspects of language as a central component of their analyses.

With many ways of understanding and using the concepts, the line between discourse and ideology can become blurry (see, e.g., Wodak and Meyer 2001). For example, both "racist ideologies" and "racist discourse" are used, but there seems to be a preference for "feminist discourse" over "feminist ideology". In both examples, the problem is accentuated by the fact that the adjective (*racist* and *feminist*) qualifying the noun *discourse* or *ideology* reflects an ideological stance. In a similar vein, we see adjectives such as "political", "religious", and "social" attached to both discourse and ideology (see Diaz and Hall 2022 [this volume]). To complicate matters even further, some scholars view discourse as ideological, while others consider ideology to be discourse (cf. Wodak and Meyer 2001; Lopes 2015). As with all concepts dealing with the social, discourse and ideology are not fully referential and entirely distinguishable – they are also associated with different theoretical and epistemological traditions (Purvis and Hunt 1993: 473–474). It is therefore not surprising that the boundaries between discourse and ideology may constitute a challenge for junior and senior scholars alike.

The problematic relation between discourse and ideology is perhaps highlighted in today's rapidly changing world. Thus, recent public debates in, for example, Northern Europe and North America, where the editors are located, have been dominated by issues such as hate speech, social injustice and discrimination, conspiracy theories, fake news, and the spread of misinformation regarding, for example, politics, climate change, and health (see, e.g., Fløttum 2019; McIntosh and Mendoza-Denton 2020). Naturally, these are not novel issues, but changes in the means by which we communicate and the accelerated speed of remote communication certainly affect how we produce and consume information, as exemplified by the rise of social media and other forms of electronic communication. At the same time, the interconnectedness of language, discourse, and ideology continues to present challenges in inquiries within "traditional" themes such as nationalism, multilingualism, language contact, and institutional language use.

This volume explores some of the divergent ways in which the concepts of ideology and discourse may be defined and applied in various branches of sociolinguistics, critical discourse studies, and applied linguistics, with a specific focus on mapping the different solutions adopted when the notion of ideology is used as a theoretical or methodological tool in work engaged with discourse. The overarching objective of the volume is to contribute to theoretical and methodological knowledge about the manifestations of discourse and ideology, particularly as they are understood within western traditions of thought. Thus, rather than providing an all-encompassing definition of discourse and ideology and their relationship, the volume aims to explore how these concepts can be defined and used jointly and separately as theoretical and/or analytical concepts, depending on the nature of the data, the definition of the concepts and their relationships, and the epistemological roots activated in each context. More specifically, we aim to provide a variety of examples of how the potentially problematic relationship between discourse and ideology can be resolved by emphasizing one or the other, or by using them in contrast or in complement.

Most chapters in this volume emphasize the analysis of ideologies in discourse studies, although some chapters question which of these concepts should be used as a primary tool of analysis, and some use both on an equal footing. The various solutions proposed in the chapters concern both the connection between the concepts on a theoretical level and how they are used as analytical tools on a methodological level.

In the remainder of this introductory chapter, we summarize some of the most prominent theorizations of discourse and/or ideology in critical and functionalist approaches to the socially infused study of language, language use, and discourse. These include broad ontologies and epistemologies, approaches, and strands, as well as individual thinkers and schools of thought that are specific to a country or a university. We conclude the chapter by presenting a summary of the contents of each chapter of this collected volume, along with our final remarks.

2 Different understandings of ideology and discourse

In order to better understand the different conceptualizations of ideology and discourse, it is important to acknowledge how they are theorized in the various strands, approaches, or schools of thought. Beginning with the Marxist definition of ideology and the notion of critique, we weave through functionalism, French discourse analysis and Foucault, cultural studies, the Essex school of discourse analysis, critical linguistics, critical discourse studies, and linguistic anthropology, ending with recent developments in critical and third-wave sociolinguistics. Our goal is to provide the reader with a quick overview and a fertile starting point for the further examination of ideology and discourse throughout the rest of the volume and beyond.

Marxist roots. Most modern views on ideology stem from Marx, who used ideology with several different meanings (Marx and Engels 2010; Eagleton 1991: 63–70). For example, Geuss (1981: 4–26) distinguishes three conceptualizations of ideology in Marx's works: descriptive ("beliefs"), positive ("worldview"), and critical ("false and misleading conscience"), although the critical dimension is the most important. In subsequent use of the concept of ideology, Eagleton (1991: 1–2) identifies up to 16 scholarly, commonsense, and political definitions. Woolard (1998) summarizes the various definitions as corresponding to three main understandings of the concept: ideology can correspond to the reflection and expression of a specific social position and its experience and interests, signifying practices linked to power, or an instrument that distorts or rationalizes reality.

An important theory with a particularly notable impact on discourse studies that engage with ideology was Althusser's reading of ideology, including his concept of *interpellation*: individuals are constituted as subjects who are aware of their agency through ideology (Althusser 1971: 150–168). Other important elements in Althusser's work include his interpretations of Freud's concept of *overdetermination* and Bachelard's concept of *epistemological break*. According to Stuart Hall, this move away from the idea of false consciousness made theorizations focusing on the linguistic and discursive composition and construction of ideologies possible (Hall [1986] 1996a: 32). Thompson's (1984: 4) theorization of ideology, emphasizing the links between ideologies and "processes of maintaining domination", has also been influential in discourse studies.

Sociology of knowledge. Karl Mannheim's *Ideology and Utopia* was published in German in 1929 and in English in 1936. Mannheim (1936) made a distinction between *particular ideologies*, corresponding for example to the distorted views related to a given situation, and *total ideologies* that are shared by a social group and create a coherence to that group's view on reality, therefore also explaining the relative nature of knowledge. In addition, he distinguished between stability-oriented ideologies and transformation-oriented utopias. Mannheim's work was very influential in the Weimar Republic and was often criticized by thinkers who would later be identified as representing Critical Theory.

Critique. The idea of critique is one of the overarching features characterizing several chapters in this volume. For Kant, critique entailed roughly the analysis and determination of the nature and limits of knowledge and the concepts on which it is founded. In Foucault's (1984: 38) interpretation, "the age of the critique" is precisely the Enlightenment: since "humanity is going to put its own reason to use, without subjecting itself to any authority", critique is necessary to define "the conditions under which the use of reason is legitimate in order to determine what can be known, what must be done, and what may be hoped".

In Critical Theory, developed within the Frankfurt School from the 1930s onwards, critique took an overtly emancipatory and liberating role. Thus, according to Horkheimer ([1972] 1982: 246), the increase of knowledge is never the only objective of the theory; rather, the goal of theory is "to create a world which satisfies the needs and powers" of human beings and emancipates them from slavery. At the same time, Critical Theory emphasizes the critique of the Enlightenment and capitalism and its cultural industry: the Enlightenment did not make good on its promise, camouflaged a totalitarian core, and led to the instrumentalization of reason (Horkheimer and Adorno 2002). In addition to this "narrow sense" corresponding to the sociological theory of the Frankfurt School, critical theories have emerged in other disciplines, and they all share the goal of unveiling the workings of ideology and power structures as an explanation for the lack of freedom in society (Bohman 2021).

Functionalism and structuralism/formalism. Saussure's theory of language and the subsequent approach known as structuralism have had an important impact on most theorizations of discourse and ideology for the last 100 years, both within and outside the study of language. In certain schools of thoughts, structuralism and functionalism are combined: this is notably the case of structural functionalism in sociology and many other fields of social sciences. In the fields of inquiry focusing specifically on the analysis of language and discourse, however, one of the dividing lines can be drawn between functionalist and structuralist approaches (Hymes 1974: 79). Accordingly, the structuralist approach to linguistics emphasizes the description of language (*langue*) as a system, whereas the functionalist concentrates on situated usage (*parole*), the functions, meanings, and consequences of language use, and the constraints and affordances related to the users and the circumstances. In fact, since both structuralist and functionalist approaches are derived from structuralism, it would be more accurate to make a division between *formalist* and *functionalist* approaches (Schiffrin 1994: x, 3). On the other hand, divisions of this kind should be approached with caution because the border between the orientations is fuzzy – for example, systemic-functional grammar draws from both.

Structuralist/formalist approaches tend to define discourse as language beyond the sentence or simply language use, as opposed to the system, whereas functionalist approaches typically focus on the conditions of existence and production of discourse as language use, with varying degrees of importance accorded to the issue of power. The formalist/structuralist view of discourse is often attributed to Saussure, although definitions in which discourse corresponds to language use, and especially spoken language, can be traced back to at least the 16th century. In functionalist approaches to the study of language, the understanding of discourse has been influenced by the input of thinkers operating in adjacent fields such as history, philosophy, and sociology. The works of Foucault and the interpretations thereof in cultural studies have been particularly influential in this respect. Regarding ideology, its analysis tends to be restricted to functionalist approaches.

French discourse analysis (see also Määttä 2022 [this volume]). This denomination is widely used in France (Maingueneau 2002; Mazière 2005; 2010): *école française d'analyse du discours* ('French school of discourse analysis') or *analyse du discours française* ('French discourse analysis'). The analysis of ideology and the theorization of both ideology and discourse were major preoccupations during the first years of this endeavor, in the late 1960s and early 1970s, characterized by "generalized structuralism", or the spread of structuralism from linguistics to adjacent disciplines such as anthropology, psychoanalysis, history, and literary theory (Gadet 1989: 2; Dosse ([1992] 2012: 155). Several intellectual traditions and fashions were conflated in this era: Althusserian Marxism, Lacan's psychoanalysis, French epistemological and philological traditions, "enunciative" linguistics (*linguistique d'énonciation*), pragmatics and analytical philosophy, content analysis and Harris' discourse analysis, as well as the ideas of the Bakhtin circle and those derived from it, such as dialogism and intertextuality (Maingueneau 1991: 9–14). Compared to subsequent ramifications, for example in British cultural studies, French discourse analysis was characterized by its entrenching in linguistics (Mazière 2005: 41).

In the early years of French discourse analysis, a strong focus was laid on the detection of the undetectable, or the ideology, in texts (Maingueneau 1991: 13). One of the most influential theorists of this approach was Pêcheux, who combined Althusserian Marxism, structuralism, and psychoanalysis in his theory of ideology and discourse (see Pêcheux 1982). However, the attempts to conceptualize ideology in connection with discourse led to a certain impasse (Williams 1999: 130). In later theorizations, ideology was less important and appears to have merged with discourse to a certain extent, as exemplified by Mazière's (2005: 10) definition of discourse: "attested manifestation of overdetermination of all individual language use".[1] In fact, by the late 1970s and early 1980s, overtly Marxist orientations gradually subsided and left room for studies focusing on, for example, interaction, pragmatics, and argumentation (Williams 1999: 130; Maingueneau 2017: 131), as well as new studies on intertextuality and interdiscursivity (e.g., Courtine 1981; Authier-Revuz 1982).

Foucault (see also Määttä 2022 [this volume]). While Foucault is considered to be one of the most important discourse scholars across disciplines, his influence in French discourse analysis remained subterranean (Maingueneau 1991: 14; Mazière 2005: 58) and hidden (Williams 1999: 125). He preferred to avoid the term "ideology", but certain aspects of his theory of discourse (Foucault 1972) were reminiscent of the predominant theories of ideology of the era, including the material power of discourse and the fact that discourse reifies and transforms the objects of which it speaks. This combination resulted in a revolutionary theory of discourse in which the characterization of a statement as belonging to a discourse depends on a complex web of relations determining the place the subject can occupy, and has to occupy, in order to utter the statement precisely as belonging to a particular discursive formation (Foucault 1972: 38, 56, 78, 95). In addition to the concept of discourse, Foucault's theorizations of power (Foucault 1980), governmentality (Burchell, Gordon, and Miller 1991), and biopolitics (Foucault 2008), among other concepts, have had a decisive impact on many branches of humanities.

British cultural studies. Stuart Hall's theory of *representation* is the most famous example of the conceptualizations produced by scholars of this school of thought, which exemplifies Foucault's impact while at the same time operating with both discourse and ideology as theoretical and methodological tools (Hall 1997; Purvis and Hunt 1993: 473). Although this research tradition, associated strongly with the University of Birmingham, is not linguistic, its sources include linguistically oriented reflections on discourse and ideology. In addition, many critical approaches to discourse and ideology have been disseminated, filtered, and transformed by cultural studies. The British approach to cultural studies developed in the 1950s, 1960s, and 1970s and shared some of the same inspirations as French discourse analysis, namely Althusser and his theory of ideology, and later Gramsci and his notion of (cultural) hegemony, explaining the some-

---

1 In French, "manifestation attestée d'une surdetermination de toute parole individuelle".

times contradictory alliances between dominant and dominated strata of society (Hartley 2003: 93). These sources were followed by an interest in the French thought represented by Lacan and Barthes, and later on especially the theory of discourse and ideology developed by Pêcheux (Sawyer 2002: 442, 445). Foucault's concept of discourse became predominant in later works of cultural studies, and according to Sawyer (2002: 435) many cultural studies scholars actually attributed their definitions of discourse to Foucault retrospectively.

The graphic guidebook to cultural studies by Sardar and van Loon (1997: 14) defines discourse as consisting of "culturally or socially produced groups of ideas containing texts (which contain signs and codes) and representations (which describe power relations to Others)". Stuart Hall defines discourse as "sets of ready-made and preconstituted 'experiencings' displayed and arranged through language" (Hall 1977: 322), or as "a group of statements which provide a language for talking about – i.e., a way of representing – a particular kind of knowledge about a topic" (Hall [1992] 1996b: 201). As for ideology, Sardar and van Loon (1997: 46) represent Althusser as saying that "ideology provides a conceptual framework through which we interpret and make sense of our lived, material conditions", whereas Hall would continue by stating that "ideology therefore produces our culture, as well as our consciousness of who and what we are". Hall (1996a: 25–26) has also defined ideology as "the mental frameworks – the languages, the concepts, categories, imagery of thought, and the systems of representation – which different classes and social groups deploy in order to make sense of, figure out and render intelligible the way society works". These definitions illustrate the intersections between discourse and ideology, and a concern about the control of representations: discourse is the material means by which ideology recreates representations that also reflect the power relations in a society.

Essex school of discourse analysis. This school of thought, which focuses on the analysis of discourse and ideology, concentrates on the examination of political discourse rather than language, but it has had considerable influence on critical approaches to language, discourse, and ideology. The most important thinkers associated with this school are Laclau and Mouffe, who draw a clear distinction between discourse and ideology (Purvis and Hunt 1993: 473). The Essex school draws largely on the same sources as French discourse analysis and British cultural studies: Gramsci, Saussure, Althusser, Lacan, Foucault, Barthes, and Derrida. One of the most important concepts in Laclau's and Mouffe's ([1985] 2001: 105) thinking is *articulation*, or "any practice establishing a relation among elements such that their identity is modified as a result of the articulatory practice", whereas discourse corresponds to "the structured totality resulting from the articulatory practice". In this understanding, discourse is closely related to schools of thought: "the category of 'discourse' has a pedigree in contemporary thought going back to the three main intellectual currents of the twentieth century: analytical philosophy, phenomenology, and structuralism" (Laclau and Mouffe 2001: x–xi). According to Laclau and Mouffe, society as a whole is a discursive construction characterized by the omnipresence of ideology. In fact, Laclau and Mouffe rarely use the concept of ideology – they equate it with objectivity and prefer to use this latter term (Jørgensen and Phillips 2002: 37).

Critical linguistics. British critical linguistics, which developed in the late 1970s mostly at the University of East Anglia, constituted the first overtly critical approach to the study of language; ideology was a key concept and became a legitimate object of linguistic inquiry (de Beaugrande 1999: 267). In line with British cultural studies and post-Marxist thought, ideology was regarded as ubiquitous. Thus, Hodge and Kress ([1979] 1993: 6) define ideology as "a systematic body of ideas, organized from a particular point of view" – ideology systematically distorts reality according to class interests, and all language is ideological, as exemplified by the title of their 1979 monograph (*Language as Ideology*). Simpson (1993: 5–6) defines ideology broadly as "the ways in which what we say and think interacts with society" and emphasizes how "dominant ideologies become ingrained in everyday discourse", therefore becoming "rationalized as 'common-sense' assumptions about the way things are and the way things should be". This idea is close to Gramsci's (1999: 663–667) theorization of *common sense*. While Hallidayan systemic-functional grammar played an important part during the first years of critical linguistics, later years were marked by the influence of French discourse analysis (Williams 1999: 29).

Critical discourse studies. Critical discourse studies (CDS), or critical discourse analysis (CDA), has its roots in critical linguistics, critical theory, and several strands of linguistics, such as pragmatics, applied linguistics, sociolinguistics, classical rhetoric, and text linguistics. The various methodological and theoretical orientations associated with this school of thought all share an interest in the links between language and power, the context of language use, and the understanding of language as a social practice (Wodak 2001). Both ideology and discourse are used as theoretical and methodological tools, but the main theorists do not regard all language as ideological. For example, Wodak (2007: 1) states that language is not inherently ideological, Fairclough (1992: 91) acknowledges that the degree of ideological investment in different types of discourses varies, and van Dijk (2006: 115, see also Van Dijk 1998; 2022 [this volume]) maintains that the "general properties of language and discourse are not, as such, ideologically marked". Regarding discourse, both Foucauldian and more traditional definitions appear to be present. For example, Fairclough (1995: 92; 2002: 164) views discourse as the social practice related to a field of action or institution, with examples such as economic, organizational, managerial, political, and educational discourses. Wodak (2001: 66) defines discourse as thematically interrelated linguistic acts that are realized in texts and genres across different fields of action. Van Dijk (2022 [this volume]) argues that the complexity of discourse makes definitions pointless, and the definition can be adapted to the kinds of data under study.

Linguistic anthropology. The long tradition of describing and classifying the languages of North American indigenous groups was a major source of inspiration for American linguistic theory, and the documentation of these languages was an important concern of anthropological linguistic research (Silverstein 2017: 97). In both sociolinguistic and linguistic anthropological work, the focus was on spoken interaction and the ethnographic method of data collection (Silverstein 2017: 104); the emphasis on interaction is also illustrated by the emergence of ethnomethodology and conversation analysis in the North American context. In these circumstances, discourse was usually conceptualized as spoken interaction and language use or "language use in social context" (Silverstein 2017: 105). Like traditional sociolinguistics, early work on linguistic anthropology did not usually engage with the concept of ideology (Labov 1979: 329). However, the merger of the agendas of linguistic anthropology and sociolinguistics paralleled the increased importance of the political dimension (Gumperz and Gumperz-Cook 2008).

Regarding the study of discourse and ideology, linguistic anthropology is known especially for the concept of *language ideology*. The post-war period was marked by the influence of European functionalism in the USA. Jakobson's work on shifters, incorporating Pierce's semiotics into functional linguistics, cleared the way for the analysis of indexicality in language use, illustrated for example by Gumperz's (1976) notion of contextualization cues and the idea that variability in language forms a strategic resource for self-representation and the enregisterment of identities (Silverstein 2017: 103, 109). According to Blommaert (2005: 171), the consideration of ideologies attached to language was a result of this evolution, coupled with the longstanding tradition of linguistic relativism and a strong emphasis on worldview. Silverstein (1979: 193) characterizes *linguistic ideologies* as "any sets of beliefs about language articulated by the users as a rationalization or justification of perceived language structure and use". His work focused especially on referential ideologies of language ("reference-and-predication", Silverstein 1979: 208). As for *language ideologies*, they are defined by Gal and Woolard (1995: 130) as "cultural conceptions of the nature, form and purpose of language" and by Irvine (1989: 255) as "cultural (or subcultural) system of ideas about social and linguistic relationships, together with their loading of moral and political interests". Woolard and Schieffelin (1994: 57) observe that the various definitions have to do with the underlying idea about ideology, with two main approaches: critical and neutral. Kroskrity (2000: 8) emphasizes the fact that the perception of language and discourse reflected by a group's language ideologies is constructed in the interest of that group.

Critical sociolinguistics. Globalization and increased academic mobility have brought together different and sometimes even antagonistic schools of thought and paradigms. In this confluence, certain transformations have also affected the critical and functionalist dimension of research on discourse and ideology. A general trend relates to the shift from the political towards identities (see also Gumperz and Gumperz-Cook 2008), as illustrated by Gee's (1999) distinction between small-d discourse (language-in-use or language as a social practice) and big-D discourses (combinations of language use and any other dimensions of interaction and semiosis, including artefacts, action, values, and beliefs, which create social identities). New conceptualizations of what critical research means include Heller, Pietikäinen, and Pujolar's (2018: 2) conceptualization of critical sociolinguistics as focusing on "questions of power and inequality" by asking "what resources are important to whom" and what the consequences of the social processes that are being studied may be. In addition, being critical means that the researchers use their "understandings about the role of language in social processes of power and inequality reflexively". In another text explaining critical sociolinguistics (Boutet and Heller 2007: 313), a clear demarcation line is drawn between this approach and critical discourse analysis. Accordingly, while both critical discourse analysis and critical sociolinguistics are interested in understanding how linguistic resources are mobilized with the aim of constructing normalized meanings that do not benefit all groups equally, critical sociolinguistics focuses on the entire process of text and discourse production rather than on fixed texts.

European third-wave sociolinguistics. A clear connection between discourse and ideology but also a distinction between the two concepts appears in a strand of European third-wave sociolinguistics (Eckert 2012), whose central figures include Jan Blommaert and Jef Verschueren. In their monograph *Debating Diversity*, Blommaert and Verschueren (1998: 26) explain that discourse is "the most tangible manifestation of ideology". By discourse, these authors refer to "a non-metaphorical, down-to-earth" concept, or "an observable instance of communicative behavior, whether verbal or not". This ontological relation between ideology and discourse is also present in Verschueren's (2012) monograph, which emphasizes empirical research and reflects the intersections between pragmatics and discourse studies (see also Verschueren 2022 [this volume]). Like critical sociolinguistics, this strand is not exactly a school of thought, and the same research could be characterized as critical sociolinguistics and (European) third-wave sociolinguists. For example, Blommaert (2005: 1–2) argues that, instead of criticizing power, critical approaches to discourse should "be an analysis of power effects, of the outcome of power, of what power does to people, groups, and societies, and of how this impact comes about". Other analyses related to the redefinition of the "critical" and the repositioning of discourse and ideology include works on language and nationalism (Blackledge 2002), migration policies in superdiverse environments (Spotti 2011), and local ecologies of multilingualism in educational settings (Milani and Jonsson 2012).

3 Summary of contents

As previously noted, this volume contains both data-driven and theoretically oriented articles representing various fields and approaches, critical discourse studies, pragmatics, applied linguistics, translation and interpreting studies, sociolinguistics, and cognitive linguistics – in many chapters, several orientations are combined. At the beginning of each chapter, the authors position discourse and ideology in relation to their work and provide definitions of the concepts as they are used within each chapter.

The chapters can be divided roughly into the following groups. Chapters 2–5 constitute both case studies and more theoretical reflections, and they are all linked to France, the French language in France and beyond, and/or "French theory". In Chapters 6 through 8, the authors engage in theoretical and methodological reflections about discourse, ideology, and how to analyze them. These are followed by case studies in relation to language contact, translation, and the ideologies of child protective work and social work with migrants, in Chapters 9 through 11. The volume concludes with a corpus-linguistic exploration of the use of the words "discourse" and "ideology" in a sample of scholarly journals in Chapter 12, and an Afterword by Christina Higgins, in Chapter 13.

Chapter 2 is a survey of existing definitions of discourse and ideology: Simo K. Määttä traces the etymology, history, and evolution of the concepts of discourse and ideology until the 1960's and 1970's, or the first years of French discourse analysis. This exploration shows how the theoretical approaches to discourse and ideology are entangled with specific political and intellectual contexts and evolve in parallel with the thought of other contemporary thinkers. In other words, this chapter demonstrates that the spread and use of such concepts are themselves dependent on complex social processes. For example, while Foucault was reluctant to use the concept of ideology, this theory of discourse contains elements from coeval theorizations of ideology. At the same time, linguistic conceptualizations of discourse were influenced by Foucault's discourse theory.

Samuel Vernet, in Chapter 3, discusses the appropriateness of the use of discourse and ideology together as related but distinct concepts, especially within the context of language education. More specifically, Vernet presents a discussion of discourse and ideology as they manifest in the context of teaching French in the francophone minority region of Acadia in Eastern Canada, and how discourses of linguistic diversity can be mobilized in the French courses that the students have to attend. A central question in this analysis is to determine to what extent talk about linguistic diversity can be characterized as a specific discourse and how it relates to ideology. Discourse, in this chapter, is understood as a set of "utterances unified by a series of rules and conditions constraining their form and content", wherein the rules are ideologically determined. Ideology, on the other hand, is conceived as a system of beliefs premised and shaped by social structures.

In Chapter 4, Mariem Guellouz examines activist counter-discourses and counter-ideologies within a recent revolutionary event in Tunisia to test the notions of performance and performativity as they relate to the concepts at hand. The question addressed in the chapter concerns the characterization of the revolutionary motto *dégage* ('get out') and the physical act of immolation in terms of performativity and counter-ideology. Guellouz stresses the importance of interpellation as a discourse-ideological phenomenon, encompassing the encountering and internalization of a culture's values through which discourse makes subjects vulnerable, but also provides a site for an emancipatory response. In this chapter, ideology is understood as being expressed through social structures determined by power relations and circulated through language and discourse.

In Chapter 5, Nadia Louar dives into a discussion about the political and epistemological implications of language and national ideologies in modern France from the perspective of critical race studies, informed by literary theory. Through a conceptualization of ideology as a mental framework for making sense of how society works and as an epistemic discourse that steers perception, Louar discusses restrictive cultural and linguistic frames through the French debate on inclusive writing, the DSK (Dominique Strauss-Kahn) case, and the *#MeToo* movement. According to Louar, epistemic shortcuts that are based on the illusion of a uniformed and universal French social body and fail to acknowledge the political and ideological underpinnings of such ideals provide a key to understanding these debates.

In Chapter 6, Jef Verschueren presents a timely discussion of the shift from mainstream acceptance of social diversity to its problematization, particularly in the European context. In the wake of growing nationalist sentiment, laden with negative attitudes toward immigration and diversity, this shift, as Verschueren notes, is observable in discourses (which are defined as an umbrella term for a variety of types of language use ranging from a single speech act to a country's legislation). Through analysis of a Belgian newspaper editorial, Verschueren specifically identifies two discursive tools: a form of anti-discourse that directly confronts alternative discourses, and a form of utopian discourse that constructs a simplified ideal image of society. Furthermore, within this work, ideology is understood as a commonsensical "pattern of meaning" or "frame of interpretation" in social relations.

Following this discussion of the "new normal" in societal debate about immigration, Elizabeth Miller, in Chapter 7, takes on an exploration of the methodological ideologies that are present in discourse-based research in the field of applied linguistics. Taking a self-reflective approach, Miller points out that ideologies are not only studied: they also drive how we conduct and perceive research, and therefore should be taken into consideration in academic endeavors. Questioning the foundations of the data production process, in which both the informants and the researcher play a crucial role, the author critiques her own discourse-based research through an overview of the beliefs regarding what "good" methodologies and data are, and their effects on the research process and product. Importantly, the chapter highlights how research practices "align with ideological norms and *create* consistency and stability in the provisional assemblages of discourse data".

In Chapter 8, Teun van Dijk presents a summary of his multidisciplinary theory of ideology integrating cognitive psychology, social psychology, sociology, and linguistics, with an emphasis on the sociocognitive and discursive aspects of ideologies. Within this chapter, ideologies are regarded as socially reproduced through discourse, namely text or talk. More specifically, ideology is conceptualized as a form of social cognition shared by members of social groups and controlling socially shared attitudes toward a variety of issues, as well as individual mental models. One of the key components of this chapter is the social and cognitive composition and genesis of ideological discourse and especially its relation to mental models. Ideological discourse reveals underlying polarization between in- and outgroups, where the ingroup may be viewed positively, and the outgroup negatively.

Elizabeth Peterson, in Chapter 9, introduces the notion of licensing, and how perceived language ideologies about English drive its use in foreign-language settings in Finland and other Nordic countries. In other words, Peterson points to, for example, how English licenses its users to speak and behave in ways that would not necessarily be appropriate or expected in their native language, and shows how perceived language ideologies about English as a first language orient the ways in which English is used in sites where English is not the native language of the majority. Here, discourse is distinguished from language as a creative and shared endeavor among people, while language ideology is employed to refer to the social hierarchy of language users, as well as beliefs and opinions related to language use and related social groups.

Diving into the realm of translation, Jyrki Kalliokoski and Anne Mäntynen discuss language ideologies and their interplay with discourses in the process of translating scholarly texts in Chapter 10. In doing so, the authors provide insights into the linguistic choices made in translations, and the process through which competing ideologies are resolved "behind the scenes" – particularly between the editor and translator. The examples analyzed in this chapter concern certain key words whose indexical dimensions and multiples layers of meaning are perceived differently by the translator and the editor. In this chapter, language ideologies are understood as a set of shared beliefs about language, specifically within its social and cultural contexts and practices. Discourse, on the other hand, is conceptualized as both as "language use as social action", as well as context-specific ways of using language.

Drawing on interactional sociolinguistics, Eleanor Lutman-White and Jo Angouri analyze negotiations of the moral order in the professional context of social work with neglected children in the United Kingdom in Chapter 11. The authors conceptualize discourse as primarily language use, and ideology as commonly held views shared by professionals. These ideologies are then acquired, expressed, and perpetuated through discourse. Through an analysis of excerpts of audio-recorded and transcribed focus group and interview data, Lutman-White and Angouri show how one ideal in child protective work can be interactionally preferable and be used as grounds to provide an exception to other, contradictory ideals. The chapter is an example of how the concepts of ideology and discourse can be used in different theoretical and methodological contexts, in this case interactive sociolinguistics.

In Chapter 12, Raquel Lázaro Gutiérrez and Jesús Manuel Tejero González conceptualize ideology as shared representations reproduced in social practices, and discourses are defined by the topics that they address. Attitudes, in turn, are defined as "expressions and manifestations of the set of beliefs that shapes a particular ideology in discourses". This in mind, Lázaro Gutiérrez and Tejero González then examine the linguistic and cultural barriers that hinder migrants' access to healthcare in Spain, and the related discourses of Spanish healthcare staff regarding migration, translation, interpretation, and mediation. Additionally, Lázaro Gutiérrez and Tejero González point out how uncovering these workers' attitudes helps tackle racist and xenophobic behaviors and misconceptions to overcome linguistic and cultural barriers in the healthcare industry more generally. The chapter analyzes a large number of data excerpts from an online discussion board that was part of a course on overcoming cultural and linguistic barriers.

To shed light on how the concepts of ideology and discourse are actually utilized by researchers, Brett Diaz and Marika Hall examine their usages in published (English-language) research articles that feature them as subjects in Chapter 13. Diaz and Hall take an empirical approach to the topic by employing corpus linguistic methods to identify, extract, and analyze instances of the uses, revealing linguistic patterns that come to define different meanings of the terms in academic practice, instead of analyzing how they are explicitly defined by researchers. Rather than endorsing particular theorizations of discourse and ideology, this chapter therefore provides a survey of patterns of their use. The analysis shows that rather than being characterized in terms of contention, the relationship between discourse and ideology is dialectical.

In the Afterword (Chapter 14), Christina Higgins remarks that the different approaches to data and analysis between the chapters appear to indicate that the epistemological approaches to discourse are not always shared, which suggests that the chapters may in fact represent several disciplines of discourse studies (rather than schools of thought or sub-disciplines). An important additional question raised by the author is that of identifying who could benefit from such analyses and where could they be helpful. Higgins also highlights the importance of researchers' self-reflection with regard to their "dispositions, identities, and genealogies", in an era where the intellectual knowledge production of scholars representing "WEIRD (western, educated, industrialized, rich, democratic) contexts" (Henrich, Heine, and Norenzayan 2010; Clancy and Davis, 2019) is overrepresented. As Higgins rightly observes, almost all chapters in this volume are produced in research-rich locations, and most of them analyze phenomena in similar settings. Following this note, the author inquires what research on discourse and ideology could gain by integrating more geographically diverse approaches. For example, an inquiry of "worldviews, histories and discursive struggle" from a Hawaiian perspective would probably focus on the concepts of moʻokūauhau ('genealogy') and moʻolelo ('history/story') instead of discourse and ideology.

4 Concluding remarks

This edited volume is the product of a journey spanning nearly half a decade. Interested in the intersections of discourse and ideology, we organized a colloquium on the topic at the American Association of Applied Linguistics (AAAL) conference in 2018. Unexpectedly, this small colloquium morphed into the beginnings of this collection of texts, right there at the conference venue, at the suggestion of Dr. Francis Hult. Things are very different now than they were then. The bulk of this project has coincided with the Covid-19 pandemic, and we are amazed and grateful for the efforts of everyone involved in putting this volume together – authors, series editors, and content editors.

During this time, we have also had the opportunity to learn from and reflect on not only the chapters presented in this volume, but also on different research practices. The chapters of this volume, and especially the Afterword, raise several important questions about the current state and future direction of discourse-analytical studies that engage with the concept of ideology, including the contingency of disciplinary boundaries upon epistemological roots, the ethical dimension of research, and the agency of the researcher.

The ethical and teleological dimension highlighted by Christina Higgins is explicitly present only in one analytical chapter, where Elizabeth Miller reflects upon the nature of authentic data and her own role as a researcher in the data production process. At the same time, many chapters represent critical traditions such as critical discourse studies, emphasizing the interlinkages between language and power, often with the aim of unraveling social issues and discriminatory practices such as racism, xenophobia, and misogyny. However, these emancipatory goals are not always made explicit, as if the potential of research as a critical tool of awareness and empowerment were regarded as a given. This raises the question as to how far the researcher should and could be more open about their own identity and agency. A related question is that of inquiring to what extent such openness is possible in current research environments, where evaluative practices such as journal rankings, individual impact factors, and tenure systems strongly emphasize scientificity and objectivity. The intersections between the researcher's origins – in terms of geography, ethnicity, race, social class, gender, etc. – and the distance between the researcher's *historical body* (Scollon and Scollon 2004) or *habitus* (Bourdieu 1990: 52–79) and their data makes this question even thornier, especially in today's globalized world, characterized by increased mobility.

While our initial focus when embarking on this collected volume was to map various definitions of discourse and ideology and their relationships, it has become evident that the epistemologies mobilized in the various definitions intersect with different conceptions of the nature of data, methods, and goals of analysis. This complexity seems to highlight the importance of reflection on the connections between the chosen epistemological framework and the heuristic value of the data and the methods of analysis. We hope that the chapters of this volume can provide useful directions for such reflection, further enriching the body of linguistically oriented discourse-analytical studies engaged with the concept of ideology.

The analysis of ideologies in linguistically oriented discourse studies may also benefit from perspectives offered by other disciplines. With so many ways of combining the concepts of discourse and ideology and their various definitions, the reader of this chapter may think that some of the approaches are simply wrong – or wonder whether it is actually possible to know anything for sure about these concepts and which theories and methods are best suited for the production of new knowledge. We deliberately leave the answers to such questions to the discretion of each reader, as the goal of this chapter is not to endorse a particular view of discourse and ideology. The prospect of a unified theory of discourse and ideology does not seem realistic at the time of this writing, and an alternative option consists of regarding the various perspectives as a richness rather than as an issue. To make progress towards a better mutual understanding of ideology and discourse, more dialogue between the disciplines is needed, including a dialogue between the different branches of discourse studies and a variety of adjacent disciplines equally interested in the same concepts. In this volume, the only contributions clearly enriched by (very different) inputs from other disciplines are Van Dijk's and Louar's chapters. A concrete next step to promote the interdisciplinary dimension could be a conference and/or a collected volume inviting scholars from completely different fields to reflect on the divergences and similarities in their understanding of discourse and ideology as well as the potential these concepts may have in understanding real-world phenomena.

References

Althusser, Louis 1971. *Lenin and philosophy and other essays*. Ben Brewster (transl.). London: New Left Books.

Authier-Revuz, Jacqueline. 1982. Hétérogénéité montrée et hétérogénéité constitutive. *DRLAV – Documentation et Recherche en Linguistique Allemande Vincennes* 26. 91–151.

Blackledge, Adrian. 2002. What sort of people can look at a chicken and think dofednod?: Language, ideology and nationalism in public discourse. *Multilingua* 21 (2–3). 197–226.

Blommaert, Jan. 2005. *Discourse: A critical introduction*. Cambridge: Cambridge University Press.

Blommaert, Jan & Jef Verschueren. 1998. *Debating diversity. Analysing the discourse of tolerance*. London & New York: Routledge.

Bohman, James. 2021. Critical Theory. In Edward N. Zalta (ed.), *The Stanford encyclopedia of philosophy*, spring 2021 edn. https://plato.stanford.edu/archives/spr2021/entries/critical-theory/ (accessed 10 February 2021).

Bourdieu, Pierre. 1990. *The logic of practice*. Richard Nice (transl.). Cambridge: Polity.

Boutet, Josiane & Monica Heller. 2007. Enjeux sociaux de la sociolinguistique: pour une sociolinguistique critique. *Langage & société* 121–122 (3–4). 305–318.

Burchell, Graham, Colin Gordon & Peter Miller (eds.). 1991. *The Foucault effect: Studies in governmentality*. Chicago: Chicago University Press.

Clancy, Kathryn B. & Jenny L. Davis. 2019. Soylent is people, and WEIRD is white: Biological anthropology, whiteness, and the limits of the WEIRD. *Annual Review of Anthropology* 48. 169–186.

Courtine, Jean-Jacques. 1981. Quelques problèmes théoriques et méthodologiques en analyse du discours. À propos du discours communiste adressé aux chrétiens. *Langages* 62. 9–128.

de Beaugrande, Robert. 1999. Discourse studies and ideology: On "liberalism" and "liberalisation" in three large corpora of English. *Discourse Studies* 1 (3). 259–295.

Diaz, Brett & Marika K. Hall. 2022. Taking a corpus-based approach to investigating Discourse and Ideology in the language sciences. In Simo K. Määttä & Marika K. Hall (eds.), *Mapping ideology in discourse studies*, 247–272. Berlin: De Gruyter Mouton.

Dosse, François. 2012 [1992]. *Histoire du structuralisme. Tome II: Le chant du cygne, 1967 à nos jours*. Paris: La Découverte.
Eagleton, Terry. 1991. *Ideology: An introduction*. London: Verso.
Eckert, Penelope. 2012. Three waves of variation study: The emergence of meaning in the study of sociolinguistic variation. *Annual Review of Anthropology* 41. 87–100.
Fairclough, Norman. 1992. *Discourse and social change*. Cambridge: Polity.
Fairclough, Norman. 1995. *Critical discourse analysis: The critical study of language*. New York: Longman.
Fairclough, Norman. 2002. Language in new capitalism. *Discourse & Society* 13 (2). 163–166.
Fløttum, Kjersti (ed.). 2019. *The role of language in the climate change debate*. London & New York: Routledge.
Foucault, Michel. 1972. *The Archeology of knowledge and the discourse on language*. M. Sheridan Smith (transl.). New York: Pantheon Books.
Foucault, Michel. 1980. *Power/Knowledge: Selected interviews and other writings 1972–1977*. Colin Gordon (ed.), Colin Gordon, Leo Marshall, John Mepham & Kate Soper (transl.). New York: Random House.
Foucault, Michel. 1984. What is Enlightenment. In Paul Rabinow (ed.), Catherine Porter (transl.), *The Foucault reader*, 32–50. New York: Pantheon Books.
Foucault, Michel. 2008. *The birth of biopolitics: Lectures at the Collège de France (1978–1979)*. Michael Senellart (ed.), Graham Burchell (transl.). New York: Palgrave MacMillan.
Gadet, Françoise. 1989. Après Saussure. *DRLAV – Documentation et Recherche en Linguistique Allemande Vincennes* 40. 1–40.
Gal, Susan & Kathryn A. Woolard. 1995. Constructing languages and publics: Authority and representation. *Pragmatics* 5 (2). 129–138.
Gee, James P. 1999. *An introduction to discourse analysis: Theory and method*. London & New York: Routledge.
Geuss, Raymond, 1981. *The idea of a critical theory: Habermas and the Frankfurt School*, Cambridge: Cambridge University Press.
Gramsci, Antonio. 1999. *Selections from the Prison notebooks*. Quintin Hoare & Geoffrey Nowell Smith (transl.). London: Electric Book.
Gumperz, John J. 1976. Language, communication, and public negotiation. In Peggy R. Sanday (ed.), *Anthropology and the public interest*, 273–292. New York: Academic Press.
Gumperz, John J. & Jenny Gumperz-Cook. 2008. Studying language, culture, and society: Sociolinguistics or linguistic anthropology? *Journal of Sociolinguistics* 12 (4). 532–545.
Hall, Stuart. 1977. Culture, media and the "ideological effect". In James Curran, Michael Gurevitch & Janet Woollacot (eds.), *Mass communications and society*, 315–348. London: Edward Arnold.
Hall, Stuart. 1996a [1986]. The problem of ideology: Marxism without guarantees. In David Morley & Kuan-Hsing Chen (eds.), *Stuart Hall: Critical dialogues in cultural studies*, 24–45. London & New York: Routledge.
Hall, Stuart. 1996b [1992]. The West and the Rest: Discourse and power. In Stuart Hall, David Held, Don Hubert & Kenneth Thompson (eds.), *Modernity: An introduction to modern societies*, 185–227. Malden, MA: Blackwell.
Hall, Stuart. 1997. *Representation: Cultural representations and signifying practices*. London, Thousand Oaks, CA & New Delhi: Sage.
Hartley, John. 2003. *A short history of cultural studies*. London, Thousand Oaks, CA & New Delhi: Sage.

Henrich, Joseph, Steven J. Heine & Ara Norenzayan. 2010. Most people are not WEIRD. *Nature* 466 (7302). 29–29.
Heller, Monica, Sari Pietikäinen & Joan Pujolar. 2018. *Critical sociolinguistic research methods: Studying language issues that matter*. London & New York: Routledge.
Hodge, Robert & Gunther Kress. 1993 [1979]. *Language as ideology*. London & New York: Routledge.
Horkheimer, Max. 1982 [1972]. *Critical Theory: Selected essays*. Matthew J. O'Donnell et al. (transl.). New York: Continuum.
Horkheimer, Max & Theodor W. Adorno. 2002. *Dialectic of Enlightenment: Philosophical fragments*. Gunzelin Schmid Noerr (ed.), Edmund Jephcott (transl.). Stanford: Stanford University Press.
Hymes, Dell. 1974. *Foundations in sociolinguistics: An ethnographic approach*. Philadelphia: University of Pennsylvania Press.
Irvine, Judith T. 1989. When talk isn't cheap: Language and political economy. *American Ethnologist* 16 (2). 248–267.
Jørgensen, Marianne & Louise Phillips. 2002. *Discourse analysis as theory and method*. London, Thousand Oaks, CA & New Delhi: Sage.
Kroskrity, Paul V. 2000. Regimenting languages: Language ideological perspectives. In Paul V. Kroskrity (ed.), *Regimes of language: Ideologies, polities, and identity*, 1–34. Santa Fe, NM: School of American Research Press.
Labov, William. 1979. Locating the frontier between social and psychological factors in linguistic variation. In Charles J. Fillmore, Daniel Kempler & William S.-Y. Wang (eds.), *Individual differences in language behavior*, 327–339. New York: Academic Press.
Laclau, Ernesto & Chantal Mouffe 2001 [1985]. *Hegemony and socialist strategy. Towards a radical democratic politics*. 2nd edn. London & New York: Verso.
Lopes, António. 2015. *Is there an end of ideologies? Exploring constructs of ideology and discourse in Marxist and post-Marxist theories*. Newcastle upon Tyne: Cambridge Scholars Publishing.
Määttä, Simo K. 2022. Discourse and ideology in French thought until Foucault and Pêcheux. In Simo K. Määttä & Marika K. Hall (eds.), *Mapping ideology in discourse studies*, 21–43. Berlin: De Gruyter Mouton.
Maingueneau, Dominique. 1991. *L'analyse du discours: Introduction aux études de l'archive*. Paris: Hachette.
Maingueneau, Dominique. 2002. École française de l'analyse du discours. In Patrick Charaudeau & Dominique Maingueneau (eds.) *Dictionnaire d'analyse du discours*, 201–202. Paris: Seuil.
Maingueneau, Dominique. 2017. Parcours en analyse du discours. *Langage & Société* 160–161 (2–3). 129–143.
Mannheim, Karl. 1936. *Ideology and utopia: An introduction to the sociology of knowledge*. Louis Wirth & Edward Shils (transl.). London: K. Paul, Trench, Trubner & Co.
Marx, Karl & Frederick Engels. 2010. *Karl Marx and Frederick Engels: Collected works, vol. 5 (Marx and Engels 1845–1847)*. Clemens Dutt, W. Lough & C. P. Magill (transl.). London: Electric Book.
Mazière, Francine. 2005. *L'analyse du discours*. Paris: PUF.
Mazière, Francine. 2010. *L'analyse du discours*, 2nd updated edn. Paris: PUF.
McIntosh, Janet & Norma Mendoza-Denton (eds.). 2020. *Language in the Trump era. Scandals and emergencies*. Cambridge: Cambridge University Press.

Milani, Tommaso M. & Rickard Jonsson. 2012. Who's afraid of Rinkeby Swedish? Stylization, complicity, resistance. *Journal of Linguistic Anthropology* 22 (1). 44–63.

Pêcheux, Michel. 1982. *Language, semantics and ideology*. Harbans Nagpal (transl.). London: MacMillan.

Purvis, Trevor and Alan Hunt. 1993. Discourse, ideology, discourse, ideology, discourse, ideology ... *The British Journal of Sociology* 44 (3). 473–499.

Sardar, Ziauddin & Borin van Loon. 1997. *Introducing cultural studies*. Cambridge: Icon Books.

Sawyer, R. Keith. 2002. A discourse on discourse: An archeological history of an intellectual concept. *Cultural Studies* 16 (3). 433–456.

Schiffrin, Deborah. 1994. *Approaches to discourse*. Oxford: Blackwell.

Scollon, Ron & Suzie Wong Scollon. 2004. *Nexus analysis: Discourse and the emerging internet*. London & New York: Routledge.

Silverstein, Michael. 1979. Language structure and linguistic ideology. In Paul R. Clyne, William F. Hanks & Carol L. Hofbauer (eds.), *The elements: A parasession on linguistic units and levels*, 193–247. Chicago: Chicago Linguistic Society.

Silverstein, Michael. 2017. Forty years of speaking (of) the same (object) language – *sans le savoir*. *Langage & Société* 160–161 (2–3). 93–110.

Simpson, Paul. 1993. *Language, ideology, and point of view*. London & New York: Routledge.

Spotti, Massimiliano. 2011. Ideologies of success for superdiverse citizens: The Dutch testing regime for integration and the online private sector. *Diversities Journal* 13 (2). 39–52.

Thompson, John B. 1984. *Studies in the theory of ideology*. Cambridge: Polity.

Van Dijk, Teun A. 1998. *Ideology: A multidisciplinary approach*. London, Thousand Oaks, CA & New Delhi: Sage.

Van Dijk, Teun A. 2006. Ideology and discourse analysis. *Journal of Political Ideologies* 11 (2). 115–140.

Van Dijk, Teun A. 2022. Ideology in cognition and discourse. In Simo K. Määttä & Marika K. Hall (eds.), *Mapping ideology in discourse studies*, 137–155. Berlin: De Gruyter Mouton.

Verschueren, Jef. 2012. *Ideology in language use. Pragmatic guidelines for empirical research*. Cambridge: Cambridge University Press.

Verschueren, Jef. 2022. The ideological grounding of the new normal: Anti-discourse meets utopia. In Simo K. Määttä & Marika K. Hall (eds.), *Mapping ideology in discourse studies*, 103–116. Berlin: De Gruyter Mouton.

Williams, Glyn. 1999. *French discourse analysis: The method of post-structuralism*. London & New York: Routledge.

Wodak, Ruth. 2001. What CDA is about – A summary of its history, important concepts and its developments1. In Ruth Wodak & Michael Meyer (eds.), *Methods of critical discourse analysis*, 1–13. London, Thousand Oaks, CA & New Delhi: Sage.

Wodak, Ruth. 2007. Language and ideology – Language in ideology. *Journal of Language and Politics*. 6 (1). 1–5.

Wodak, Ruth & Michael Meyer. 2001. *Methods of critical discourse analysis*. London, Thousand Oaks, CA & New Delhi: Sage.

Woolard, Kathryn A. 1998. Introduction: Language ideology as a field of inquiry. In Bambi B. Schieffelin, Kathryn A. Woolard & Paul V. Kroskrity (eds.), *Language ideologies: Practice and theory*, 3–47. New York & Oxford: Oxford University Press.

Woolard, Kathryn A. & Bambi B. Schieffelin. 1994. Language ideology. *Annual Review of Anthropology* 23. 55–82.

Simo K. Määttä
Chapter 2
Discourse and ideology in French thought until Foucault and Pêcheux

Abstract: Since many, if not most, of the early sources of critical approaches to discourse and ideology come from France, the parallel and sometimes divergent development of these concepts may help to explain some of the contradictions present in today's theorizations and applications. This chapter provides a succinct account of the etymology, history, and evolution of the concepts from their first usage until the early years of French discourse analysis in the late 1960s and early 1970s. The focus rests on the similarities, overlaps, and coincidences in the theorizations of some of the most important thinkers for the critical study of discourse, particularly Michel Foucault and Michel Pêcheux. The goal is to explain how the theory of discourse and ideology is contingent upon the political and intellectual context and the relations between theorizations coming from different sources. The chapter concludes by arguing that the divergence of later approaches and the frequent difficulty of integrating discourse and ideology are due to different factors. These include the polysemy and diverse historical usages of the word *discours* in French and other languages and the fact that Foucault's concept of discourse is a hybrid configuration integrating several contemporary ideas, including Althusserian considerations of ideology.

Keywords: discourse, ideology, discourse analysis, French discourse analysis, critical discourse analysis, Foucault, Pêcheux

1 Introduction

French theorizations of ideology and discourse are a source of inspiration for many scholars positioning themselves within critical approaches to language and discourse. However, the complex relationships between different theorists are not often discussed, although making such connections explicit may help clarify some of the contradictions and dilemmas that are present, especially when discourse and ideology are used jointly as theoretical and methodological tools. This chapter presents a concise overview of the history of the concepts of discourse and ideology from the first attested usage and definitions to a sample of French theorists of the late 1960s and the early 1970s. The focus is on the usage of the concepts in the study of language, and the goal is to explain the context in which different theorizations of these concepts have arisen, as well as to offer paths for a more detailed inquiry of the relationship between the concepts in cases in which combining them becomes a problem. In addition, the chapter aims to explain both the affordances and the constraints that have motivated the choices of thinkers who have applied concepts and models coined by other thinkers in different theoretical frameworks.

The label "French discourse analysis" is used in this chapter as a translation of the French terms *analyse du discours* (or *AD*) *française* ('French discourse analysis') and *école française d'analyse du discours* ('French school of discourse analysis'). These denominations are commonly used in France to refer to the linguistically oriented discourse analysis of the 1960s and 1970s, whose main concerns included the scientific study of ideology and political discourses (Maingueneau 2002; Mazière 2005: 41). The chapter specifically focuses on Michel Foucault's and Michel Pêcheux's ideas about discourse and ideology because of these thinkers' importance in critical approaches to language, discourse, and ideology outside France. The following two sections provide a brief summary of the etymology and early usage of the words *discourse* and *ideology*. Subsequently, I examine the confluence of ideas characterizing the French intellectual environment in the 1960s, especially with regard to linguistics and adjacent disciplines. This presentation of the context is followed by a succinct outline of Foucault's theory of discourse and Pêcheux's linguistic approach to discourse and ideology, as well as a discussion of the dissemination of Foucault's thought in France and elsewhere. To conclude, I argue that many of the current challenges of using both ideology and discourse as theoretical and/or analytical tools stem from the ways in which the concepts of language, discourse, and ideology – as well as the relations between these concepts – have been theorized and used in the past.

As this chapter is a survey of the diverse usages of the concepts, it does not endorse a particular definition of discourse or ideology.

2 Ideology

The first attestation of the French word *idéologie* is from 1796, in a treaty on the faculty of thought authored by the political scientist and philosopher Antoine Destutt de Tracy (1754–1836). In this first understanding (Destutt de Tracy 1796: 324–328) ideology referred to a vigorous *science of ideas* with foundations in the philosophy of Enlightenment. According to Destutt de Tracy (1801: 3, 183), the premises of this science were laid by the philosopher and epistemologist Étienne

Bonnot de Condillac (1714–1780). Destutt de Tracy's particular goal was to create a rational and scientific basis for political and social reforms (Hayward 2007: 77–78) and to avoid "nebulous metaphysics"[1] (Destutt de Tracy 1801: 355). In fact, ideology was conceived as forming part of zoology and destined to unveil the intellectual faculties of the human being (Destutt de Tracy 1801: 1). Destutt de Tracy (1796: 324) states that as a science of ideas, ideology is "very wise, for it does not imply anything that is doubtful or unknown; it does not remind the mind of any idea of cause". In addition, he argues, the meaning of ideology is clear because everyone knows what an idea is – although not many people know it *well*.

A negative meaning of ideology, referring to a "group of ideas with no connection to reality", is attested to have appeared by the year 1800 in the French language (TLFi 2002; Rey 1992, s.v. *idéologie*). The timing coincides with Napoléon Bonaparte's derogatory usage of the term *idéologue* when referring to Destutt de Tracy and like-minded thinkers, who opposed Napoléon's reign despite having initially supported him (Canguilhem 1977: 36; Nicholls 1999: 123). By accusing the ideologues of "hollow metaphysics", while presenting himself as a man of political and social realism, Napoléon therefore subverted the image of these ardent positivists.

Both the neutral and the derogatory meanings coexisted during the decades that followed. An association with political groups was documented for the first time in French in 1842 (TLFi 2002, s.v. *idéologie*): In this acceptation, *ideology* referred to a doctrine that inspires or appears to inspire a government or political party. This shift in meaning coincides with the early writings of Karl Marx (1818–1883), who lived in Paris from 1843 to 1845 and in Brussels from 1845 to 1848, after having been expelled from France.

Larrain (1983: 42) identifies two dimensions in Marx's theory of ideology: *positive* (referring to the construction of social consciousness) and *negative* (distorted thought). While the negative connotation prevails in Marx's thinking, it is difficult to find an all-encompassing definition of ideology in his works (Wolf and Leopold 2021). Geuss (1981: 4–26; see also Eagleton 1991: 63–70) distinguishes at least three different dimensions in Marx's works: *descriptive* (beliefs), *positive* (worldview), and – the most important in terms of Marx's general theory – *critical* (false and misleading conscience). Thus, ideology makes contingent phenomena, ideas, and especially social flaws appear as natural, accepted, necessary, and corresponding to the well-being and interest of all, although they in fact favor the ruling class. All of these characteristics are hidden by a deceptive surface structure (Wolf and Leopold 2021; Rosen and Wolff 1996: 235–236).

---

[1] Translations from French texts are mine unless stated otherwise.

Language plays an important role in such ideological processes. For example, in *The German Ideology*, written between 1845 and 1846, Marx and Engels (2010: 36–37) emphasize how the perception of the world and the production of conceptualizations, ideas, and ideologies are connected with the materiality of everyday life. Hence, ideology is also connected to material activity and its development rather than being independent. Language per se is "practical, real consciousness" (Marx and Engels 2010: 44). This work also includes severe criticism against Destutt de Tracy's theory of ideology.

Regarding later usage, Eagleton (1991: 1–2) recognizes 16 scholarly, everyday, and political definitions of ideology. The everyday or commonsense meaning can be summarized as "opinions and beliefs of a particular group or a distorted worldview typical of that group", and typically entails a negative connotation and the opposition between the ideological and that which is regarded as knowledge and is true, accurate, empirical, or pragmatic (Eagleton 1991: 2). As for the scholarly definitions, they correspond roughly to two predominant ways of thinking. In the Marxist tradition, ideology is regarded as "illusion, distortion, and mystification", whereas the sociological line of thought views ideologies as "schematic, inflexible ways of seeing the world, as against some modest, piecemeal, pragmatic wisdom" (Eagleton 1991: 3–4).

Many Marxist thinkers of the twentieth century have had a decisive influence on the development of critical approaches to language. One of the predecessors of later theories of discourse and ideology was Soviet linguist Valentin N. Vološinov (1895–1936). His work *Marxism and the Philosophy of Language* was published in Russian in 1929, in English in 1973, and in French in 1977.[2] For Vološinov ([1973] 1986: 10–13, 70–82), ideology was a fundamental characteristic of language: wherever there are signs, there is ideology, and the truth and fairness of all signs is subject to an ideological assessment. More precisely, ideology is located in the intercommunicative space between individuals where signs and ideologies are materialized. Consequently, the specific contexts in which linguistic signs are materialized also constitute *ideological contexts*, and these contexts – rather than the Saussurean abstract object of language – should be the object of linguistics.

The Italian Marxist thinker Antonio Gramsci (1891–1937) developed the concept of *hegemony* to conceptualize the ways in which the dominant classes create consent and incorporate their values in order to dominate other social groups ideologically. Gramsci (1999: 634) argues that ideology is "a conception of the world that is implicitly manifested in art, in law, in economic activity, and

---

2 In the French translation, the work was originally attributed to Mikhail Bakhtin. Vološinov's name is also spelled Voloshinov.

in the manifestations of individual and collective life". Gramsci (1999: 687; see also Fairclough 2010: 62) viewed ideologies as inherently active, which is visible, among other things, in the social effects that they have. In addition, Gramsci highlights the importance of the media, the education system, and other *ideological apparatuses* as instruments by which cultural hegemony is created. Gramsci's main theses are included in his *Prison Notebooks*, which he wrote between 1929 and 1935. The first French translation is from 1953, and the first selections in English are from 1971.

The ideas of French philosopher Louis Althusser (1918–1990) have been particularly influential in the study of language and discourse. As Hall ([1986] 1996: 32) elucidates, by moving away from the conception of ideology as consisting merely of false consciousness, Althusser made possible subsequent theorizations emphasizing the linguistic and "discursive" components of ideology. According to Althusser's reading, Marx's thought from the *German Ideology* onwards constituted an *epistemological break*,[3] breaking from the ideological and philosophical heritage characterizing his early works, substituting real science for ideology, and obliterating the distinction between the subject and the object (Althusser and Balibar 1970: 25–28, 41–43). Another important concept in subsequent analyses of discourse has been *overdetermination*, a notion Althusser borrowed from Freud: A single observable effect can in fact have multiple causes, although one of them would be sufficient to cause the effect (Althusser 1969: 101). Applied to social structures, overdetermination means that the changes affecting them are linked to numerous contradictions, and events can be related to multiple circumstances whose combinations may trigger unpredicted ruptures and social changes (Althusser 1969: 100). The third important notion is *interpellation*. According to Althusser (1971: 150–168; see also Fairclough 1992: 30), the individual becomes a subject aware of their agency because of the prevailing social practices and especially ideological practice, namely ideological state apparatuses, such as the education system, law, family, religion, and the media; ideology has a material existence in the practice(s) of these apparatuses. Hence, ideology constitutes individuals as subjects and is always present – as Marx and Engels had said, it emanates from material reality rather than the subject and projects the relationship between the subject and reality rather than reality itself (Althusser 1971: 159 and *passim*). Thus, when an individual is hailed or interpellated to be a subject, that subjecthood has been given already, and ideology merely mirrors this identity.

---

3 This concept was coined by Bachelard (1938) in *La Formation de l'esprit scientifique* (translated into English in 2002).

In sum, an initially "idealistic" definition of ideology was redefined by Marx and Engels and has been developed further mostly by Marxist thinkers. Thinkers who did not participate in the Marxist venture include Mannheim (1936), who distinguished between *particular ideologies* corresponding roughly to individual, distorted views, and *total ideologies* shared by social groups, shaping their interpretation of reality and bearing witness to the relational nature of all knowledge.

3 Discourse

While *ideology* is a relatively recent word coined for a specific purpose, the word *discourse* has a much longer history. The noun is derived from the Latin verb *discurrere*, whose main meaning was 'to run around'. The participle *discursus* had the meaning 'speech', 'conversation', and 'talk' in Late Latin, and its first attestation (*discours*) in written French sources with the meaning 'story, (written or oral) talk' is from 1503 (TLFi 2002, s.v. *discours*). The word was included in the French Academy's first dictionary with the following main meanings: 'assembly of words (*paroles*) with the aim of explaining what one thinks', 'conversation' (*entretien*), and 'oral or written talk' (Académie française 1694, s.v. *discours*). Examples of discourse furnished by this dictionary include "ordinary (*familier*) discourse, eloquent discourse, and formal (*soutenu*) discourse". The meaning 'succession of words that constitute language' was in use by 1613 (TLFi 2002, s.v. *discours*).[4] Similar meanings were present in seventeenth-century English dictionaries: Phillips's (1658, s.v. *discourse*) *The New World of Words* defines discourse as "Speech, Talk, Conversation, Reasoning" and, in a logical sense, also "that rational Action of the Mind by which we form any new Judgment from others before made, or whereby we can infer or conclude one thing from another".

Interestingly, the ways in which discourse is understood in both structuralist and functional approaches to language (see Hymes 1974: 79 for this distinction) stem from these early definitions. For example, in Saussure's *Course in General Linguistics*, whose first French edition is from 1916 and the first English translation from 1959, discourse means simply 'speech' and 'language use' (de Saussure 1983: 14, 123; 1971: 31, 170–171; 1959: 14, 121). Hence, these usages are similar to the ones attested at least in the early seventeenth century. As a result, the "standard usage" of the term *discourse*, corresponding to the definition "unit of language larger than a sentence", did not emerge in the 1940s or with Saussure; it was

---

[4] This definition is also reflected in the compound *partie du discours*, 'part of speech', whose first attestation in French is from 1637 (Rey 1992, s.v. *discours*).

present in the earliest attested meanings of the word (cf. Sawyer 2002: 434, 436). Another important usage, in the sense "language use", is also derived from definitions that predate the emergence of modern linguistics. Thus, the "ideologue" Destutt de Tracy (1803: 23) defines discourse as "all usage of a language, all production of signs".

In the previous section, we saw that a politicized usage of the term *ideology* emerged quite soon after the coinage of the term, changed the meaning of the word, and had a decisive influence on the subsequent scholarly usage of the notion. The case of discourse is quite different because scholarly definitions have their roots in everyday usage. In fact, the relatively neutral meanings "speech" or "talk" are still common in, for example, many Romance languages.

Regarding subsequent scholarly definitions, they are notoriously manifold and complex, even if one considers only those that are used in disciplines that study language. One way to draw a line is to make a distinction between *formalist* and *functional* linguistics (Schiffrin 1994: x, 3). The formalist approach would maintain that discourses are linguistic units that are larger than a sentence and seek to answer the question of how language is organized into such units. In discourse analysis, this perspective is represented famously by Harris (1952: 3), according to whom language occurs "in connected discourse". The functionalist approach is more concerned with language use and endeavors to know how language is used "to convey information about the world, ourselves, and our social relationships" (Schiffrin 1994: x). Other definitions of discourse pertaining to the functionalist paradigm include "language-in-action", "language as social practice", "systematic meaning-making within such a specific social practice", and "characteristic language use of a group or a person" (Schiffrin 1994: 20–43; Maingueneau 2005: 64–72). However, the division between functionalist and formalist (or structural) approaches represents a continuum of different perspectives on language, and the definitions of discourse emerging within these approaches reflect their stance on the nature, function, and functioning of language – in other words, their *language ideology* (see, e.g., Gal and Woolard 1995; Kroskrity 2000).

4 French thought in relation to language and discourse in the 1960s

The intellectual atmosphere in France in the late 1960s was dominated by structuralism in linguistics and especially in literary theory, as well as Althusser's reading of Marxism and Jacques Lacan's reading of psychoanalysis, particularly affecting the study of texts and writing (Maingueneau 1991: 10–11). Different approaches focusing on texts and writing appeared simultaneously: Jacques Derrida's grammatology, Foucault's archeology, Julia Kristeva's semanalysis, and Roland Barthes' pleasure of the text (Sarfati 2005: 88–89). In linguistics, where structuralism had started to have a certain impact from the mid-1950s onwards, semiotic structuralism had reached its peak, although generative grammar, North American distributionalism, functionalist approaches, Bakhtinian dialogism, and analytical philosophy were gathering more importance (Dosse [1992] 2012a: 80–88, 249–261; [1992] 2012b: 13–28, 72–73).

Compared to the other fields of the humanities, linguistics was widely regarded as having managed to perform an epistemological break in the Althusserian sense and become a "real" science (Maingueneau 1991: 12). The autonomous character of language was also underscored in structuralism as a whole, and in the aftermath of the events of May 1968, structuralism and linguistics gained a firm foothold in universities (Dosse 2012a: 266; 2012b: 146, 160–168). By the late 1960s, structuralism had become "generalized" in the sense that it had spread to adjacent disciplines beyond linguistics, including thinkers, such as Claude Lévi-Strauss, Barthes, Lacan, and Foucault (Gadet 1989: 2; Dosse 2012b: 155). They all had a decisive impact on the evolution of the theory of discourse (and ideology).

Lévi-Strauss met Roman Jakobson in New York, where both resided after having fled from the Nazi regime, and came to know linguistic structuralism and especially structural phonology (Dosse 2012a: 38). Subsequently, Lévi-Strauss was to become one of the leading figures of structuralism in France and beyond. One of the main concerns of Lévi-Strauss's writings in the 1940s and 1950s was language's relationship to social and cultural phenomena, such as myths and rites. A key component of this relationship was the *unconscious*, which Lévi-Strauss (1949: 25–26; 1963: 203) regards as a vacuum responsible for the symbolic function. The unconscious, whose laws are the same for all human beings, imposes the structural laws according to which specific individual or collective stories and images become *a discourse* (or *language*, in the English translation). Myth, Lévi-Strauss (1955: 430) argues, should not be "treated as language" because it "*is* language: to be known, it has to be told; it is part of human speech".[5] In a paper written in 1956 and published in 1958, he claims that the structure of discourse –

---

5 In the "complemented and modified" French translation of this paper originally written in English, "myth is an integral part of language (*langue*); it is known through speech (*parole*), and it pertains to discourse" (*discours*; Lévi-Strauss 1958: 230).

"which is not altogether random" – could be one of the objects of a comparative structural analysis (Lévi-Strauss 1958: 98; 1963: 85).

Barthes was one of the thriving forces behind the development of French discourse analysis. At the height of the structuralist venture, he called for a linguistics of discourse that could study the regularities of language beyond the sentence level, or the organization of the message of a "language" above or superior to the "language of the linguists" (Barthes 1966: 3). Barthes (1966: 3, 5) contends that the foundations of discourse analysis had been laid down by Benveniste (1966: 119–131) in his text dealing with the levels of linguistic analysis. Other precursors of discourse analysis, Barthes explains, included Lévi-Strauss, who had shown that the basic structural units of mythical discourse form larger units and combinations, and Tzvetan Todorov, who had established the distinction between story (*histoire*) and discourse. Barthes also refers to Harris's 1952 article on discourse analysis (this text was not translated into French until 1969).

Lacanian psychoanalysis was particularly important in this era of French thought, and it is visible in Althusser's thinking and French discourse analysts' theorizations of the subject (Mazière 2010: 17–18). Lacan (1966: 155 *et passim*) popularized the idea that discourse is not just the actual production of speech but can be understood metaphorically as the presence or the voice of the "Other", and that these discourses or voices can be multiple. In addition, he argued that the realm of things is created in and through language: words create coherence to perceptions, and language enables the presence of objects even when they are physically absent. A key notion in Lacan's thinking, namely the *unconscious*, was based on Lévi-Strauss' reformulation of the concept (Dosse 2012a: 138–154).

The peak of "generalized" structuralism also coincided with growing awareness of the dialogic nature of *parole* and the concept of *intertextuality*. This concept stems from Vološinov's work, and his ideas, as well as those of other scholars of the Bakhtin circle, had been known in France since the mid-1960s through Julia Kristeva, who gave a talk on Bakhtin's theories of language in Barthes's seminar in 1966 and coined the term *intertextuality* to account for Bakhtin's concept of dialogism (Limat-Letellier 1998). Her articles on intertextuality were published in 1966 and 1967 and included in her book *Semiotikè* (Kristeva 1969). The English translation of Vološinov's work became available in 1973, and Marcellesi and Gardin (1974) discussed its contents in their influential work *Introduction à la sociolinguistique*.

A central idea in Bakhtin's circle was that we do not "own" our words because they have been, are, and will be used by others, and they inevitably refer to other instances of language use. This conjecture was in some ways compatible with Lacan's ideas about the split subject and the inescapable presence of the discourse of the "Other". Simultaneously, the speaking subject was also deconstructed within "enunciative" linguistics (*linguistique énonciative*). Benveniste's (1966: 251–266) paper on the nature of pronouns, first published in 1956, is generally regarded as the starting point of this approach, seeking to explain the expression of subjectivity in language and emphasizing the unique nature of each *act of énonciation* by which statements (*énoncé*) are produced. This act brings to the fore the subject and the relation between the subject and the addressee (Benveniste's 1966: 262), as well as the fact that the person responsible for the *énonciation* is not irreducible to the subject of the statement that is produced. For Benveniste (1970: 13–14), discourse is a "manifestation of *énonciation*" and "produced every time one speaks"; it implies the conversion of language (*langue*) into an "instance of discourse". In other words, discourse is speech insofar as it is considered in relation to the act of "enunciation" and its contingencies, including the speaker, the addressee, and the circumstances.

The concept of *énoncé* is notoriously polysemic. For Benveniste (1970: 13), it refers to the result of the act of enunciation by which the speaker appropriates language and constitutes itself as subject. But *énoncé* can also refer to the actualization of a clause, a structured sequence of clauses, a sequence of clauses on the level of language (*langue*), and a sequence of actualized clauses (Kerbrat-Orecchioni 2006: 33).

The theory of *énonciation* has close affinities with speech act theory (Benveniste 1966: 267–285; Sarfati 2005: 11, 18), but its impact outside the Francophone world has been reduced due to the problem of translating its key concepts, such as *énonciation* and *énoncé* (Angermüller 2007: 29–30). In France, the theory of *énonciation* was triumphant: in the late 1960s, many linguists argued that linguistic structuralism per se was *passé*; enunciative linguistics had become an alternative to mainstream linguistics, focusing increasingly on formal syntax (Gadet 1989: 2).

5 Foucault's theory of discourse in *The Archeology of Knowledge*

Foucault's background was Nietzschean and Heideggerian rather than Marxist (Foucault 1988; Sarfati 2005: 99, 102; Dosse 2012a: 432–434). While Foucault or at least some of his ideas have been characterized as structuralist (e.g., Gadet 1989: 2; Purvis and Hunt 1993: 489; Williams 1999; Dosse 2012a, 2012b), his aim was to move beyond hermeneutics and structuralism (Dreyfus and Rabinow [1982] 1983). In one interview, Foucault (1980c: 56) described himself as an antistructuralist. However, the intellectual currents of the era are, of course, visible in his theory of discourse. For example, the contribution of enunciative linguistics is clearly present in Foucault's *The Archeology of Knowledge* (published in French in 1969 and in English in 1972), which constitutes the most explicit exposition of the theory of discourse in his œuvre. Examples of the connection with the *théorie de l'énonciation* include the numerous occurrences of the terms enunciation (*énonciation*) and statement (*énoncé*) and their role in *discourse*.

Foucault (1969: 153; 1972: 117) defined discourse as "a group of statements (*énoncé*) in so far as they belong to the same discursive formation". In addition, instead of "signifying elements referring to contents or representations", discourses should be regarded as "practices that systematically form the objects of which they speak". Admittedly, while "discourses are composed of signs", they do more than just designate things with these signs, and are therefore "irreducible to the language (*langue*) and to speech (*parole*)"; the goal of discourse analysis is to describe and uncover this "more" (Foucault 1969: 66; 1972: 49). In other words, the unity of discourse is based "on the space in which various objects emerge and are continuously transformed" and "the rules that make possible the appearance of objects during a given period of time" (Foucault 1969: 46; 1972: 32–33). The existence of such objects is contingent upon "a complex group of relations" that exist "between institutions, economic and social processes, behavioral patterns, systems of norms, techniques, types of classification, modes of characterization" (Foucault 1969: 61; 1972: 45). This theorization of discourse was revolutionary because it focused on the conditions of existence and the consequences of discourse instead of its linguistic forms.

The description of a formulation as a statement, Foucault continues, should not be conflated with the analysis of the author's explicit or implicit intention or their relationship to the contents of the formulation. Rather, this description consists of "determining what position can and must be occupied by any individual if he is to be the subject of it" (Foucault 1969: 126; 1972: 95–96). Accordingly, the existence of a statement is related to that which can and cannot be said from a particular position. As a result, affirming "the Earth is round or that species evolve does not constitute the same statement before and after Copernicus, before and after Darwin" (Foucault 1969: 136; 1972: 103). While the basic meaning of the words is the same, the web of relations to other propositions and the entire complex of the statements' conditions of production have changed, and they do not belong to the same discourse.

Another important notion in relation to discourse is *discursive formation* (Foucault 1969: 53; 1972: 38), defined as a detectable dispersion and regularity among "objects, types of statement, concepts, or thematic choices", with this regularity manifesting itself in "an order, correlations, positions and functionings, transformations". The discursive formation is used in lieu of "words that are already overladen with conditions and consequences" and are inadequate to describe this dispersion, "such as 'science', 'ideology', 'theory', or 'domain of objectivity'".

Foucault's (1970) inaugural lecture at the *Collège de France*, titled *L'ordre du discours* in French, is included as an appendix in the English edition of *The Archeology of Knowledge* with the title *Discourse on Language* (Foucault 1972: 215–237). This translation had been published previously in April 1971 in *Social Science Information* with the title *Orders of Discourse* (Foucault 1971). In the new translation (Foucault 1981), the title is *The Order of Discourse*. The control and materiality of discourse are powerfully foregrounded in this text: "[...] in every society the production of discourse is at once controlled, selected, organised and redistributed according to a certain number of procedures whose role is to ward off its powers and dangers, to gain mastery over its chance events, to evade its ponderous, formidable materiality" (Foucault 1981: 52). In addition, "[...] discourse is not simply that which translates struggles or systems of domination, but is the thing for which there is struggle, discourse is the power to be seized" (Foucault 1981: 52–53).[6]

Interestingly, the material power of discourse is reminiscent of the active force and effect of ideologies in Gramsci's theory and the materiality of ideology in Marx's and Engel's and subsequent theorizations. In fact, Balibar (1989) argues that a combat with Marx's ideas characterizes Foucault's entire work. Purvis and Hunt (1993: 476, 489) contend that Foucault's notion of discourse is very similar to the main thrust of ideology in Western Marxism, namely a positive or "sociological" version of ideology, emphasizing the outcome of a specific social position and a sphere of struggle of competing ideologies. In addition, the argument of discourses systematically forming, shaping, and changing the contours of their objects relates to Vološinov's idea of ideological contexts.

Regarding *interdiscursivity*, Foucault (1969: 128–131, 206–208, 225; 1972: 97–99, 158–159, 172) states that the borders of a statement are always occupied by other statements, and these borders create the context, so that the context of the same sentence is different in texts pertaining to different genres or in different situations of language use. In addition, the borders are controlled by the "enunciative field" (*champ énonciatif*), namely the constraints determining what can

---

[6] In the earlier translation (Foucault 1971: 8), these passages are rendered as follows: "[...] in every society the production of discourse is at once controlled, selected, organised and redistributed according to a certain number of procedures, whose role is to avert its powers and its dangers, to *cope with* chance events, to evade its ponderous, *awesome* materiality" and "*speech* is no mere verbalisation of conflicts and systems of domination, but that *it is the very object of man's conflicts*" (emphasis mine).

and cannot be said from a particular position. This associated field comprises a complex web, including textual context and its relationships to genre and situation, and implicit or explicit references, as well as potential future statements made possible by the statement in question. In sum, all statements reactualize other statements in different ways, and a statement is one only insofar as it occupies a position in an enunciative field.

6 Linguistic approaches to discourse analysis in the 1960s and 1970s

Understanding the workings of ideology was a major impetus during the first years of the linguistic study of discourse in France, and discourse analysis emerged as an instrument allowing a scientific study of the ideological deformations of social relations. Following Althusser, everything was perceived as being ideological (Williams 1999: 73), and ideology was paralleled with the unconscious, as theorized in (Lacanian) psychoanalysis. The goal was to decipher and *analyze* the hidden layers of meaning in texts. The emergence of discourse analysis was also a natural extension of a long tradition of philological and didactic textual analysis, but the focus shifted from literary texts toward political and other authoritative texts (Maingueneau 1991: 9–14, 22). At the same time, the connection with linguistic thought was clear (Marandin 1979: 18). The relations between linguistics and discourse analysis were under constant reevaluation during these early years of French discourse analysis, characterized as a program of Marxist semantics examining the conditions of production of discourse and the links between discourse and society, on the one hand, and discourse and ideology on the other (Sarfati 2005: 6–7, 105).

One of the most influential discourse analysts of these early years was Michel Pêcheux (1938–1983), whose first paper on discourse analysis focused on the relationship between content analysis and discourse analysis (Pêcheux 1967). In his monograph on the automatic analysis of discourse, Pêcheux (1969) attempted to apply the distributionalist method theorized by Harris (Puech 2005: 104; Angermuller, Maingueneau, and Wodak 2014). Foucault's thought is also clearly visible in this work: according to Puech (2005: 104–105), Pêcheux borrowed the notion of discursive formation from Foucault's *The Archeology of Knowledge*, published the same year. Pêcheux's aim was to "rectify" the notion by making it compatible with structuralist thought and by resolving the problem of theorizing the relations between linguistics, history, and Marxist and Lacanian theorizations of the subject.

In his later, more theoretical works, Pêcheux attempted to combine Althusserian Marxism, structuralism, and psychoanalysis. For example, Pêcheux and Fuchs (2014: 91; 1975: 10–11) argue that "ideology interpellates individuals as subjects".[7] At certain historical moments of confrontation, class relations are organized into ideological formations consisting of "a complex set of attitudes and representations that are neither 'individual' nor 'universal'" and in which different political and ideological positions maintain "among themselves relations of antagonism, alliance or domination". Discourse (or *le discursive*, 'the discursive'), in turn, consists of (one of the) material aspects of ideological materiality (Pêcheux and Fuchs 1975: 11; 2014: 91–92). In other words, discourse is contingent upon ideology: "the discursive *species* belongs […] to an ideological *genre*". Citing ideas exposed in a previous text (Haroche, Henry, and Pêcheux 1971: 102), Pêcheux continues by stating that ideological formations contain interrelated discursive formations that determine the rules of what one can and what one has to say from a particular position. Examples representing different textual genres are given as possible manifestations of such choices: "a harangue, a sermon, a pamphlet, a statement, a program etc.". As regards the boundaries of discursive formations, they are defined by the "strictly unsayable since it determines it". However, from the viewpoint of discursive formation, this unsayable is not to "be confused with the subjective space of enunciation, the imaginary space that provides the speaking subject's movement within the reformulable" (Pêcheux and Fuchs 1975: 21; 2014: 95). Pêcheux and Fuchs (1975: 23–24; 2014: 96)[8] also note that discourse should not be confused with speech or language use (*parole*) in the Saussurean sense, nor with the way of speaking or linguistic competence contingent upon a social position, although discursive processes have a linguistic base.

These excerpts, which contain several ideas that were present in Foucault's *The Archeology of Knowledge* (although this linkage is not mentioned), exemplify a certain difficulty of defining discourse. In fact, Pêcheux's usage of the concept is sometimes contradictory, and in some formulations, discourse appears to refer to language use or talk: "individuals are 'interpellated' as speaking subjects (as subjects of their discourse) by the discursive formations which represent 'in language' the ideological formations that correspond to them" (Pêcheux 1982: 156).

---

7 Althusser's manuscript exposing the idea of interpellation had circulated at least since 1969 (Bidet 2017); it was published the following year (Althusser 1970). An English translation of the text appeared in *Lenin and Philosophy and Other Essays* (Althusser 1971).
8 All pages of the French text are not included in the selection of pages translated in Pêcheux and Fuchs 2014. For a more detailed analysis of this paper, see Thompson 1984: 232–254.

However, in the same passage, by citing Henry (1977: 118–122), Pêcheux specifies that there is a constitutive reduplication of the subject of discourse, who is both responsible for the contents posed and a "universal subject".

The word *interdiscourse* was first attested in a collective work by Culioli, Fuchs, and Pêcheux (1970: 7) and defined as the "effect of a discourse on another discourse". According to Paveau (2008), this note was probably written by Pêcheux. However, as explained above, the concept had previously appeared in Foucault's (1969, 1972) *The Archeology of Knowledge*, where the adjective *interdiscursif/ve* ('interdiscursive') was used four times, in addition to passages where the phenomenon was described without naming it.

In *Language, Semantics and Ideology*, Pêcheux (1982: 113) argues that the "contradictory material objectivity of interdiscourse" is dissimulated by all discursive formations and the transparent meanings formed within them.[9] Hence, interdiscourse is the space of conflicts and contradictions in which discursive formations unfurl (Paveau 2008: 97). Pêcheux's opaque formulation led to a certain impasse in future research: Interdiscourse is observable only in the marks (*traces*) that it leaves in the observable discourse. New formulations of interdiscourse would appear in the early 1980s (see, e.g., Courtine 1981: 54; 1982: 250; Authier-Revuz 1982), following the weakening of Marxist prerogatives in the French intellectual scene from the mid-1970s onwards (Éribon 1991: 266; Williams 1999: 130). At the same time, Pêcheux's impact would be important, for example, in Brazil and in critical discourse analysis.

7 Foucault's position in French thought in France and beyond

The examples given in the previous section show that in addition to Lacanian psychoanalysis and Althusserian Marxism, both the theory of enunciation and Foucault's theorizations of discourse, discursive formation, and interdiscursivity left a strong mark in Pêcheux's work. However, Foucault was not credited, which may have been linked to Foucault's non-participation in the Marxist venture (Éribon 1991: 52–53, 139; Purvis and Hunt 1993: 487–488; Dosse 2012b: 117–119). The most important difference between Foucault and the "mainstream" French discourse analysis of the 1960s and 1970s was Foucault's avoidance of referring to Marx and his reluctance to use the term *ideology* – although he had used this

---

9 French original : *Les vérités de La Palice* (Pêcheux 1975: 146–147).

term 26 times in *The Order of Things* (Foucault 1966, 1970). Foucault (1980c: 118) did not agree with the non-material dimension of ideologies in certain theories and argued that the concept implies almost inevitably an opposition between ideology and truth, as well as the recognition of a phenomenological, constitutive subject. In addition, Foucault's (1983: 211) deliberate refusal to cite Marx in the 1960s and 1970s was related to his unwillingness to gratify dogmatic Marxists, although he mentions ideology several times in a seemingly neutral fashion in interviews and particularly in one of the most important collected volumes of his thought in English, namely *Power/Knowledge* (Foucault 1980a).

Another explanation for Foucault's dismissal among French discourse analysts was the fact that he did not develop an exact methodology for discourse analysis, which meant that his influence remained subterranean (Maingueneau 1991: 14). His theory of discourse was not linguistic (Purvis and Hunt 1993: 490), and according to Mazière (2005: 55–56), his theorizations were to a certain extent useless for those who considered language and discourse as interdependent notions and who viewed the discursive formation as containing essentially linguistic forms. In addition, he was not interested in political discourse like linguistically oriented discourse analysts; his main interest had always been the historical analysis of the "different modes by which, in our culture, human beings are made subjects" (Foucault 1982: 777).

In the early 1970s, Foucault started to move gradually beyond reflections centered on language, discourse, and enunciation toward concepts such as power, biopower, and governmentality. He viewed power not only as negative, repressive, or restrictive, but also as manifest in the effects it produces in relation to desire and knowledge (Foucault 1980b: 59): Power produces discourse, induces pleasure, and traverses and produces things (Foucault 1980c: 119). Developing an idea he had expressed in *The Order of Discourse* (Foucault 1970; 1981), he regarded truth as one of the effects of power and considered that each society ratifies certain discourses as representations of the truth (Foucault 1980c: 131). Finally, while relations of power are everywhere and interwoven with all kinds of social relations, the existence of resistances is a condition *sine qua non* for the existence of power (Foucault 1980d: 142).

Foucault became immensely popular in the USA, which, according to Cusset (2003: 11–15), was related to a "structural misunderstanding" stemming from a different organization of the academic field in France and the United States. Foucault and other theorists such as Baudrillard, Derrida, Deleuze, Guattari, Lacan, Lévi-Strauss, and Lyotard were all regarded as representatives of French "poststructuralism" or "French Theory". Typically, literary studies and French departments were the ports of entry for these thinkers into the U.S. academy (Cusset 2003: 86–117).

The theories of these thinkers, conflated under the common denominator of French Theory, constitute a prime example of denationalized (Bourdieu 2002: 3) "traveling theories" (Said 1984: 226–247). Often, these theoreticians were recycled by U.S. scholars, so that especially in the Anglophone world, many scholars know their thought only through the interpretation and explanation provided by another scholar (Cusset 2003: 302–303). In fact, Sawyer (2002) argues that the concept of discourse was attributed to Foucault retrospectively in British cultural studies to refer to a concept that had been formed earlier in relation to other French scholars, such as Althusser, Lacan, and Pêcheux. As a result, Sawyer contends, many connotations of the notion of ideology and of other Marxist and Lacanian theorizations were attached to discourse, and the difference between the two concepts became blurred. However, as I wish to have shown in this chapter, while all currents present in the French thought of the late 1960s and early 1970s influenced each other, Foucault's concept of discourse was already a hybrid construction, and Pêcheux's theorizations were often reformulations of Foucault's conceptualizations.

Bennett (2017) thinks that exoticism played an important role in making Foucault so popular among English-speaking scholars. According to her, a double exoticization took place in order to market Foucault for English-speaking readers: He was presented as a French theorist whose writing is complex and as a thinker whose works were disseminated in rather opaque translations. In other words, the translations of Foucault's works did not follow the tendency of "domesticated" translations, in which fluency outweighs accuracy, as is usually the case for translations from other languages into English, especially in the United States (Venuti 1995: 1). The unstable meaning of Foucault's key concepts both in French and in English translations has been discussed by several scholars (e.g., Bennett 2017: 233; Sawyer 2002: 434, 437; Cusset 2003: 101).

Translation automatically entails a new context and a new set of indexical links to other voices, meanings, words, texts, and discourses, because the situation and the context in which the text is produced is different (Blommaert 2006). An example of such shifts from Foucault's writing is the couple *discours–discourse*, even though the French and the English word share the same etymology and appear to denote the same references. Foucault used the word profusely in *The Order of Things*, published in French in 1966 (*Les mots et les choses*, 'The words and the things') and in English in 1970. Hence, the concept was familiar to his readers both in the Francophone and the Anglophone world by the time *The Archeology of Knowledge* was published in French in 1969 and in English in 1972. However, in *The Order of Things*, the usage appears to correspond mostly to the meaning "representation" (Foucault 1966: 93–96; [1970] 1989: 86–90), or appears in his discussion of French scholars of the classical period, especially Condillac, who uses the concept mostly in the sense of language production about a specific topic. However, in the following quote from Condillac, the usage is strangely similar to Foucault's later theory of discourse: "Where there is discourse, representations are laid out and juxtaposed; and things are grouped together and articulated" (Foucault 1966: 322; 1989: 338–339). One of the key elements of discourse, namely statement (*énoncé*), was also known to Foucault's translators and readers: It had been used in the English translation of *The Order of Things* six times as an equivalent of five different French words (*constat* [twice], *parole*, *propos*, *déclaration*, and *affirmation*) – but not *énoncé*.

8 Conclusion

In this very succinct overview of the etymology and history of the concepts of discourse and ideology and their importance in French discourse analysis in the 1960s and 1970s, I have analyzed only a small sample of the thinkers who have used these concepts in their work. Both terms have been essentially polysemic throughout their history, and both have been politicized. The "neutral" and "scientific" notions, such as the definition of discourse as language use beyond the sentence or of ideology as a belief system, have been present since the first attested usages in French and English texts. They have not been invented by any branch of linguistics.

The analysis of the early years of French discourse analysis shows that the operationalization of the concept of ideology in linguistically oriented discourse analysis led to somewhat complex and opaque definitions. One problem resided in the clash between the constraints created by certain forms of Marxist thought and the linguistic definitions of language that were prevalent in this era. An additional problem was occasioned by Foucault's theory of discourse and his notions of discursive formation and interdiscursivity, which incorporated many of the coeval theorizations of ideology within them. When these conceptualizations were surreptitiously integrated into linguistically oriented discourse analysis dominated by Marxism, the boundaries among the concepts grew increasingly blurry.

Subsequently, French theorizations of discourse and ideology, and especially Foucault's thoughts about discourse, have travelled through several translations, interpretations, and schools of thought, entering into contact with multiple epistemologies and conceptual configurations. This journey has increased the polysemy of the concepts and created several models for understanding the relationship between the two. A glimpse of the history of the concepts shows that the interrelationship has perhaps never been easy and may contribute to fathoming out some of the current dilemmas in defining them.

References

Académie française. 1694. *Le Dictionnaire de l'Académie Françoise*, dédié au Roi. Paris: Jean Baptiste Coignard.
Althusser, Louis. 1969. *For Marx*. Ben Brewster (transl.). London: Allen Lan.
Althusser, Louis. 1971. *Lenin and philosophy and other essays*. Ben Brewster (transl.). London: New Left Books.
Althusser, Louis & Étienne Balibar. 1970. *Reading Capital*. Ben Brewster (transl.). London: New Left Books.
Angermuller, Johannes. 2007. Qu'est-ce que le poststructuralisme français? À propos de la notion de discours d'un pays à l'autre. *Langage et société* 120. 17–34.
Angermuller, Johannes, Dominique Maingueneau & Ruth Wodak. 2014. Michel Pêcheux: From ideology to discourse. In Johannes Angermuller, Dominique Maingueneau & Ruth Wodak (eds.), *The discourse studies reader: Main currents in theory and analysis*, 89. Amsterdam & Philadelphia: John Benjamins.
Authier-Revuz, Jacqueline. 1982. Hétérogénéité montrée et hétérogénéité constitutive. *DRLAV – Documentation et Recherche en Linguistique Allemande Vincennes* 26. 91–151.
Bachelard, Gaston. 1938. *La formation de l'esprit scientifique. Contribution à une psychanalyse de la connaissance objective*. Paris: J. Vrin.
Balibar, Étienne. 1989. Foucault et Marx. L'enjeu du nominalisme. In Association pour le Centre Michel Foucault (ed.), *Michel Foucault philosophe: rencontre internationale, Paris, 9, 10, 11 janvier 1988*, 54–77. Paris: Seuil.
Barthes, Roland. 1966. Introduction à l'étude structurale des récits. *Communications* 8. 1–27.
Bennett, Karen. 2017. Foucault in English: The politics of exoticization. *Target* 29 (2). 222–243.
Benveniste, Émile. 1966. *Problèmes de linguistique générale I*. Paris: Gallimard.
Benveniste, Émile. 1970. L'appareil formel de l'énonciation. *Langages* 5 (19). 12–18.
Bidet, Jacques. 2017. Le sujet interpellé: au-delà d'Althusser et de Butler. *Actuel Marx* 61. 184–201.
Blommaert, Jan. 2006. How legitimate is my voice? A rejoinder. *Target* 18 (1). 63–76.
Bourdieu, Pierre. 2002. Les conditions sociales de la circulation internationale des idées. *Actes de la recherche en sciences sociales* 145. 3–8.
Canguilhem, Georges. 1977. *Idéologie et rationalité dans l'histoire des sciences de la vie*. Paris: Vrin.
Courtine, Jean-Jacques. 1981. Quelques problèmes théoriques et méthodologiques en analyse du discours. À propos du discours communiste adressé aux chrétiens. *Langages* 62. 9–128.
Courtine, Jean-Jacques. 1982. Définition d'orientations théoriques et construction de procédures en analyse du discours. *Philosophiques* 9 (2). 239–264.
Culioli, Antoine, Catherine Fuchs & Michel Pêcheux. 1970. *Considérations théoriques à propos du traitement formel du langage*. Paris: Dunod.

Cusset, François. 2003. *French theory: Foucault, Derrida, Deleuze & Cie et les mutations de la vie intellectuelle aux États-Unis*. Paris: La Découverte.
de Saussure, Ferdinand. 1959. *Course in general linguistics*. Wade Baskin (transl.). New York: Philosophical Library.
de Saussure, Ferdinand. 1971. *Cours de linguistique générale*. Charles Bally, Albert Sechehaye & Albert Riedlinger (eds.). Paris: Payot.
de Saussure, Ferdinand. 1983. *Course in general linguistics*. Roy Harris (transl.). London: Duckworth.
Destutt de Tracy, Antoine. 1796. Mémoire sur la faculté de penser. In *Mémoires de l'institut national des sciences et art pour l'an IV de la République. Sciences morales et politiques. Tome premier*, 283–450. Paris: Baudouin.
Destutt de Tracy, Antoine. 1801. *Projet d'éléments de l'idéologie à l'usage des écoles centrales de la République française*. Paris: Didot.
Destutt de Tracy, Antoine. 1803. *Éléments d'idéologie. Seconde partie: Grammaire*. Paris: Courcier.
Dosse, François. 2012a [1992]. *Histoire du structuralisme. Tome I: Le champ du signe, 1945–1966*. Paris: La Découverte.
Dosse, François. 2012b [1992]. *Histoire du structuralisme. Tome II: Le chant du cygne, 1967 à nos jours*. Paris: La Découverte.
Dreyfus, Hubert L. & Paul Rabinow. 1983 [1982]. Introduction. In Hubert L. Dreyfus & Paul Rabinow, *Michel Foucault: Beyond structuralism and hermeneutics*, 2nd edn. with an afterword and an interview with Michel Foucault, xvii–xxvii. Chicago: University of Chicago Press.
Eagleton, Terry. 1991. *Ideology: An introduction*. London: Verso.
Éribon, Didier. 1991. *Michel Foucault*. Betsy Wing (transl.). Cambridge, MA: Harvard University Press.
Fairclough, Norman. 1992. *Discourse and social change*. Cambridge: Polity.
Fairclough, Norman. 2010. *Critical discourse analysis: The critical study of language*, 2nd edn. Harlow: Longman.
Foucault, Michel. 1966. *Les mots et les choses. Une archéologie des sciences humaines*. Paris: Gallimard.
Foucault, Michel. 1969. *L'archéologie du savoir*. Paris: Gallimard.
Foucault, Michel. 1970. *L'ordre du discours. Leçon inaugurale au Collège de France prononcée le 2 décembre 1970*. Paris: Gallimard.
Foucault, Michel. 1971. Orders of discourse. Rupert Swyer (transl.). *Social Science Information* 10 (2). 7–30.
Foucault, Michel. 1972. *The archeology of knowledge*. Alan M. Sheridan Smith (transl.). New York: Pantheon Books.
Foucault, Michel. 1980a. *Power/Knowledge: Selected interviews and other writings 1972–1977*. Colin Gordon (ed.). Colin Gordon, Leo Marshall, John Mepham & Kate Soper (transl.). New York: Random House.
Foucault, Michel. 1980b. Body/Power. Colin Gordon (transl.). In Colin Gordon (ed.), *Power/Knowledge: Selected interviews and other writings 1972–1977*, 55–62. New York: Random House.
Foucault, Michel. 1980c. Truth and power. Colin Gordon (transl.). In Colin Gordon (ed.), *Power/Knowledge: Selected interviews and other writings 1972–1977*, 109–133. New York: Random House.

Foucault, Michel. 1980d. The eye of power. Colin Gordon (transl.). In Colin Gordon (ed.), *Power/Knowledge: Selected interviews and other writings 1972–1977*, 146–165. New York: Random House.
Foucault, Michel. 1981. The order of discourse. Ian McLeod (transl.). In Robert Young (ed.), *Untying the text: A post-structuralist reader*, 51–78. Boston, London & Henley: Routledge & Kegan Paul.
Foucault, Michel. 1982. The subject and power. Leslie Sawyer (transl.). *Critical Inquiry* 8. 777–795.
Foucault, Michel. 1983. Structuralism and post-structuralism: An interview with Michel Foucault (by Gérard Raulet). *Telos* 55. 195–211.
Foucault, Michel. 1988. The return of morality. Thomas Levin & Isabelle Lorenz (transl.). In Lawrence D. Kritzman (ed.), *Politics, philosophy, culture: Interviews and other writings 1977–1984*, 242–254. London & New York: Routledge.
Foucault, Michel. 1989 [1970]. *The order of things: An archaeology of the human sciences*. Alan M. Sheridan Smith (transl.). London & New York: Routledge.
Gadet, Françoise. 1989. Après Saussure. *DRLAV – Documentation et Recherche en Linguistique Allemande Vincennes* 40. 1–40.
Gal, Susan & Kathryn A. Woolard. 1995. Constructing languages and publics: Authority and representation. *Pragmatics* 5 (2). 129–138.
Geuss, Raymond. 1981. *The idea of a critical theory: Habermas and the Frankfurt School*. Cambridge: Cambridge University Press.
Gramsci, Antonio. 1999. *Selections from the prison notebooks*. Quintin Hoare & Geoffrey Nowell Smith (ed. & transl.). London: Electric Book.
Hall, Stuart. 1996 [1986]. The problem of ideology: Marxism without guarantees. In David Morley & Kuan-Hsing Chen (eds.), *Stuart Hall: Critical dialogues in cultural studies*, 24–45. London & New York: Routledge.
Haroche, Claudine, Paul Henry & Michel Pêcheux. 1971. La sémantique et la coupure saussurienne: langue, langage, discours. *Langages* 24. 93–106.
Harris, Zellig. 1952. Discourse analysis. *Language* 28 (1). 1–30.
Hayward, Jack. 2007. *Fragmented France: Two centuries of disputed identity*. New York & Oxford: Oxford University Press.
Henry, Paul. 1977. *Le mauvais outil. Langue, sujet et discours*. Paris: Klincksieck.
Hymes, Dell. 1974. *Foundations in sociolinguistics: An ethnographic approach*. Philadelphia: University of Pennsylvania Press.
Kerbrat-Orecchioni, Catherine. 2006. *L'énonciation. De la subjectivité dans le langage*. Paris: Armand Colin.
Kristeva, Julia. 1969. *Semiotikè. Recherches pour une sémanalyse*. Paris: Seuil.
Kroskrity, Paul V. 2000. Regimenting languages: Language ideological perspectives. In Paul V. Kroskrity (ed.), *Regimes of language: Ideologies, polities, and identity*, 1–34. Santa Fe, NM: School of American Research Press.
Lacan, Jacques. 1966. *Écrits*. Paris: Seuil.
Larrain, Jorge. 1983. *Marxism and ideology*. London: MacMillan.
Lévi-Strauss, Claude. 1949. L'efficacité symbolique. *Revue de l'histoire des religions* 135 (1). 5–27.
Lévi-Strauss, Claude. 1955. The structural study of myths. *The Journal of American Folklore* 68 (270). 428–444.
Lévi-Strauss, Claude. 1958. *Anthropologie structurale*. Paris: Plon.

Lévi-Strauss, Claude. 1963. *Structural anthropology*. Claire Jacobson & Brooke Grundfest Schoepf (transl.). New York: Basic Books.
Limat-Letellier, Nathalie. 1998. Historique du concept d'intertextualité. In Marie Miguet-Ollagnier & Nathalie Limat-Letellier (eds.), *L'intertextualité*, 17–64. Besançon: Presses universitaires de Franche-Comté.
Maingueneau, Dominique. 1991. *L'analyse du discours: Introduction aux études de l'archive*. Paris: Hachette.
Maingueneau, Dominique. 2002. École française de l'analyse du discours. In Patrick Charaudeau & Dominique Maingueneau (eds.), *Dictionnaire d'analyse du discours*, 201–202. Paris: Seuil.
Maingueneau, Dominique. 2005. L'analyse du discours et ses frontières. *Marges linguistiques* 9. 64–75.
Mannheim, Karl. 1936. *Ideology and utopia: An introduction to the sociology of knowledge*. Louis Wirth & Edward Shils (transl.). London: K. Paul, Trench, Trubner & Co.
Marandin, Jean-Marie. 1979. Problèmes d'analyse du discours. Essai de description du discours français sur la Chine. *Langages* 55. 17–88.
Marcellesi, Jean-Baptiste & Bernard Gardin. 1974. *Introduction à la sociolinguistique: la linguistique sociale*. Paris: Larousse.
Marx, Karl & Frederick Engels. 2010. *Karl Marx and Frederick Engels: Collected works, vol. 5 (Marx and Engels 1845–1847)*. Clemens Dutt, W. Lough & C. P. Magill (transl.). London: Electric Book.
Mazière, Francine. 2005. *L'analyse du discours*. Paris: PUF.
Mazière, Francine. 2010. *L'analyse du discours*, 2nd updated edn. Paris: PUF.
Nicholls, David. 1999. *Napoleon: A biographical companion*. Santa Barbara: ABC-CLIO.
Paveau, Marie-Anne. 2008. Interdiscours et intertexte. In Driss Ablali & Margareta Kastberg Sjöblom (eds.), *Linguistique et littérature: Cluny, 40 ans après*, 93–105. Besançon: Presses Universitaires de Franche-Comté.
Pêcheux, Michel. 1967. Analyse de contenu et théorie du discours. *Bulletin d'Études et Recherches Psychologiques* 3. 211–227.
Pêcheux, Michel. 1969. *Analyse automatique du discours*. Paris: Dunod.
Pêcheux, Michel. 1975. *Les vérités de La Palice*. Paris: Maspero.
Pêcheux, Michel. 1982. *Language, semantics and ideology*. Harbans Nagpal (transl.). London: MacMillan.
Pêcheux, Michel & Catherine Fuchs. 1975. Mises au point et perspectives à propos de l'analyse automatique du discours. *Langages* 37. 7–80.
Pêcheux, Michel & Catherine Fuchs. 2014. Development and perspectives of the automatic analysis of discourse. In Johannes Angermuller, Dominique Maingueneau & Ruth Wodak (eds.), *The discourse studies reader: Main currents in theory and analysis*, 90–97. Amsterdam & Philadelphia: John Benjamins.
Phillips, Edward. 1658. *The new world of words, or universal English dictionary*. London: [Printed for] R. Bentley, I. Phillips, H. Rhodes & I. Taylor.
Puech, Christian. 2005. L'émergence de la notion de « discours » en France et les destins du saussurisme. *Langages* 159. 93–110.
Purvis, Trevor & Alan Hunt. 1993. Discourse, ideology, discourse, ideology, discourse, ideology ... *The British Journal of Sociology* 44 (3). 473–499.
Rey, Alain. 1992. (ed.) *Dictionnaire historique de la langue française*. Paris: Dictionnaires Le Robert.

Rosen, Michael & Jonathan Wolff. 1996. The problem of ideology. *Aristotelian Society Supplementary Volume*, 70 (1). 209–242.
Said, Edward. 1984. *The world, the text, and the critic*. London: Faber & Faber.
Sarfati, Georges-Élia. 2005. *Éléments d'analyse du discours*. Paris: Armand Colin.
Sawyer, R. Keith. 2002. A discourse on discourse: An archeological history of an intellectual concept. *Cultural Studies* 16 (3). 433–456.
Schiffrin, Deborah. 1994. *Approaches to discourse*. Oxford: Blackwell.
Thompson, John B. 1984. *Studies in the theory of ideology*. Cambridge: Polity.
TLFi 2002 = ATILF, CNRS & Université de Lorraine. 2002. *Trésor de la langue française informatisé*. http://atilf.atilf.fr/ (accessed 9 January 2021).
Venuti, Lawrence. 1995. *The translator's invisibility. A history of translation*. London & New York: Routledge.
Vološinov, Valentin Nikolajevitš. 1986 [1973]. *Marxism and the philosophy of language*. Ladislav Matejka & I. R. Titunik (transl.). Cambridge, MA: Harvard University Press.
Williams, Glyn. 1999. *French discourse analysis: The method of post-structuralism*. London & New York: Routledge.
Wolff, Jonathan & David Leopold. 2021. Karl Marx. In Edward N. Zalta (ed.), *The Stanford encyclopedia of philosophy*, Spring 2021 edn. https://plato.stanford.edu/archives/spr2021/entries/marx/ (accessed 9 January 2021).

Samuel Vernet
Chapter 3
Teaching French in Acadia: From a discourse of linguistic diversity to a standard ideology

Abstract: This chapter exposes a sociolinguistic ethnographic inquiry conducted at the Université de Moncton in Acadia, a francophone minority region in Canada. The research aimed at studying what variety of French was taught, how, and why. After a contextualization of Acadia, the ethnographic data are presented. Then, the chapter proposes to use the notions of discourse and ideology together to achieve a good understanding of a complex situation where Acadian French practices are both praised and sanctioned by teachers. Discourse is understood as a set of utterances unified by a series of rules and conditions constraining their form and content. These rules are regarded as ideologically determined, leading to a definition of the notion of ideology as a system of beliefs that both emerges from the social structures and shapes them. The chapter concludes by arguing that a discourse of linguistic diversity can be mobilized for the benefit of a standard ideology.

Keywords: critical sociolinguistics, ethnography, Acadia, linguistic diversity, standard ideology

1 Introduction: Discourse, ideology, and the analysis of linguistic domination

In this chapter, the notion of "discourse" is understood as a set of utterances unified by a series of rules and conditions constraining their form and content. These rules are regarded as ideologically determined. The notion of "ideology" is then understood as a system of beliefs that both emerges from the social structures and shapes them. The purpose of this chapter is to show how the discourse of linguistic diversity can be mobilized in French courses in Acadia for the benefit of a standard ideology.

This chapter aims to explain the appropriateness the notions of discourse and ideology can have for a critical approach to discourse analysis when they are used jointly. I start by describing an ethnographic sociolinguistic inquiry carried out in the region of Acadia in New Brunswick, a francophone minority region in Eastern Canada, where I conducted PhD fieldwork in 2013–2014. My doctoral research aimed at studying what variety of French was taught, how, and why. The field of inquiry was the Université de Moncton, a French-speaking university where French courses are mandatory for all students and delivered within the bachelor's program. Acadians have been living among an anglophone majority for centuries; as a result, English is obviously a dominant language in Acadia. It is certainly possible to live entirely in English in Acadia, but perhaps not to do the same in French. Moreover, the research documented a second process of domination, namely the domination of Standard French[1] in Acadian society over vernacular practices, leading to a crossed minorization situation. The latter domination process is "erased" (Irvine and Gal 2000) by the first one as the status of the French-speaking minority is interiorized and becomes part of an essentialized Acadian identity (Vernet 2020, 2021). That is why I took an interest in describing the power relations within individuals' relationship with linguistic practices. Within this framework, the notions of discourse and ideology became necessary theoretical and methodological tools.

After presenting the field of inquiry more precisely, I will describe some relevant data excerpts. These data concern the use of the term *linguistic diversity* in the French courses at the Université de Moncton. As we will see, teachers and administrators make use of this notion as a category to include all vernacular practices. In class, in front of the students, and in interviews in front of me, teachers profusely praised the social and cultural virtues of linguistic diversity. Yet, vernacular practices are systematically penalized on the exams, and confined to private and personal spheres of language use (Vernet 2019). Initially, I interpreted this phenomenon as an example of contradictory doublespeak; however, in this text, I argue that an analysis combining the notions of discourse and ideology brings out the coherence of such a situation. In this chapter, these data will be presented in detail and analyzed, first as a discourse, then as emanating from an ideology. I want to show that if we observe the utterances that refer to "linguistic diversity" as a "discourse" unified by its conditions of emergence, we can then link these conditions to a dominant ideology which constrains the content and the linguistic form of utterances. Analyzing the discourse then sheds light on the ideology; and ideology is a fundamental notion allowing the understanding of power relations that I seek to highlight.

---

1 While it is impossible to delimitate "Standard French", it is important to note that it is an exogenous variety, widely picked up in textbooks and dictionaries published in France and sometimes in Québec. Henceforth, I will use Standard French without quotes, while being aware that naming such a vague set of uses contributes to its essentialization and that the very possibility to delineate the linguistic forms of any standard can be considered a myth (Lippi-Green [1997] 2012: 55–63).

2 Framing the field

Acadia is a historical francophone minority region in Eastern Canada. I say "historical" because today it does not correspond to any administrative border. Instead, Acadia corresponds to the places in the Maritime Provinces where the French settled during the seventeenth century, and where francophones still live today. This region was almost entirely ceded to the British in 1713 (Peace of Utrecht).[2] The francophones have been minoritized, both demographically as in terms of political power, for more than three centuries. Since the end of the nineteenth century, Acadians have successfully fought for cultural recognition and linguistic rights (LeBlanc and Boudreau 2016). They have gained recognition in the form of public francophone schools, hospitals, official bilingualism, etc., and today they have a more secure situation than ever in their history. Nevertheless, they have not achieved equality with the English-speaking majority.[3]

The linguistic ecology of Acadia is inherited from that history. French in Acadia is a spectrum in which three blended sets of linguistic practices can be identified. First, the so-called traditional Acadian designates all the phonetic, lexical, morphological, and syntactic elements that were present in the first settlers' French (Massignon 1962; Péronnet 1989). Second, the normative French called "standard" is official, taught, and disseminated by the media and institutions. That set of linguistic practices comes from reference books mostly published in France, and to a certain extent in Québec, meaning that it replicates linguistic patterns from France. Third, from the secular contact with the English-speaking majority, a full-fledged variety called Chiac has developed. It integrates English lexical elements in a French morphological and syntactical framework (Perrot 1995; King 2008). Several phenomena are linked to this variety. Indeed, it evokes identity, and social and cultural issues for Acadians, and constitutes the language of socialization for a significant part of them, particularly (but not only) in Southeastern New Brunswick, around the city of Moncton (Comeau and King 2011). At the same time, it is perceived by many (especially in institutions) as proof of the gradual anglicization of the French-speaking minority (Boudreau 1996).

However, it would be impossible to settle the Chiac debate within this chapter. Besides, linguistic issues regularly raise public debates in Acadia. Given

---

2 For more information about Acadian general history, see Landry and Lang (2014), and about the "French period", Faragher (2005).
3 For more information about inequalities between Anglophone and Francophone communities, see, for example, Forgues, Beaudin, and Béland (2006), and for a general overview about the vitality of the Acadian community, see Allard and Landry (1998).

the context, it is often the issue of the "quality" of French[4] that comes up (Arrighi and Violette 2013). French, in its standard form, is taught throughout undergraduate studies. At the Université de Moncton, two French courses are mandatory for all students: written communication and oral communication. The level of French is subject to a test prior to registering at the university. This test determines whether the student will take only these two courses, or whether they will have to complete one or two remedial courses. That is why, when I arrived in Moncton to understand what kind of French was taught, how, why, etc., it was particularly relevant to attend these courses.

My attention ended up being drawn to the domination of Standard French over vernacular practices. The double minorization of Acadian French mentioned above (regarding English on the one hand, and Standard French on the other hand) can be seen in the phenomenon of self-depreciation of vernacular French. For the French-speaking minority, this phenomenon legitimates only the Standard alongside English in the spheres of power (that is, in institutions, at work, in politics, in the media, etc.), making it a tool for social selection.

This situation of complex minorization is certainly not unique to Acadia. However, at the Université de Moncton, sociolinguistics is a powerful and visible scientific discipline. Professors, and even the administration, share a common ground of sociolinguistic knowledge. Since the mid-1990s, they have been trying to engage thinking about linguistic norms (Vernet and Määttä 2019) within the French courses. At the time of the inquiry, French courses taught Standard French, while claiming to be "taking linguistic diversity into account".

3 The ethnographic corpus

To understand how teachers try to meet these two goals, I chose an ethnographic approach. Ethnography allows the construction of a multimodal corpus where different types of data can be crossed to shed light on one facet of the problem,[5] each in its own way. At the end of a research project, the researcher has gathered a vast amount of data. Once transcribed, these data form a set of utterances that have a content and a linguistic form; both can be analyzed to understand "what is

---

[4] The debate on the quality of French is overarching all over Francophone Canada, including Québec, where French is not in the same minority situation (Cajolet-Laganière and Martel 1995; Laforest 1997).
[5] To find out more about ethnography, read Wolcott ([1999] 2008), and about this approach applied to linguistics and sociolinguistics, see Duranti (1997) or Blommaert (2018).

said". In addition, the interpretation of data allows us to identify that which is not said. Such a content analysis involves the inherent risks of interpretation – wrong interpretations and over-interpretation (Lahire 1996). I will illustrate that point with some data of my inquiry in Acadia.

The chapter is based on an inquiry that took place in 2013–2014. I attended the two compulsory French courses, recorded and transcribed them, and collected the pedagogical materials and the administrative documents linked to the French courses since 1992. Finally, I interviewed the French teachers – 12 of the 16 of teachers who were teaching French at the time. During the investigations, I came across problematic data related to the relationship of individuals to linguistic diversity.

In what follows, I will first present an excerpt of the syllabus of the oral communication course. Then, five excerpts of teachers in class and in interviews will illustrate teachers' stances toward linguistic practices and linguistic norms. Finally, one excerpt gives an overview of the evaluation grids used in class. This sample is intended to be representative of the way in which linguistic diversity is taken into account in the classroom. This chapter focuses on theoretical reflection; consequently, in this section, I will only describe the examples. The analyses are proposed in Section 4 and contribute to the theorization of the notions of discourse and ideology. The extracts are presented in French and translated into English; translations are mine unless otherwise noted. Since the analysis of the transcripts focuses on the semantic content, I have not included prosodic features or pauses and false starts. Instead, I have "normalized" the texts by dividing them into sentences and clauses through punctuation marks. All the teachers cited were working as French teachers at the Université de Moncton in 2013–2014.

As noted above, in French classes, a normative standard French is taught. However, at the same time, linguistic diversity is claimed to be an asset. In the syllabus of the oral communication course, the main goal of the course is worded as follows:

(1) *Assurer une meilleure maîtrise d'une variété standard à l'oral et en valoriser l'usage dans la vie universitaire et professionnelle en tenant compte de la diversité linguistique du milieu.*

[Improve oral skills in a Standard variety and promote its use in academic and professional life while taking into account the linguistic diversity of the environment.]

Strictly speaking, the term "linguistic diversity" is vague enough to include any linguistic practice: It is up to the teacher to explain to the class what it contains. During the first lecture, immediately after reading the passage in example 1, Teacher 1 explains this point orally to the class:

(2) Professeure 1: *Le milieu, surtout ce milieu-ci, est très bilingue, vous allez vous en apercevoir. Puis un peu partout y a des contacts de langue et puis ça colore la langue française et des fois on a de la difficulté à faire le tri entre ce qui est standard et ce qui ne l'est pas. Je crois que ça pose problème souvent parce qu'il y a des transferts qui se font de l'oral populaire familier à l'écrit et ça se fait aussi de cet oral-là à l'oral standard, à un oral qui se veut standard. Y a tout un travail à faire dans la distinction des niveaux ou des registres de langue, ça veut dire qu'il y a une partie du cours où nous visons à connaitre la différence entre le standard et les autres niveaux de langue.*

[Teacher 1: The environment, especially this one, is very bilingual, you will notice. Everywhere, there are language contacts, and it colors the French language and sometimes we have difficulties sorting out what is Standard from what is not. I believe this is often a problem because there are language transfers from popular, familiar, oral to written and also from this oral to Standard oral, an oral which is supposed to be standard. There is work to be done to distinguish language levels or language registers; that means that during the course, we will learn to identify the difference between Standard and other language levels.]

Basically, "linguistic diversity" comprises all linguistic practices that are not Standard French. This restricted meaning of the word "diversity" is relatively common and contributes to essentializing the language practices considered as a cultural heritage linked to minority groups (to go further, see the analysis of the word "diversity" by Muehlmann 2007). So how do teachers "take diversity into account"? Generally, by having meliorative stances on vernacular practices. Here are two representative examples; the first one, from Teacher 2 in example 3, takes place in front of her class, and the second one, from Teacher 1 in example 4, takes place during an interview with me:

(3) Professeure 2: *La langue a beaucoup varié dans le temps, donc on l'a vu le français n'est plus exactement ce qu'il était en 1604,[6] ça a évolué. Y a une variation géographique donc ça varie selon les régions, y a une variation sociale aussi, si vous prenez un ouvrier, il parlera pas de la même façon qu'un médecin ou un avocat par exemple, donc c'est là où y a des différences parfois socio-économiques donc selon les métiers. Est-ce que ça veut dire qu'un ouvrier parle moins bien qu'un avocat, non, ça veut juste dire que c'est différent.*

[Teacher 2: Language has changed a lot over time. As we saw, French is not exactly what it was in 1604,[6] – it has evolved. There is a geographical variation, so it varies according to regions; there is a social variation also. If you take a worker, he won't speak the same way as a doctor or a lawyer, for instance, so there are socio-economic differences depending on professions. Does it mean that a worker speaks poorly compared to a lawyer? No, it just means that it is different.]

---

6 The year 1604 is the date of the establishment of the first French settlement in Canada, Port-Royal, in the Bay of Fundy.

(4) Professeure 1: *Ils [les étudiants] aiment les anglicismes, ils aiment ces anglicismes, les archaïsmes, des régionalismes, ces mots non-standard ont un charme il faut le dire, ils aiment s'en servir.*

[Teacher 1: [Students] like Anglicisms; they like these Anglicisms, archaisms, regionalisms; these non-Standard words have a certain charm, it should be said – they like to use them.]

Meliorative utterances are sometimes essentializing and regularly counterbalanced by normative remarks, especially concerning the degree of tolerance that teachers should or should not have. Example 5 is the immediate continuation of the previous example 4; Teacher 1 explains some of the rules governing her decision-making:

(5) Professeure 1: *Des archaïsmes, de vieux termes acadiens (...)[7] je pense à des anglicismes, ça je n'accepte pas. Certains anglicismes, pas tous, parking je peux accepter, ceux qu'on voit dans les dictionnaires, baby-sitting, et qui sont acceptés. Je les accepte. Mais si y a un équivalent en français, walkman, je pourrais pas l'accepter parce que baladeur est l'équivalent, tu vois ? parking, baby-sitting, je l'accepte parce qu'il n'y a pas de marque d'usage dans le dictionnaire Petit Robert ou Larousse pour dire que ce n'est pas du français standard.*

[Teacher 1: Archaisms, old Acadian terms [...] – I think about Anglicisms, [and] I don't accept that. Some Anglicisms, not all of them – *parking*, I can accept it – those that we see in dictionaries, *baby-sitting*, and which are accepted. I accept them. But if there is a French equivalent – *walkman*, I cannot accept it because *baladeur* is an equivalent, see? *Parking, baby-sitting* – I accept those because there are no usage labels in the Larousse or Petit Robert dictionaries to say that they are not Standard French.]

The balance between meliorative utterances about linguistic diversity and normative attitudes reaches the point where many teachers explicitly express a duality: claiming the importance of the vernacular practices on the one hand and restraining their use on the other. During an interview, Teacher 3 gives a good example of that duality constructed with the pivotal word *mais* ('but'):

(6) Professeure 3: *À un moment y a quelqu'un qui a dit ça « moi je parle vraiment mal ». Hey je veux pas entendre ça dans mon cours, c'est pas vrai, c'est pas vrai que tu parles mal, c'est pas vrai. Puis le chiac, ben je dis, moi je veux que vous maitrisiez la variété de langue standard mais ne perdez jamais votre chiac. C'est votre identité, c'est vous-autres ça tu sais, c'est comme si j'essayais de vous enlever votre prénom, je peux pas vous enlever votre prénom, mais c'est la même chose. Mais j'ai dit le chiac c'est correct, mais là où ça devient incorrect c'est quand on utilise le chiac dans une situation formelle, là ça fonctionne plus.*

---

7 A series of examples has been cut.

[Teacher 3: At one time somebody said that "I speak really badly". Hey, I do not want to hear that in my course, that is not true, that is not true that you speak badly, it is not true. The Chiac, I say, well, I want you to master the standard variety of language, but never lose your Chiac. It is your identity, it is you, you know. It is like I tried to erase your name – I can't erase your name, it is the same thing. But I say the Chiac is good, but where it is not good, it is when we use the Chiac in a formal situation; there it doesn't work anymore.]

However, "linguistic diversity", which "must be taken into account" (example 1), has, in fact, no place on exams, which are strictly limited to normative French. The most striking example is the evaluation grid distributed during the first lesson of the oral communication course. In general, this scale depends on the type of exercise, but it guides the teacher's choices all along the semester. The grid presents two columns, one for "positive points" and one for "points to be improved"; there are four main categories evaluated, subdivided into 17 criteria, each having at least one sub-criterion in each column. In that grid, some criteria unambiguously reject vernacular practices, as we can see in example 7 (elements within quotes are direct translations):

(7) The criterion "Diction – Pronunciation" indicates that a "socially acceptable pronunciation" is a positive point, while an "archaic pronunciation" is to be improved.

In the criterion "Morphology", it is indicated that the "gender neutralization"[8] should be avoided.

In the criterion "Syntax", it is indicated that "Frequent use of the 'added value' *que* (*quand que*)"[9] should be avoided.

In the criterion "Vocabulary", it is indicated that "Anglicisms, improprieties, pleonasms, archaisms" should be avoided.

"Anglicisms" and "archaisms" are other names for "Chiac" and "traditional Acadian"; however, their connotation is negative.

Therefore, we observe meliorative utterances on vernacular practices related to identity issues, common heritage, culture, and socialization. At the same time, the same people impose restrictions on vernacular usage, accompanied by a constant penalization (sometimes with discriminatory wording, as in the grid described above). These observations raise the following question: that of how to

---

8 In Canadian French (not only Acadian French), it is common to neutralize the gender (masculine or feminine) of some pronouns: *ce, cette* ('this') become [stə], and *tous, toutes* ('all') become [tut].

9 In Acadian French, it is also common to double the conjunction *quand* ('when') by another conjunction, *que* ('that').

interpret people saying one thing and its opposite (even sometimes in the same sentence). A simple content analysis leads to the conclusion that there is a contradiction. Is there incoherence, self-delusion, or even lies? Of course, the answer is no, and the purpose of this chapter is to show how these data are coherent and ideologically rational. In what follows, I will first analyze this talk about linguistic diversity as forming a discourse; then I will try to understand the role of ideology. The analysis of the conditions of existence of these utterances will allow me to argue that a certain context (sometimes facing the class, sometimes the sociolinguist, for example) strongly constrains the form and the content of utterances.

4 Theoretical analysis of the data

4.1 The discourse of diversity

This section will address the following question: To what extent can all the utterances about "linguistic diversity" be considered a *discourse*? This question will allow me to discuss the notion of "discourse", which is difficult to grasp because of a multiplicity of definitions and uses depending on scientific fields and approaches (Määttä 2014: 64–65).

a. Thematizing the discourse

Analyzing power relations between groups requires a critical approach. French critical theory has traditionally linked discourse to the social structures that generate it (Pêcheux 1975; Angermüller 2004). Critical discourse analysis (CDA) was born in Europe following this social critique. CDA aims to understand the legitimization processes of social domination and inequalities (Heller and McElhinny 2017: 235–237). It usually defines discourse as a social practice (Fairclough and Wodak 1997) or as a "general mode of semiosis" (Blommaert 2005: 2). Fairclough (1992: 231) details his three-dimensional analysis as: 1) analyze discourse as text (linguistic level), 2) analyze discourse as a discursive practice (intertextuality, dialogism, circulation, performativity), and 3) analyze discourse as a social practice (power relations and ideologies). Those broad definitions allow different and transdisciplinary theorizations of the notion of discourse. In fact, in CDA, discourse is an analytical tool rather than a theoretical concept, built by the researcher from a heuristic perspective in order to explain a social phenomenon. That is why what is called *discourse* is generally a set of utterances gathered primarily according to a thematic criterion. For instance, an alternation between a *discourse of profit* and a *discourse of pride* has been analyzed in the relationship of the francophone minority in Canada to language practices (Duchêne and Heller 2012; Arrighi 2013). Utterances are then conceived as the observable and analyzable trace of discourse; they are its materiality.

Foucault tried for years to delineate the notion of discourse, and the definitions he gives are not exactly the same in different texts. In his most cited definition, he argues that discourse is "a group of statements for which a group of conditions of existence can be defined"[10] (Foucault 1972: 117). In fact, in this approach, there is a *discourse* when, among a set of utterances, we are able to identify the rules of the discursive formation, meaning the rules governing the formation of a) objects, b) enunciative modalities, c) concepts, and d) theoretical options (each of these elements constitutes a full chapter of Foucault's [1972: 40–71] *The Archaeology of Knowledge*). Foucault's concepts are not all relevant to the analysis of my data. For instance, I will not use the notion of "discursive formation". I would rather employ the notion of ideology that Foucault preferred not to use (Määttä and Pietikäinen 2014: 6). More importantly, what Foucault calls the "object of discourse" corresponds rather to the CDA conception of discourse. In fact, the criteria Foucault (1972: 40–71) used to specify the "objects of discourse", namely *surface of emergence*, *authorities*, and *grids of specifications*, can constitute good arguments from a CDA perspective to consider all the utterances about linguistic diversity as a discourse.

In the data from the Université de Moncton, several utterances thematize linguistic diversity. This theme emerged in Acadia at the end of the sixties, in the heart of social and cultural struggles for recognition. For instance, Brault, in 1969, makes the *Éloge du chiac* in the eponymous documentary film (Brault 1969), while large-scale strikes hit the young Université de Moncton (Boudreau 2016: 29–34; Brault and Perreault 1971). Over the years, education, and particularly French teaching at the Université de Moncton, has become one of the major authorities establishing linguistic diversity as an object (other authorities could be media or literature; see again King 2008). The academic institution, with its teachers and administration, has designated, named, and described linguistic diversity, as we can see in examples 2 and 7 in the previous section. Teachers largely contributed to building grids of specification by dividing linguistic diversity into small subcategories, each having a special treatment in class. For example, a lin-

---

10 In the most recent editions of *The Archaeology of Knowledge*, the words "conditions of existence" are replaced by "discursive formation", which are a literal translation of the French text. For my part, I prefer to use the term "utterances" rather than "statements", which is also a closer translation of the French word "*énoncé*", used by Foucault.

guistic practice that is considered a borrowing can be tolerated. On the contrary, however, a linguistic practice that is considered an Anglicism must be penalized. Furthermore, lexical, morphological, syntactical, or phonetical practices do not have the same treatment. This has led to evaluation grids comprising dozens of criteria, as example 7 shows.

Thus, while I do not take Foucault's concepts entirely as they are, his materialist[11] approach to discourse provides valuable help in understanding how and why the existence of discourse and its linguistic forms are ideologically conditioned – and how discourse supports and reproduces ideologies. In order to show this link, I will now describe the *discourse of linguistic diversity* using three criteria proposed by Foucault: modalities of enunciation, concepts, and theoretical options.

b. Describing the discourse of linguistic diversity

If linguistic diversity constitutes a discourse, it is relevant to look for shared enunciative modalities among the utterances. This means asking two crucial questions in CDA: Who has the legitimacy and authority to speak about linguistic diversity? And from what institutional position? In all the data, there are no occurrences of linguistic diversity proffered by the students. Hence, these specific terms are not reclaimed by field actors. These terms can only be found in administrative documents (written by teachers in charge, teachers who temporarily assume an administrative position, or external consultants, generally linguists), and in the words of teachers, in class in front of students, and in interviews in front of me. We can clearly delineate the enunciative modalities of linguistic diversity: This notion is used by teachers and researchers speaking from an institutional position to persons (students) who are predisposed to recognize the authority of teachers in matters of language, and in doing so, to accept what comes from them. This is what Bourdieu (1984: 103) calls an "authority-belief linkage".

As mentioned earlier, linguistic diversity is composed of a complete taxonomy of linguistic practices – in other words, a set of concepts enacted by this

---

[11] This term refers to a Marxist approach in the social sciences (Godelier 1980) from which the so-called "French" discourse analysis is derived, notably by Michel Pêcheux, and subsequently, Foucault and his theorization of discourse. The notion of "materialism" has here two meanings. At a linguistic level, the analysis focuses on the concrete study of linguistic marks in the discourse. At a supra-level, following the idea that "the subject is not the source of meaning" (Maldidier and Pêcheux 1990: 89, my translation), it seeks to link these linguistic traces to social structures and their history, in a given context.

authority. The examples from the data samples above illustrate this taxonomy: *bilingualism* (2), *language contacts* (2), *colloquial French* (2), *geographical variation* (3), *Anglicisms* (4, 5, 7), *archaisms* (4, 5, 7), *regionalisms* (4), and *Chiac* (6). All these concepts are subcategories of linguistic diversity produced by persons in a position of authority (here, teachers and researchers). More important than the labels themselves is the relationship between these concepts: succession, concomitance, contradiction, erasure, etc. For example, in the data, *bilingualism* is concomitant with *language contacts*. In example 2, these two labels designate close realities: the dominant presence of English in francophone lives. Also concomitant are *Anglicisms*, *archaisms*, and *regionalisms* in the enumeration in examples 5 and 7. Even if they label different linguistic practices, they co-occur to exemplify "non-standard" practices opposed to Standard French. Some concepts composing linguistic diversity are in contradiction to each other, in the sense that their label indexes different representations and attitudes. For example, *language contacts* and *Anglicisms* qualify the same linguistic practices, although they appear in slightly different contexts. *Language contact* has a more meliorative connotation ("It colors the language" [2]) and appears in descriptive contexts; *Anglicisms* has a negative connotation and appears to be opposed to the *standard* and qualified as a language mistake in evaluation grids, as in example 7. The same happens with *(traditional) Acadian*, which has a positive connotation, and *archaisms*, negatively connoted and penalized in class and on exams. Finally, it is significant that when it comes to describing *linguistic diversity*, the labels erase Standard French, while on a linguistic basis we could think that diversity comprises all linguistic practices, including the normative ones. It is as though the dominant practices were taken for granted, while "the rest of it" had to be described and distributed in specific spheres of use, as we see in example 6. In fact, the rules governing the relation between the concepts are ideologically determined, and I will come back to this idea below.

The last criterion I borrow from Foucault (1972: 65) is what he calls "the formation of strategies". I would rather use another of his terms and describe the formation of "theoretical choices". The way linguistic diversity is thematized, the enunciative modalities, and the concepts, makes different theoretical options possible. Foucault urges us to identify the points of diffraction of discourse (i.e., where exactly different choices are possible) and to determine the theoretical choices that were made, as well as those that were not.

In the data, there are several points of diffraction. For instance, while Anglicisms (bilingualism, language contacts, etc.) "color the language" (2), they are penalized on the exams and considered a "point to be improved" (7). Chiac, a crucial part of students' identity, is unacceptable at university or at work (6). These two examples contain meliorative remarks with conditions of use imposed.

Hence, at least two theoretical options are offered: Accept linguistic variation in class and on exams or refuse it. In practice, some teachers try marginally to choose the first option, but it is limited to a light lexical sprinkling of vernacular uses and is by far a minority standpoint. In fact, if the discourse of linguistic diversity does theoretically allow such a choice, the second theoretical option is clearly dominant. The next question is: Why is there such a power imbalance between these options? That brings us again to ideology, which tends to select one of the options.

4.2 Standard ideology

In previous sections, I have analyzed "linguistic diversity" as a discourse. From concrete, describable, and analyzable utterances in context, I described the modalities of enunciation of this discourse, the concepts it contains, and their relations, and determined the theoretical options it allows. If we are now interested in understanding *why* all these elements are organized that way (and not another), we are dealing with ideology. In this section, I propose a definition of the notion of ideology and analyze the data accordingly. It should allow me to clearly specify the differences between *discourse* and *ideology* and, in doing so, to establish how these two notions can be useful, when used in close connection, to understand power relations and situations of social domination.

a. General definition

Ideology is a highly contested notion. The definition of this term often depends on the researcher's positionality. There is a relative consensus on one aspect of this notion: Ideology is a systematic set of converging thoughts, beliefs, or representations. In what follows, I will provide a brief overview of some relevant dissensus points, to shed light on the most useful definition here.

The first dissensus point is the relationship of ideology with truth and materiality. Several traditions relate ideology to false ideas, such as the Marxist tradition that considers ideology a manipulation of the masses (Marx and Engels [1932] 1988), although ideologies result from the state of structural power relations inside a society. This means that ideology is deeply anchored in concrete conditions of life. More recently, the sociological branch of methodological individualism has regarded ideologies as dogmas opposed to a factual reality. Within that perspective, one can regard ideologies as ethereal beliefs, unproven and unfounded claims, even if they may be supported by scientific argumentation, meaning that people are rationally believing falsities (see, e.g., Boudon [1986] 1991; or before, Shils 1968).

The second dissensus point is the relationship between ideology and social domination and conflictuality. In the tradition of social critique, ideology is tightly related to power (Thompson 1984), participating in the reproduction of social order. Logically, ideology is then supported by institutions and people in a dominant position: those who own the means of production for Marx and Engels (1988), the Nation-State for Althusser (1971), and an elite possessing simultaneously the material, cultural, and symbolic capital for Bourdieu and Boltanski (1976). But for others, ideology refers only to political traditions, which permits a focus on marginal, extremist, fanatical political movements (Bronner 2009). One step beyond on the way to depoliticization, some schools of thought exclude conflictuality from the definition, bringing the notion of ideology close to "culture" or "worldview" (Friedrich 1989; Woolard 1998).

A third dissensus point is the relation between ideology and agency. In some theories, an interiorization of ideology obliterates almost all possibilities of free will, as in Marx's alienation of self. Contrarily, methodological individualism places a high degree of agency in individuals to explain the macro sociological movements. Some scholars have tried to explain the circular relationship between individuals and social structures through new concepts: Althusser (1971), inheritor of the Marxist tradition, developed the notion of "interpellation", whereas Giddens (1984) developed the notion of "reflexivity".

I endorse an intellectual filiation with Marxist tradition (Haroche, Henry, and Pêcheux 1971), with a slight modification, however, concerning the possibility of agency. We could therefore define *ideology* as an institutionalized and interiorized system of beliefs that emanates from the social structures, contributes to justifying and reproducing the social conditions of life, and regulates the authorized/legitimate ways of expressing, acting, and thinking. This definition has three important consequences. First, the "true/false" criterion is not relevant. Ideology is a strongly coherent and rational political system of beliefs. It comes with a set of discourses, arguments, and justifications of an established social order. However, as Eagleton (1991: 26) notices, it does not mean that ideology "doesn't involve falsity, distortion, and mystification". Second, ideology comes from dominant sources – at least, authorized and legitimate ones. It can certainly be a state, its institutions, or media, but it can also be dominant inside a restricted group – regarding society, a given ideology can be marginal, but inside a particular group, it may be dominant. Third, except for totalitarian systems, determinist definitions of ideology fail to explain why unequal and violent systems reproduce. That is why agency must be considered. If there is alienation and restriction of free will, they emanate from a subtle play of interests – rarely with people's awareness – between individuals, groups, and dominant powers. In this "game", discourses are important, as they are performative,[12] reinforcing ideology or – with more difficulty – fragilizing it.

b. Toward a definition of the standard ideology

If we accept the idea that discourse can be delineated by describing its object, its enunciative modalities, the relations between its concepts, and the theoretical choices it allows, we could perhaps say that ideology resides in the rules that govern the formation of these criteria. Consequently, addressing ideology is asking the question *why*: Why did linguistic diversity become an object of discourse, and why from teachers? The minority status has been part of Acadians' collective memory for centuries. The Université de Moncton was founded in the early sixties through the merger of several private Catholic institutions in New Brunswick, with the goal of being an institution for Acadians' empowerment. For many decades, the French courses have been designed to be appropriate for a French minority population. Teaching normative French has always been obvious, but taking vernacular practices into account has become inevitable, following the recognition movements and the increasing pride in vernacular practices (Boudreau 1996). In the mid-nineties, a first administrative report recommended developing the students' thinking about the sociolinguistic situation (Heller et al. 1994). The French courses have logically catalyzed the linguistic issues. Teachers face the imperative of teaching normative French, while being challenged by the growing legitimacy of vernacular French they now cannot ignore. As Heller (2006: 65–66) writes:

> There is a tension between the status and authority accorded to the standard and the authenticity accorded to the Canadian French vernacular. Both kinds of French are necessary to support the legitimacy of the school: the first in terms of the school's claims to prepare young francophones for the modern world, social mobility, and access to global networks and the second in terms of its claim to be uniquely able to respond to the needs of an oppressed, marginalized and distinct minority group.

Little by little, a discourse of linguistic diversity emerged, alongside new discourses justifying the teaching of Standard French, related to its potential value in markets (Heller 2011: 145–172; Duchêne and Heller 2012).

---

[12] This is a very fertile and much-debated notion. I will consider, with Fish (1980) or Langton (2012), for example, that all utterances have a performative potential. The performative power of discourses would therefore rely on their capacity to materialize ideologies (see footnote 11).

The rules governing the repartition of the concepts, their concomitance, their opposition, etc., depend on ideological power balance. In class, as the examples show, vernacular practices are categorized and subcategorized, sorted, classified, and labelled. *Bilingualism* or *Acadian French* are positively described, situated in their history, and legitimized as a crucial identity issue, but only in specific spheres of language use: in private, in family, between friends, and so forth. In class and on exams (as well as at work or in the media), *Anglicisms* and *archaisms* are nonetheless systematically penalized. *Acadian French* or *archaisms* designate the same linguistic reality, but the concepts are different and denote a different relationship that depends on ideological criteria. As Vernet (2019) shows, we could say the same about Anglicisms: If they are used in France, they can be tolerated, as France is still perceived as the epicenter of Standard French. But if Anglicisms appear in Canadian French, they are penalized. Hence, when discourse allows several theoretical options (such as to accept or refuse the use of specific terms), ideology selects one. As the discursive frame is open to legitimizing the vernacular practices as much as possible, this will not happen, except marginally.

As a result, the global discursive construction gives a restricted space and role to vernacular French outside the social spheres of power. This leads us to believe that these different varieties of French are not in competition, and that they rather coexist in the same social environment, in different spheres of language use. This brings us back to Ferguson's (1959) theory of consensual diglossia where the "low variety" does not compete with the "high variety". This notion was highly contested, first by Ferguson (1991) himself, but also in general as a notion that does not fit to contemporary relationships between language practices (Jaspers 2017). Nevertheless, this discursive construction is the solution teachers use to reconcile two politically opposed goals: a) teaching a normative form of French close to what they think are the most international norms, while b) protecting the vernacular usage, as it is a crucial part of Acadian identity. However, in the process, the discursive construction contributes to depoliticizing Acadian French, while Standard French is reinforced in its dominant position in society. This is close to what Woolard (2016: 7) calls "an ideology of sociolinguistic naturalism", meaning that this kind of discursive construction, which both promotes linguistic diversity due to the identity of the community and the standard as a neutral vehicle of communication, contributes to essentializing language practices and thinking of linguistic forms as "independent of willful human intervention".

To summarize, ideology is the system that politically places Standard French in a position of dominance. Different discourses converge to justify and reinforce Standard French as the sole legitimate variety, that is, the standard ideology (Milroy and Milroy 1999; Fuller 2012; Lippi-Green [1997] 2012). This ideology builds the conditions of existence of the discourse of linguistic diversity and makes its appearance among teachers inevitable. This discourse is partially constituted by "pro-diversity" utterances (and attitudes) – which play a legitimizing role for the standard ideology, and by "anti-diversity" utterances (and attitudes), which directly express the standard ideology. In this perspective, "discourse" is both the product and the producer of ideology: Ideologies shape discourses, and discourses are performative, reinforcing and reproducing ideologies. Inside that performative circle resides free will, the agency of social actors: By changing discourses, even marginally, ideologies begin to change.

5 Conclusion

To conclude, I will come back to the definitions of *discourse* and *ideology* to defend the idea that we do need both (Määttä 2014) to understand the global picture of social domination situations. It must be borne in mind that each element of the definitions proposed here focuses on the study of power relations and social domination processes. These definitions are not universal and may not be relevant in another theoretical framework, or another discipline.

Discourse is a scholarly construction based on the identification of a certain unity among a varied set of utterances. This unity involves themes, enunciative modalities, concepts, and theoretical options. Utterances are the only analyzable trace we have; in other words, they are the materiality of discourse (Foucault 1971: 10–11). Ideology is a system of beliefs that both emanates from the social structures and shapes them. It regulates the authorized/legitimate ways of expressing, acting, and thinking, justifying, and reproducing the social conditions of living. In that perspective, discourse is an actualization of ideology, and analyzing discourse allows us to understand ideology. If discourse analysis is supported by concrete, visible, describable linguistic marks, analyzing ideologies is an interpretative act. Analyzing discourse *and* ideology is, nonetheless, necessary, as it is the key to finding a global coherence among the profusion of utterances – which sometimes seem to contradict one another.

When teachers produce a meliorative discourse on linguistic diversity while penalizing it systematically, their practice is motivated by a language ideology that establishes Standard French as the most valuable variety. At the same time, teachers are aware that crushing a vernacular with an exogenic vehicular French is not desirable or even possible, in times of recognition of Acadians' culture and identity. In addition, it stimulates a high linguistic insecurity among students (and teachers as well). Meliorative discourse, therefore, appears as a "protecting balm", while the comeback of "Ferguson's diglossia" appears as a willingness to engage in a consensual coexistence of linguistic varieties.

This approach to *discourse* and *ideology* shows that there is, in fact, a strong coherence in the collection of data I have presented. In this kind of fieldwork, if the two concepts of "discourse" and "ideology" are not used in close relation, I could be inclined to think that the participants are incoherent, irrational, or even that they lie. This would be a particularly pretentious and condescending mistake, giving the impression that I have a *truth* that the participants in the study do not have.

References

Allard, Réal & Rodrigue Landry. 1998. French in New-Brunswick. In John Edwards (ed.), *Language in Canada*, 202–225. Cambridge: Cambridge University Press.
Althusser, Louis. 1971. *Lenin and philosophy and other essays*. Ben Brewster (transl.). New York: New Left Books.
Angermüller, Johannes. 2004. 'French Theory' in den USA. Diskursanalytische Betrachtungen eines internationalen Rezeptionserfolgs. *Sociologia Internationalis* 42 (1). 71–101.
Arrighi, Laurence. 2013. Un bagage linguistique diversifié comme capital humain: esquisse d'un (nouveau) rapport aux langues en Acadie. *Revue de l'Université de Moncton* 44 (2). 7–34.
Arrighi, Laurence & Isabelle Violette. 2013. De la préservation linguistique et nationale: la qualité de la langue de la jeunesse acadienne, un débat linguistique idéologique. *Revue de l'Université de Moncton* 44 (2). 67–101.
Blommaert, Jan. 2005. *Discourse: A critical introduction*. Cambridge: Cambridge University Press.
Blommaert, Jan. 2018. *Dialogues with ethnography: Notes on classics, and how I read them*. Bristol: Multilingual Matters.
Boudon, Raymond. 1991 [1986]. *L'idéologie ou l'origine des idées reçues*. Paris: Points.
Boudreau, Annette. 1996. Les mots des jeunes Acadiens et Acadiennes du Nouveau-Brunswick. In Lise Dubois & Annette Boudreau (eds.), *Les Acadiens et leur(s) langue(s)*, 137–155. Moncton: Éditions d'Acadie.
Boudreau, Annette. 2016. *A l'ombre de la langue légitime. L'Acadie dans la francophonie*. Paris: Classiques Garnier.
Bourdieu, Pierre. 1984. *Questions de sociologie*. Paris: Minuit.
Bourdieu, Pierre & Luc Boltanski. 1976. La production de l'idéologie dominante. *Actes de la recherche en sciences sociales* 2. 4–73.
Brault, Michel (dir.) 1969. *Éloge du Chiac* [Documentary]. Canada: National Film Board of Canada.
Brault, Michel & Pierre Perrault (dir.). 1971. *L'Acadie, L'Acadie?!?* [Documentary]. Canada: National Film Board of Canada.
Bronner, Gérald. 2009. *La pensée extrême: comment des hommes ordinaires deviennent des fanatiques*. Paris: Denoël.

Cajolet-Laganière, Hélène & Pierre Martel. 1995. *La qualité de la langue au Québec*. Québec: Institut québécois de recherche sur la culture.

Comeau, Philip & Ruth King. 2011. Media representations of minority French: Valorization, identity, and the Acadieman phenomenon. *Canadian Journal of Linguistics* 56 (2). 179–202.

Duchêne, Alexandre & Monica Heller (eds.). 2012. *Language in late capitalism: Pride and profit*. London & New York: Routledge.

Duranti, Alessandro. 1997. *Linguistic anthropology*. Cambridge: Cambridge University Press.

Eagleton, Terry. 1991. *Ideology: An introduction*. London: Verso.

Fairclough, Norman. 1992. *Discourse and social change*. Cambridge: Polity.

Fairclough, Norman & Ruth Wodak. 1997. Critical discourse analysis. In Teun A. Van Dijk (ed.), *Discourse as social interaction*, 258–284. London, Thousand Oaks, CA & New Delhi: Sage.

Faragher, John M. 2005. *A great and noble scheme. The tragic story of the expulsion of the French Acadians from their American homeland*. London & New York: W. W. Norton & Co.

Ferguson, Charles A. 1959. Diglossia. *Word* 15. 325–340.

Ferguson, Charles A. 1991. Epilogue: Diglossia revisited. *Southwest Journal of Linguistics* 10 (1). 214–234.

Fish, Stanley. 1980. *Is there a text in this class? The authority of interpretive communities*. Cambridge, MA: Harvard University Press.

Forgues, Éric, Maurice Beaudin & Nicolas Béland. 2006. *L'évolution des disparités de revenu entre les francophones et les anglophones du Nouveau-Brunswick de 1970 à 2000*. Moncton: Institut canadien de recherche sur les minorités linguistiques.

Foucault, Michel. 1971. *L'ordre du discours*. Paris: Gallimard.

Foucault, Michel. 1972. *The archeology of knowledge*. Alan M. Sheridan Smith (transl.). New York: Pantheon Books.

Friedrich, Paul. 1989. Language, ideology, and political economy. *American Anthropology* 91. 295–312.

Fuller, Janet M. 2012. Ideologies, bilingualism, and monolingualism. In Annick de Houwer & Lourdes Ortega (eds.), *The Cambridge handbook of bilingualism*, 119–134. Cambridge: Cambridge University Press.

Giddens, Anthony. 1984. *The constitution of society. Outline of the theory of structuration*. Cambridge: Polity.

Godelier, Maurice. 1980. Le marxisme dans les sciences humaines. *Raison présente* 55. 105–118.

Haroche, Claudine, Paul Henry & Michel Pêcheux. 1971. La sémantique et la coupure saussurienne: langue, langage, discours. *Langages* 6 (24). 93–106.

Heller, Monica. 2006. *Linguistic minorities and modernity*. London & New York: Continuum.

Heller, Monica. 2011. *Paths to post-nationalism: A critical ethnography of language and identity*. New York & Oxford: Oxford University Press.

Heller, Monica, Normand Labrie, Danielle Cyr, Jürgen Erfurt, Micheline Doiron, Denise Wilson, Florian Levesque & Roselyne Roy. 1994. *Le perfectionnement en français à l'Université de Moncton*. Toronto: Centre de recherches en éducation franco-ontarienne.

Heller, Monica & Bonnie McElhinny. 2017. *Language, capitalism, colonialism. Toward a critical history*. Toronto: University of Toronto Press.

Irvine, Judith T. & Susan Gal. 2000. Language ideology and linguistic differentiation. In Paul V. Kroskrity (ed.), *Regimes of language: Ideologies, policies, and identities*, 35–84. Santa Fe: School of American Research Press.

Jaspers, Jürgen. 2017. Diglossia and beyond. In Ofelia García, Nelson Flores & Massimiliano Spotti (eds.), *The Oxford handbook of language and society*, 179–196. New York & Oxford: Oxford University Press.

King, Ruth. 2008. Chiac in context. Overview and evaluation of Acadie's Joual. In Miriam Meyerhoff & Naomi Nagy (eds.), *Social lives in language – sociolinguistics and multilingual speech communities. Celebrating the work of Gillian Sankoff*, 137–178. Amsterdam & Philadelphia: John Benjamins.

Laforest, Marty. 1997. *États d'âmes, états de langue*. Québec: Nuit Blanche Éditeur.

Lahire, Bernard. 1996. Risquer l'interprétation. Pertinences interprétatives et surinterprétations en sciences sociales. *Enquête* 3. 61–87.

Landry, Nicolas & Nicole Lang. 2014. *Histoire de l'Acadie*. Montréal: Septentrion.

Langton, Rae. 2012. Beyond belief: Pragmatics in hate speech and pornography. In Ishani Maitra & Mary Kate McGowan (eds.), *Speech and harm: Controversies over free speech*, 72–93. New York & Oxford: Oxford University Press.

LeBlanc, Mélanie & Annette Boudreau. 2016. Discourse, legitimization, and the construction of acadianité. *Signs and Society* 4 (1). 80–108.

Lippi-Green, Rosina. 2012 [1997]. *English with an accent: Language, ideology and discrimination in the United States*. London & New York: Routledge.

Määttä, Simo K. 2014. Discourse and ideology – Why do we need both? In Laura Callaghan (ed.), *Spanish and Portuguese across time, place and borders. Studies in honor of Milton A. Azevedo*, 63–77. New York: Palgrave Macmillan.

Määttä, Simo K. & Sari Pietikäinen. 2014. Ideology. In Jan-Ola Östman & Jef Verschueren (eds.), *Handbook of pragmatics online*. Amsterdam & Philadelphia: John Benjamins. https://benjamins.com/online/hop/ (accessed 14 February 2022).

Maldidier, Denise & Michel Pêcheux. 1990. *L'inquiétude du discours*. Paris: Éditions des Cendres.

Marx, Karl & Friedrich Engels. 1988 [1932]. *The German ideology*. Clemens Dutt (transl.). Buffalo: Prometheus Books.

Massignon, Geneviève. 1962. *Les parlers français d'Acadie*. Paris: Klincksieck.

Milroy, James & Lesley Milroy. 1999. *Authority in language. Investigating standard English*. London & New York: Routledge.

Muehlmann, Shaylih. 2007. Defending diversity: Staking out a common global interest? In Alexandre Duchêne & Monica Heller, *Discourses of endangerment*, 14–34. New York: Continuum.

Pêcheux, Michel (ed.). 1975. Analyse de discours, langue et idéologies. [Special issue]. *Langages* 37.

Péronnet, Louise. 1989. *Le parler acadien du sud-est du Nouveau-Brunswick: éléments grammaticaux et lexicaux*. New York, Bern, Frankfurt am Main & Paris: Peter Lang.

Perrot, Marie-Ève. 1995. *Aspects fondamentaux du métissage français/anglais dans le chiac de Moncton (Nouveau-Brunswick, Canada)*. Paris: Université de la Sorbonne Nouvelle dissertation.

Shils, Edward A. 1968. *The concept and function of ideology*. New York: Crowell Collier & Macmillan.

Thompson, John B. 1984. *Studies in the theory of ideologies*. Berkeley: University of California Press.

Vernet, Samuel. 2019. La 'diversité linguistique' dans un modèle d'enseignement du français standardisé: les cours de français à l'Université de Moncton. In Ali Reguigui, Julie Boissonneault, Leila Messaoudi, Hafida El Amrani & Hanane Bendahmane (eds.), *Languages in context*, 363–380. Sudbury, Ontario: Université Laurentienne, Département d'études françaises.

Vernet, Samuel. 2020. Au-delà de la notion de 'minorité linguistique' en Acadie: penser le croisement des processus de minorisation. In Karine Gauvin & Isabelle Violette (eds.), *Minorisation linguistique et inégalités sociales. Rapports complexes aux langues dans l'espace francophone*, 45–67. New York, Bern, Frankfurt am Main & Paris: Peter Lang.

Vernet, Samuel. 2021. Entre français standard et vernaculaire acadien, l'invisibilisation du conflit linguistique. In Geneviève Bernard Barbeau, Franz Meier & Sabine Schwarze (eds.), *Conflit sur/dans la langue: perspectives linguistiques, argumentatives et discursives*, 99–117. New York, Bern, Frankfurt am Main & Paris: Peter Lang.

Vernet, Samuel & Simo K. Määttä. 2019. L'Université de Moncton, la langue et les normes. Enjeux acadiens, échos finlandais. *Revue de l'Université de Moncton* 50. 49–85.

Wolcott, Harry F. 2008 [1999]. *Ethnography: A way of seeing*, 2nd edn. Lanham: AltaMira Press.

Woolard, Kathryn A. 1998. Language ideology as a field of inquiry. In Bambi Schieffelin, Paul V. Kroskrity & Kathryn A. Woolard, *Language ideology: Theory and practice*, 3–47. New York & Oxford: Oxford University Press.

Woolard, Kathryn A. 2016. *Singular and plural. Ideologies of linguistic authority in 21st century Catalonia*. New York & Oxford: Oxford University Press.

Mariem Guellouz
Chapter 4
Ideology and emancipation through the prism of performativity: Immolation and mottos of struggle as moments of popular counter-discourse

> It is not consciousness that determines life, but rather life that determines consciousness.
> (Marx and Engels 2010: 37)

Abstract: This chapter aims to rethink ideology and counter-ideology by confronting them with three conceptual notions – performance, the performative, and performativity – to explain what an instance of activist counter-discourse is, be it a silent act, such as immolation or a motto of struggle during an uprising. Counter-ideology is negotiated from within the split between the collective practice of resistance and the individuals' desire for emancipation. In this framework, relationships between ideologies and language are made manifest by studying discursive practices that are no longer reducible to the site of truth calling for unveiling; instead, they are presented as a space of ideological event production. Neither collectively subjected/alienated nor individually liberated/emancipated. I postulate the existence of a revolutionary subject shown or performed through the tension between corporeal and non-corporeal assemblages in the passing of a represented socio-political performance – here, a revolutionary event. These considerations are developed starting from a recent revolutionary event in Tunisia, where the act of immolation of the young street vendor Mohammed Bouazizi on a public square in Sidi Bouzid on December 17, 2010, became the first of a series of acts of resistance leading to the downfall of dictator Zine Elabidine Ben Ali on January 14, 2011.

Keywords: ideology/counter-ideology, performance, discourse, immolation, Tunisian revolution

---

Note: I am grateful to Cécile Canut, Luca Greco, Simo Määttä and Félix Danos for their feedback on earlier versions of the chapter.

https://doi.org/10.1515/9781501513602-004

1 Introduction

What do an individual and silent act of immolation and a collective and polyphonic motto of struggle have in common? Though it does not call for an immediate answer, this question forces us to reflect upon the complexity of subjective positionings of resistance in relation to mottos of subjection. Woven from the thread of relations between discourses, voices, and embodiments, the process of subjectivation requires a subject to position itself beyond the dead-end dichotomy of choosing between subjugation and uprising. Inscribed in a heterogeneous, complex, non-linear trail of attempts at resistance – whether silent, voiced, hidden, announced, impromptu, or organized – the subject combines desire and dignity to redefine its relations to power and to the real. It would be easy to qualify any process of subjection as ideology, though this would risk significantly reducing or extending the concept, which is one of the most commented upon in academic literature (Thompson 1987; Eagleton 1991).

I do not wish to address ideology as a vacuous, abstract notion (cf. Costa 2017). Instead, I want to identify it in discursive materiality and contextualize it in social and political performances. To do this, I will first focus on the mottos of struggle of the Tunisian Revolution to examine counter-ideology as performance, that is, as a social space – a woven assemblage[1] of discourses, institutions, individuals, and practices – where revolutionary action is performed. Is there such a thing as a performance of revolution? How are the actions of revolutionary subjects performed? What transforms an individual and spontaneous act of immolation into a political and social performance? I start with the idea that mottos of struggle can only be performative if they are inscribed in performance space. The aim is not to understand them as elements of a revolutionary process but as a means of acting out the revolutionary event they index (Silverstein 2003) by creating and contextualizing it. This chapter falls within the scope of *political sociolinguistics* (Canut et al. 2018) while also taking up performance as an operational concept (Greco 2017, 2018). It aspires to go beyond the limits of a form of discourse analysis that seeks to reveal what ideologies hide by apprehending discourse from the point of view of whichever political practice it indexes (Silverstein 2003).

These theoretical considerations will be developed starting from a recent revolutionary event in Tunisia (2010/2011), where the act of immolation of the young

---

[1] This concept was theorized by Deleuze and Guattari and refers to the multi-semiotic nature of subjects and things (see Section 3).

street vendor Mohammed Bouazizi on a public square in Sidi Bouzid on December 17, 2010, became the first of a series of acts of resistance leading to the downfall of dictator Zine Elabidine Ben Ali. On January 14, 2011, one month after the immolation of Bouazizi, thousands of people gathered at the very center of Tunis, on Avenue Habib Bourguiba, in front of the Ministry of the Interior. The location was a site of trauma linked to police brutality – a place of torture that Tunisians could not approach, photograph, or film for nearly 23 years during Ben Ali's regime. Throughout this month, from the immolation to the mottos of struggle (*dégage*, 'leave', 'get out'), several utterances, actions, instances of public speech, gatherings, sit-ins, and demonstrations marked the revolutionary process. Section 2 discusses the relationship between ideology and the subject, and Section 3 addresses the connections between performance, emancipation, and discourse. In Section 4, I analyze the act of immolation as a necropolitical performance, and in Section 5, I examine mottos of struggle as moments of emancipation. Section 6 concludes the chapter with a discussion of performativity and counter-ideology as potential explanatory grids for the acts described in this chapter.

2 Ideology beyond the subject

The difficulty of defining the concept of ideology does not only lie in the term's polysemy; it also rests on the diverse theoretical and disciplinary positionings that constitute it. The concept draws extensively from the effects and evolutions of its exegesis, which itself is often ideological. A neutral conception defining ideology as a set of representations, beliefs, or ideas is confronted with a critical conception that presents it as a system of reproduction of social relations of domination (Thompson 1987; Eagleton 1991). Althusser (1970) and his structuralist interpretation of Marx's work epistemologically broaden the notion of ideology. Thanks to this, we can shift this concept's scope away from its negative meanings (e.g., the dominant bourgeois ideology) toward a theory of subjects' practices within their conditions of existence and their recognition processes. Althusser broadens the concept of ideology through the concept of *interpellation*. He accounts for its discursive determinants as a means of access to the production of subjectivity. This theory of ideology as legitimation or reproduction (Sobel 2013) imposes a structuralist perception of the social and alienated subject. A society without an ideology of repression is possible, but it does not rule out the production of new ideologies, reincarnated through other means. For Althusser, ideology should be placed in psychoanalysis, whose structuralist definition of the unconscious could only resonate with the Marxist definition of the subject. Althusser's interest in Lacanian psychoanalysis in the 1960s goes against the grain of a hostile period for this discipline, which Polack qualifies as "ambient obscurantism". Althusser points out the importance of the issue of the unconscious in the elaboration of a structuralist theory of capital and revolution. In addition, echoes of a Lacanian definition of the "unconscious structured as a language" (Polack 2020: 55) can be identified in Althusser's definition of ideology and subject. For example, he takes up the psychoanalytic blueprint in which "the obviousness of a first utterance hides a more profound meaning that the philosopher, just as the psychoanalyst, must bring to light. This obstetrics accompanies the affirmation of an 'epistemological break' whose principle could be applied to his own domain of reflection" (Polack 2020: 56).

However, this theoretical alliance does not exclude a few theoretical divergences between a symbolic approach and a more materialist approach where the subject is "socially fabricated, fashioned, and alienated". The subject is not only a producer but also "an object of production, localizable in the time and space of institutions" (Polack 2020: 57). Ideology is expressed by complex and heterogeneous means, through discursive and social practice constructed within power relations and relations of domination between speakers and institutions and subjects. The question then is that of understanding how meaning serves as a power process and how it is manifested in implementing such processes, contradicting the idea of ideology as an illusion and reaffirming its active part in signifying reality. As Thompson (1987: 16) explains, "ideology operates through language and language is a medium of human action; it is equally necessary to consider the fact that ideology is partially constitutive of what, in our societies 'is real'. Ideology is not a pale reflection of the social world, but a part of this world, a creative and constitutive element of our social life". Therefore, the critique of ideology unveils the roll-out of relationships of domination within historically situated and socially marked power processes.

However, I would instead address the question of the emancipated subject in a revolutionary counter-ideological framework by proposing an analysis of two emblematic political events of the Tunisian revolution: immolation and the motto *dégage* ('piss off/get out/leave'). I propose to analyze each as a form of social performance in which an act of emancipation is produced, placing myself within the continuity of Canut's work, which offers an innovative epistemological network whose theoretical and methodological implications are far-reaching. This line of thought can be summarized by a question that is essential to any research on the relations between discourse and emancipation: "What are the linguistic marks that make it possible for us to prove that social emancipation is occurring?" (Canut 2021: 95).

3 Performance, emancipation, and discourse

By affirming that ideology interpellates individuals into subjects, Althusser places the question of discourse at the center of the theory of ideology. Language constitutes the subject and recognizes it, making it recognizable. Thus, the subject is not autonomous but divided, traversed by utterances that comprise it and embodied in material relations between sites of power and institutions. While constituting the subject, discourse subjugates, imposes an order, and hierarchizes systems of domination. This paradox of subjectivity enables Butler (1997) to understand the pair of vulnerability and agency as forming a reversible relationship, with one feeding the other. Discourse makes subjects vulnerable through interpellation, but it is also through discourse that an emancipatory response becomes possible. Butler points out the contradiction between the constitutive dimension of language and its injurious dimension. We are constituted as subjects through language, and through language, our subjectivity is denied, dismissed, and attacked. Language calls into existence, and language denies existence: "We ascribe an agency to language, a power to injure, and position ourselves as the objects of its injurious trajectory. We claim that language acts, acts against us, and the claim we make is a further instance of language, one which seeks to arrest the force of prior instance" (Butler 1997: 1).

To recognize and be recognized – such is the strength of interpellation. The recognition of sex[2] is a speech act ("it's a girl!"), and the attribution of a name already assigns subjectivity to its assignee. What are the discursive specificities of interpellation that constitute us and make us vulnerable? The subject is interpellated but can also counter-interpellate, emancipate itself, by freeing itself of the modalities of interpellation. Counter-interpellation (Lecercle 2019) is construed as a form of agency embodied through polysemiotic struggle practices that I denote in this study as a counter-ideology. Faced with the reproduction of repressive systems organized by ideologies of domination that are embodied by repressive state apparatuses, the subject can free itself from class, sex, and race assignation and pursue a path of emancipation. Sobel proposes leaving the "field of positive analysis" and reductive dichotomies that oppose the social and phenomenological subject by accounting for one's "own ethico-political thickness, or at least a thickness that is irreducible to its own functional flattening as the cog of a social relation reproduction machine" (Sobel 2013).

---

[2] I use sex in this case to refer to a biological and medical categorization, which is to differentiate from the social construction of gender.

The concept of *assemblage* (Deleuze and Guattari (1987)) allows me to go beyond a purely linguistic definition of subjectivity and to include a multi-semiotic and performative dimension in its analysis. Deleuze and Guattari propose surpassing the signifier's imperialism and language system's imperialism and considering subjects as multi-semiotic wholes traversed by discourses, institutional concerns, corporealities, rhythms, desires, and intensities. The concept of collective assemblage of *enunciation*[3] helps address the question of emancipation as a set of practices related to political and desiring forces. I wish to break free of a binary view of the subject defined by two modes of subjectivation: determined/subjugated/alienated or emancipated/agentive/resistant. Thus, I aim to avoid the dead end of an opposition between the dominant and dominant ideologies to account for the notions of desire and dignity through a more dynamic definition of counter-ideology as an active, polyphonic, and dialogical process. It is an illusion to attribute absolute individual free will to an emancipated subject, because emancipation is a dialectic that brings together, through its very action, the biographies of the individuals and the history of the group formed by them. Neither collectively subjected/alienated nor individually liberated/emancipated (Canut 2021), I postulate the existence of a revolutionary subject shown or performed through the tension of corporeal and non-corporeal assemblages in the passing of a represented socio-political performance – here, a revolutionary event.

This article favors a conceptualization of performance in its link with discourses as indexicalizations rather than symbolizations using a revolutionary event as a locus of ideological performance. In this sense, discourse is linguistically produced, socially and politically determined, and articulated to a dialogical process. What I define as counter-discourses are the activist ones targeted against the legitimate and the official state discourse production. I use counter-ideology in the meaning of an emancipatory assemblage that creates articulations between language, bodies, and institutions. Suppose the ideology is linked to the robust and dominant discourse. In that case, the counter-interpellation is a counter-discourse of resistance and protest against all forms of state domination on its citizens (Lecercle 2019).

In this framework, relationships between emancipation and language are made manifest by analyzing discursive practices that are no longer reducible to the site of truth calling for unveiling; instead, they are presented as a space of ideological event production. This article aims to rethink ideology and counter-ideology by confronting them with three conceptual notions: performance, the performative, and performativity, to make explicit what an instance of activist counter-discourse

---

[3] The French word *énonciation*, which can be translated as 'enunciation', refers to the production of any linguistic act by a subject.

is, be it a silent act – such as immolation – or a motto of struggle during an uprising.[4] Ideology is negotiated from within the split between the collective practice of resistance and the individuals' desire for emancipation. In what follows, I propose an analysis of the framework of the Tunisian Revolution, where silent immolation was an emblematic catalyst. I postulate that scenes of immolation and the mottos of struggle (*dégage*) are performances that cite other scenes and reiterate them; they are themselves reiterable in the infinite context of social struggle.[5]

The difficulty of grasping the concept of performance is, without a doubt, linked to the word's polysemy and the problems posed by its translation (Helbo 2011). The circulation of the term across various disciplines and multiple viewpoints reinforces the semantic blurring linked to it. Related to multiple fields, including arts, sports, language, and theory, the concept of performance is at risk of becoming a catch-all term. Considered to be a floating signifier (De Toro 2011), the notion of performance has also been discussed in terms of the relevance of its interdisciplinary scientific usage. The work of Bernard Schechner (2006) emerged in the wake of *Performance Studies*. While it gives the notion complete scientific legitimacy, it also makes it more fragile by recognizing the porosity of its scientific boundaries and by including all social practices within it:

> Performances [...] occur in many different instances and kinds. Performance must be constructed as a 'broad spectrum' or 'continuum' of human actions ranging from ritual, play sports, popular entertainments, the performing arts (theatre, dance, music), and everyday life performances to the enactment of social, professional, gender, race, and class, roles, and on to healing (from shamanism to surgery), and the internet. (Schechner 2006: 2)

Retracing the critical chronology of the term, De Toro (2011) starts from the works of Goffman and Kaprow, who place the spectator and theatrality at the center of their approach and confronts these to the definitions proposed by Schechner (2006). In doing so, De Toro demonstrates the conceptual dead-end in which *Performance Studies* lie. Performance is an issue that touches upon social and artistic practices. Referring to Barthesian theory, the author thus offers a semiological definition of performance: "The postmodern theatrical performance does not perform a word [*parole*] or a spectacle, but an issue. An issue becomes central, not only for theater, but for the whole postmodern culture. What becomes thea-

---

[4] For the concepts of performativity and performative, see Austin (1970).
[5] Other slogans appeared within the months that followed the Tunisian revolution including "RCD *dégage*" and "Ghannouchi *dégage*", and the expression *dégage* was even used in advertisement discourse, where the Tunisian supermarkets Mercury Market used the phrase "*Dégage* la vie chère*" [Expensive life, piss off!]. Since 2011, it remains a part of the political vocabulary in the Arab world. Events in Egypt illustrate its durability and prevalence. Indeed, new uses such as "Morsi *dégage*" or "Sisi *dégage*" or even "Macron *dégage*" have appeared.

tralized, and thus intentionally semiotized, is the relation between the present and the past" (De Toro 2011: 82). As an effect of postmodernity, performance questions the status of the postmodern subject. Greco (2018) sheds valuable light on these theoretical discussions by suggesting three categories to define performance: artistic, discursive, and theoretical.

Performance is a form of semiosis that allies dynamic relations between text and daily, social, or artistic theatrality. It is an indexical system that exceeds oppositional dichotomies between speech acts and non-speech acts. Performance is neither theatrality nor staged text; it indexes productions of subjectivity that link any text to its witnessed contextualization. Performance is an event that "is situated within and rendered meaningful with reference to relevant contexts" (Bauman 1975: 298).

Immolation, taken as a silent, performative discourse without words, indexes a text of resistance. The motto of struggle *dégage*, understood as a poetic-political act, was deployed as a performance that indexed relations of emancipation from the repressive state apparatus. By sacrificing itself on the stage of tragedy, the subject of immolation transforms its act into a public and civic offering. It would be inappropriate to portray political immolation as an artistic performance or spectacle, and I refuse such a romantic analogy that denies the necessity of popular violence in any emancipatory process. Immolation appears to me as a performative act that, while appropriating public space, catalyzes an event of necropolitical resistance[6] (Mbembe 2006), as I will explain in the next section. Is death a public or private process? One dies through an institutional and performative act (the time of death being pronounced by a doctor, for example, or formula being pronounced by a religious authority). The subject of immolation appeals to citizens as its witness and transforms the political community (*la Cité*) into a site of collective mourning. Through this gesture, the subject inserts its act into an ideological performance of resistance.

Therefore, it is not the context that makes the performative, but the performative that recreates the act of communication in a new context.

4 Immolation: A necropolitical performance?

On December 17, 2010, in Sidi Bouzid, a young street vendor, Mohammed Bouazizi, publicly immolated himself after being a victim of humiliation and intimidation by the police. The scene took place at the very center of Ben Ali's dictatorial and

---

[6] Importantly, one must note that Mohammed Bouazizi did not die on site, but a few days later at the hospital.

repressive regime (Dakhlia 2011). In this specific historical and political context,[7] the act of immolation in question inscribed itself in a series of other militant gestures, such as hunger strikes, the chaining of bodies to one another, and physical mutilation. Qualified as an act of suicide by some, of resistance or desperation by others, immolation occupies the public space and links different levels of sensoriality and corporeality together.

Spivak (1988) qualifies immolations as "ritual performances" where suicide and sacrifice are conflated. The practice of "sati" by Indian widows is legitimated through topological ritualization: a woman can perform *this* type of "(non) suicide" (Spivak 1988: 299).

The public ignition of the body places immolation at the center of a more global reflection about free choice and the desire of subjects who, refusing to submit to external biopolitics, emancipate themselves in the act of annulling their subjectivity. Immolation, by contrast, reveals an agency manifested in the dual choice of the status of non-agent and of silence as counter-discourse. Because it is a (non-) suicide (Spivak 1988), immolation is embodied in a citational performance that engages social milieu, class, and the entire collectivity (Yousfi 2015). What transforms an individual and a spontaneous act of immolation into a political and social performance? Beyond the presence of spectators or observers and the carrying out of this action in public space, immolation stages a suffering body that responds to the violence of state subjection with self-violence. The scene of immolation is a praxis that refuses state violence through the choice of resignifying death. Working from a biopolitical perspective, Uzzell (2012) sees the act of immolation as a gesture of resistance toward the domination of the sovereign. Unlike the discourse of repression, immolation is a counter-discourse that performs the agency of the suffering subject, who, through the choice of self-violence, engages each of the bodies of the collectivity.

By setting fire to a live body, the subject of immolation states both a refusal and a free choice (*I declare that I prefer my violence to yours*) and engages the witness-subjects (*I bequeath the legacy of my act to you*) through dialogical effects in a trajectory of resistance. The subject of immolation is collective, the performativity of whose act is necessarily construed by the witness-subject (Ben Yakoub 2018). Between a non-agentive actor (the subject of immolation) and a fictive agent or witness (the spectator as an ethic dative), immolation is a performance that goes beyond typical dichotomies opposing the speech act and the non-speech act. Can

---

[7] The media, newspapers, and social networks were closely monitored and scrupulously controlled. Practices of torture, intimidation, and corruption were regular and normalized in and by the police regime.

immolation be considered performative? By immolating themselves in a context of ideological repression, the subject radicalizes activist discourse to the point of silence. Thus, the act of immolation is a refusal of violence all while bringing violence unto oneself; it is both language-based and embodied, intimate, and in need of a public witness.

By de-legitimizing the leader and their apparatuses, the performance of immolation acts on reality and disrupts the structures of representation that legitimate state violence. Rethinking the Foucauldian and biopolitical definition of the leader as the sole bearer of the power to give life or death, Mbembe (2006) uses the concept of necropolitics to enable an understanding of subjects as living dead, evolving under the threat of possible execution, and legitimized by policies of exploitation, violence, and the selection of bodies. Choosing the execution of one's own body to protest necessarily links resistance and self-destruction:

> The extraction and looting of natural resources by war machines goes hand in hand with brutal attempts to immobilize and spatially fix whole categories of people or, paradoxically, to free them as a way of forcing them to scatter over broad areas no longer contained by the boundaries of a territorial state. As a political category, populations are then disaggregated into rebels, child soldiers, victims, or refugees, or civilians who are incapacitated through mutilation or simply massacred on the model of ancient sacrifices, while, after enduring a horrific exodus, the "survivors" get confined in camps and zones of exception.
>
> (Mbembe 2006: 52)

By refusing the status of living dead, immolation makes it possible for the subject to choose the radicality of death as the worthiest form of life. In Tunisia, this act served as historical catharsis – a site of popular testimony and an atemporal event. Hachad (2013) offers a meticulous analysis of the immolation of Bouazizi, which she compares to a political and artistic manifesto as a witness to a crisis – a call and denunciation that gives the one who produces it the status of a political leader. I agree with Hachad's analysis but do not share her interpretation. By equating the act of immolation with a (political or artistic) manifesto, Hachad sets aside the silent and bodily dimensions of immolation. Immolation is not an "exhibitionistic" act, and it does not stage a form of violence; it indexes a biopolitical relation to life and the body. Bouazizi's action is not simply "revealing" or "liberating" or "revolutionary". It is a performance that creates a counter-ideology by interpellating the world and witnesses to the act. Unlike body art performances or those carried out by Orlan (mentioned by Hachad 2013), immolation neither experiments with nor represents anything (Ben Yakoub 2018). It radicalizes the axis of distinction between life and death by relying on necropolitics. It is not a manifesto; it is an ethical and political break. For Hachad, immolation bears witness to a crisis that it aims to transform. In my analysis, immolation is considered a performance of activist counter-discourse. It transforms spectators into ethical witnesses and not only testifies about violence but also creates the same legacy for which the witnesses are responsible. From silence, it gives birth to a powerful articulation between discourse and ideology. Immolation does not say anything but opens a textual space of testimonies and commentaries for the community's eyes. The narration of immolation by those who have or have not seen it is an unavoidable rationalization of the performative act. In this sense, the performative nature of immolation is necessarily linked to a constative, namely an action that describes what is happening instead of simultaneously performing and explaining the act like a performative (see Austin 1970).

The performativity of immolation transforms the spectator into a witness and the witness into a political actor who acts by confiscating the leader's necropolitical legitimacy. The silence of immolation opens the space of protest embodied by activist discourse in confrontational struggles between repressive state apparatuses and popular counter-ideologies.

5 Performing the revolution: Mottos of struggle as moments of emancipation

Following the revolution, the utterance *dégage* [degaʒ] played an essential role in the academic field. It must be noted that the word is phonologically modified in its usage in Tunisia, where protesters often chanted *digage* ([digaʒ], Guellouz 2017) instead of *dégage*[8] ('piss off', 'leave', 'get out'). When analyzing this utterance, several works adopted a pragmatic point of view, seeing *digage/dégage* as the perfect illustration of a performative.

For example, Jrad (2011a, 2011b) titles one of her articles: *Quand dire c'est faire la révolution*, which can be translated as "How to bring about a revolution with words".[9] This raises the question concerning the relevance of understanding *digage/dégage* as a performative. My analysis starts from a filmed sequence that

---

[8] Various phonetic occurrences of the utterance were observed throughout the Arab revolution: *degage* [dəgaʒ], *digage* [digaʒ], and *dijège* [diʒɛʒ]. I noted the following phrasings, written on placards, flyers, or leaflets: "Ben Ali *dégage*", "Moubarak *dégage*", "Khadafi *dégage*", and, more seldom, "Bachar *dégage*", or even "Alliot-Marie *dégage*". After the revolution, the utterance went through a series of derivations. It can be used in certain contexts as a characterizer, e.g., The *Dégage* Revolution, where it serves as an attributive adjective. Additionally, the title of some books such as *Dégage! A Revolution!* or *Dégage: The Tunisian Revolution* are proofs of the emblematic character that the expression took on.
[9] The French title being an explicit reference to the translation of Austin's *How to Do Things with Words*.

has become foundational in the history of the Tunisian revolution.[10] The scene unfolds as follows: the standing crowd occupies the space in front of the Ministry of the Interior. A rise in tension is vocalized through a polyphonic voice that shouts: "Ohhhhhhhh". Hands wave synchronously in the air. The rhythm changes and rapidly becomes binary, accompanied by hand movement. The crowd starts to yell with a hand gesture that signifies departure: *diga-ge, diga-ge/déga-ge*.[11] A drop in tension is embodied through applause and whistles, which mark the end of the sequence (Ben Yakoub 2018).[12]

Figure 4.1: Demonstrators in Habib Bourguiba street in front of the ministry of interior, January 2011. Photo © Maxppp/ZUMAPRESS.com.

This scene was ritualized and rapidly became a repeatable sequence in each gathering during the weeks that followed the revolution, echoing the three-part codification of the initial sequence:
1. Rise in tension: shouting
2. Catharsis: *digage/dégage*
3. Drop in tension: applause

---

[10] https://www.dailymotion.com/video/xgn01o (accessed 2 December 2021).
[11] The tri-syllabic structure of the word is yelled by the Tunisian crowd in a bi-syllabic rhythm.
[12] For Ben Yakoub (2018: 254), bodies spontaneously assembled in front of the Ministry of the Interior, the nervous system and central site of regulation of the regime. "*Dégage!*" – this one collective-performative movement, translated in one performative word – toppled the dictator and planted the seeds of a possible regime change.

Digage/dégage cannot be analyzed by separating the linguistic act from praxematic elements but must be taken as a polysemiotic whole that cannot be extracted from its bodily, gestural, textual, rhythmic, and prosodic assemblage. To properly grasp the ideological reach of the scene, it is necessary to analyze it by articulating the semiotic and pragmatic dimensions that make it possible to apprehend the contextualization processes that transformed this into a motto of struggle. Beyond the political context of its production, the analysis must focus on the term's metapragmatic contextualization (Bauman and Briggs 1990). The question here is not limited to activist discourse situated in its global social and political context. The question aims to understand the establishment of a process of contextualization where rhythm, verb choice, the imperative mode, register, language choice, corporality, prosody, and sequentialities as "contextualization cues"[13] all index an ideological relation to institution and the spectators or witnesses. Bauman and Briggs (1990: 73) consider performance "the enactment of the poetic function, a highly reflexive mode of communication". As an assemblage, *dégage* enacts poetics, not of the order of the symbolic or representation; it creates context and transforms ideological power relations. In this sense, protestors do not chant a term from within a given context. They create and recreate a contextualization of new ideological relations. Performed and contextualized, *dégage* enacts a reflexive poetic dimension negotiated in interactions between protesters and power figures that become spectators and witnesses of the revolt. In this sense, context is not objective but is constructed ideologically. First, the legitimacy of *dégage* is de-centered through the decontextualization of usage and the confiscation of this motto of powerful speech. Following this "entextualization" (Blommaert 2006; Silverstein and Urban 1996), *dégage* is cited in activist discourse and recontextualized as a performed motto of struggle. The tensions between decontextualization and recontextualization are where ideological relations appear inside this political performance of the motto *dégage*. The following definition by Silverstein and Urban (1996: 13) captures well the entextualization process taking place in the case of *dégage*: "The entextualized discourse, however, whether we are focused on the interactional or denotational plane, or both, can maintain its status as emblematic of the culture only if there are periodic reperformances or re-embeddings in actual discourse contexts that count and projectively 'the same'". It is indeed relevant to apprehend entextualization through performance and repetition.

---

[13] See Gumperz (1976) for this term.

Any performance decontextualizes praxematic speech when staging it and recontextualizes it by reinventing this speech in new ideologies. The theoretical inputs by Bauman and Briggs (1990) and Bauman (1996) on this subject are precious. They enable us to understand how performance – through the implementation of decontextualization and recontextualization – becomes the site of ideological theater. In an article about entextualization in a Mexican festival drama, Bauman (1996: 301) shows how the concept of entextualization can be thought through its performativity: "The performance forms of a society tend to be among the most markedly entextualized, memorable, and repeatable forms of discourse in its communicative economy". I primarily share this perspective in the following analyses of the performance of "*dégage*" in Tunisia.

A popular and polyphonic choir was heard emanating from the body of the crowd, which chanted in a shared rhythm and grouped choreography: *di-gage, di-gage*. Political poetics reinvented the event's ideological context by inverting power relations between people and leaders. *Dégage*, as a motto of struggle, was performed in public space. Bodies, voices, and rhythms intertwined, forming a space of performativity where speech acts and non-speech acts could no longer exist apart from one another.[14] The utterance *dégage*, analyzed above, draws its performativity from its inscription within a political and social performance, to which it points while deploying itself. The appropriation of public space in a dictatorship constitutes the catalyst of such a performative act.

Through the reinvention of a relation to public space, the sociopolitical performance of immolation and *dégage* enabled assembling words and bodies, performing a desire for emancipation. Likewise, through its iteration and citationality, the narration of the dégage speech act makes it exist as a performative via a constative gesture. The performative is detachable from its context and recontextualizable within the infinity of future discourses since "it is citation's essential characteristic to be not only extracted but transplanted, grafted, and to still perform in other contexts" (Cotton 2016). Performance indexes performative desires of emancipation. The motto *dégage* does not reveal a hidden counter-ideology – it creates one, comments on it, rationalizes it, and makes a revolutionary text out of it.

I have intended to show how *dégage*, as embedded in a ritualized scene, is not a performative in the Austinian sense. Rather, it is a performative because it

---

[14] Kerbrat-Orecchioni opts for a reflection that considers the possible "linkages" between speech acts and non-speech acts and provides us with a glimpse of the possibility of an epistemology that would enable us to consider the specificities of each act without "sacrificing the intrinsic heterogeneity of speech acts and non-speech acts [and to know] how one can give to the actional function the place it deserves without sacrificing other (ideational, relational, etc.) functions of speech" (Kerbrat-Orecchioni 2004: 42, my translation).

indexes a reversal of social relations between repressive state apparatuses and symbolic power. Thus, the performativity of popular emancipation is embodied in a conventional power relation through the assemblage of corporeal and non-corporeal practices, of desires and determinations that make performance. In this sense, I agree with Cotton's non-Austinian definition of the performative:

> Far from depending on a law or on pre-existing rules, on a "Me" or on an "I", or even on a context, the performative is the possibility to create, while reiterating them, this *me*, this context, these rules, and these laws. The performative thus creates an absolute and necessary break between past and present, it ushers into the future. (Cotton 2016: 15)

As an answer to the sovereign's motto of order, *dégage* is a counter-interpellation that comments on the ideology of domination and appears as a metapragmatic process. The resistant subject performs and records, creates anew, and repeats what has already been said. At the same time, it is determined by the discourses of subjection it reproduces by resignifying them through a reversal of meaningful effects. Performance is the site of constative statements and performativity.

Making *dégage* a symbol of the Tunisian revolution runs the risk of romanticizing social struggles in which the slogan would serve as a magic word. Adopting a Derrida-inspired critique of Austin, Judith Butler warns against a theological construction of "the subject as the causal origin of the performative act" through divine or magical power (Butler 1997: 50). Taking *dégage* as an illocutionary performative would leave out the importance of symbolic power (Bourdieu 1991) of all the social conditions necessary for the felicity of the utterance.

The immolation and the struggle mottos such as *dégage* are articulated in a way that they are both considered counter-discourses that indexicalize counter-ideologies. The immolation was a silent discourse that opened the way to the *dégage* and other emblematic revolutionary slogans (Carle 2019). A quiet and individual act gives birth to a collective and polyphonic discourse. Both discourses invite us not to limit the performativity of counter-ideologies to the binary opposition between individual and collective practices or between corporeal and non-corporeal (discursive) acts. The articulation between them depicts the emancipation moments as an assemblage of bodies, subjectivities, and desire for emancipation.

6 Performativity or counter-ideology?

Ideology is not intrinsically linked to the dominant class but the reproduction of social systems of production of power relations. Domination is not a homogeneous and fixed whole, either; it is also fluctuating and differentiated depending on the context of production and interaction.[15] Accounting for the continuum that enables the dialogical circulation of discourses through social fields and classes is a necessary pathway to apprehending ideology and counter-ideology, interpellation and counter-interpellation, as discursive practices. Here, the subject is an agent, mainly because of processes of invention, resignification, semantic shift, or rejection of uses. As Hall (1985: 113) makes explicit: "Contrary to the emphasis of Althusser's argument, ideology does not therefore only have the function of 'reproducing the social relations of production'. Ideology also *sets limits* to the degree to which a society-in-dominance can easily, smoothly and functionally reproduce itself". The discourse of ideology, when it is confiscated and uttered by a subject, embeds itself in the process of agency embodied through the choice of life and death of a subject within necropolitics, through the appropriation of forbidden public space, and the deployment of mottos of struggle against the sovereign who engages in processes of semantic resignifications. These processes involve an interdiscursive shift from a discourse of domination to a discourse of emancipation, as the analysis of the motto *dégage* shows.

Are performativity and ideology two faces of the same social-relational process? What are the advantages and downfalls of extending the notion of ideology to that of performativity? To these questions, Ambroise, Salle, and Sobel (2015: 26) answer:

> Doesn't it [performativity] function as a kind of euphemism aimed at softening the reach in terms of social critique that the terms ideology, fetishism, economism or reification have – these concepts having most likely not said their last word? One might then ask how the extended use of such a term is more heuristic than another concept, such as that of "symbolic power" elaborated by Pierre Bourdieu, who, himself, took up Austin's discoveries about the efficacy of language.

Ideology or performativity? The use of one or the other of these two notions implies an ethical positioning by the researcher trying to move away from or reaffirm the structuralist Marxist legacy that inhabits the notion of ideology. For my part, I do not want to oppose one to the other. I have unfolded the notion of coun-

---

15 Commenting on Althusser's uses of the concept of ideology, Rancière reminds us that "bourgeois ideology is a system of power relations that are reproduced daily by bourgeois ideological state apparatuses; proletarian ideology is a system of power relations posited through the struggle of the proletariat and other dominated classes against all forms of bourgeois exploitation and domination: forms of resistance to ideological effects materially produced by the bourgeois division of labor, forms of systematizations of anti-capitalist struggles, forms of control of the masses upon the superstructure: a system of power relations that is always only a fraction because it defines further conquests, always temporary because it is produced not by apparatuses, but by movements of struggle" (Rancière 1973, my translation).

ter-ideology as an ideology of emancipation and resistance and its relations to the performative and performance within the specific political framework of a revolutionary event. Not seeking to do away with the ideological reach of the theoretical use of utterances, I have shown – through the analysis of two key moments of the Tunisian revolution, immolation and *dégage* – that political performance is ideology at work. The illusion lies in the separation of what, in the performative, is of corporeal or non-corporeal nature, since ideological performance, far from being simply a relation of symbolic power or social class, is a field of the unfolding of subjective desires, desires for dignity, for life, or death (Ajari 2019). The notion of agency runs the risk of giving too much importance to the individuality of actors who would "consciously" develop subjective processes of struggle (Marignier 2020). The risk of such an approach is to conceive performativity as an apolitical phenomenon that falls beyond the bounds of ideological determinations, and which can thus potentially be used at the service of neoliberal logic (Yousfi 2020). Over the categories of *subjects* and *people*, *civil society* is preferred; over the idea of collective resistance, that of individual subversion; and over that of activist, the notion of stakeholder. Beyond these dichotomies, this article has offered a disjunctive resolution that, while recognizing the alienating aspect of ideological discourse, also acknowledges its subjectivizing power.

The concept of assemblage, which I borrow from Deleuze and Guattari (1987), takes discourse as an agentive machine enacted through praxis. From two symbolic moments of the Tunisian revolution, I have used the concept of counter-ideology to test the notions of *performance* and *performative*. Counter-ideology is a collective assemblage of enunciation that unfolds here in the context of a political crisis, as a performance of counter-interpellation – in other words, a poetico-political *metapragmatics*.

References

Ajari, Norman. 2019. *La dignité ou la mort. Ethique et politique de la race*. Paris: La découverte.
Althusser, Louis. 1970. Idéologie et appareils idéologiques d'État: notes pour une recherche. *La Pensée. Revue du rationalisme moderne* 151. 3–38.
Ambroise, Bruno, Grégory Salle & Richard Sobel. 2015. L'économie entre performativité, idéologie et pouvoir symbolique. *L'Homme & la Société* 197 (3). 13–30.
Austin, John L. 1970. *Quand dire c'est faire*. Gilles Lane (transl.). Paris: Seuil.
Bauman, Richard. 1975. Verbal art as performance. *American Anthropologist* 77 (2). 290–311.
Bauman, Richard. 1996. Transformations of the word in the production of Mexican festival drama. In Michael Silverstein & Greg Urban (eds.), *Natural histories of discourse*, 301–329. Chicago: University of Chicago Press.

Bauman, Richard & Charles Briggs. 1990. Poetics and performance as critical perspectives on language and social life. *Annual Review of Anthropology* 19. 59–88.

Ben Yakoub, Joaquim. 2018. Performing self-sacrifice, despite everything or despite oneself? Embodying a necropolitical space of appearance in the Tunisian Revolution. In Marina Gržinic & Aneta Stojnić (eds.), *Shifting corporealities in contemporary performance: Danger, im/mobility and politics*, 251–274. New York: Palgrave MacMillan.

Blommaert, Jan. 2006. Language ideology. In Keith Brown (ed.), *Encyclopedia of language & linguistics*, 2nd edn., 510–522. Oxford: Elsevier.

Bourdieu, Pierre. 1991. *Language and symbolic power*. John B. Thompson (ed.). Gino Raymond & Matthew Adamson (transl.). Cambridge: Polity Press.

Butler, Judith. 1997. *Excitable speech: A politics of the performative*. London & New York: Routledge.

Canut, Cécile. 2021. Agencements et indexicalités: signifier la subjectivation politique. *Langage et société* 172. 95–123.

Canut, Cécile, Feli Danos, Manon Him-Aquilli & Caroline Panis. 2018. *Le langage, une pratique sociale. Éléments d'une sociolinguistique politique*. Besançon: Presses universitaires de Franche-Comté.

Carle, Zoé. 2019. *Poétique du slogan révolutionnaire*. Paris: Presses de la Sorbonne Nouvelle.

Costa, James. 2017. Faut-il se débarrasser des "idéologies linguistiques"? *Langage et société* 160–161 (2–3). 111–127.

Cotton, Nicholas. 2016. Du performatif à la performance: "la performativité" dans tous ses états. *Sens public*. http://www.sens-public.org/article1216.html (accessed 30 January 2021).

Dakhlia, Jocelyne. 2011. *Tunisie, le pays sans bruit*. Paris: Actes Sud.

Deleuze, Gilles & Felix Guattari. 1987. *A thousand plateaus: Capitalism and schizophrenia*. Brian Massumi (transl.). Minneapolis: University of Minnesota Press.

De Toro, Fernando. 2011. Performance: quelle performance? In André Helbo (ed.), *Performance et savoirs*, 65–102. Louvain-la-Neuve: De Boeck Supérieur.

Eagleton, Terry. 1991. *Ideology: An introduction*. London: Verso.

Greco, Lucas. 2017. La performance au carrefour des arts et des sciences sociales: quelles questions pour la sociolinguistique? *Langage et société* 160–161 (2–3). 301–317.

Greco, Lucas. 2018. Performance. In Loïc Ballarini, Laurent Di Filippo, Stéphane Dufour, Béatrice Fleury, Nicolas Hubé, Mustapha Krazem, Michelle Lecolle, Caroline Masseron, Caroline Pernot, Anne Piponnier, Brigitte Simonnot, Marieke Stein & Jacques Walter (eds.), *Publictionnaire: Dictionnaire encyclopédique et critique des publics*. http://publictionnaire.huma-num.fr/notice/performance/ (accessed 7 January 2021).

Guellouz, Mariem. 2017. The construction of "Tunisianity" through sociolinguistics practices from the Tunisian independence to 2016. *Journal of Arabic and Islamic studies* 16. 290–298.

Gumperz, John J. 1976. Language, communication, and public negotiation. In Peggy R. Sanday (ed.), *Anthropology and the public interest*, 273–292. New York: Academic Press.

Hachad, Naima. 2013. "Dégage!" C'est la révolution: En guise de manifeste pour les révoltes arabes de 2010–2012. *Lignes* 40 (1). 133–150.

Hall, Stuart. 1985. Signification, representation, ideology: Althusser and the post-structuralist debates. *Critical Studies in Mass Communication* 2 (2). 91–114.

Helbo, André (ed.). 2011. *Performance et savoirs*. Louvain-la-Neuve: De Boeck Supérieur.

Jrad, Nabiha. 2011a. La révolution tunisienne des slogans pour la démocratie aux enjeux pour la langue. *Archivio anthropologico mediterraneo* 13 (2). 41–54.

Jrad, Nabiha. 2011b. Quand dire c'est faire la révolution, Tunis, *La lettre de l'IRMC* 6. https://irmc.hypotheses.org/182 (accessed 7 January 2021).

Kerbrat-Orecchioni, Catherine. 2004. Que peut-on "faire" avec du dire? *Cahiers de linguistique française* 26. 27–43.

Lecercle, Jean Jacques. 2019. *De l'interpellation. Sujet, langue, idéologie*. Paris: Amsterdam.

Marignier, Noémie. 2020. Pour l'intégration du concept d'*agency* en analyse du discours. *Langage et société* 170 (2). 15–37.

Marx, Karl & Frederick Engels. 2010. *Karl Marx and Frederick Engels: Collected works, vol. 5 (Marx and Engels 1845–1847)*. Clemens Dutt, W. Lough & C. P. Magill (transl.). London: Electric Book.

Mbembe, Achille. 2006. Nécropolitique. *Raisons politiques* 21 (1). 29–60.

Polack, Jean-Claude. 2020. *Politique(s) de L'inconscient*. Paris: Érès.

Rancière, Jacques. 1973. Sur la théorie de l'idéologie politique d'Althusser. *L'Homme et la société* 27. 31–61.

Schechner, Bernard, 2006. *Performance studies: An introduction*. London & New York: Routledge.

Silverstein, Michael. 2003. Indexical order and the dialectics of sociolinguistic life. *Language and Communication* 23. 193–229.

Silverstein, Michael & Greg Urban (eds). 1996. *Natural histories of discourse*. Chicago: The University of Chicago Press.

Sobel, Richard. 2013. Idéologie, sujet et subjectivité en théorie marxiste: Marx et Althusser. *Revue de philosophie économique* 14 (2). 151–192.

Spivak, Gayatri. 1988. Can the subaltern speak? In Cary Nelson & Lawrence Grossberg (eds.), *Marxism and the interpretation of culture*, 271–313. Basingstoke: Macmillan Education.

Thompson, John B. 1987. Langage et idéologie. Pierre Achard (transl.). *Langage et société* 39. 7–30.

Uzzell, Jacob. 2012. *Biopolitics of the self-immolation of Mohamed Bouazizi*. https://www.e-ir.info/2012/11/07/biopolitics-of-the-self-immolation-of-mohamed-bouazizi/ (accessed 7 January 2021).

Yousfi, Hela. 2015. *L'UGTT, une passion tunisienne: enquête sur les syndicalistes en révolution (2011–2014)*. Paris: Karthala.

Yousfi, Hela. 2020. National sovereignty for Arab countries: A utopia? *Historical materialism*. https://www.historicalmaterialism.org/blog/national-sovereignty-for-arab-countries-utopia (accessed 7 January 2021).

Nadia Louar
Chapter 5
Language trouble.s
Universalist ideology and inclusive language in France

Abstract: Taking the French debates about inclusive writing as a starting point, I discuss the political and epistemological implications of language and national ideologies in contemporary France. I show how prescribed linguistic practices hinder French culture from thinking outside the universalist box and acknowledging its de facto cultural pluralism. Drawing on two episodes that propelled an important cultural shift, the Strauss-Kahn case (*l'affaire DSK*) and France's backlash over #MeToo movements, I examine the restrictive cultural and linguistic frames that French elites, in particular, use to reinforce their hegemony and France's patrimonial ideology.

Keywords: epistemology, inclusive writing, inclusivity, universalist ideology, French language, #metoo, *L'affaire DSK*

Terminology: In this essay, I use the term *ideology* drawing on sociologist and cultural theorist Stuart Hall's definition: "By ideology I mean the mental frameworks – the languages, the concepts, categories, imagery of thought, and the systems of representation – which different classes and social groups deploy in order to make sense of, figure out and render intelligible the way society works" (Hall [1986] 1996: 25–26). Stretching slightly the scope of Hall's definition, I then consider ideology as being conveyed by an *epistemic discourse* that polices modes of perception and cognition through cultural and social inculcation by dint of discursive practices. We may thus simply think of ideology as a kind of dressage that informs how one thinks, understands, and interprets reality. Hence, the term *episteme* is understood in Foucauldian terms as *the order of things*, that is, how norms have been posited and naturalized in Western societies – norms referring to the knowable, the thinkable, and the feasible; in other words, "the space of order" within which knowledge is constituted. Foucault ([1970] 1989: xxiv) first described the concept of episteme as "those configurations within the *space* of knowledge which have given rise to the diverse forms of empirical science".[1]

---

[1] In French, "[...] les configurations qui ont donné lieu aux formes diverses de la connaissance empirique" (Foucault 1966: 13).

Before the philosophical concept of episteme drifted toward the social sciences and was emancipated from its Foucauldian boundaries, it signified the conditions of the possibilities of knowledge and thought in a particular society and culture.² It is in that sense that I approach the notional field of epistemology in this essay. In a similar critical vein, I understand the term *discourse* as a wide set of linguistic practices in their relations with power structures (see, e.g., Foucault 1980).

1 Language trouble.s

The debates about inclusive writing in France have been particularly virulent in recent years. They reached their apex in the fall of 2017, after the French educational publishing house Hatier published a textbook intended for elementary school children in which they could read the sentence: "Grâce aux agriculteurs.rice.s, aux artisan.e.s et aux commerçant.e.s, la Gaule était un pays riche" [Gallia was a rich country thanks to [male and female] farmers, [male and female] artisans, and [male and female] traders]. The feminization and addition of the median period at the end of masculine nouns proved the final straw. The Académie française (2017) – the immortal bastion of the French language – wrote an impassioned declaration about "the mortal peril" threatening the French language. French Education Minister Jean-Michel Blanquer condemned the "repeated attacks on the French language" and banned the new spelling in official texts. French Minister for Gender Equality Marlène Schiappa declared herself against teaching inclusive writing to children (Lorriaux 2017). The polarization on the issue of French spelling and grammar rules unfolded mostly along gender and partisan lines. But the for-or-against inclusive writing polemic was primarily academic. It involved French feminist scholars, linguists, and grammarians who debated the formation and evolution of grammatical genders in the history of the French language. As #MeToo movements were taking the world by storm, France was grappling with its feudal culture of sexual violence and gender inequality, and the picayune squabbles about French spelling were aptly instrumentalized by uninformed public figures to advance various agendas.

---

2 Foucault put it very clearly in his 1971 debate with Noam Chomsky: he wants to understand "the content of various knowledges which is dispersed into a particular society, permeates through that society, and asserts itself as the foundation for education, for theories, for practices" (Chomsky 2015).

Before delving into the scandal of inclusive writing *à la française*, let us recall some basic facts about French. Like most Romance languages, French is gendered. A noun is either masculine or feminine, and the adjective and many verbs agree with it in number and gender. The corresponding grammar rule is that the masculine overrides the feminine (in French, *le masculin l'emporte sur le féminin*). Accordingly, if one male student and ninety-nine female students are in a classroom, the subject pronoun that refers to them is masculine. French historian Éliane Viennot, one of the foremost proponents of inclusive writing, contends that the grammatical precept was politically motivated when it was endorsed in the seventeenth century (Viennot 2014). Viennot is also a signatory of a celebrated manifesto against the *règle scélérate* ('villainous rule') of the masculine overriding the feminine. According to the manifesto, signed by 314 school and university teachers, this rule was designed to "induce mental representations that lead women to accept the domination of one sex over another as well as all forms of social and political minoritization of women".[3] Opponents have derided this interpretation and rejected *en bloc* the concept of linguistic gender bias. Some disgruntled anti-inclusivists went so far as to decry "feminazi" attitudes toward the French language. At the other end of the political spectrum, and in an equally radical vein, socialist senator Laurence Rossignol exposed the stand against inclusive writing as "the new banner under which reactionaries are gathering" (Leicester 2021). It is worthy to note here that in 2016, Rossignol, then minister for women's rights, compared women who choose to wear Islamic dress to "American Negroes" who supported slavery (Radio Monte Carlo 2016). What such lapses in language suggest is that the political left–right axis in France does not seamlessly align along ideological lines. It is a fact that language policies aimed at addressing gender inequalities often overlook the racial and/or cultural element. Inclusive writing in the French context is thus not to be confused with political correctness. Rather, it is a set of orthographic and discursive practices that feminize masculine nouns by adding the suffix *e* (e.g., *professeur / professeure*) and introducing a median period in the plural to denote both genders (e.g., *professeur·e·s*). While opponents deplore the futility of the issue, proponents contend that inclusive language furthers gender parity.

Whether gendered languages contribute to sexist behavior and trigger gender inequality is an enduring question that continues to elicit conflicting answers in

---

[3] The French quotation reads: "La répétition de cette formule aux enfants, dans les lieux mêmes qui dispensent le savoir et symbolisent l'émancipation par la connaissance, induit des représentations mentales qui conduisent femmes et hommes à accepter la domination d'un sexe sur l'autre, de même que toutes les formes de minorisation sociale et politique des femmes" (Abdesslem et al. 2017).

the scientific community. As a non-specialist, I will cautiously leave aside the contentions of cognitive and/or anthropological linguists to focus instead on a simpler question: why is the French language such an ideological minefield? The conflagration of emotions and opinions about the various practices of inclusive writing – whether they be morphological or lexical, or reimpose proximity agreements or median periods – clearly indicates that the stakes are higher than conflicting linguistic allegiances and gender-neutral practices.

The comments of socialite and philosopher Raphaël Enthoven on Europe 1 Radio[4] crystallize the arguments and expose the ideological dimensions of the *trouble* (in the Butlerian sense)[5] that inclusive writing brings to the fore. Enthoven (2017) claims that inclusive writing is "an assault on syntax by egalitarianism" and compares it to Newspeak, the propagandist language of George Orwell's dystopian novel *Nineteen Eighty-Four*.[6] Enthoven then compares inclusive writing to a lobotomy: "C'est le cerveau qu'on vous lave quand on purge la langue" [Bowdlerizing is simply brainwashing]. He finally likens the suggested linguistic changes to the removal of Confederate statues in the US. Little did he know how significant his cynical analogy sounded to those for whom toppling the statues of slave traders or grammar patriarchy reflected the same political struggle.

In any event, Enthoven's histrionic claims were surely part of a performance for the benefit of his listeners. However, his criticism touches upon the crux of the matter: an increasing anxiety about an imperiled French cultural *patrimoine* rooted in a fiercely contested universalist model. "Inclusive" elicits distinctions and particularisms incompatible with French essentialist notions of citizenship. It conjures up a reckoning with histories of discrimination conflicting with French secular republican ideals. That an Anglicism is used to qualify linguistic attitudes reflecting gender diversity is revelatory of the cultural lacunae in the French discourse on identity. Indeed, although the word *inclusif* exists in French, it is in the sense of the English loanword "inclusive" that it is currently used. *Inclusif*, or *inclusive* in the feminine, refers to an American conception of inclusion and a social model of diversity that, in fact, contradict the tenets of French society.

---

4 One of the leading radio broadcasting stations in France.
5 In Butler's (1990) seminal *Gender Trouble: Feminism and the Subversion of Identity*, the term "trouble" signifies a departure from the norms.
6 In the "Principles of Newspeak", the appendix of the novel, Orwell (1949: 236) writes: "[t]he purpose of Newspeak was not only to provide a medium of expression for the world-view and mental habits proper to the devotees of Ingsoc, but to make all other modes of thought impossible".

Color- and gender-blind conceptualizations of national belonging have strategically aligned with prescriptive language policies that thwarted the inclusion of terms denoting divergent identities. The political fictions devised by the French republic offered instead a homogeneous nation built upon a unitary standard language. These ideological narratives remained the mainstay of contemporary political discourses. A tweet against inclusive writing on 15 November 2017 by Minister of Education Jean-Michel Blanquer is indicative of the extent to which the myth of an unbroken and exclusive French continues to have currency: "Il y a une seule langue française, une seule grammaire, une seule République" [There is only one French language, only one grammar, only one Republic].[7] For his part, President Macron conjures up the heroic figure of the French teacher on International Francophonie Day 2018, and draws from the same political imaginary to promote his linguistic politics: "The French teacher", he claims, "is the central figure who forges the mind, sensitivity, memory and curiosity, because grammar, vocabulary, etymology and very often literature are the fertile ground where our lives take root" (Macron 2018).

Language in France is not merely a tool of communication; it is the site of ideological projections that easily turn into injunctions. It partakes of an ideological apparatus that promotes the myth of national unity and instills habits of speech and mentalities that maintain social and cultural hierarchies. The universalist episteme that informs these hierarchies has hindered the possibility of divergent epistemologies and forms of reflexive thinking that challenge France's self-deceiving and conceited republican values. Reflexive thinking lies in the ability to turn one's critical gaze upon oneself and reckon with one's cognitive blind spots or, as Žižek (2004) explains, "the unknown knowns – the disavowed beliefs, suppositions and obscene practices we pretend not to know about, even though they form the background of our public values". Nothing captures this bias better than the linguistic hubris that posits French as the natural expression of universal truth and equity.[8]

But this national conceit has been crumbling as French society becomes more diverse and the gulf between political discourse and social facts untenable. Republican ideals have indeed fallen short as governing institutions remain bogged down in parochial mindsets that clash with the cultural pluralism of French society. This political schism plays out in dramatic fashion in the media. While a new breed of public intellectuals denounces the decline of French civilization, global protest

---

7 https://twitter.com/jmblanquer/status/930813255211208707 .
8 The myth of *the universality of the French language* is epitomized in Rivarol's (1794: 49) still-celebrated statement according to which "what is not clear is not French" (in French, "ce qui n'est pas clair n'est pas français").

movements against systemic racism and sexism have forced the country into its own moment of reckoning. It is in the context of a country beset by its contradictions and ever-growing disparities that the virulence of the debate about inclusive writing can be best understood. The controversial term *inclusive* crystallizes the ideological quagmire and conceptual chaos in which France finds itself: on the one hand, French citizenry as it really is, and on the other, its unconceivable reality. One may think of it as the "unthought known" of the Francocentric patriarchal narrative, that is, what is known but not yet thought (see Bollas 1987).

Indeed, France's inability to conceive of itself through the prism of inclusivity and develop a lexicon that captures its diversity is due to the generational disparities in its thinking. It is indeed a generational problem – as the gap is defined by Bachelard (2002: 24–25) in *The Formation of the Scientific Mind:*

> When we contemplate reality, what we think we know very well casts its shadow over what we ought to know. Even when it first approaches scientific knowledge, the mind is never young. *It is very old, in fact, as old as its prejudices.* When we enter the realms of science, we grow younger in mind and spirit and we submit to a sudden mutation that must contradict the past [emphasis mine].

Drawing on the philosopher's interpretation, I will argue that France approaches its social reality with its old, prejudiced mind and therefore fails to think outside "the space of the thinkable". In Bachelard's (2002: 24) theory on knowledge, this cognitive "inertia" is described as an "epistemological obstacle".

2 The ideological plane of the unthinkable

The workings of ideologies on cognition are manifested in the contemporary "quarrels between the Ancients and the Moderns" around issues of "inclusivity".[9] The very term remains the object of ferocious attacks and puzzling contradictions. Such was the case when President Macron advocated for "inclusive patriotism" in his April 2019 speech[10] to respond to outpourings of civil and social unrest (Macron 2019). The oxymoron might have *stirred something from the field of the possible and disturbed a certain order on the plane of the thinkable*, to paraphrase Samuel Beckett (Cohn 1984: 139), if the French president had not in the same breath claimed "an ambitious republican reconquest of *the banlieues*" and condemned

---

9 The quarrel between the ancients and moderns is a recurrent theme in the European history of ideas. It always opposes the traditionalists against the innovators of the times. The term is part of French literary history but is now loosely used to distinguish between the old and the new.
10 He borrowed the phrase from Mounk (2018).

"political Islam" to finally reaffirm "that distinctive art to be French".[11] But if, for the proponents of inclusion, "inclusive patriotism" sounded merely contrived, for cultural conservatives it signified "minorities' tyranny" and alerted them to "the actual scale of the project to destroy French civilization" (see, e.g., Lefebvre 2019).

The adjective *inclusive* conjures up the specter of American cultural dominance and politics of identity inimical with "the art" of being French. Inclusive writing and inclusive patriotism thus recall histories of discrimination mostly imputed to US history. Its emergence in the French context erodes the surface of the universalist model and angers its gospelers. Illustrative in this respect is Macron's critical reaction to American media following their coverage of his "anti-Muslim measures" after a particularly shocking terrorist attack on a French teacher on 16 October 2020. He personally called *The New York Times* to refute their political analysis and lecture the Americans about the singularity of the French model. His arguments relied on a repetitious and sterile "us versus them/you" paradigm that lays bare the fault lines of the French ideological discourse:

> There is a sort of misunderstanding about what the European model is, and the French model in particular", he said. "American society used to be segregationist before it moved to a multiculturalist model, which is essentially about coexistence of different ethnicities and religions next to one another. [...] Our model is universalist, not multiculturalist. [...] In our society, *I don't care* whether someone is Black, yellow or white, whether they are Catholic or Muslim, a person is first and foremost a citizen". (Smith 2020)

That the president equates his particular position with an all-encompassing universalism shows the extent to which discursive practices of exclusion are instrumental in maintaining the prevailing narrative and shaping habits of unthinking (*la pensée qui ne pense pas,* 'thinking that does not think'). Another example of the unthinking of French thought can be found in the comments made by philosopher Michel Onfray in the wake of the murder of African American George Floyd by the police in the summer of 2020. Repeating Emmanuel Macron's lines almost verbatim, Onfray declares on Radio Monte Carlo's (2020) show *Grandes Gueules* ('big mouths') on 3 June 2020: "I, for one, am a universalist. I am a child of the Enlightenment and classical reason. I have never considered that someone was good or bad because of their skin color. This is not my concern" (my translation).[12]

---

11 *Banlieue* is a French word that designates poor and very diverse suburban communities. French *banlieues* are often compared to ghettos and conjure up stereotypical images of poverty, ethnic populations, and social unrest.
12 In French: "Moi, je suis universaliste, je suis un enfant des Lumières et de la raison classique et je n'ai jamais considéré que quelqu'un était bien ou mal parce qu'il avait telle couleur de peau ou telle religion. Ce n'est pas mon propos".

Overlooking the problems of unconscious bias and systemic discrimination, the "thinker" is unable to think beyond his preconceptions and resorts to an ideological cliché. Yet behind the cliché loom the real lack of concern and the refusal to reckon with the diverse demographics of the French population.

These examples are not isolated. The kind of universalist Newspeak used by politicians and intellectuals subsumes the prevailing racial discourse and the epistemic paralysis endemic to French national ideology. France is, in fact, stuck in its ideological morass and cannot think it through. In *Black Skin, White Masks*, Frantz Fanon memorably diagnoses this alarming state of affairs as cognitive dissonance:

> Sometimes people hold a core belief that is very strong. When they are presented with evidence that works against that belief, the new evidence cannot be accepted. It would create a feeling that is extremely uncomfortable, called cognitive dissonance. And because it is so important to protect the core belief, they will rationalize, ignore and even deny anything that doesn't fit in with the core belief. (Fanon 1967, back cover)

The "French model" is always brandished as a guarantee against prejudices. It functions as an ideological fortification that keeps alternative epistemic models likely to threaten its "core belief" at bay. It is an unrepentant model that stirs passions but ignores the social realities and lived experiences in today's France. It deploys a politics of avoidance and ignorance that translates into a patrimonial lexicon and ancillary discursive practices that dismiss as non-French inclusive conceptions of identity. Such terms as *communautarisme* ('communitarianism'), *société victimaire* ('victim society'), or *islam politique* ('political Islam') polarize public discourse along ethical lines and signpost a national route that proscribes divergence. In the words of French journalist Natacha Polony, "*this factory of conformist thinking* [...] accounts for the growing gap between citizens' aspirations and the policies implemented during the past several decades" (Polony 2020, translation and emphasis mine).[13]

In the concluding part of this chapter, I will briefly examine the specific ways in which patrimonial ideology,[14] another phrase for cultural hegemony, has reframed two of the most defining moments in the recent history of sexism and sexual violence in France: the "#MeToo" movement and the Strauss-Kahn case (in French, *L'affaire DSK*).

---

[13] In French : "*Cette fabrique de la pensée conforme* [...] explique le décalage croissant entre les aspirations des citoyens et les politiques menées depuis plusieurs dizaines d'années".
[14] For the "effect of patrimony" (in French, *effet patrimoine*), see de Kerorguen (1981).

3 Inclusivity and its discontents

As suggested above, the disproportionate reactions both for and against inclusive writing are symptomatic of a "dissensus" that plays itself out in particular kinds of speech situations. Dissensus is a concept theorized by French philosopher Jacques Rancière that describes the fundamental clash that pits one against another and the incompatible grids of intelligibility according to which each sees, hears, understands, and speaks. As Rancière (2010: 218) makes clear, dissensus does not describe a situation in which one says "white" and another says "black", but a situation in which one says "white" and another says "white", but they do not understand or hear the same thing by it. The concept of dissensus allows for a deeper understanding of the *trouble* around the notion of inclusivity, whether it be associated with spelling or nationalism. Where one sees cultural diversity, another conceives a threat to national unity.

The language used in France to portray Dominique Strauss-Kahn's (often abbreviated as DSK in France) arrest in New York City on 14 May 2011 and the global women's movement triggered by the long-awaited Weinstein indictment in 2018 are perfect illustrations of dissensus and its divergent regimes of intelligibility. One may be tempted to think that these regimes correspond to antithetic ideological postures such as one modern, young,[15] and inclusive, promoting full and equal citizenship for people of different races, religions, and sexualities; and the other ancient, old, and patrimonial, safeguarding the traditional ways of the French world. It is true to a certain extent. However, the reactions to the arrest for rape in a Hilton hotel in New York City of Dominique Strauss-Kahn, then head of the International Monetary Fund and contender for the 2012 French presidential election, brought a wave of supporters spanning the political spectrum. Their support confirmed that the French right–left divide only operates within a very white and very male political world and promptly recedes when "the old guard" is at risk; but more importantly, it corroborated a uniformity of thought and language among the French elites.

In France, the episode was first framed in "French versus American" cultural terms, unsurprisingly setting American puritanism in opposition to French marivaudage. Hence, the political and intellectual elites in France resorted to literary tropes and feudal topoi to characterize their peer's sexual entitlement. One of the most striking was the infamous *troussage de domestique* ('stripping' or 'having forced sex with a servant'), used by journalist Jean-François Kahn to deride what he "felt sure must have happened" between his VIP friend and the

---

15 "Young" according to the Bachelard paradigm young/old as mentioned above.

hotel maid.[16] Kahn used an idiomatic phrase that describes the sanctioned licentious male behavior toward female servants dating back the *Ancien Régime* ('old regime'). Similarly, Bernard-Henry Lévy pretexted the Gallic charm and art of seduction of his esteemed friend to explain his "sexcapades" (my word): "Charming, seductive, yes, certainly; a friend to women and, first of all, to his own wife" (Lévy 2011). Jean-Marie Le Guen, French politician of the Socialist Party and former member of the National Assembly, returned, for his part, to the inexorable "spirit of the Enlightenment and the libertines who, in the 18th century, closely linked political, economic, and moral freedom". This, he claimed, is what "allowed peace and the emancipation of individuals" (Jérôme 2011).

The unapologetic sexist rhetoric used by the defenders is characteristic of the unaccountability that comes with unquestioned intellectual credibility and political legitimacy. It exemplifies the epistemic shortcuts the French culture takes when confronted with its own violence. Nowhere is the complicity between linguistic practices and power structures more blatant than in situations in which cultural capital is exploited for the ideological gains of the dominant caste. France's political and literary culture provides the authoritative lens through which sexual abuse perpetrated by patricians ought to be read. Any other reading belongs to the realm of the unthinkable. This partly explains the cognitive shock at the sight of an unkempt and handcuffed Dominique Strauss-Kahn flanked by New York City's Special Victims Unit authorities. If the image of the former IMF director's "perp walk" hurt French sensibilities, the depiction of *L'affaire DSK* in France reached novelistic proportions. In a discerning article about the literary exploitation of the *affaire* by the media, Keri Yousif notes that Laclos's canonic novel *Les Liaisons dangereuses* [in English, *Dangerous Liaisons*) was a main frame of reference:

> Strauss-Kahn is cast in the role of Valmont, the decadent *Ancien Régime* aristocrat who uses his power and status to seduce and corrupt women. And like Valmont's deflowering of Cécile, Strauss-Kahn was accused of forcing the Sofitel maid to succumb to his sexual desires against her will.
> (Yousif 2013: 900)

The literary interpretations of the DSK case limn a portrait that sets him apart from the average citizen and their ordinary fate. Phillippe Sollers's reading is exemplary in this respect. A psychoanalyst and one of the leading figures of the

---

[16] I deliberately leave aside the racial element involved in this case. But it is important to note here that the maid in question was Black and from a former French colony. These facts certainly add a critical layer of complexity, which are unfortunately beyond the scope of this study.

avant-garde, Sollers (2011) declares himself "fascinated by the character of DSK". He recasts DSK as a "republican monarch" who still lives under the rules of the *Ancien Régime* and the Salic Law.[17] He presents him as a larger-than-life character who does not abide by general rules. Although critical of the man, Sollers's criticism is informed by a scholastic mode of reasoning that estheticizes DSK's criminal offense according to the dominant ideological coordinates of the elites. He transfigures the "perp" into a fallible "republican monarch" and defuses misogynistic arrogance as hubris. As John Kekes aptly reminds us in his analysis of Robespierre's murderous ideological tyranny: "The justification of monstrous actions by appealing to a passionately held ideal, elevated as the standard of reason and morality, is a characteristic feature of political ideologies in power" (Kekes 2006).

Similar ideological assumptions and beliefs shaped the critical response of prominent French women to the "#MeToo" movement in France. In a now-infamous open letter published in the newspaper *Le Monde* on 9 January 2018, one hundred female academics, entertainers, and writers posed as the hermeneuts of French sexual norms and denounced what they considered the gross generalizations of the movement about gender relations in France. "Rape is a crime", the women write. "But insistent or clumsy flirting is not a crime, nor is gallantry a chauvinist aggression" (Safronova 2018). The anachronistic vocabulary with which they avail themselves to condemn the "excesses" of #MeToo revived the most hackneyed gender and sexual stereotypes. Their much-commented vindication relied mostly on a Manichean dualism that reduced sexual harassment to bothersome accosting and legal empowerment to victimhood. The backlash was highly mediatized, and the most famous of the signatories, the actress Catherine Deneuve, bore the brunt of the opprobrium. She promptly issued a statement apologizing "solely" to the victims. Her apology (Deneuve 2018), printed in the newspaper *Libération*, was well received. "I fraternally salute all women victims of odious acts who may have felt aggrieved by the letter in *Le Monde*", she writes. "It is to them, and them alone, that I apologize". And yet, more than her collective *cri de cœur*, her letter of contrition (not so contrite in reality) is remarkable for its lack of understanding of the real issues. It seamlessly aligns with a cultural elitist discourse that remains unaware of its own sexual and social biases and ideological conceptions of reality:

> I ultimately signed this text for a reason that I believe is essential: the danger of cleaning in the arts. Are we going to burn the Pléiade edition of Sade's works or label Leonardo da Vinci a pedophile artist and erase his paintings? Remove the Gauguins from museums? Destroy

---

[17] Frankish civil law from around 500 AD, known for its misogyny.

Egon Schiele's drawings? Ban Phil Spector's records? This climate of censorship leaves me speechless and worried about the future of our societies.[18]

Like Sollers, Deneuve is unable to think through the actual stakes of the global social movement and construes it through an esthetic lens that ignores actuality. It is as if both Deneuve and Sollers are unable to access a reality for which they do not have reference. Their responses epitomize the epistemic shortcuts French culture takes when confronted by narratives that do not conform to their ideal scenario. Both thus obliterate historical or juridical questions through an appeal to art. The reality is that DSK is not the literary figure that Sollers conjures. And Deneuve's first line is a *non sequitur*: An accusation of rape is not about censoring artists.

4 Conclusion

Through prescriptive language policies, France has established a fictional uniformity to foster a sense of national belonging. But global cultural shifts and social media have whittled down the paradigm of unity that upholds the myth of French universalism. The rhetorics of avoidance and ignorance of the debates on inclusivity and gender parity (and what these entail in terms of emancipatory political attitudes) show that intellectual intimidation and political coercion have long conspired in France to maintain the hierarchical order in place. This essentialist policing of French culture resides in a controlled language that shapes reality. It relies on a strong and unopposed centralized culture and language. But social media and the global circulation of cultural models have introduced vernacular ways of knowing and a language that definitely *trouble* the French linguistic and cultural norms. France's responses to the overpowering cultural shift translate into national anxieties and predictable anti-American rhetoric over "certain social science theories imported from the United States" (Onishi 2021). Revealing its own entanglement in the ideologies it sets out to challenge, the French establishment rises up against a "made in the USA" intellectual matrix and condemns its "leftist cancel culture". Rather than turning an analytical gaze back upon itself and its

---

18 My translation. In French: "J'ai enfin signé ce texte pour une raison qui, à mes yeux, est essentielle: le danger des nettoyages dans les arts. Va-t-on brûler Sade en Pléiade ? Désigner Léonard de Vinci comme un artiste pédophile et effacer ses toiles ? Décrocher les Gauguin des musées ? Détruire les dessins d'Egon Schiele ? Interdire les disques de Phil Spector ? Ce climat de censure me laisse sans voix et inquiète pour l'avenir de nos sociétés".

own institutional cancelling practices, the French establishment looks askance at academic disciplines and social discourses on the other side of the Atlantic to rationalize the failure of its universal agenda and attendant domestic politics.

But the failure can no longer be rationalized. The recent rise of grassroots social movements has forced France to reckon with its social, economic, and political realities. The global circulation of ideas that digital cultures and social media make possible elicits new forms of critical awareness, or conscientization, to use Freire's ([1970] 2000) concept, that challenge hegemonic cultural trends with full force. What France obviously fails to understand is that the global cultural impact of powerful social movements, such as Black Lives Matter or #MeToo, is not the result of an American stranglehold on French culture but a conjunctural response to France's own domestic, untenable structural inequalities. The ideological war that the French governing and cultural institutions wage against their old foe is, in fact, symptomatic of their inability to think critically about contemporary France and interrogate its exclusionary ideologies. Thus, those who have been excluded from the hierarchies of knowledge and dismissed from the very discussions that involved them are not simply taking to the streets: they are thinking and talking back.

The politico-intellectual morass in which France finds itself today comes precisely from the speech situation that I earlier identified as dissensus. In Rancière's conceptualization of politics, this particular situation pertains to a certain "moment when those who are excluded from the political order or included in it in a subordinate way, stand up and speak for themselves" (Corcoran 2010: 6). The new technologies of communication and the alternative epistemes that they facilitate render visible and audible new models of political subjectivities. A diversity of voices and faces is thus steadily permeating French institutions and *troubling* its regime of thought and perception. New portraits of national identity are emerging and opening a thinkable pathway toward inclusive and pluralist conceptions of Frenchness. Or so we hope.

References

Abdesslem, Malika et al. 2017. Nous n'enseignerons plus que « le masculin l'emporte sur le féminin ». *Slate*[FR], 7 November 2017. http://www.slate.fr/story/153492/manifeste-professeurs-professeures-enseignerons-plus-masculin-emporte-sur-le-feminin (accessed 29 October 2021).

Académie française. 2017. *Déclaration de l'Académie sur l'écriture dite « inclusive »*, 26 October 2017. http://www.academie-francaise.fr/actualites/declaration-de-lacademie-francaise-sur-lecriture-dite-inclusive (accessed 12 December 2020).

Bachelard, Gaston. 2002. *The formation of the scientific mind*. Mary McAllester Jones (transl.). Manchester: Clinamen.
Bollas, Christopher. 1987. *The shadow of the object: Psychoanalysis of the unthought known*. New York: Columbia University Press.
Butler, Judith. 1990. *Gender trouble: Feminism and the subversion of identity*. London & New York: Routledge.
Chomsky, Noam. 2015. Human nature: Justice versus power. Noam Chomsky debates with Michel Foucault, 1971. *Chomsky.Info*. https://chomsky.info/1971xxxx/ (accessed 30 October 2021).
Cohn, Ruby (ed.). 1984. *Disjecta: Miscellaneous writings and a dramatic fragment*. New York: Grove Press.
Corcoran, Steven. 2010. Editor's introduction. In Jacques Rancière, *Dissensus: On politics and aesthetics*, 1–24. London & New York: Continuum.
de Kerorguen, Yan. 1981. L'effet patrimoine. *Esprit* 60 (12). 99–106.
Deneuve, Catherine. 2018. Rien dans le texte ne prétend que le harcèlement a du bon, sans quoi je ne l'aurais pas signé. *Libération*, 14 January 2018. https://www.liberation.fr/debats/2018/01/14/catherine-deneuve-rien-dans-le-texte-ne-pretend-que-le-harcelement-a-du-bon-sans-quoi-je-ne-l-aurais_1622399/ (accessed 6 February 2021).
Enthoven, Raphaël. 2017. Le désir d'égalité n'excuse pas le façonnage des consciences. *Europe 1*, 26 September 2017. https://www.youtube.com/watch?v=D6QdIUzMCeo (accessed 6 February 2021).
Fanon, Frantz. 1967. *Black skin, white masks*. Charles L. Markmann (transl.). New York: Grove Press.
Foucault, Michel. 1966. *Les mots et les choses. Une archéologie des sciences humaines*. Paris: Gallimard.
Foucault, Michel. 1980. Truth and power. Colin Gordon (transl.). In Colin Gordon (ed.), *Power/Knowledge: Selected interviews and other writings 1972–1977*, 109–133. New York: Random House.
Foucault, Michel. 1989 [1970]. *The order of things: An archaeology of the human sciences*. A. M. Sheridan Smith (transl.). London & New York: Routledge.
Freire, Paulo. 2000 [1970]. *Cultural action for freedom*. Loretta Slover (transl.). Cambridge, MA: Harvard Educational Review.
Hall, Stuart. 1996 [1986]. The problem of ideology: Marxism without guarantees. In David Morley & Kuan-Hsing Chen (eds.), *Stuart Hall: Critical dialogues in cultural studies*, 24–45. London & New York: Routledge.
Jérôme, Beatrice. 2011. M. Le Guen défend « l'exemple des libertins ». *Le Monde*, 20 May 2011. https://www.lemonde.fr/politique/article/2011/05/20/m-le-guen-defend-l-exemple-des-libertins_1524932_823448.html www.jstor.org/stable/24268430 (accessed 17 December 2020).
Kekes, John. 2006. Why Robespierre chose terror: The lessons of the first totalitarian revolution. *City Journal*, Spring 2006. https://www.city-journal.org/html/why-robespierre-chose-terror-12935.html (accessed 28 December 2020).
Lefebvre, Barbara. 2019. De l'écriture inclusive au patriotisme inclusif, ou l'hyper-individualisme en marche. *Figaro Vox*, 26 April 2019. https://www.lefigaro.fr/vox/politique/de-l-ecriture-inclusive-au-patriotisme-inclusif-ou-l-hyper-individualisme-en-marche-20190426 (accessed 18 December 2020).

Leicester, John. 2021. In the French language, steps forward and back for women. *ABC News*, 8 May 2021. https://abcnews.go.com/International/wireStory/french-language-steps-forward-back-women-77572240 (accessed 29 October 2021).

Lévy, Bernard-Henry. 2011. Dominique Strauss-Kahn: Bernard-Henri Lévy defends IMF director. *The Daily Beast*, 16 May 2011. https://www.thedailybeast.com/dominique-strauss-kahn-bernard-henri-levy-defends-imf-director?ref=scroll (accessed 18 December 2020).

Lorriaux, Aude. 2017. « Quand on est féministe, on est forcément énervée, pas épilée et pour le point médian! ». *Slate^{FR}*, 22 November 2017. http://www.slate.fr/story/154148/marlene-schiappa-ecriture-inclusive-interview (accessed 6 February 2021).

Macron, Emmanuel. 2018. Ambition for the French language and multilingualism – Speech by M. Emmanuel Macron, President of the Republic, at the Institut de France. *France in the United Kingdom, French Embassy in London*, 20 March 2018. https://uk.ambafrance.org/spip.php?page=article&id_article=27334 (accessed 6 February 2021).

Macron, Emmanuel. 2019. Conférence de presse à l'issue du Grand Débat national. *Elysée*, 19 April 2019. https://www.elysee.fr/emmanuel-macron/2019/04/25/conference-de-presse-grand-debat-national (accessed 6 February 2021).

Mounk, Yascha. 2018. *The people vs. democracy: Why our freedom is in danger and how to save it*. Cambridge, MA: Harvard University Press.

Onishi, Norimitsu. 2021. Will American ideas tear France apart? Some of its leaders think so. *The New York Times*, 9 February 2021. https://www.nytimes.com/2021/02/09/world/europe/france-threat-american-universities.html (accessed 26 February 2021).

Orwell, George. 1949. *Nineteen eighty-four*. London: Secker & Warburg.

Polony, Natacha. 2020. Affaire Duhamel: des réseaux de pouvoir? Vraiment? *Marianne*, 14 January 2020. https://www.marianne.net/agora/les-signatures-de-marianne/affaire-duhamel-des-reseaux-de-pouvoir-vraiment (accessed 6 February 2021).

Radio Monte Carlo. 2016. Marché de la mode islamique: « C'est irresponsable », juge la ministre des droits des femmes. *Bourdin direct*, 30 March 2016. https://rmc.bfmtv.com/emission/marche-de-la-mode-musulmane-c-est-irresponsable-juge-la-ministre-des-droits-des-femmes-962915.html (accessed 29 October 2021).

Radio Monte Carlo. 2020. Le Grand Oral de Michel Onfray, philosophe et créateur de la Revue Front Populaire. *Le grand oral de GG*, 3 June 2020. https://rmc.bfmtv.com/mediaplayer/video/le-grand-oral-de-michel-onfray-philosophe-et-createur-de-la-revue-front-populaire-0306-1252432.html (accessed 29 October 2021).

Rancière, Jacques. 2010. *Dissensus: On politics and aesthetics*. Steven Corcoran (ed. & transl.). London & New York: Continuum.

Rivarol, Antoine de. 1794. *De l'universalité de la langue française; discours qui a remporté le prix à l'Académie de Berlin*. Paris: Bailly et Dessenne.

Safronova, Valeriya. 2018. Catherine Deneuve and others denounce the #MeToo movement. *The New York Times*, 9 January 2018. https://www.nytimes.com/2018/01/09/movies/catherine-deneuve-and-others-denounce-the-metoo-movement.html (accessed 29 December 2020).

Smith, Ben. 2020. The President vs. the American media. *The New York Times*, 15 November 2020. https://www.nytimes.com/2020/11/15/business/media/macron-france-terrorism-american-islam.html (accessed 6 February 2021).

Sollers, Philippe. 2011. *Philippe Sollers sur DSK, extraits*, 6 June 2011. https://www.youtube.com/watch?v=al0uYChjxf4 (accessed 27 December 2020).

Viennot, Éliane. 2014. *Non, le masculin ne l'emporte pas sur le féminin! Petite histoire des résistances de la langue française*. Donnemarie-Dontilly: Éditions iXe.

Yousif, Keri. 2013. Les liaisons dangereuses: Media, literature, and « l'affaire » Strauss-Kahn. *The French Review* 86 (5). 898–911.

Žižek, Slavoj. 2004. What Rumsfeld doesn't know that he knows about Abu Ghraib. *In These Times*, 21 May 2004. https://inthesetimes.com/article/what-rumsfeld-doesn-know-that-he-knows-about-abu-ghraib (accessed 2 January 2020).

Jef Verschueren
Chapter 6
The ideological grounding of the new normal: Anti-discourse meets utopia

Abstract: This article explores the shift from earlier overt and mainstream acceptance of societal diversity (combined with an underlying homogeneistic ideology) to the overt problematization of diversity (combined with explicit homogeneism). Two discursive tools are seen to be at work: a form of anti-discourse directly confronting alternative discourses (labeled "politically correct"), and a form of utopian (strongly identitarian) discourse constructing a simplified ideal image of society. An illustration related to the domain of language ideology will analyze how the two can be combined to ground the so-called new normal, even when that is clearly not the intention.

Keywords: discourse, ideology, language ideology, the new normal

1 Introduction

For the purposes of this contribution, I handle the following notions of discourse and ideology. For me, coming from the field of linguistic pragmatics, *discourse* is a cover term for any type of language use, from a single speech act or tweet, via a fleeting conversational exchange, to a university lecture or even the entire body of a country's legislation.[1] The notion of *ideology* bears on any pattern of meaning or frame of interpretation, experienced as commonsensical, pertaining to social relations in the (broadly conceived) public sphere.[2] Ideology surfaces most visibly in language use or discourse. *It is through discourse that ideologies are shaped, maintained, and reproduced.* This also turns ideology into a clearly empirical object of investigation. Since the patterns of meaning involved are felt

---

[1] In other words, the scope of discourse studies I envisage corresponds largely to what is represented in standard reference works such as Schiffrin 1994, Jaworski and Coupland 1999, and Angermüller, Maingueneau, and Wodak 2014. The specificity of my position is that for me all usage-oriented discourse studies belong to a broadly conceived field of linguistic pragmatics, simply defined as the science of language use.

[2] I am seriously indebted to Eagleton 2007 and Thompson 1990 for the development of my view of ideology.

to be "just normal", they are rarely questioned in discourse related to the social "realities" at issue. This means that analytical attention, while not ignoring what is said explicitly, must focus strongly on implicit meanings carried along in the discourse, keeping in mind that discrepancies between the levels of explicit and implicit meaning are by no means exceptional. Linguistic pragmatics provides excellent instruments for analyzing meaning beyond what is literally "said". It lends itself, therefore, to ideology research.[3]

From the above definitions it follows that there is nothing "innocent" about the relation between ideology and discourse. Thompson (1990) defined ideology as meaning in the service of power and ideology research as the study of the ways in which meaning serves to establish and sustain relations of domination. The patterns of meaning that emerge and spread through discourse are not simply abstract constellations of ideas. They form the basis for social action. Refusing to go along with Thompson's exclusively negative perspective, I believe this may be highly beneficial. Also anti-racism, for instance, may be seen as an ideology. But often unquestioned frames of interpretation are the harmful engines of detrimental social and political processes, involving Thompson's "relations of domination", which may be quite detached both from individual intentionality and from purposeful courses of action. This is what the following pages will try to illustrate with reference to a much-observed phenomenon, the appearance of a "new normal" in public life in much of Europe and North America (and in some places beyond). What I am referring to is the expanding acceptance of harshening public discourse, as witnessed in the political discourse of Trump and others of his ilk, as well as on social media platforms.

I will narrow down my attention to aspects related to the power dynamics between local majorities and new minorities resulting from migration flows (which, of course, is not the only ideology-laden theme of public concern). My questions will be: (i) How is this new normal grounded ideologically, and what are the main constitutive tendencies? (ii) And how do these tendencies appear in types of discourse where we would not expect them to have lodged themselves?

The first of these questions will be approached in general terms in Section 2, focusing mainly on observations within a European context. Section 3 moves to the second question, providing an analysis of one concrete example in which

---

[3] For a book-length account of these ideas and their implications for discourse-based ideology research, see Verschueren 2012. This is hardly the place for a lengthy discussion of the field of pragmatics. Just note that pragmatics has sometimes been defined as the study of implicitness (cf. Östman 1986). The analytical tools referred to are, to mention just the most obvious ones, the notions of indirect speech acts, presuppositions, and implicatures (classical descriptions of which already date back to Levinson 1983).

a language-ideological issue is brought to bear on majority-minority relations. What is analyzed in Section 3 is inevitably tied to a local context, in this case in Belgium. In particular, it is meant to illustrate how strongly discourse may be imbued with ideological ingredients, the consequences of which the authors might themselves strongly disapprove of. It demonstrates, in other words, the power of ideology.

2 The new normal and its ideological grounding

At the end of the previous century, it was still "normal" or "mainstream" in public discourse to explicitly accept diversity in society, welcoming migration as a form of enrichment. More often than not, this went along with an underlying homogeneistic ideology feeding into a model of integration that allowed for superficial differences (say, food and dress codes – as long as the latter were not interpretable as too strictly Islamic) while upholding the norms and values that were presented as fundamental to western societies (such as freedom and equality, but also extending to proficiency in the local language).[4] In other words, the concept of integration was an instrument to control diversity while displaying openness and tolerance.

The discrepancy between surface acceptance and veiled rejection was reinforced by the fact that the extreme right was already setting the agenda, with mainstream political parties trying to reduce its popular appeal by moving as closely as possible in its direction, rather desperately forgetting that people tend to opt for the original. Yet, the extreme right was still presented as somehow deviant, non-European, and undemocratic. This undemocratic nature, however, was conceived within the confines of a reductionist interpretation of the complex notion of democracy in terms of a binary adjectival contrast between democratic and undemocratic, allowing all mainstream parties to define themselves as democratic without asking themselves any further questions about what that should mean in view of the politically (not just semantically) complex noun. A textbook example was the treatment of the nationalist and anti-migration party *Vlaams Blok* in Belgium. All self-defined "democratic" parties agreed they would never form a coalition with them to govern, at any level. But even after the party had been condemned in court for racism and discrimination, it was allowed to resurrect, almost the following day, under the different name *Vlaams Belang*, inheriting all earlier parliamentary seats as well as all party finances. The courage to consider sanctions, in tune with

---

[4] This contrast between explicit levels of acceptance and fundamental but largely implicit rejection of diversity was analyzed in Blommaert and Verschueren 1998.

a conviction for racism and discrimination, was obviously lacking, which raises the question to what extent the court decision was taken seriously. By the time this happened in 2004, mainstream parties had already busily been displaying their own ambivalence towards diversity.

Against that background, there is no denying that meanwhile, during the past two decades and seriously accelerating since 2010, a "new normal" has emerged which explicitly problematizes diversity and equally explicitly promotes the homogeneistic ideology that presents the ideal model of society as a uniformly coherent entity. In the process, the extreme right has been relabeled "radical" rather than "extreme", further underscoring the already apparent gravitational direction of the mainstream.

What are the ideological anchoring points of this shift, which has also been called the "multiculturalism backlash"?[5] We can discern two major ingredients: an anti-discourse, dialectically opposing other (sometimes imagined) discourses, and a utopic discourse, constructing an ideal-society ideology.

The newly dominant public discourse on minorities has an agenda which, as already said, was set by the extreme right. Its practitioners, however, include a significant segment of the traditional left trying to navigate the rough waters of political debate without getting wet. They go along with a caricature of multiculturalism as the naïve and detrimental acceptance of everything different or exotic, a radical form of cultural relativism.[6] The most concrete reproaches around which this *anti-discourse* is centered is the inability to see the "reality" of diversity, the refusal to understand the reactions of "the people", and the injunction against "telling the truth" which is all said to be part of political correctness. The most vocal warrior against political correctness may be the immensely popular Canadian psychologist Jordan Peterson, who claims the absolute validity of IQ tests on the basis of which ethnic groups can be ranked on an intelligence scale. This, according to him, is a much better explanation of underachievement than any form of discrimination, or a better explanation of success than patterns of privilege.[7]

An interesting case of reverse political correctness (if one wants to use that term at all) has installed a "new realism" which describes the defense against

---

[5] I am borrowing the title of Vertovec and Wessendorf 2010. This book contains chapters on how the shift manifests itself in western democracies, from the United Kingdom to the Netherlands, France, Denmark, Switzerland, Germany, and Spain.

[6] For a well-informed discussion of the fictional nature of this kind of multiculturalism as ever having been part of European policies, see Schinkel 2018.

[7] See for instance *The Munk Debate on Political Correctness*, 24 May 2018, available at www.youtube.com/watch?v=MNjYSns0op0 (accessed 31 March 2020).

attacks on multiculturalism as cultural Marxism, as an assault on freedom of expression, even as educational censorship.[8] Angela Merkel, David Cameron, and Nicolas Sarkozy displayed their personal "realism" in 2010–2011 by officially declaring multiculturalism a "failure".[9] Going a step further, accusations of people's talk or behavior as racist or xenophobic are now said to be counterproductive, and to *make* people racist and xenophobic. Thus, safe-conduct is provided for the freedom to describe in particular Islam as the new Nazism or worse. Islam is presented as either unadapted or as unadaptable to "western" values. It is placed under generalized suspicion, and zealously enlightened condescension is shown in the attempt to protect Muslim women by forbidding them to cover their hair in certain public functions. At the same time, racism and discrimination are said to be relative, invoked mainly to cover up personal failure. Flemish politician Liesbeth Homans, then Minister for Integration and Equal Opportunities, famously declared in 2013, "Racism is a relative concept. I deplore that the word is used so quickly today. Is there still racism? Probably yes. From the autochthon population directed to the allochthon population? Probably yes. The other way around? That too. But today, racism is mostly used as an excuse for personal failure".[10]

The other side of the coin is a *utopic discourse* giving center stage to the notion of (national) identity. Ideas about (the need for) national identity are behind the political positioning of Le Pen in France, Wilders in the Netherlands, Van Grieken in Belgium, Orbán in Hungary, many of the Brexiteers in the United Kingdom, and a long list of others. Usually, lots of other considerations are thrown into the mix to form political movements and parties. Moreover, identitarianism is not foreign to a wide range of formations in the political middle ground.[11] Indicative, for instance, is the noticeable urge of mainstream Flemish political parties since the 1990's to have "Flemish" (*Vlaams*) in their name, a clearly ethnic-linguistic concept. Since there is no informational need for this adjective – all major political families in Belgium having split many decades ago between independent Flemish and francophone parties – the Gricean maxim of quantity (Grice 1975) tells us that more is meant than what is literally said. The "more" is an appeal

---

[8] The term "new realism" is borrowed from Prins and Saharso 2010.
[9] It would be wrong to simply associate this with David Cameron's "muscular liberalism". The ideological grounding went far beyond European liberalism. It was not only to be found also among Christian democrats (Merkel being an example), but even among socialists; in Flanders the adjective *flinks* was coined to combine *flink* ('firm') with *links* ('left').
[10] For an extensive account of this relativization of racism, see Zienkowski 2017.
[11] Among the mainstream politicians who felt obliged to write about the need for (national) identity care, we find Besson 2009 in France or De Wever 2019 in Belgium. For a general look at identitarianism, specifically in Europe, see Zúquete 2018.

to identity, the basis for a political program which, at best, treats diversity as an interesting curiosity or a minor nuisance. This now goes along with open pleas against too much migration. And it is "normal" these days to say that people coming from some countries "naturally" don't "fit". Clearly, in this field utopia meets the anti-discourse. Saying that people don't fit is based on views of a homogeneous ideal society, and it is just a matter of "telling the truth", of confronting political correctness.

Another aspect of mainstream utopic discourse is the professed belief that openness and tolerance are natural and indisputable ingredients of western identities. Xenophobia does not emerge until an overdose of foreignness (for which the concept "threshold of tolerance" was coined in the 1990's) renders it impossible to maintain toleration. I hope there is no need to argue how this not only represents an idealized image of the self, but also imposes normative uniformity.

More relevant to the remainder of this paper: normative homogeneity also pertains to language. In spite of widespread multilingualism of an everyday kind (with dozens of languages in all major urban areas) and the promotion of multilingualism of an elitist kind (with knowledge of the languages of international business being a valuable commodity), societal monolingualism is often imposed as a norm. An extreme though not isolated case is Flanders, where the maintenance of immigrants' languages (and even traces of them in their Dutch) tends to be interpreted as an unwillingness to integrate, and where a lack of proficiency in Dutch can even be used as an argument to deny someone the right to social housing.

In the following section, I will stay in the Flemish/Belgian context, analyzing a piece of text to illustrate the way in which the above ingredients of a widespread ideological process get anchored into discourse related to the topic of language. I will show that this even happens in discourse produced by someone who clearly would not like to be associated with the "new normal", as defined above, and who stays far away from the crude formulations circulating in the public and semi-public realms. It is this common type of disjunction between intentions and the meaning that is effectively generated or implicitly supported that makes ideologies such powerful catalysts of socio-political processes.

3 Language as an ideological playing field

The context for the text to be analyzed is the following. October 2016. The Brussels public school network (*Gemeenschapsonderwijs*), in collaboration with VUB (*Vrije Universiteit Brussel*, the Free University of Brussels), announced their initiative to start offering Arabic language teaching in a few schools outside of regular class hours. This could have been presented as a straightforward language maintenance service (of the same kind as had already been agreed upon with the Polish and Chinese communities in the Belgian capital). Given the reigning language-ideological mentality, in combination with the specific target group generally perceived as "problematic", this was bound to spark controversy. Thus, it was clear that attention would have to be paid to justification. One anticipatory response-controlling measure was the explicit argument that teaching Arabic in schools would keep youngsters of Arabic descent out of the Koran schools. This argument, by the way, keeps coming up in official statements until today, six years later. In the left-of-center newspaper *De Morgen*, the "opiniating editor-in-chief" (*opiniërend hoofdredacteur*) Bart Eeckhout, whose usually outspoken open attitude in migration-related matters is beyond doubt, wrote the following editorial when the initiative was first made public.

Original text (numbering added) *De Morgen* 15/10/2016, p. 2 (editorial)	English translation
Lessen Vlaams-Arabisch (1) Er wordt uit erg diverse hoeken afwijzend gereageerd op het plan van het Gemeenschapsonderwijs in Brussel om op de eigen scholen lessen Arabisch in te richten voor kinderen die dat vrijwillig willen volgen. (2) Sommige seculieren zien er een zoveelste bewijs in van *soumission*, onderwerping aan de druk van islamisering van de samenleving. (3) Maar ook sommige mensen met migratieroots, met name in de moslimgemeenschap, reageren defensief, omdat ze er bemoeienis in zien met hun godsdienst – hoewel taalonderricht daar in principe niets mee te maken heeft.	**Flemish-Arabic classes** (1) From quite diverse corners there are negative reactions to the plans of the public education network in Brussels to organize, in their own schools, classes in Arabic for children who want to follow them voluntarily. (2) Some seculars see in this yet another illustration of *soumission*, giving in to the pressure of islamization of society. (3) But also some people with roots in migration, specifically in the Muslim community, react defensively, because they see in this interference with their religion – though in principle language education has nothing to do with this.
(4) Toch vergissen al die critici zich. (5) Naschoolse lessen Arabisch hebben geen impact op het andere taalonderwijs. (6) Of alleszins geen negatieve. (7) Er is ruim wetenschappelijk bewijs dat een goede kennis van de thuistaal kinderen juist vertrouwen geeft om ook andere talen sneller aan te leren. (8) Kennis van een extra taal is sowieso geen slechte zaak in een diverse omgeving als een grootstad.	(4) Yet, all those critics are mistaken. (5) After-school classes in Arabic have no impact on other language education. (6) Or at least not a negative one. (7) There is ample scientific proof that a good knowledge of the home language strengthens children's confidence to learn other languages faster. (8) Knowledge of an extra language, at any rate, is not a bad thing in the diverse environment of a big city.

(continued)

Original text (numbering added) *De Morgen* 15/10/2016, p. 2 (editorial)	English translation
(9) Maar ook de moslims die wantrouwig reageren, vergissen zich. (10) Een van de achterliggende overwegingen om Arabisch binnen de officiële schoolmuren te halen, is om de aantrekkingskracht van Koranscholen af te remmen. (11) Dat vinden allicht niet alle moslims een fijne strategie, maar we moeten toch maar eens een eerlijke en open discussie houden over die Koranscholen.	(9) But also the Muslims who react with suspicion are mistaken. (10) One of the underlying reasons to bring Arabic inside the official school walls is to contain the attraction of Koran schools. (11) Probably not all Muslims find this a nice strategy, but let's have an open and honest discussion about those Koran schools.
(12) Het recht op de inrichting van zo'n Koranschool wordt gegarandeerd door de grondwettelijke vrijheid van vereniging en godsdienstbeleving. (13) Daar moeten we niet angstvallig aan willen tornen. (14) Maar dat wil niet zeggen dat we het moeten toejuichen dat zovele kinderen in hun vrije tijd een wel erg specifiek godsdienstonderricht krijgen. (15) Koranscholen zijn verbonden aan een moskee. (16) Niet elk schooltje is dus identiek, maar je mag toch zeggen dat kinderen er soms minstens impliciet ondergedompeld worden in een orthodoxe, conservatieve interpretatie van de islam. (17) Slechts één oppervlakkig voorbeeld: deze krant staat voor het standpunt dat vrouwen zich net als mannen moeten kunnen kleden zoals ze zelf willen – met hoofddoek of zonder. (18) Maar het hart bloedt bij het beeld van jonge meisjes die op de Koranschool verplicht collectief de hoofddoek moeten opzetten. (19) Met vrije keus heeft dat weinig te maken.	(12) The right to organize such a Koran school is guaranteed by the constitutional freedom of association and religious practice. (13) We should not fearfully tamper with this. (14) But that does not mean that we must applaud that so many children get a, say, very specific religious education in their free time. (15) Koran schools are linked with a mosque. (16) Therefore not every school is identical, but one can truly say that children are sometimes drenched at least implicitly in an orthodox, conservative interpretation of Islam. (17) Just one superficial example: this newspaper takes the position that women, just like men, must be allowed to dress as they please – with or without headscarf. (18) But the heart bleeds at the image of young girls who are obliged to collectively put on the headscarf at the Koran school. (19) That has little to do with free choice.
(20) Moslims hebben net als eenieder het recht om hun godsdienst vrij te beleven. (21) Maar ze zouden moeten beseffen dat het samenbrengen van grote groepen kinderen in clubs die soms waarden verspreiden die haaks staan op die van de seculiere maatschappij – vrijheid, gelijkwaardigheid – onnodige barrières opwerpt die het	(20) Muslims have the right to practice their religion freely, just as anybody else. (21) But they should realize that bringing together large groups of children in clubs which sometimes spread values that are not compatible with those of secular society – freedom, equality – creates unnecessary barriers to living together. (22) Therefore, also the Muslim community can

Chapter 6 The ideological grounding of the new normal: Anti-discourse meets utopia — 111

(continued)

Original text (numbering added) De Morgen 15/10/2016, p. 2 (editorial)	English translation
samenleven bemoeilijken. (22) Daarom heeft ook de moslimgemeenschap alle baat bij degelijke, open lessen Vlaams-Arabisch binnen de schoolmuren.	only benefit from professional, open Flemish-Arabic classes within the school walls.

What I can present within the confines of this article is not at all a full-scale pragmatic analysis. In order to do so, I would have to go through the minutiae of deictic positioning, lexical choice, code and style, patterns of information structure, mood and modality, presupposition-carrying expressions and constructions, indicators of metapragmatic awareness, and many more (cf. Verschueren 2012). Instead, I will focus on the overall rhetorical structure, asking questions about coherence and sequencing, and about the overall frames of interpretation embodied by the text.

The title of this editorial, to begin with, may be puzzling. What does "Flemish-Arabic classes" mean? The phrase, which comes back in the final sentence (22) as well, clearly lacks any denotational value. Is it a slightly infelicitous way to concisely refer to the fact that the teaching of Arabic that is at issue takes place in Flemish schools in Brussels rather than in the francophone schooling network? Such a contraction would make sense in the title. But why does it recur in the text, where "open Flemish-Arabic classes within the school walls" could easily have been replaced by the much more transparent "open Arabic classes within the Flemish school walls"? Is it perhaps a clumsy way to dismiss fears that the Flemishness of education in Flemish schools would be under threat by the teaching of Arabic?

Whatever the answer to that question may be, unease with the topic radiates from sentence (1). Not only does it start out with descriptive reference to "negative reactions", it immediately introduces attenuating details that could avert criticism, assumed to be seen as legitimate by the intended audience: do not worry, the public education network does not make extraordinary efforts at accommodation (they organize classes "in their own schools"), and children are not forcibly drenched in Arabic (it's only "for children who want to follow them voluntarily"). In other words, the surreptitious suggestion is that the cherished monolingual utopia is not truly endangered.

Then two of the "diverse corners" from which "negative reactions" have come are brought onto the stage in (2) and (3). Both "some seculars" and "some people with roots in migration" bring in the issue of religion, associating Arabic with Islam. However, a false contrast is set up by appending "though in principle language education has nothing to do with this" only to the associative link that is made by "some people with roots in migration" and not directly to the more or less identical conflation for which "some seculars" are responsible.

Keeping an open mind, one could anaphorically extend the scope of "though in principle language education has nothing to do with this" back to sentence (2). But the following paragraphs reinforce the false contrast by separately addressing and countering the criticism of "some seculars" in sentences (5) to (8) and the Muslim criticism from sentence (9) onwards. True enough, "seculars" are not literally identified as the holders of the beliefs argued against in (5) to (8), but a clear separation between the two target groups is indicated by the opening string "But also the Muslims, [...]" in (9).

In fact, two quite illogical moves are made, illustrating the problematically muddled meeting of anti-discourse and utopia. First of all, sentence (5) aggravates the false contrast by introducing a radical change of "footing" which does not at all fit the content of (2) by acting as if the seculars' criticism had nothing to do with the anti-discourse casting suspicion on everything Islamic, but simply with the utopic discourse promoting societal – and in particular linguistic – homogeneity. Content-wise, there is nothing wrong with sentences (5) to (8) in themselves. But the fact that this paragraph is disconnected from (2), which it nevertheless is supposed to counter, illustrates the journalist's strong awareness of language-ideological thinking within a utopic homogeneistic framework, which is expected (or observed, without being made explicit in this text) to play a crucial role in negative reactions to the public schooling network's initiative to pay attention to Arabic. Clearly, there is a strongly felt need to explicitly defend a course of action which could just as well be regarded as "normal" or merely practically useful.

The second illogical move concerns the sequencing of sentences (9) and (10). While (9) declares that there are no good reasons for suspicion on the part of Muslims, sentence (10) actually presents what really was the reason for such suspicion in the first place: the explicitly professed motivation for the initiative as an attempt to keep youngsters of Arabic background out of the Koran schools (which were the only places for children's education in Arabic until then). It is hardly surprising, given this loudly and repetitively expressed motivation, that some people felt religion was being interfered with.

What follows, sentence (11) onwards, is simply a defense of the official justification that teaching Arabic within the regular school context (albeit on a purely voluntary basis and outside of regular class hours) could greatly diminish the attractiveness of the Koran schools. The mixture of language and religious issues is simply carried along without being questioned any further. Moreover, the defense is completely in line with the classical anti-p.c. strategy of having "an open and

Chapter 6 The ideological grounding of the new normal: Anti-discourse meets utopia — 113

honest discussion" (in [11]) in contrast to an assumed politically correct avoidance of the "truth". Sentences (12) to (21) contain three CONCESSION + BUT episodes:

(i) On freedom of association and religion:

(12)–(13): freedom of association and religion is constitutionally protected

BUT

(14)–(16): religious education in many Koran schools is too conservative.

Koran schools are indeed private initiatives connected with mosques. The Belgian constitution guarantees freedom of association (and of religious practice), so that officially objecting is out of the question. But the "very specific religious education" mentioned in (14) euphemistically expresses the opinion that – though legally protected – what happens in many of the Koran schools may be unadapted to "our" society. This is made somewhat more explicit with reference to the "orthodox, conservative interpretation of Islam" in (16), which is ("at least implicitly" – to bounce back the journalist's wording) condemned. What is reflected here is the generalized suspicion of Islam, which makes it virtually impossible for Muslim communities in Belgium, in spite of the equally constitutionally guaranteed freedom of education, to obtain official recognition for Islamic schools (in spite of the vast network of specifically Catholic schools throughout Belgium, and the expanding network of – sometimes very orthodox – Jewish schools in a city like Antwerp).

(ii) On women's self-determination (for instance in relation to dress codes):

(17): women should be free to wear a headscarf or not

BUT

(18)–(19): young girls are often obliged to cover their hair.

The unadaptedness suggested in episode (i) is illustrated here with reference to the never-ending debate on headscarfs. The relevance of the position taken by "this newspaper" (in [17]) is doubtful, since the idea "that women, just like men, must be allowed to dress as they please" is hardly newspaper-specific. That very idea, however, is rather naïve. No-one is really allowed to dress as he or she pleases. Even if dress codes are not very specific, there are codes. If they are not explicit (as in a resort warning such as "No shoes, no shirt, no service"), you can always test the implicit ones by watching the reactions when someone deviates from the unwritten norms. On the other hand, freedom is an important principle. This applies, however, as much to the acceptance as to the rejection of a norm. In some communities there is pressure on women to cover their hair, just as in comparable communities there is pressure on men to let their beards grow. What we see too often, and what is clearly displayed in (18)–(19), is a disbelief in individual women's abilities to exercise their freedom of choice, a lack of trust, or a form of enlightened condescension. There is no mention of the possibility to stay away from contexts where there is an obligation. Children are of course limited in the range of decisions they can take for themselves. They may be sent to the Koran schools by their parents. But also parents have the freedom to raise their children according to principles of their own choosing. And what is so terrible in headscarfs that the sight of them makes "the heart bleed" (in [18])? Perhaps even children wear them with pride.

(iii) On freedom of religion again:

(20): Muslims are free to practice their religion as they see fit

BUT

(21): they should not clash with secular values.

Again a display of suspicion. There is no debate about how exactly secular values are under threat. Yet, debate should be the basis of any liberal democracy.

The text ends in (22) with a *non sequitur*: "Therefore" suggests a logical conclusion, but there is no real connection between the string of retracted concessions and the final claim that, again, mixes linguistic and religious issues.

As is usually the case when analyzing discourse in view of ideological processes, the most telling ingredients of meaning are those that are absent, those that are either so self-evident that they are "forgotten", or that are simply not part of the utterer's frame of interpretation. The latter seems to be the case when it comes to reasons for teaching minority languages. A rather non-committal statement is made about the usefulness of knowing "an extra language" in "the diverse environment of a big city" (in [8]). The journalist also refers to the importance of the "home language" as a basis for learning other languages (in [7]).[12] But the important issue of structural support for language maintenance – which is completely lacking in Belgium – is not touched upon, let alone the right of people to expect such support. In the context of Brussels this is all the more surprising. Brussels has two official languages, French and Dutch. But Arabic has overtaken Dutch as the second most common native language in the city.

---

12 Note that "home language" is itself not an unproblematic notion. It suggests actual confinement to the home or private sphere, which is where politicians might want to keep it – but it rarely stays there.

4 Derailed reflexivity and complicity

When relations between groups of people are at issue, there are no courses of action without ideological foundations. But constellations of ideas in terms of which we interpret social reality and orient our behavior, are not the products of individual minds. Some people, however, can do more than others to steer ideological developments, in particular people with power (such as politicians) or with influence (politicians again, but also artists, intellectuals, and media personalities). In today's world, however, all those corners of society seem to suffer from a form of derailed reflexivity.

Reflexive awareness of how we have to tune our messages in to what we assume our interlocutors to know and think is an absolute prerequisite for the successful use of language as a communicative tool. This capacity derails, however, when an attempt to "score" communicatively loses sight of the essential concerns related to the field of action which the communicative act fits into. In politics this happens when the hunt for votes makes politicians join the choir of voices singing the praise of national identity and the dangers of (too much) diversity. Intellectuals fall into the trap when trying to maintain popular credibility by distancing themselves from the so-called political correctness of multiculturalism. Journalists obviously belong to the category of intellectuals, but their attempt to maintain credibility may be further complicated by the commercial demands of the media concerns they are working for. Their role, therefore, is both extremely difficult and important. As we have seen from the analysis of a single text, complex constellations of seemingly commonsensical ideas tend to be reproduced and perpetuated with clearly unintended but wide-ranging practical and moral consequences.

All of this implies that responsibility for ideological processes is widely shared. This responsibility must be taken seriously, which requires a high degree of healthy reflexivity, quasi-permanent vigilance, constantly questioning one's own unspoken assumptions. If one does not succeed in doing so, a charge of complicity cannot be avoided. In fact, a form of complicity is inevitable anyway, but constant awareness of this simple fact may help us to avert detrimental consequences. This is a tall order for everyone. Only sustained education, aimed uncompromisingly at an ecology of discourse in the public sphere, can create the proper frame of mind at a wide-enough societal level. Recognizing this form of shared responsibility, however, provides everyone with the power to contribute.[13] When talking about the ideological grounding of ideas, briefly, we should

---

[13] The notions of derailed reflexivity, complicity, and an ecology of the public sphere are discussed at length Verschueren 2022.

not only analyze its ingredients and its anchoring points, but we should also recognize that they are "located" in people, collectively and individually – no-one being able to avoid a share of the responsibility.

References

Angermuller, Johannes, Dominique Maingueneau & Ruth Wodak (eds.). 2014. *The discourse studies reader: Main currents in theory and analysis*. Amsterdam & Philadelphia: John Benjamins.

Besson, Éric. 2009. *Pour la nation*. Paris: Bernard Grasset.

Blommaert, Jan & Jef Verschueren. 1998. *Debating diversity: Analysing the discourse of tolerance*. London & New York: Routledge.

De Wever, Bart. 2019. *Over identiteit* [About identity]. Gent: Borgerhoff & Lambrigts.

Eagleton, Terry. 2007. *Ideology: An introduction* (New and updated edn). London: Verso.

Grice, Paul. 1975. Logic and conversation. In Peter Cole & Jerry L. Morgan (eds.), *Syntax and semantics 3: Speech acts*, 41–58. New York: Academic Press.

Jaworski, Adam & Nikolas Coupland (eds.). 1999. *The discourse reader*. London & New York: Routledge.

Levinson, Stephen C. 1983. *Pragmatics*. Cambridge: Cambridge University Press.

Östman, Jan-Ola. 1986. *Pragmatics as implicitness*. Berkeley: University of California at Berkeley dissertation.

Prins, Baukje & Sawitri Saharso. 2010. From toleration to repression: The Dutch backlash against multiculturalism. In Steven Vertovec & Susanne Wessendorf (eds.), *The multiculturalism backlash: European discourses, policies and practices*, 72–91. London & New York: Routledge.

Schiffrin, Deborah. 1994. *Approaches to discourse*. Oxford: Basil Blackwell.

Schinkel, Willem. 2018. Against 'immigrant integration': For an end to neocolonial knowledge production. *Comparative Migration Studies* 6 (31). https://doi.org/10.1186/s40878-018-0095-1 (accessed 12 October 2020).

Thompson, John B. 1990. *Ideology and modern culture*. Cambridge: Polity.

Verschueren, Jef. 2012. *Ideology in language use: Pragmatic guidelines for empirical research*. Cambridge: Cambridge University Press.

Verschueren, Jef. 2022. *Complicity in discourse and practice*. London: Routledge.

Vertovec, Steven & Susanne Wessendorf (eds.). 2010. *The multiculturalism backlash: European discourses, policies and practices*. London & New York: Routledge.

Zienkowski, Jan. 2017. Asserting racism's relativity: An interpretive and functional analysis of Flemish nationalist re-articulations of the problematic of racism. *Journal of Multicultural Discourses* 12 (2). 149–165.

Zúquete, José Pedro. 2018. *The identitarians: The movement against globalism and Islam in Europe*. Notre Dame, IN: Notre Dame University Press.

Elizabeth R. Miller
Chapter 7
Hiding in plain sight: Methodological ideologies in discourse research in applied linguistics

Abstract: This chapter discusses a methodological ideology that often is (re)constructed in and informs many discourse-focused research practices. Its primary focus is on the often-unnoticed contradictions between discourse researchers' interpretive, post-foundational, and non-essentialist theoretical frameworks and their materializing and essentializing methodological practices that are (seemingly) necessary for conducting data collection and discourse analysis. I demonstrate this contradiction by re-examining many familiar methodological and analytical practices that I have adopted in my own research as an applied linguist. The chapter then offers a brief exploration of recent contributions to discursive research by a still-small but growing body of scholars whose work aligns with new materialist perspectives and whose efforts seem to achieve ideological alignment across theory and methods. In highlighting this alignment, I do not suggest that new materialist approaches should be taken up in all discourse research, however, as they introduce many new complexities and research dilemmas. I close the chapter by acknowledging that many post-foundational discourse scholars (including myself) may well choose to persist with familiar and standardized data-generating practices but must recognize them as often based in positivist practices and human-centric perspectives.

Keywords: post-foundational, interpretivist, research epistemologies, cartographies of communicability, data as material

1 Introduction

In using the term "discourse research" in this chapter, I am addressing scholarly work in which the primary research content is constructed of words, whether produced in interaction, published texts, field notes, interviews, or some other data collection format. That said, my understanding of the scope of what discourse entails is far more complex and points to why it is essential to consider discourse and ideology together. Early in my academic career, James Gee's (1990) highly influential definitions of "big-D" and "little-d" discourses shaped my understanding of discourse. "Little-d" **d**iscourse, as most readers likely know, referred to verbal interactions or written utterances, while "big-D" **D**iscourse referred to the complex intersections between identities, practices, contexts, ideologies, artifacts, language-in-use, and other symbolic systems. These intersections, according to Gee (1990: 143), help constitute our ways of "thinking, feeling, believing, valuing, and acting" and are "used to identify oneself as a member of a socially meaningful group or 'social network'". In order to make one's discursive activity "identifiable" or to be identified as "playing a socially meaningful 'role'" (Gee 1990: 143) in a social network, one typically draws on and re-enacts "common sense" practices and/or values for a given context. In this way discourses and ideologies regarding what is socially valued and deemed "appropriate" by particular groups of social actors inevitably implicate each other.

More recently, I have drawn on Verschueren's (2012) comprehensive book-length guide for researching ideology in language use. In line with Gee's approach to discourse, Verschueren (2012: 4) examines how "mundane and everyday processes" produce social meanings, shape human relationships, sustain values, and produce powerful norms. However, whereas Gee's focus on discourse tended to emphasize the role of "common sense" values in (de)legitimizing particular social identities, Verschueren's emphasis in interrogating ideology focuses on how meaning and (often inequitable) social values or norms are constituted via discursive acts or practices. For example, Verschueren (2012: 7) contends that in order to research ideology, one can and must examine mundane discursive acts (among many other social phenomena). The forms of discourse to be examined include "the ways in which beliefs, ideas, or opinions are discursively used; i.e., their *forms of expression* as well as *the rhetorical purposes* they serve" (italics in the original).

Informed by Gee's and Verschueren's approaches to discourse and ideology, my scholarly focus in this chapter is on a small set of normative research practices that are frequently used by many discourse-oriented scholars and the ideological assumptions that shape and are (re)constituted through these methods. I seek to show that these ideological assumptions enable and, in fact, lead many post-structural discourse scholars to treat words and utterances as commonsensically recognized forms of data.

I write this as a North American applied linguist whose discursive research practices have centered on concerns related to identity, ideology, agency, and emotions in language learning and teaching with a research focus on using words as data. My geographical situatedness influenced my approach to analyzing discourse. North American discourse research has tended to emphasize the analysis of language in use, typically spoken interactions, with value assigned to careful, detailed empirical observations (Miller 2018). This perspective contrasts with the more philosophical approaches to discourse theory as developed by "Continental European theorists" from the 1970s and 1980s, such as Michel Foucault or Jacques Lacan (Angermuller, Maingueneau, and Wodak 2014: 5). My scholarly coming of age as a graduate student took place during the late 1990s and early 2000s. At the same time, the field of applied linguistics and language learning studies was expanding to include a broader range of theoretical frameworks. These included, most notably, sociocultural theory along with a range of post-foundational approaches such as social constructionist, poststructuralist, performativity, and feminist perspectives. A broader range of discursive data collection and analytic methodologies such as conversation analysis, narrative inquiry, (micro)ethnography, positioning analysis, among others, began to gain legitimacy over this same time period. I do not have the space in this chapter to explore the complex history of shifting epistemologies and ontologies related to the research frameworks and methodologies adopted by the applied linguistics research community over the past three decades (but see Pennycook 1994, 2010, 2018). Instead, I have decided to focus on only one component of the discursive research enterprise: ideologies regarding discourse data.

Now widely accepted, theoretical frameworks such as social constructionism, poststructuralism, performativity, and some forms of narrative inquiry that are drawn upon in applied linguistic research explicitly reject the possibility of gaining unmediated access to social reality or of uncovering universal truths. These approaches disallow treating language, identity, or social context as essentialized, stable, or objective constructs in the world, viewing them rather as fluid, distributed, co-constructed, situated, fragmented, and performed constructs. While there are important distinctions among post-foundational approaches, one can find among them a shared orientation to "our social, cultural, historical and political realities [as] constituted by discursive practices" (Miller and Kubota 2013: 231). These interpretive and post-foundational frameworks have often been juxtaposed against positivist perspectives, and in nearly all cases, positivism is treated as the perspective to be abandoned and avoided and is, in fact, often cast about as "a term of abuse" as Brinkmann wryly notes (cited in Demuth and Terkildsen 2015: 137).

While post-foundational discourse research has proliferated over the past two decades, so too have publications that provide guidance on how to select and implement particular research methodologies. Although methodology publications continue to emphasize quantitative approaches, there appears to be a growing appetite among scholars (and recognized by publishers) for established, standardized methodological guidelines that focus on qualitative approaches which incorporate discourse, materialized as words, as their primary data. This burgeoning publishing industry is particularly remarkable when we consider that the first *Handbook of Qualitative Research* (Denzin and Lincoln 1994) was published by Sage Publications only a little more than twenty-five years ago. At around that time, Lazaraton (1995: 485) lamented that there were "to date no qualitative research methods texts written for and by applied linguists". In August 2020, I did a simple search on the Sage Publishing website using "discourse analysis textbooks" as my search terms under "Qualitative Research". The company's website returned fifty-six "results" or names of published textbooks that provide methodological guidance on how to conduct discourse analysis, twenty-one of which had been published since 2015. Many other academic publishers have likewise contributed to this current and still-growing appetite among discourse scholars for standardized protocols, clarity, and scholarly rigor when it comes to doing research with words.

2 Epistemological contradictions in producing discourse data

While the reasons for the current strong appetite for methodology texts are most certainly complex and multiple, Brinkmann (cited in Demuth and Terkildsen 2015: 137) attributes it, in part, to the "whole battle of positivism" that first emerged in the 1970s and 1980s and the ensuing need for qualitative researchers to demonstrate "scientific" rigor without recourse to concepts such as reliability, validity, and/or generalizability that form the foundation of positivist research.[1] Brinkmann acknowledges the very practical need for scholars to be able to assign recognized labels to their methodological practices in order to persuade funders or reviewers or editors that their research is legitimate. However, he and others, including researchers who claim the label of "post-qualitative" scholars (discussed below), have argued that many of the normative methodological and analytic practices used by qualitative researchers lead to an interesting epistemological contradiction. Though aligning with a theoretical orientation to non-positivist, interpretive and/or post-foundational work, researchers' standardized methodological practices of collecting, coding and finding themes or patterns in their qualitative data often "stay within a quantitative logic" and align with a positivist ideology (Demuth and Terkildsen 2015: 145).

In addressing these concerns elsewhere, Brinkmann (2014: 720) published a provocative article titled "Doing without Data" in which he comments that he

---

[1] Brinkmann is commenting on research in the field of psychology in this particular publication, but his observations are pertinent for all fields using post-foundational, discursive methods.

has become "skeptical [. . .] of the very idea of data as such". He clarifies that qualitative researchers too often seem to treat their data as "the givens" that they then "collect" and "code" (Brinkmann 2014: 721). This orientation to collectable, codable data is, he argues, true to the word's Latin root *dare*, which means to "to give", but he adds that the notion of data as *given*, rather than *taken*, has long been shown to be a "myth" (e.g., Dewey [1929] 1960; Sellars [1956] 1997). Brinkmann (2014: 721) proposes that we instead talk about data as "creata" or then simply as "materials" (cited in Demuth and Terkildsen 2015: 153) in order to emphasize their status as created, physical things in the world. On the substance of discourse data, he claims: "It's not just given. It's made. It's done. It's a material thing" (cited in Demuth and Terkildsen 2015: 153). Brinkmann continues:

> They [data] are not there to be picked up. They are there because we have created situations that enable them to be taken. We translate all the time from verbal interaction to the – if we talk about interviewing – to the sound recorder, to the transcription, to the software package, to whatever . . . . It is just a series of translations from different kinds of materials and there are sensible ways of translating and there are bad ways of translating. I am not saying that anything goes. (cited in Demuth and Terkildsen 2015: 153–154)

In emphasizing the created status of research materials, Brinkmann argues that researchers, in fact, assign the status of data to discursive acts that they have selectively extracted from a research encounter. An interviewee's utterances, for example, become data through being treated as such, methodologically and ideologically.

In the introductory chapter to their comprehensive volume on research methods in applied linguistics, Paltridge and Phakiti (2015: 19) use the term "post-positivist" to identify researchers who may use qualitative data such as interviews or observations but who maintain a "critical realist ontology (to maintain as much objectivity as possible)" by relying on methods such as triangulation, member-checking, and/or intra- and inter-code reliability. They contrast this approach to constructivist or hermeneutical research in which the researcher "forms interpretations or constructions, from a close understanding of the [discursive] data (e.g., observations, notes, interview recordings)" (Paltridge and Phakiti 2015: 19). However, I would argue that it is this latter approach that is particularly susceptible to inadvertently incorporating conflicting epistemologies (both positivism and interpretivism) into its methodologies. Though post-foundational researchers shun essentialist perspectives, emphasizing the dialogical, dynamic and co-constructed character of social realities in collecting and analyzing our discursive content, i.e., the meanings-captured-in-words, we often construct objectivity through creating standardized representations of what was said or written or intimated in some fashion in our research processes. That is, we often treat interview transcripts or field notes or other written texts as given or found data which have a kind of ontological stability that can hold and carry the same meaning even as they are translated from one site and modality to another.

St. Pierre (2013) argues, along with a growing number of feminist scholars who are working to promote "post-qualitative" research (e.g., Benozzo 2021; Jackson 2013, 2017; Lather 2017; Lather and St. Pierre 2013; MacLure 2013; St. Pierre 2014, 2021; St. Pierre and Jackson 2014), that most qualitative, discursive research continues to adhere to positivist epistemologies. She writes, "I believe that qualitative research methodology – too often confused both epistemologically and ontologically [. . .] encouraged some bizarre combination of interpretivism and positivism in thinking about data by insisting, with interpretivism, that data be textualized, and, with logical positivism, that words in those texts can be brute, sense data" (St. Pierre 2013: 224). To this she adds, "The rationale seems to be that if qualitative data can't be numbers (pure and uncontaminated by humans) then words will have to do [. . .] Words become quasi-numbers" (St. Pierre 2013: 224).

Elsewhere, St. Pierre and a colleague discuss the "incommensurability" often found in "interpretive" research that codes and textualizes data as part of its methodology schema given that such practices are "thinkable and doable only in a Cartesian ontological realism that assumes data exist out there somewhere in the real world to be found, collected, and coded using the 'Cartesian principle of breaking down the difficulty into as many parts as may be necessary for finding the solution'" (Derrida [1967] 1978: 287, cited in St. Pierre and Jackson 2014: 715). This positivist ideology of "data" can be recognized even when we describe our discursive data as co-constructed or as performatively mobilized in some fashion, such as when interview data are treated as "interaction" with careful attention given to how the researchers' utterances frame and mobilize the interviewee's utterances as I have done in my own research.

3 Cartographies of communicability

Anthropologist Charles Briggs has long brought a cautionary perspective to the taken-for-granted methodologies adopted in qualitative research though he focused primarily on research interviewing (e.g., Briggs 1986). More than a decade ago, he published an insightful discussion on the ideologies that inform our research processes of creating "subjects, texts, knowledge and authority" (Briggs 2007: 552). In looking specifically at narratives of infanticide produced during the 1990s in Venezuela, Briggs (2005: 325) explored their "cartography of communicability" or the mapping of who and what is incorporated into a narrative in ways that are entirely "familiar, knowable". He adds that the cartography of communicability for these particular narratives of violence include "detectives [who] pry clues out of witnesses, physicians, and the material world of 'evidence' and force confessions. Judges retell violent narratives in their decrees and sentences. Reporters expose lies and provide 'the public' with the 'real' story. Activists and defense attorneys resignify the same plot in counternarratives of violence" (Briggs 2005: 318).

These textualized reports are then received as reasonably faithful representations of "what happened", or as Briggs (2005: 323) puts it, these crime narratives project an "iconicity" to or "mimesis" between the event and the account. Even as we recognize that information is selected and texts are carefully edited or crafted, the narrativized version of the event comes to be treated as an "immutable mobile" (Latour 1988), which, as Briggs (2005: 321) argues, means that these now-textualized accounts are "seemingly able to travel anywhere, crossing scales, social fields, countries, and racial boundaries without shifting, presumably, meaning". I have described this work in some detail because it helps us to understand Briggs' (2005: 318) argument that through exploring how the cartography of these violence narratives was mapped and created he could identify "resemblances of methods, objects, and perspectives" in his own scholarly research practices. He argues, therefore, that researchers "need to ponder not just the content of messages but how the ideological construction of their production, circulation, and reception shapes identities and social 'groups' and orders them hierarchically" (Briggs 2005: 275). Bourdieu (1996) explores similar concerns in aligning with the notion that researchers' methodological concerns do not lie between choosing positivism or interpretivism, or, as he puts it, "between a science which effects a construction and one which does not". Bourdieu argues that researchers must instead strive to develop awareness of their "inevitable acts of construction and the equally inevitable effects which they produce" (Bourdieu 1996: 18) and describes researchers' efforts to develop such awareness as "perilous" work (Bourdieu 1996: 33).

Talmy (2010) draws on Brigg's notion of cartographies of communicability in exploring the ideologies that often inform interview research in applied linguistics. Like Briggs, he critiques the manner in which discourse data produced in interviews are often

> [. . .] ontologically ascribed the status of "reports" of respondents' biographical, experiential, and psychological worlds, with the interview thus conceptualized as the epistemological conduit to those worlds: the interviewer reveals what "really" happened, or what participants "actually" felt through the technology of the interview, with closer approximations of reality depending on the interviewer's skill at developing rapport, for example, or not asking leading questions. (Talmy 2010: 131)

Talmy thus highlights the need to examine not only the *whats* or the content of interview talk but also the *hows* or the methods and processes by which meanings and knowledge are worked up in an interview situation (see Holstein and Gubrium 1995, 2003, for more on the notion of the active interview). Talmy (2011) skillfully demonstrates one approach an applied linguist can use in order to treat "interviews as social practice" rather than in the post-positivist "interviews as research tools" orientation. Using conversation analysis conventions, he shows how the themes and ideologies regarding the language and immigration identities of students at the high school where his research was based were co-constructed *in* the interview interactions themselves. As such, Talmy contends that he and his participants were not merely talking about the topic of interest; they are producing those very same identities and ideologies in the process of conducting the research. This work is exemplary in its effort to reveal the cartographies of communicability at work in producing a research account. I fully endorse Talmy's (2010: 143) call for "heightened reflexivity" regarding scholars' research methods and the "status ascribed to interview data". And yet, even here, even when urging scholars to examine and report on the "interactional and interpersonal circumstances of the local production" of data, Talmy (2010: 142) does not question the ideologies informing his use of transcription conventions developed in the field of Conversation Analysis which attempt to provide a textualized representation of the intonation, pausing, voice-quality, and turn-taking activity that occurred in the research interview. In producing a highly detailed rendering of the audio qualities and embodied actions as well as the words spoken in the interview interactions, Talmy (2011) has created a mimetic account, an immutable mobile, in which the ineffable is transformed into something material. This material representation, in the form of an interview transcript, is treated by him and his readers as a more or less faithful rendering of what transpired.

Though I take a critical stance in the above paragraph, I find Foucault's (1988: 154) notion of critique useful to include here: "Critique is not a matter of saying that things are not right as they are. It is a matter of pointing out on what kinds of assumptions, [on] what kinds of familiar, unchallenged, unconsidered modes of thought the practices that we accept rest" (cited in St. Pierre 2014: 4). Furthermore, I write this, not as someone who has avoided such practices, but as a researcher who is often fully complicit in furthering such taken-for-granted epistemological contradictions.

4 Exploring cartographies of communicability in discourse research

In this section, I aim to critique some of my own materializing and essentializing research processes in light of Briggs' perspectives on cartographies of communicability and Brinkmann's and others' views of data as created rather than taken/found materials as a way of demonstrating how positivist ideologies of data infuse our post-foundational work. The study involved interviews with immigrant small business owners living in the United States who had learned English after arriving in the country as adults. This project adopted dialogical (Bakhtin 1981) and performativity (Butler 1997) frameworks in which social realities are regarded as co-constructed, performed, situated, fragmented, and dynamic. Though my work with these interviews appears in a number of publications, I will focus on how I conceptualized the discursive data in a research monograph (Miller 2014). In this book, I draw explicitly on Briggs and state that I view my research and writing processes as "productive and constitutive work" (Miller 2014: 135). I seek to avoid the research model of "mining" my interviewees for true, authentic accounts as Talmy (2010, 2011) warned against, and directly commented on my participation in the production of my interviewees' accounts through the form my questions took and through my interactional behaviors in the interview situation. And yet, despite this theoretical framing of my methodological practices, I still maintain a positivist orientation to the discursive data in my study through treating them all too often as "brute, sense data" and even as "quasi-numbers" (St. Pierre 2013: 224) that fit comfortably within a normative, recognizable cartography of communicability.

4.1 Recruiting and materializing particular research participants

I first examine the mundane research practice of identifying and recruiting research participants. In discussing this aspect of my methodology, I drew on Rosenblatt's (2002) notion of the "imagined subject". As I argue in my book, by identifying my research participants as imagined subjects, "I do not conjure something out of nothing, but I do selectively 'address' and thus constitute particular kinds of speaking subjects – a kind of 'foreclosure' (Butler 1997: 139) that both constrains and enables interviewees to speak and act in legitimated, recognizable ways for the purpose of my research" (Miller 2014: 29). On this topic, Briggs (2007: 558) further argues, "The process of recruitment, interviewing and analysis generally involves inserting individuals into systems of social classification – according to gender, race, age, income, or relationship to a particular event". While the eighteen individuals involved in my study could all be factually identified as *adult immigrant small business owners who learned English after childhood*, these selves were not simply waiting to be verbalized or released in the interview talk. The imagined selves noted above had to be materialized throughout the research process, from recruitment procedures, to developing interview questions, to analyzing and writing about these subjects.

In the book, I created a table (see Table 3.1 in Miller 2014: 32) composed of columns with the participants' pseudonyms, their gender, their countries of origin, and the types of businesses that they owned. By creating a textual diagram such as this, I projected an "iconicity" between the research participants and my entextualized "data", as Briggs (2007) might argue. That is, this kind of representation "project[s] seemingly direct, automatic, and natural connections . . . on the basis of [participants] sharing the same features in the same relations" (Briggs 2005: 323). In order to create the data I was interested in, I took embodied individuals whom I encountered in dynamic and complex material and social environments and stripped away much of this complexity in order to develop a case that these individuals were sufficiently similar participant types for my study. Michael (2004: 14) comments on the need to "discipline" the interfering "noise" of research so that "sociological data might be 'gatherable'". Clearly the data for my study are not waiting to be taken but are rather crafted through my identification, recruitment, materialization, entextualization, and, ultimately, essentialization of particular characteristics of people who could produce relevant discursive material.

4.2 Collecting data vs. creating materials

I will now consider one example of how I sought to substantiate one set of interpretations of the discursive data created in my study. In a chapter that focused on how interviewees positioned themselves as (in)agentive and (not) responsible in relation to learning English and other languages after arriving in the U.S., I argued that all of the interviewees portrayed themselves as highly agentive and as undertaking effortful actions and measures in order to learn English. However, I perceived that these same individuals portrayed their learning of their customers' or employees' non-English languages as an unproblematic and even enjoyable process of just "picking up" the language.

Following standard methodological protocols, I gave numerous examples from my transcribed interview data to supply evidence that the above claims are justified. One of these examples can be found in the following Excerpt 1 (which uses Conversation Analysis conventions for marking intonation) taken from my interview with Tony, a Vietnamese sandwich shop owner. I cast it as one demonstration of how interviewees treated their on-the-fly language learning encounters in their businesses as unplanned, unproblematic, relatively easy, and often as pleasurable. In the chapter, I noted how my question regarding whether Tony's customers ever learn any Vietnamese from him (line 1) serves to mobilize his response. I also pointed out that my supportive and positive assessments (*yeah, yes, excellent, very good*) produced at appropriate turn-taking moments in the interaction enabled Tony to produce this account (i.e., a different, less welcoming reception might have curtailed it or even rendered it unsayable).

Excerpt 1: *Tony teaches and learns a little bit of language*
1. Int: Do do customers ever learn any Vietnamese from you?
2. Tony: Oh yeah.
3. Int: Yeah?
4. Tony: Some uh Laos customer,
5. Int: Okay.
6. Tony: they come they come to order my sandwich,
7. Int: Yeah.
8. Tony: and they ask me about my language
9. Int: Yes yes.
10. Tony: And I teach them a little bit, then I ask them
11.   [about their language.
12. Int: [Yes.
13. Tony: They teach me a little bit.
14. Int: Excellent.
15. Tony: They teach me a little bit of Laos?
16. Int: Uh huh?
17. Tony: And Thai?
18. Int: Uh huh?
19. Tony: And Hmong?
20. Int: Yeah.
21. Tony: A little bit. Yeah.
22. Int: Very good.   (Miller 2014: 66)

Despite my explication of the co-construction of the talk in the face-to-face encounter between Tony and me, I was silent on the communicative cartography that enabled me to turn this embodied encounter in a noisy sandwich shop into a digitally rendered audio recording which was then translated into a tidy, linear stretch of words on a page. As Briggs (2005: 327) argues, photographs and directly quoted discourse function as "indexical icons demonstrating the reality of their referent". In this case, the entextualization of the interview talk gives proof that Tony and I were both somewhere together and that he, the research participant, actually produced these words. We typically interpret the entextualization of research encounters "in this fashion" (Briggs 2005: 327). But as Briggs further contends, "following Bakhtin, [we recognize that] reproducing texts involves transformations of form, context, and meaning *that preclude exact replication*" (Briggs 2007: 562, italics added).

Further, the particular emplacement of this transcript in the larger text, determined as a means for providing evidence for my broader claims, can make it seem "predisposed" to appear here; that is, we accept that this bit of transformed text can be "fitted into collective portraits and transported into professional texts and contexts" (Briggs 2007: 558) with no change in meaning. We might say that its construction within and as part of the larger text projects its own communicable cartography in which we orient to this discursive event as able to move through time, space, and modalities relatively unscathed. There is no possibility of my "representing" the former event as it really transpired even if I had included photographic images or links to audio or video recordings of the interaction. Though such additional details and data modalities could have provided richer or "thicker" information, it remains impossible for me to deliver the actual encounter anywhere else. From spoken interaction to audio recording to transcription to analysis and interpretation and then finally to entextualized placement and representation in the published text, this discursive content is not given, a thing that can be moved from location to location unchanged. It is clearly material that I carefully worked up at each stage of the research process.

4.3 Dialogic exchange vs. power relations

We can further critique the manner in which this exchange between interviewer and interviewee is entextualized in terms of dialogic relations. The interviewer and interviewee are constructed as equal partners in their placement and textual formatting in the transcript. The turn-taking seems to roll along, with one turn eliciting the next, in an easy, non-coercive fashion. Kvale (2008: 13) addresses the "masking of power" that is often constructed in research data. As he notes, "dialogical research may suggest mutuality and egalitarianism where qualitative interviewers with their gentle, unassuming non-directive approaches enter into authentic personal relationships with their subjects" (Kvale 2008: 13). He adds that such representations create "an illusion of mutual interests in a conversation" (Kvale 2008: 13) when we, of course, know that it typically takes place only for the interests of the interviewer. (There are, of course, interviews or other research encounters where researchers' power is constrained or stymied by uncooperative interviewees, but these are usually regarded as problematic interviews.)

In my analysis of the above transcribed talk, I did not explicitly comment on my non-coercive approach with Tony, but its textualized representation fits with the communicative cartography that we all recognize. The questioner (me) controls the talk but does so in a "gentle, unassuming non-directive" style, mostly because that style of interviewing typically leads to greater volubility by the interviewee. It is a way to create better research material. Though many have argued that interviews can "give voice" to individuals who would not otherwise be heard, it is typically only the researcher who "claims the right to juxtapose these voices and convert them into public discourse, that is, to make them travel" (Briggs 2007: 565) from one situation to another, across scales, and through converting those voices from one modality to another after the interview is over.

Thus, instead of being an egalitarian, power-free encounter, one might better view such dialogic interactions as benevolently "manipulative" (Kvale 2008: 14). While power relations between researcher and the researched have been given intense scrutiny (Bengtsson and Fynbo 2018; Briggs 2002; Herzog 2012; Slembrouck 2004), the production and reception of entextualized research materials are often seen as purely mechanical processes when in fact these practices serve to "infuse" such materials with "authority and value" (Briggs 2007: 565). Denzin (2013) addresses the role of power in research, not between the human individuals involved but in terms of how our data/materials are used to provide evidence. He argues:

> [It] is not a question of evidence or no evidence. It is rather a question of who has the power to control the definition of evidence, who defines the kinds of materials that count as evidence, who determines what methods best produce the best forms of evidence, whose criteria and standards are used to evaluate quality evidence. The politics of data, the politics of evidence, cannot be separated from the ethics of evidence. (Denzin 2013: 354)

His comments remind us that discourse data such as interview interactions are not only collected and curated objects. They are also always political in the sense of being produced for the benefit of the more powerful participants in their creation: the researchers (see also Bucholtz 2000; Ochs 1979).

5 New materialism, materialization, and complexifying discursive data

One of the recent developments in discourse scholarship in applied linguistics from the past decade is research that adopts a "materialist orientation" Canagarajah (2018: 268, see also Canagarajah 2017, 2020; Fleming et al. 2018; Higgins and Ikeda 2019; Sharma 2020; Toohey 2019). I do not have space to provide a comprehensive overview of new materialist approaches in applied linguistics given their complexity and variability, so I will only briefly address their relevance to the discussion of ideologies of discourse data as material. Like most new materialists, Toohey (2019: 3) draws on the work of Deleuze and Guattari ([1987] 2005) in discussing researchers' need to account for complex 'assemblages'[2] or entanglements of "the animate and inanimate [. . .] material people, animals, objects, nature, discourses, and so on" and their interrelations and processes of "becoming together". As such, materials, discourses and all other phenomena are *all* regarded as *material* that is continually created anew, always becoming, in a continual "dynamic and shifting entanglement of relations" (Barad 2007: 35, cited in Toohey 2019: 4). Such a view upends the primacy given to discourse for the discourse analyst, however expansive and inclusive our understandings of discourse as social practice, in the "big-D" sense of discourse, might be. That is, I along with many other post-foundational scholars have regarded discourse as that which "render[s] experience sensible, orderly, [and] meaningful" (Gubrium and Holstein 2012: 341) even as we have distanced ourselves from viewing discourse as a representational object (i.e., treating language as a tool that represents other things and meanings). In taking this sense-making perspective, we have necessarily relied on materializing and entextualizing processes in order to create "data" that we can analyze and interpret and understand in our research endeavors, thus contributing to the epistemological contradictions between positivism and post-foundationalism as discussed above.

By contrast, new materialist epistemologies (and ontologies) assign materiality to all aspects of the research endeavor (Fox and Aldred 2017), what many refer to as a "flattened ontology" in which "empirical data" are not privileged because they are regarded as "no more authentic or closer to reality than something else (e.g., philosophical theory)" (Brinkmann 2017: 117). For this reason, Canagarajah contends that new materialist methodologies require that researchers "track the complex circuits at work whereby discursive and material forms are inextricable yet irreducible" (Coole and Frost, 2010: 27, cited in Canagarajah 2018: 271). Matter is treated as agentive and semiotic just as "human living, thinking, and acting is always material" (Brinkmann 2017: 116). I would argue that the effort to render all of the intersecting components of research as material, or treating *everything* as "data", presents a more ideologically coherent approach, particularly for schol-

---

[2] Deleuze and Guattari used the French term *agencement*. This term has been translated into English as 'assemblage'.

ars who explicitly reject positivism, post-positivism, and who embrace post-foundational theories.

At the same time, new materialists regard assemblages of discourse, matter and other phenomena as inherently "unstable and unable to be contained in language" (St. Pierre and Jackson 2014: 717), and thus the research enterprise and the concept of analyzing discourse data are not only greatly complexified in a new materialist world, they become different beasts altogether. Lather (2017: 81), in fact, describes new materialist work as "post-praxis or praxis 2.0" and argues that it is "ruined from the start" – i.e., it is impossible to assign a meaning or even several authoritative meanings given the "limits of our [human] knowing". However, she also adopts a hopeful stance in noting that this "praxis without guaranteed subjects or objects" holds the promise of enabling researchers to explore and create "as yet completely unthinkable conditions and the potential of given arrangements" (Lather 2017: 81). Likewise, Jackson (2017: 671) argues for "thinking without method" and variously describes method as normative, dogmatic, and an apparatus of capture. Thinking without method is necessary, from her perspective, in order to enter into new ways of thinking such as "how we welcome a people to come, a world to come, a movement beyond ourselves, rather than simply affirming what we are". Likewise, Brigstocke and Noorani (2016: 2) pose the question: "What new intersections among research, invention, and political agency might emerge when voices have to be assembled rather than merely amplified, and when new methods of listening need to be invented?" (cited in Pennycook 2018: 130).

This hopeful stance to what might be – a brave new world of research – is still more speculative than practiced, still more a call to adopt such approaches and ideas than clearly demonstrated in research studies (e.g., Pennycook 2018). There is much that can be critiqued in new materialist orientations to research as well (see Brinkmann 2017; Greene 2013; Larsen-Freeman 2019 for substantive critiques). In commenting briefly on the efforts taken by new materialists and by critiquing at length the epistemological contradictions that often inform discourse research, my position here is not to advocate for one research ideology over another, but rather to urge scholars to not take the taken-for-granted for granted. There is no exteriority in research according to Piattoeva and Saari (2020); that is, researchers cannot stand outside of "data infrastructures", whether they are comprised of words or numbers, because they are inevitably entangled in them (Piattoeva and Saari 2020: 4). As Ramanathan (2008: 20) has proposed, applied linguists – and all discourse scholars, for that matter – always need "to carefully scrutinize the language we use [. . .] to probe as far as possible our unacknowledged foundational assumptions, and to admit that our representations are most precariously poised and partial even though for the moment they are all we have;

they are our provisional truths". As I close this chapter, I do not want to leave the impression that methodological eclecticism should become the new method in discourse studies, but rather I hope to promote an awareness of how discourse analytic and methodological practices align with ideological norms and *create* consistency and stability in the provisional assemblages of discourse data that we will most likely continue to work with.

References

Angermuller, Johannes, Dominique Maingueneau & Ruth Wodak. 2014. The discourse studies reader: An introduction. In Johannes Angermuller, Dominique Maingueneau & Ruth Wodak (eds.), *The discourse studies reader: Main currents in theory and analysis*, 1–14. Amsterdam & Philadelphia: John Benjamins.
Bakhtin, Mikhail M. 1981. *The dialogic imagination: Four essays by M. M. Bakhtin*. Michael Holquist (ed.). Caryl Emerson & Michael Holquist (transl.). Austin, TX: University of Texas Press.
Bengtsson, Tea T. & Lars Fynbo. 2018. Analysing the significance of silence in qualitative interviewing: Questioning and shifting power relations. *Qualitative Research* 18 (1). 19–35.
Benozzo, Angelo. 2021. Post qualitative research: An idea for which the time has come. *Qualitative Inquiry* 27 (2). 167–170.
Briggs, Charles L. 1986. *Learning how to ask: A sociolinguistic appraisal of the role of the interview in social science research*. Cambridge: Cambridge University Press.
Briggs, Charles L. 2002. Interviewing, power/ knowledge, and social inequality. In Jaber F. Gubrium & James A. Holstein (eds.), *Handbook of interview research: Context and method*, 911–922. London, Thousand Oaks, CA & New Delhi: Sage.
Briggs, Charles L. 2005. Mediating infanticide: Theorizing relations between narrative and violence. *Cultural Anthropology* 22 (3). 315–356.
Briggs, Charles L. 2007. Anthropology, interviewing, and communicability in contemporary society. *Current Anthropology* 48 (4). 551–580.
Brinkmann, Svend. 2014. Doing without data. *Qualitative Inquiry* 20 (6). 720–725.
Brinkmann, Svend. 2017. Humanism after posthumanism: Or qualitative psychology after the "posts". *Qualitative Research in Psychology* 14 (2). 109–130.
Bourdieu, Pierre. 1996. Understanding. *Theory, Culture & Society*, 13 (2). 17–37.
Bucholtz, Mary. 2000. The politics of transcription. *Journal of Pragmatics* 13. 1439–1465.
Butler, Judith. 1997. *Excitable speech: A politics of the performative*. London & New York: Routledge.
Canagarajah, Suresh. 2017. The nexus of migration and language: The emergence of a disciplinary space. In Suresh Canagarajah (ed.), *The Routledge handbook of migration and language*, 1–28. London & New York: Routledge.
Canagarajah, Suresh. 2018. Materializing 'competence': Perspectives from international STEM scholars. *The Modern Language Journal* 102 (2). 268–291.
Canagarajah, Suresh. 2020. English as a resource in a communicative assemblage: A perspective from flat ontology. In Christopher H. Hall & Rachel Wicaksono (eds.),

Ontologies of English: Conceptualising the language for learning, teaching, and assessment, 295–314. Cambridge: Cambridge University Press.

Deleuze, Gilles & Felix Guattari. 2005 [1987]. *A thousand plateaus: Capitalism and schizophrenia*. Brian Massumi (transl.). Minneapolis: University of Minnesota Press.

Demuth, Carolin & Thomas Terkildsen. 2015. The future of qualitative research in psychology: A discussion with Svend Brinkmann, Günter Mey, Luca Tateo, and Anete Strand. *Intregrated Psychological and Behavioral Science* 49 (2). 135–161.

Denzin, Norman K. 2013. The death of data? *Cultural Studies ↔ Critical Methodologies* 13 (4). 353–356.

Denzin, Norman K. & Yvonna S. Lincoln. 1994. *Handbook of qualitative research*. London, Thousand Oaks, CA & New Delhi: Sage.

Dewey, John. 1960 [1929]. *The quest for certainty: A study of the relation of knowledge and action*. New York: Capricorn Books.

Fleming, Douglas, Monica Waterhouse, Francis Bangou & Maria Bastien. 2018. Agencement, second language education, and becoming: A Deleuzian take on citizenship. *Critical Inquiry in Language Studies* 15 (2). 141–160.

Fox, Nick J. & Pam Alldred. 2017. *Sociology and the new materialism: Theory, research, action*. London, Thousand Oaks, CA & New Delhi: Sage.

Gee, James P. 1990. *Social linguistics and literacies: Ideology in discourses*. Bristol, PA: The Falmer Press.

Greene, Jennifer C. 2013. On rhizomes, lines of flight, mangles, and other assemblages. *International Journal of Qualitative Studies in Education* 26 (6). 749–758.

Gubrium, Jaber F. & James A. Holstein. 2012. Theoretical validity and empirical utility of a constructionist analytics. *The Sociological Quarterly* 53 (3). 341–359.

Holstein, James A. & Jaber F. Gubrium. 1995. *The active interview*. London, Thousand Oaks, CA & New Delhi: Sage.

Holstein, James A. & Jaber F. Gubrium. 2003. Inside interviewing: New lenses, new concerns. In James A. Holstein & Jaber F. Gubrium (eds.), *Inside interviewing: New lenses, new concerns*, 1–32. London, Thousand Oaks, CA & New Delhi: Sage.

Herzog, Hanna. 2012. Interview location and its social meaning. In Jaber F. Gubrium, James A. Holstein, Amir B. Marvasti & Karyn D. McKinney (eds.), *The SAGE handbook of interview research: The complexity of the craft*, 207–217. London, Thousand Oaks, CA & New Delhi: Sage.

Higgins, Christina & Maiko Ikeda. 2019. The materialization of language in tourism networks. *Applied Linguistics Review* 12 (1). 123–152.

Jackson, Alecia Y. 2013. Posthumanist data analysis of mangling practices. *International Journal of Qualitative Studies in Education* 26 (6). 741–748.

Jackson, Alecia Y. 2017. Thinking without method. *Qualitative Inquiry* 23 (9). 666–674.

Kvale, Steinar. 2008. Qualitative inquiry between scientific evidentialism, ethical subjectivism and the free market. *International Review of Qualitative Research* 1 (1). 5–18.

Larsen-Freeman, Diane. 2019. On language learner agency: A complex dynamic systems theory perspective. *The Modern Language Journal* 103 (s1). 61–79.

Lather, Patti. 2017. Thirty years after: From research as praxis to praxis in the ruins. In Helen Janc Malone, Santiago Rincón-Gallardo, & Kristin Kew (eds.), *Future directions of educational change*, 71–87. London & New York: Routledge.

Lather, Patti & Elizabeth A. St. Pierre. 2013. Introduction: Post-qualitative research. *International Journal of Qualitative Studies* 26 (6). 629–633.

Latour, Bruno. 1988. *The pasteurization of France*. Alan M. Sheridan & John Law (transl.). Cambridge, MA: Harvard University Press.

Lazaraton, Anne. 1995. Qualitative research in applied linguistics: A progress report. *TESOL Quarterly* 29 (3). 455–472.

MacLure, M. 2013. Researching without representation? Language and materiality in post-qualitative methodology. *International Journal of Qualitative Studies* 26 (6). 658–667.

Michael, Mike. 2004. On making data social: Heterogeneity in sociological practice. *Qualitative Research* 4 (1). 5–23.

Miller, Elizabeth R. 2014. *The language of adult immigrants: Agency in the making*. Bristol, England: Multilingual Matters.

Miller, Elizabeth R. 2018. Interaction analysis. In Luke Plonsky, Peter De Costa, Aek Phakiti & Sue Starfield (eds.), *The Palgrave handbook of applied linguistics research methodology*, 615–638. London: Palgrave Macmillan.

Miller, Elizabeth R. & Ryuko Kubota. 2013. Second language learning and identity. In Julia Rogers Herschensohn & Martha Young-Scholten (eds.), *Cambridge handbook of second language acquisition*, 230–250. Cambridge: Cambridge University Press.

Ochs, Elinor. 1979. Transcription as theory. In Elinor Ochs & Bambi B. Schieffelin (eds.), *Developmental pragmatics*, 43–71. New York: Academic Press.

Paltridge, Brian & Aek Phakiti (eds.). 2015. *Research methods in applied linguistics: A practical resource*. London & New York: Bloomsbury Publishing.

Pennycook, Alastair. 1994. Incommensurable discourses? *Applied Linguistics* 15 (2). 115–138.

Pennycook, Alastair. 2010. Critical and alternative directions in applied linguistics. *Australian Review of Applied Linguistics* 33 (2). 16.1–16.6.

Pennycook, Alastair. 2018. *Posthumanist applied linguistics*. London & New York: Routledge.

Piattoeva, Nelli & Antti Saari. 2020. Rubbing against data infrastructure (s): Methodological explorations on working with (in) the impossibility of exteriority. *Journal of Education Policy*, 1–21. https://doi.org/10.1080/02680939.2020.1753814 (accessed 6 October 2020).

Ramanathan, Vaidehi. 2008. Applied linguistics redux: A Derridean exploration of Alzheimer life histories. *Applied Linguistics* 29 (1). 1–23.

Rosenblatt, Paul C. 2002. Interviewing at the border of fact and fiction. In Jaber F. Gubrium & James A. Holstein (eds.), *Handbook of interview research: Context and method*, 893–910. London, Thousand Oaks, CA & New Delhi: Sage.

Sellars, W. 1997 [1956]. Empiricism and the philosophy of mind. In Herbert Feigl & Michael Scriven (eds.), *The foundaations of science and the concepts of Psychology and Psychoanalysis*, 253-329, 7th printing. Minneapolis, MN: University of Minnesota Press.

Sharma, Bal K. 2020. A new materialist perspective to studying L2 instructional interactions in engineering. *International Journal of Bilingual Education and Bilingualism*. 1–19. https://doi.org/10.1080/13670050.2020.1767030 (accessed 6 October 2020).

Slembrouck, Stef. 2004. Reflexivity and the research interview: Habitus and social class in parents' accounts of children in public care. *Critical discourse studies* 1 (1). 91–112.

St. Pierre, Elizabeth A. 2013. The appearance of data. *Cultural Studies ↔ Critical Methodologies* 13 (4). 223–227.

St. Pierre, Elizabeth A. 2014. A brief and personal history of post qualitative research: Towards "post inquiry". *Journal of Curriculum Theorizing* 30 (2). 2–19.

St. Pierre, Elizabeth A. 2021. Post qualitative inquiry, the refusal of method, and the risk of the new. *Qualitative Inquiry* 27 (1). 3–9.

St. Pierre, Elizabeth A. & Alecia Y. Jackson. 2014. Qualitative data analysis after coding. *Qualitative Inquiry* 20 (6). 715–719.
Talmy, Steven. 2010. Qualitative interviews in applied linguistics: From research instrument to social practice. *Annual Review of Applied Linguistics* 30. 128–148.
Talmy, Steven. 2011. The interview as collaborative achievement: Interaction, identity, and ideology in a speech event. *Applied linguistics* 32 (1). 25–42.
Toohey, Kelleen. 2019. The onto-epistemologies of new materialism: Implications for applied linguistics pedagogies and research. *Applied Linguistics* 4 (6). 937–956.
Verschueren, Jef. 2012. *Ideology in language use: Pragmatic guidelines for empirical research.* Cambridge: Cambridge University Press.

Teun A. van Dijk
Chapter 8
Ideology in cognition and discourse

Abstract: In this chapter, I present a summary of a multidisciplinary theory of ideology and how ideologies are socially reproduced through discourse. It is assumed that ideologies, just as knowledge, are forms of social cognition, and shared by the members of social groups. Ideologies control socially shared attitudes about specific social issues and indirectly the mental models of individual group members. These subjective ideological models control specific ideological practices, in general, and ideological discourse, in particular – which in turn may ultimately contribute to the confirmation or the modification of the ideology.

My framework is multidisciplinary. It integrates a cognitive psychological, social psychological, sociological and linguistic (discourse analytical) approach to ideologies, their mental organization, their social and political functions, as well as their acquisition and reproduction by public text and talk. Since the sociopolitical conditions and functions of ideologies are best known, this paper will specifically focus on the sociocognitive and discursive aspects of ideologies (there are thousands of books on ideology, so I do not provide references to them; the same is true for the relevant literature on social cognition, social identity theory, and other theories that contribute to a general theory of ideology, for which I refer to my previous publications).

Keywords: ideology, social cognition, discourse, ingroup and outgroup, polarization

1 Discourse studies

The main perspective of this paper is discourse analytical, and hence focuses on how ideologies are socially acquired and reproduced by text and talk. Since this discourse analytical perspective has been generally ignored in sociopolitical approaches to ideology, I shall briefly summarize the current state of the study of discourse – without many further references to the many areas of Discourse Studies (for detail, see the following general handbooks and introductions: Blommaert 2005; De Fina and Georgakopoulou 2020; Gee and Handford 2012; Tannen, Hamilton, and Schiffrin [2001] 2015; Stivers and Sidnell 2011; Van Dijk 2011).

Discourse Studies (DS) is a cross-discipline that emerged from the early 1960 onwards in all disciplines of the humanities and the social sciences, initially in anthropology, sociology, linguistics and psychology.

In *linguistics*, DS developed as a critical reaction against structuralist and generative grammars that limited the study of language to formal grammars of isolated sentences, instead of accounting for the structures of socially situated discourse. Thus, linguistic theories of discourse showed how discourses are locally and globally coherent sequences of sentences, and have many structures beyond those studied in sentence grammars. Besides the phonological study of sounds, the syntax of sentence structures, and the semantics of word and sentence meanings, theories of discourse also describe meaning at more global (macro) levels of discourse, schematic structures such as those of stories or argumentations, as well as style, rhetoric, conversational interaction or the pragmatics of speech acts, among other levels and structures of text and talk (for linguistic approaches to discourse, see Tannen, Hamilton, and Schiffrin 2015).

In *anthropology* in the early 1960s, the research direction called the "ethnography of speaking" focused on the structures and the contexts of "communicative events" in different cultures, and thus showed how discourse structures may vary across the world, as is the case for storytelling, media discourse or political discourse. Later, this research was continued and expanded in what became known as linguistic anthropology (see Bauman and Sherzer 1974).

In the early 1970s, *sociology* saw the emergence of a more qualitative microsociology focusing on interaction, in general, and on conversation, in particular, within a framework called ethnomethodology. With its sophisticated, detailed analysis of the structures and strategies of talk, Conversation Analysis became a prominent form of discourse study in most of the humanities and social sciences (see Stivers and Sidnell 2011).

Also in the early 1970s, *cognitive psychology*, interested in the actual processes and mental representations involved in language use, went beyond the sentence level as studied in traditional grammars, and began to develop theories for the production and comprehension of discourse. It was shown that – and how – "knowledge of the world" plays a fundamental role in these processes, for instance by establishing the local and global coherence relations of discourse. In cognitive theories of discourse processing, a central notion relating general, socioculturally shared knowledge with actual discourse structures is that of (mental) models, that is, subjective representations in Episodic Memory (part of Long Term Memory) of events and personal experiences (see Graesser, Gernsbacher, and Goldman 2003).

Initially, *social psychology* hardly participated in the general Discursive Turn in the humanities and social sciences, although many relevant aspects of discourse could and should be accounted for precisely in social psychological terms, such as the relations between individuals and groups, social identity, interaction and communication, attribution, self-presentation, impression management, as well as ideology. However, within social psychology there has been a development called "Discursive Psychology", specifically interested in the account of text and talk as social interaction (see Potter and Wetherell 1987).

After half a century of spectacular developments in and across these and other disciplines, Discourse Studies today is a flourishing cross-discipline, with its own university programs, journals, international congresses and organizations.

Although much integration and cooperation characterizes the field, there are dozens of sometimes very technical specializations, such as Discourse Grammars, Conversation Analysis, Argumentation Analysis, Narrative Analysis, Genre studies, Rhetoric, Stylistics, Pragmatics, each with a full array of qualitative and quantitative methods. Crucial though for most forms of discourse study is a detailed, systematic and explicit description of the structures and strategies of text and talk, as well as their cognitive foundations and social, political and cultural functions.

Within this multidisciplinary framework of the study of discourse, ideology in this paper will be studied as the sociocognitive basis of ideological discourses of the members, institutions and organization of ideological groups. Crucial in this case is to identify discourse structures that typically express or enact underlying ideologies, and thus may contribute to the "application" and reproduction of ideologies in society.

Within the field of Discourse Studies, ideologies are typically studied in the perspective of Critical Discourse Studies, e.g., on racist, sexist or classist domination and social inequality and the resistance against these forms of power abuse (see, e.g., Caldas-Coulthard and Coulthard 1995; Fairclough 1995; Flowerdew and Richardson 2018; Hart 2011; Lazar 2005; Machin and Mayr 2012; Richardson et al. 2013; Van Dijk 2008b).

Given the many areas of discourse studies in several disciplines, this paper specifically deals with notions developed in cognitive and social psychology, and how these play a role in the production of ideological discourse and its structures. But since ideologies – as forms of social cognition – are developed and shared by social groups in sociopolitical contexts, obviously a broader, multidisciplinary approach of ideology is crucial, as advocated in other research not reviewed here (see Van Dijk 1998).

In the social sciences, it is often expected of discourse analysts to give a "definition" of discourse. The complexity of discourse is such, however, that such a definition is pointless. In the same way, not even a handbook of sociology will provide a "definition" of society. The whole of all areas of discourse studies provides such "definitions". But to distinguish the use of "discourse" in this paper from more philosophical uses of "discourse" in such expressions as "the discourse of modernity" in political science, this paper refers to discourse(s) only as (i) specific instances of language use, that is, of text or talk in their communicative, cognitive and sociopolitical and cultural contexts, and (ii) sometimes as a generic expression, e.g., to refer to political or media discourse.

2 Ideologies as social cognition

Ideologies have many properties, but their core property is that they are a kind of socially shared beliefs as these are represented in the minds of members of social groups (for details of this conception of ideology, see Van Dijk 1998). This implies, first of all, that ideologies, by definition, are not individual, but essentially collective, and hence forms of socially distributed cognition. There are however personal *uses* of ideologies, e.g., in individual discourses, as there are also personal uses of socially natural languages shared by the members of linguistic communities. It is therefore theoretically important to relate ideologies as socially shared systems of beliefs, on the one hand, with the individual ideological practices – such as text and talk – of its members, on the other hand.

Unfortunately, cognitive psychology has no theory of the way ideologies are stored and organized in the mind. However, it has some theories about other forms of social cognition, such as knowledge, its organization and location in the mind-memory-brain (for many references, see Van Dijk 2014). Thus, socially shared, generic "knowledge of the world" is usually located in what is called "Semantic Memory", part of Long Term Memory (LTM), and organized by frames, scripts and other hierarchical schematic structures of concepts, prototypes and other mental units. Actually, today not much more is known about the mental (or neurological) organization of knowledge – and this remains one of the major areas to explore in the cognitive sciences.

I shall assume that ideologies, as another form of socially shared beliefs, also are stored in LTM, and based on the system of knowledge. For instance, ideological beliefs about immigration presuppose minimum knowledge of the very concepts of immigration and immigrants. Typical of ideologies, and different from knowledge, is that ideological beliefs are evaluative: They are based on norms and values. They say what is good or bad, or what is (not) to be done by the group members. When we say that ideologies are part of social cognition, this means that such is the case for the socially shared beliefs that define ideologies, which should not be confused with the *expression* or manifestations of ideologies in discourse or social practices.

Ideologies are not only very general, fundamental, socially shared beliefs, but also basic social beliefs that control more specific ideological beliefs: social *attitudes*. For instance, ideological beliefs on immigration may be based on an underlying racist ideology, an antiracist ideology, a neoliberal, a nationalist or a socialist ideology. Compared to the more specific beliefs on social issues, that is, social attitudes such as immigration, abortion or homosexual marriages, among many others, thus, ideologies need to be relatively stable. They develop and change slowly, and are slowly acquired by the members of an ideological group. Socialism, feminism, neoliberalism, and environmentalism took decades to develop, and one does not become a socialist or feminist overnight.

Although we may have some informal ideas about the typical contents of ideologies as they are typically expressed in the discourse of ideological leaders, it is as yet unknown what the cognitive structures of ideological systems are. One property of these systems however seems quite plausible: They are polarized, and thus also define social ingroups and outgroups: *Us* vs. *Them*.

Thus, ideologies are probably basic self-representations of groups: Who are we? Besides this fundamental ideological Identity, it is likely that ideologies also represent the characteristic Actions and activities of a group as their Aims, Norms and Values, Reference groups and Resources. In other words, an ideology may be organized by a mental schema of fundamental categories defining social groups. Thus, the professional ideology of journalists may feature Making News as central activity, with the Aim of informing the public, with the values of objectivity or fairness, with the public and the state as reference groups, and the fundamental resource of information – defining the basic interest concern of the group, to be defended at all costs. Similar basic structures may organize feminist, anti-feminist, racist or anti-racist, liberal or socialist ideologies.

In other words, ideologies are developed as shared mental representations so as to represent fundamental characteristics of social groups as related to other (competing, opposed) social groups, so as to organize and control the social practices that optimize the success and reproduction of the group and its interests.

Ideologies may be further organized by their *underlying norms and values*, for instance in terms of liberal-progressive or conservative ideologies, implementing such values as equality, justice, independence or freedom as applied to various social domains, e.g., freedom of the press or freedom of enterprise. Note though that each ideology makes its own self-interested use of culturally shared values: The Freedom of the market claimed by a business company is quite different from the Freedom of the press claimed by journalists.

2.1 Attitudes

Ideologies are derived from and control more specific ideological attitudes, as shown above, for instance on immigration, abortion, gay marriage or the death penalty. These are the meso-level social representations as they are explicitly known, advocated and expressed in public debate, rather than the more general, and more abstract underlying ideologies that organize them. Attitudes are socially shared by social groups, and acquired by discourse and communication in the group, such as media, the internet, textbooks, novels as well as everyday conversations based on them, possibly combined with models of personal experiences.

Also the structures of attitudes are as yet unknown, if we ignore for a moment the simplistic traditional distinction between cognitive, evaluative and conative dimensions, as hypothesized in traditional social psychology of attitudes (Eagly and Chaiken 1993). As is the case for all social representations, attitudes must have an overall, schematic organization for them to be able to organize specific social practices or discourse.

For instance, attitudes on immigration, first of all, may be organized by underlying polarized racist (or antiracist) and nationalist ideologies, representing Us vs. Them. A racist attitude would then represent the immigrants as outgroups that are different and deviant and that represent a threat to Us, Our country, Our culture, Our economy, etc. – further specified by the stereotypical representation of social (out) groups, following such categories as Identity, Origin, Goals, Appearance, Beliefs and Character. Such schemas may typically be derived from detailed analysis of stories about immigrants and arguments about immigration – though always adapted to (and hence transformed by) the context of communication, as we shall see below.

3 Ideological mental models

Whereas attitudes and ideologies are socially shared by groups, and hence necessarily are more abstract and generic and by definition (must) apply to many concrete social situations, we need a theoretical notion that relates such social representations to concrete experiences and practices of the members of ideological groups.

Fortunately, in the early 1980s, cognitive psychology developed a concept that ideally satisfies these conditions: mental models (Johnson-Laird 1983; Van Dijk and Kintsch 1983). Mental models are also mental representations, but stored in Episodic, Autobiographical memory (the "personal" part of LTM). They are personal, and subjective, and not only feature subjective knowledge of a situation or event, but also personal opinions and emotions. In other words, mental models are multimodal, subjective representations of a situation or event, and hence also called situation models. They theoretically account for what we call *experiences* in everyday life.

As is the case for other mental representations, models have a schematic structure, consisting of a Setting (Time, Place), Participants (and their Identities, Roles and Relationships), an Action/Event, as well as the Goals and Knowledge of the participants, and often personal opinions and emotions.

Mental models are the subjective representations of events/experiences we tell stories about or write news reports about. Conversely, when we understand discourse, we do so by construing a mental model of the discourse in our Episodic Memory. This mental model in turn may be the basis of what we later remember of an earlier text or talk – rather than the text or talk itself.

Mental models thus embody not only information from discourse, but also from underlying, socially shared knowledge and ideologies. This means that models may be biased twice: First by the ideologies of the groups a person belongs to, and secondly, more personally by a person's own autobiographical experiences, goals and interests as they have been accumulated in their lives, on the one hand, and as they are (made) relevant in the current interactional and communicative situations on the other hand.

We see that mental models are the ideal (mental) interface between underlying, socially shared attitudes and ideologies, on the one hand, and concrete, situated, personal discourse and other social practices on the other hand. Thus, an experience of a dominant ingroup member with an outgroup member, as is the case for racist encounters, or reading about ethnic or immigration events in the press or social media, or watching a program, or movie on TV give rise to a mental model – a subjective interpretation – that may be influenced by underlying racist ideologies and attitudes or by the personal experiences (old mental models) of people. This also explains why in discourse (and hence in interviews) on immigrants or minorities, dominant group members do not always show a neatly coherent ideological picture: In social practices, as well as in text and talk, socially shared ideology is always mediated by personal motivation, goals, interests, experiences and the ad hoc context. It is in this way that we explain how ideologies are *used* by individual citizens. Thus, ideologies also may be (slowly) changed and adapted to new social situations, experiences and interests of people on the basis of ingroup communication and an increasing new consensus.

Although generic attitudes and ideologies are typically evaluative, they probably do not feature "embodied" emotions (groups have no bodies; and members can communicate and share beliefs and opinions but not feelings), mental models of concrete experiences are multimodal and embodied, and hence may feature emotions. This accounts for the fact that ideological practices and discourse often show emotions of anger or fear, as is typically the case in racist text and talk.

Mental models are the individual mental basis of specific instances (tokens) of text and talk. Thus, they form the mental "plan" for what we tell other people about our personal experiences or about events we have witnessed or read/heard about. Since mental models are always individually biased by earlier experiences (old models) as well as personal goals, motivation, or interests, they may be biased compared to the discourse from which they are derived. Thus, the recipients of media messages may each have a slightly different interpretation (model) of what they have heard or read. Due to shared sociocultural knowledge as well as pervasive group attitudes and ideologies, mental models are usually quite similar, but their unique contents are always in last instance personal and contextual. We see that the notion of mental model accounts both for the similarity as well as the diversity and variability of ideological experiences and discourse – as we also know from polls, interviews, storytelling and everyday storytelling.

Given the theory summarized above, it should be repeated that ideologies, as forms of shared social cognition, are defined for (ideological) groups of people, and not as personal beliefs, although individual group members typically make personal *uses* of such ideologies, depending on their personal situation and experiences. This means that ideologies should not be defined in terms of personality characteristics of people, as is proposed in some psychological approaches (see, e.g., Jost 2009).

4 Context models

Language users not only form mental models of their personal experiences or of the situation and events a discourse is *about*, but also of the communicative situation *in which* they are *now* engaged. I call these special mental models *context models*, because they represent the relevant aspects of the communicative situation to which a discourse is adapted and hence more or less appropriate (Van Dijk 2008a, 2009). Thus, whereas the situation models mentioned above are the basis for the *semantics* of discourse, context models represent the conditions of *pragmatic* appropriateness.

Thus, we may have a specific experience, for instance of a car accident, represented in a personal model of the accident. But given that model, we tell a story about the accident in a very different way to our friends than when we provide a declaration to the police or the insurance company, or write a news report about it if we are a journalist. In other words, context models may dramatically change the style and even the contents of underlying "semantic" models, because they require the speaker or writer to adapt their discourse to the specific conditions of the communicative situation: the current Setting (Time, Place), the Participants (and their Identity, Role or Relations), the current social Action, as well as the Goals and the Knowledge of the participants – all different when we talk to friends, the police or write a news report.

Context models also explain why ideological mental models need not always be expressed as such in discourse. Indeed, sexist or racist speakers may feel free to express their opinions to their buddies, in specific informal situations, but may well hide or mitigate these in communicative situations in which the expression of these opinions would be against personal interests, e.g., in a job interview, writing an article in the newspaper, or in a conversation with ideological opponents. Context models are thus the filter that ultimately shapes ideological text and talk.

Concluding this brief theoretical account of the sociocognitive aspects of ideology, we see that the relation between ideology and discourse is very indirect, and mediated by different cognitive structures at different levels: first specified as socially shared attitudes about social issues, then individualized in personal mental models of experiences and finally filtered by the constraints of context models. This also explains why it is not easy to simply "read off" ideologies from text or talk, or to observe them in other social practices. We always need to examine in detail what the personal, contextual biases are. It is by comparison of different speakers and in different communicative situations that we may eventually infer ideologies from specific instances of text and talk.

4.1 Ideologies are not necessarily negative

It also has become obvious that unlike both classical and contemporary conceptions of ideology, my conception of ideology is not necessarily negative. Indeed, as the basic social representations of groups (and their identity, goals, interests, etc.), ideologies as defined here of course also hold for groups or social movements that struggle *against* dominant groups, as was and is the case for socialism, feminism, antiracism, pacifism and environmentalism – which would be *utopias* in Mannheim's terminology (for racist ideologies, see Van Dijk 1984, 1987, 1991, 1993; for antiracist ideology, see Van Dijk 2021). This is theoretically consistent because ideologies of both dominant and dominated groups have the same cognitive structures and the same sociocognitive, social and political functions, namely to control social practices and hence ideological discourse of group members, in one case in order to legitimate domination, and in the other case to resist domination. Of course, this does not mean, as some commentators of this generalized notion of ideology have suggested, that such a broad notion of ideology invalidates a critical approach to ideology – defined exclusively as the ideology of dominant groups. Of course, this argument does not hold, because what we want to struggle against, also theoretically, are forms of domination, and it is imperative that we do so on the basis of adequate theoretical notions. In the same way, we do not exclusively use the notion of power in order to study abuse of power, but also as part of the empowerment of dominated groups (see also Van Dijk 2008b).

5 Ideological discourse structures

Any empirical study of ideology defined as a basic sociocognitive system of beliefs shared by the members of social groups requires a study of the social practices of these groups. Besides many other ideological practices – such as discriminatory actions based on sexist or racist ideologies, or strikes, demonstrations, protests as activities of resistance of socialist, feminist or pacifist group members – public discourse is one of the most prominent ideological activities.

Since discourse is often more "articulate" than other social activities, especially because language users thus make explicit their underlying ideologically based opinions and attitudes which are only implicit in non-verbal action, discourse is by far the richest source for the study of ideology. Indeed, most ideologies develop first of all because of the founding discourses of "ideologues" and other leaders, and thus spread among, and are accepting among specific social target groups – as was and is the case for resistance ideologies such as socialism, feminism, pacifism and environmentalism (for some recent monographs on discourse and ideology, see, e.g., De Saussure and Schulz 2005; Hart 2014; Pütz, Neff-van Aertselaer, and Van Dijk 2004).

Obviously, not all members of ideological groups have the same explicit, articulate and extensively argued ideological discourse, but even in mundane, everyday discourse features personal opinions and explanations have an ideological basis, even when such expressions of personal mental models also show how socially shared ideologies are being personally "applied" or "used" – and hence also deviated from – by individual members.

5.1 Methods of ideological discourse analysis

Despite the theoretical and methodological sophistication of contemporary Discourse Studies, there is no such thing as a standard "Ideological Discourse Analysis". *All* discourse analysis and its methods depend on many factors and conditions, such as the type of discourse (e.g., editorials in the press or parliamentary debates), the aims of the investigators, the specialization of the investigators, time budget and other resources of a project, and so on. Analyses may be more quantitative, especially when there is a large amount of data, or qualitative, or a combination of the two.

Although Ideological Discourse Analysis (IDA) generally examines the details of the meaning of discourse, and hence favor various types of semantic analysis, ideologies may indirectly be expressed at several levels of discourse. Indeed, even a special intonation in spoken discourse may in a specific context be intended and/or interpreted as sexist or racist.

This again also shows the crucial importance of *context*, and hence the context models participants construe for the communicative situation, as defined above. The same utterance (e.g., "Immigrants cause problems") may be used in a racist or antiracist speech, depending first of all on context (such as the identity, role, goals, intentions, etc. of the speaker and recipients) and then on the overall topic or the local co-text of (a) speech. In other words, it seldom will be the case that words or even whole sentences as such are sexist, racist or feminist. It always depends on context and co-text.

Despite the fact that there is no standard IDA, and analysis always – as any text! – depends on the research context as summarized above (participants, goals, etc.), it does not mean that IDA is arbitrary and without systematic methods. First of all, given my theory of ideology, a discourse is by definition only ideological if it is produced by a member of an ideological group with which the ideology is shared, e.g., when someone speaks or writes *as a feminist*. This means that purely personal discourses cannot be ideological by this criterion, as when someone tells a personal story about a domestic accident. But as soon as people tell a story as being antiracist, or male, party member, progressive or a professional, then – under further conditions – such a story may well be ideological. More generally, though, many if not most public discourses, as produced by organizations and institutions, are ideological, not only because they tend to concern public issues or affairs, but because the authors are by definition members of groups with group identities, goals, interests, etc.

Against this general background, we may now formulate some general properties of ideological discourse as they may be studied by different discourse analytical methods. It must be stressed though that Discourse Analysis is NOT as such a method, but rather a discipline, which I prefer to call Discourse Studies. There is not a *method* of Discourse Analysis, any more than there is a *method* of Social Analysis, Political Analysis, Cognitive Analysis or Cultural Analysis. Also in the field of Discourse Studies there are many methods. Some are more linguistically oriented, whereas others are just like any other quantitative or qualitative method of the humanities or the social sciences, including those of rhetoric, narrative and argumentative analysis, corpus study, ethnography, participant observation, interviews (of many types), focus groups, polls, content analysis, and so on. True, by definition, any method used in Discourse Studies uses discourse data – as in fact most methods of the social sciences involve forms of text or talk. And it is also true that the methods of Discourse Studies take these forms of text and talk seriously, by specifically also (though not exclusively) focusing on the detailed structures of such text and talk – beyond just using them only as a source of opinions or attitudes, for instance. Finally, Discourse Studies will typically (though not exclusively) use qualitative methods, rather than quantitative ones. Hence, traditional Content Analysis may well be part of a discourse analysis, but in principle not the *only* part.

5.2 Polarized ideological discourse

We have seen that many ideologies have a polarized structure, simply because they represent the opposed interests of social groups. This polarized structure is often summarized by the pronoun pair *Us* vs. *Them*, representing what social psychology has traditionally called ingroups and outgroups, respectively. Groups represent themselves as groups, and part of this self-presentation is a representation of their relations to specific other groups, such as enemies or allies, clients or bosses, dominant and dominated groups.

We have also seen that ideologies are possibly construed in terms of specific *ideological schemas*, featuring such categories as Identity, Actions, Goals, Norms and Values, Resources, and so on. If related to outgroups, thus, we may expect discourse of group members not only to express the main aspects of the self-representation of a group (who we are, what we want, etc.), but also of the specific outgroups, and *their* characteristics. Typically the self-representation of most (though not all) ideologies is positive, and if the relevant reference group is a competing or opponent group, or more generally interpreted as a threat to the interests of the ingroup, outgroup representations tend to be negative. These properties of ideologies are consistent with prevailing views in the psychology of intergroup relations.

Since these general properties also influence more specific ideological attitudes (as a sexist ideology will influence attitudes about sexuality or equal rights of women) and these attitudes in turn often combine with the personal experiences of individual group members, also the personal models of specific events will tend to be polarized and feature concrete instantiations of general ideological categories, such as those of Identity, Actions and Goals of ingroup and/or outgroup members, for instance in storytelling on personal experiences.

Note finally that before such ideological models are actually expressed in text and talk they need to be adapted to the communicative situation, as defined by the context models of the speakers. Even if their model of an experience may be quite racist or sexist, speakers may adapt their discourse to the perceived ideology of the recipient. Thus, racist models may be toned down in situations where antiracist participants are dominant.

Under these general constraints, there are four complementary ideological strategies in discourse, according to the following schema, which I have called the Ideological Square (Van Dijk 1998):
1. Emphasize *Our* GOOD things!
2. Emphasize *Their* BAD things!
3. De-emphasize *Our* BAD things!
4. De-emphasize *Their* GOOD things!

This is a very simple general strategy – as it should be for fast, online ideological control of discourse. But, its implementation at all levels of discourse provides for a large number of quite sophisticated ideological structures in discourse. Thus, the strategy applies, for instance, by (de)emphasizing global discourse topics, local meanings, the lexicon, metaphors, pictures, and so on. In the remainder of the chapter, I will give some examples selected from my previous work on racism in discourse (Van Dijk 1984, 1987, 1991, 1993; Wodak and Van Dijk 2000).

5.3 Topics

Nearly all studies of racist discourse show that discourse topics, defined as semantic macrostructures, tend to be negative in much political and media discourse. Depending on country, period, political orientation and type of newspaper, the following main topics are usually defined and enhanced as a problem or as a threat to *Us*:
– Immigration
– Ethnic (e.g., religious, linguistic, etc.) differences
– Terrorism, crime and deviance
– Housing and labor market
– Use of social services

On the other hand, Our negative aspects, such as Our racism, are often ignored, mitigated or attributed to marginal groups (e.g., football hooligans, Neo-Nazis) in society, whereas Our positive aspects, such as Our democracy or Our tolerance, tend be highlighted, whereas Theirs, such as Their contribution to the economy and cultural diversity is usually ignored or downplayed. Indeed, minorities and immigrants hardly appear in many dominant topics of political or media discourse, as is the case for the economy, the arts or science.

5.4 Local meanings

At the level of the local meanings of sentences, the strategy applies in the description of actors and actions, as well as in implications, presuppositions, metaphors, granularity, and so on. Here are a few examples, taken from a debate on benefits for asylum seekers in UK parliament on March 5, 1997, initiated by Conservative MP, Ms. Gorman. In the following examples, for instance, we find *enhanced negative actor description* of an asylum seeker, for instance in terms of extreme generalization (*never*), contrasted to a positive, emphatic description of Our elderly:

(1) In one case, a man from Romania, who came over here on a coach tour for a football match [...] decided that he did not want to go back, declared himself an asylum seeker and is still here four years later. He has never done a stroke of work in his life. Why should someone who is elderly and who is scraping along on their basic income have to support people in those circumstances? (Gorman).

(2) [...] those people, many of whom could reasonably be called economic migrants and some of whom are just benefit seekers on holiday, to remain in Britain (Gorman).

The following example continues the representation of Our people as victims of Them, with a *general normative statement* (*it is wrong*), in a classical polarized structure of Us and Them:

(3) It is wrong that ratepayers in the London area should bear an undue proportion of the burden of expenditure that those people are causing (Gorman).

Often examples feature several of the semantic moves associated with the ideological strategies:

(4) But the escalating number of economic and bogus asylum seekers who have come here, not because of persecution but because of the economic situation in this country and the benefits it affords them, has caused great concern (Gorman).

Thus, we here find a *negative lexical description* of the outgroup (*bogus*), emphasis or *hyperbole* (*escalating*), the well-known move of the *numbers game* (*number*), usually with specific statistics, a *denial* of merit of the case, such as their negative situation (*not because of persecution*), an *implied negative action description* ("abuse of benefits") and an enhanced (*great*) populist move referring to the *negative attitudes* among the (British) people (*caused great concern*).

To mark that a discourse not only has negative (personal) opinions about the Others, it is quite common that speakers emphasize that what they talk about are the *facts*. They typically do so with various kinds of evidentials, which refer to the sources of knowledge, such as the press and the courts:

(5) The Daily Mail today reports the case of a woman from Russia who has managed to stay in Britain for five years. According to the magistrates court yesterday, she has cost the British taxpayer £40,000. She was arrested, of course, for stealing (Gorman).

In its *negative Other description* (*stealing*), this example also shows two instantiations of the *numbers game* (*five years, £40,000*), an economic description of Us, the ingroup (*the British taxpayer*) and a *presupposition* that one may expect such behavior of asylum seekers (*of course*). Often, however, no sources or evidence are necessary, but only personal impressions to make attributions of *negative actor descriptions* (*illegally, not bona fide*), the *number game* (*costs*):

(6) I am sure that many of them are working illegally, and of course work is readily available in big cities (Gorman).

(7) Goodness knows how much it costs for the legal aid that those people invoke to keep challenging the decision that they are not bona fide asylum seekers (Gorman).

(8) Now they are going to be asked to pay £35 to able-bodied males who have come over here on a prolonged holiday and now claim that the British taxpayer should support them (Gorman).

Besides the example of the numbers game in (8), the rhetoric of this example also features a form of *irony*, when the arrival and support of asylum seekers is described as a prolonged holiday, further enhanced by the *concrete actor description* (*able-bodied males*) as an *implied argument* that if any group does not deserve support it is strong men. Again, the ingroup is not just described as the British, but as the British taxpayer, a *populist denomination* that emphasizes that ordinary citizens pay for asylum seekers.

Populist moves may get very concrete, as is typically the case in the following *colloquial metaphors:*

(9) Such things go on and they get up the noses of all constituents (Gorman).

(10) It would open the floodgates again, and presumably the £200 million a year cost that was estimated when the legislation was introduced (Gorman).

Apart from the usual *numbers game* move (£ 200 million), this last example also features a metaphor (*open the floodgates*) that is especially frequent in discourse on immigration (*waves of immigrants*, etc.), and conveys an embodied threat of drowning in so many asylum seekers. Again, these are not facts, but *guesswork* (*estimated*) and part of a *counterfactual* (*would*). Note also the *passive voice* (was estimated) which conceals a concrete agent: *Who* made the estimate? That is, not only the semantics but also the syntax may express part of the ideological meaning of a discourse.

The ideological square shows that negative other-presentation is usually combined with positive self-presentation, as is the case in the following example of another Conservative MP in the same debate:

> (11) Britain has always honoured the Geneva convention, and has given sanctuary to people with a well-founded fear of persecution in the country from which they are fleeing and whose first safe country landing is in the United Kingdom (Wardle).

Thus, many of the debates on immigrants or minorities in many parliaments begin with positive nationalist statements on Our democracy, tolerance, generosity. When combined in one sentence, an initial positive self-presentation may be followed by a negative Other presentation, in such *disclaimers* as the *apparent denial* ("I have nothing against Blacks, but [. . .]"). In this debate, thus, the speaker uses another typical disclaimer, which I call one of *apparent empathy*:

> (12) I understand that many people want to come to Britain to work, but [. . .] (Gorman).

Indeed, a few years earlier, Sir John Stokes formulates the following *positive self-presentation* about the UK in his very negative speech on immigrants, at the same time establishing a nationalist polarization between the UK and Other countries:

> (13) I believe that we are a wonderfully fair country. We stick to the rules unlike some foreign Governments. (Sir John Stokes, May 15, 1990).

Of course, the English are not the only ones: here are examples of *nationalist self-glorification*, in the same year, from France, Germany and the USA (see Van Dijk 1993 for background and analyses of these examples):

> (14) Our country has for a long time been open to foreigners, a tradition of hospitality going back, beyond the Revolution, to the Ancien Régime. (France, Mr. Mazeaud, July 9, 1990).
>
> (15) I know no other country on this earth that gives more prominence to the rights of resident foreigners as does this bill in our country. (Germany, Mr. Hirsch, February 9, 1990).
>
> (16) This is a nation whose values and traditions now excite the world, as we all know. I think we all have a deep pride in American views, American ideals, American government, American principle, which excite hundreds of millions of people around the world who struggle for freedom. (United States, Mr. Foley, August 2, 1990).

6 Conclusions

Ideologies are forms of social cognition, the basis of the shared representations of social groups. As mental self-presentations, they are organized by a schema featuring some of the characteristics of groups, such as their Identity, Actions, Norms and Values, Goals, as well as Reference Groups. They are often polarized by positive properties being attributed to the ingroup and negative ones to outgroups. They embody general cultural values (such as freedom or justice), but translated into the specific interest domains of the ingroup (e.g., freedom of the market). Ideologies, as defined here, are not limited to dominant groups. They may also characterize the social representations shared by dominated groups, with the same sociopolitical functions – but in a different direction: not to legitimate but to struggle against domination.

Ideologies are derived from, facilitate and organize more specific socially shared attitudes about prominent social issues, such as those on immigration, abortion, gay marriage, and so on. These attitudes are the meso-level of ideological influence and debate, that is they represent the topics of ideological debate. Many of the properties of the more abstract underlying ideologies – such as those of racism and anti-racism – are applied in the attitudes they organize, as is the case for positive self-presentation and negative other-presentation.

Whereas ideologies and attitudes are socially shared, they also influence the experiences of the members of the group, that is, the mental models of Episodic Memory, representing concrete events, such as encounters with immigrants or the arrival of asylum seekers. Again, these models may specify for concrete situations some of the properties of the underlying attitudes and ideologies shared by the ingroup.

These mental models are the subjective basis of concrete stories and argumentation, for instance in everyday storytelling, news reports or parliamentary debates. For such discourse to be appropriate, mental models of personal experiences are not expressed directly, but filtered by subjective context models that represent the communicative situation: We tell the same personal experience differently to different people. Thus, also ideological discourse depends on how speakers represent the identity (and power) of the recipients, the current goals of the communicative interaction, the knowledge and ideologies of the recipients (racist talk is more explicitly racist among one's racist buddies than in front of an antiracist boss).

Ideological discourse at all levels is organized by an ideological square that represents underlying polarization between ingroup and outgroup: emphasis on Our good things and Their bad things, and mitigation of Our bad things and Their good things. Applied at all levels of discourse, these ideological strategies control the selection of discourse topics, lexical items, metaphors, syntactic structures (such as nominalization and passive voice) that conceal Our negative agency (e.g., *discrimination*, instead of *We discriminate*), and a host of semantic moves, such as negative actor description, the numbers game, disclaimers, and so on.

And conversely, when constantly repeated, more or less explicitly, in much dominant public discourse, such as that of politics, media or education, ingroup members may form biased mental models of specific (e.g., ethnic) events, generalize such models to more general attitudes as these are more broadly adopted and communicated in public discourse, and finally into basic ideologies that provide the foundation and organization of these attitudes.

The circle of the reproduction of ideologies is thus closed, relating mental but socially shared representations on the one hand with social practices in general, and discourse in particular at the personal level of society, and with the social position of groups and their (lack of) power and interests on the other hand.

References

Bauman, Richard & Joel Sherzer (eds.). 1974. *Explorations in the ethnography of speaking*. Cambridge: Cambridge University Press.
Blommaert, Jan. 2005. *Discourse. A critical introduction*. Cambridge: Cambridge University Press.
Caldas-Coulthard, Carmen R. & Malcolm Coulthard (eds.). 1995. *Texts and practices: Readings in critical discourse analysis*. London & New York: Routledge.
De Fina, Anna & Alexandra Georgakopoulou (eds.). 2020. *The Cambridge handbook of discourse studies*. Cambridge: Cambridge University Press.
De Saussure, Louis & Peter J. Schulz (eds.). 2005. *Manipulation and ideologies in the twentieth century. Discourse, language, mind*. Amsterdam & Philadelphia: John Benjamins.
Eagly, Alice H. & Shelly Chaiken. 1993. *The psychology of attitudes*. Fort Worth, TX: Harcourt Brace Jovanovich.
Fairclough, Norman. 1995. *Critical discourse analysis. The critical study of language*. London: Longman.
Flowerdew, John & John E. Richardson (eds.). 2018. *The Routledge handbook of critical discourse studies*. London & New York: Routledge.
Gee, James P. & Michael Handford (eds.). 2012. *The Routledge handbook of discourse analysis*. London & New York: Routledge.
Graesser, Arthur C., Morton A. Gernsbacher & Susan R. Goldman (eds.). 2003. *Handbook of discourse processes*. Mahwah, NJ: Erlbaum.
Hart, Christopher (ed.). 2011. *Critical discourse studies in context and cognition*. Amsterdam & Philadelphia: John Benjamins.
Hart, Christopher. 2014. *Discourse, grammar and ideology. Functional and cognitive perspectives*. London & New York: Bloomsbury Academic.

Johnson-Laird, Philip N. 1983. *Mental models. Towards a cognitive science of language, inference, and consciousness.* Cambridge, MA: Harvard University Press.

Jost, John T. 2009. "Elective affinities": On the psychological bases of left-right differences. *Psychological Inquiry* 20 (2–3). 129–141.

Lazar, Michelle (ed.). 2005. *Feminist critical discourse analysis. Gender, power and ideology in discourse.* Houndsmills: Palgrave MacMillan.

Machin, David & Andrea Mayr. 2012. *How to do critical discourse analysis: A multimodal introduction.* London, Thousand Oaks, CA & New Delhi: Sage.

Potter, Jonathan, & Margaret Wetherell. 1987. *Discourse and Social Psychology: Beyond Attitudes and Behaviour.* London, Thousand Oaks, CA & New Delhi: Sage.

Pütz, Martin, JoAnne Neff-van Aertselaer & Teun A. van Dijk. 2004. *Communicating ideologies: Multidisciplinary perspectives on language, discourse, and social practice.* New York, Bern, Frankfurt am Main & Paris: Peter Lang.

Richardson, John E., Michael Krzyżanowski, David Machin & Ruth Wodak (eds.). 2013. *Advances in critical discourse studies.* London & New York: Routledge.

Stivers, Tanya & Jack Sidnell (eds.). 2011. *Handbook of conversation analysis.* Oxford: Wiley-Blackwell.

Tannen, Deborah, Heidi E. Hamilton & Deborah Schiffrin (eds.). 2015 [2001]. *The handbook of discourse analysis*, 2nd edn. Chichester: Blackwell-Wiley.

Van Dijk, Teun A. 1984. *Prejudice in discourse. An analysis of ethnic prejudice in cognition and conversation.* Amsterdam & Philadelphia: John Benjamins.

Van Dijk, Teun A. 1987. *Communicating racism: Ethnic prejudice in thought and talk.* London, Newbury Park, CA, & New Delhi: Sage.

Van Dijk, Teun A. 1991. *Racism and the press.* London & New York: Routledge.

Van Dijk, Teun A. 1993. *Elite discourse and racism.* London, Newbury Park, CA & New Delhi: Sage.

Van Dijk, Teun A. 1998. *Ideology: A multidisciplinary approach.* London, Thousand Oaks, CA & New Delhi: Sage.

Van Dijk, Teun A. 2008a. *Discourse and context. A socio-cognitive approach.* Cambridge: Cambridge University Press.

Van Dijk, Teun A. 2008b. *Discourse and power.* Houndmills: Palgrave MacMillan.

Van Dijk, Teun A. 2009. *Society and discourse. How social contexts influence text and talk.* Cambridge: Cambridge University Press.

Van Dijk, Teun A. (ed.). 2011. *Discourse Studies: A multidisciplinary introduction.* 2nd, one-volume edition. London, Thousand Oaks, CA & New Delhi: Sage.

Van Dijk, Teun A. 2014. *Discourse and knowledge: A sociocognitive approach.* Cambridge: Cambridge University Press.

Van Dijk, Teun A. 2021. *Antiracist discourse. From abolition to Black Lives Matter.* Cambridge: Cambridge University Press.

Van Dijk, Teun A. & Walter Kintsch. 1983. *Strategies of discourse comprehension.* New York: Academic Press.

Wodak, Ruth & Teun A. van Dijk (eds.). 2000. *Racism at the top: Parliamentary discourses on ethnic issues in six European states.* Klagenfurt: Drava Verlag.

Elizabeth Peterson
Chapter 9
Licensing through English

Abstract: An observation about pragmatic borrowing from English into various recipient languages is what has been termed "licensing", which, along with semantic bleaching and perceived positive politeness, has been advanced as a motivation for borrowing pragmatic forms from English (see Andersen 2014). In this chapter, the notion of licensing is explored further, drawing on observations from, for example, Matras ([2009] 2020). It has already been proposed that the borrowing of certain English-sourced linguistic items allows a speaker to engage in discourse behavior that is not seen as native (or possibly even appropriate) in the recipient culture or language (Peterson 2017). In this chapter I broaden the perspective of previous research to look at longer stretches of discourse and language choice, demonstrating that perceived ideologies about characteristics of English in native-speaker settings are driving mechanisms in how English is used in foreign language settings, in this case Finland.

Keywords: English language and linguistics, language contact, Finnish, language ideology, licensing, bilingualism

1 Introduction

An observation about pragmatic borrowing from English into various recipient languages is what has been termed "licensing", which, along with semantic bleaching and perceived positive politeness, has been advanced as a motivation for pragmatic borrowing from English (Andersen 2014; Peterson 2017). In this chapter, the notion of licensing is explored further, drawing on observations from, for example, Matras (2020). In previous work (Peterson 2017), I have used the term *licensing* to refer to the borrowing of certain English-sourced linguistic items which offer a speaker the opportunity to engage in linguistic behavior that is not seen as appropriate or customary in the recipient culture or language. In this chapter I broaden the perspective to look at longer stretches of discourse and

---

Note: I am grateful to the editors of this volume for their attentive and constructive feedback on earlier versions of the chapter, as well as for allowing me to take on exploratory content. In addition, my gratitude goes to the external reviewers, who offered critical and extremely helpful recommendations. The usual disclaimers apply.

https://doi.org/10.1515/9781501513602-009

at language choice, demonstrating that perceived ideologies about characteristics of English in native-speaker settings are driving mechanisms in how English is used in foreign language settings, in this case Finland.

The focus of this chapter is the use of English-sourced elements in recipient languages for social and pragmatic effect. Such elements often include pragmatic markers and other discourse elements (Andersen 2014), but the same principles can apply to larger elements of discourse, for example language choice involving English during a conversation (Matras 2020). These issues are examined in locations – primarily in Finland in this chapter – and by speech communities where English has no official status, but where it is used as a widespread lingua franca or foreign language. Thus, key themes in this chapter are language contact and the use of English as a foreign language.

In this chapter, *discourse* is treated as something distinctive from language in that discourse is regarded not as an abstract system but as a shared phenomenon whereby "people draw on the knowledge they have about language, knowledge based on their memories of things they have said, heard, seen, or written before to do things in the world: exchange information, express feelings, make things happen, create beauty, entertain themselves, and so on" (Johnstone [2002] 2008: 3). That is, whereas language can be considered as an abstract system, separate from its speakers and the contexts in which they find themselves, discourse is something which is actively created and shared by humans through language (in association with other semiotic tools, e.g., gestures) as they conduct their daily lives. As with other definitions of discourse (see, for example Fairclough [1992] 2009), discourse is regarded as something that is on the move, with people making use of existing discourse while at the same time adding or subtracting layers of meaning.

The concept of *ideology* in this chapter borrows largely from the use of the term in the field of linguistic anthropology (e.g., Woolard 1998) and subsequently in sociolinguistics (e.g., Lippi-Green [1997] 2012; Milroy 2001). The concept of *language ideology* in this chapter refers to language as a symbolic but also concrete component of the social standing of certain kinds of language users relative to others. In this chapter, language ideology is furthermore viewed as beliefs and opinions connected to language use and particular social groups and how the groups themselves are perceived. These ideologies do not have to be real; the point is that they are believed and imagined, even if they are largely stereotyped (Hekanaho 2020; Woolard 1998). Language-related ideologies in Finland, for example, could be that Finnish is difficult for foreigners to learn, or that Finnish does not exhibit social class distinctions.

The information in this chapter is divided into five main parts. The first topic is to clarify the concept of *licensing*, and in particular what is meant by *licensing through English*. This explanation is supplemented with information about the type of language contact that characterizes licensing. The exploration of *licensing through English* occurs through four main vantage points: the lexical level, the level of code-switching and phraseology, language choice, and ideologies about the use of English within the receiving community. While the focus of this chapter is primarily the setting of Finland, the information and ideas advanced are in no way limited to Finland: the use of English is widespread, and ample evidence demonstrates that similar phenomena occur in other locations, as well.

2 Background

The main premise of this chapter comes from two overlapping areas of study. The first has to do with the discourse practices of bilingual individuals, namely a phenomenon known as *licensing*, an established concept that is investigated in fuller detail here. A second relevant area has to do with the status and use of English among different foreign language communities in the world today, and the language contact and ideological outcomes that tend to characterize this linguistic relationship.

2.1 Licensing

In his influential work on language contact, Matras (2020) has used the term *licensing* to describe when bilingual speakers employ word-forms from an "outside" language when interacting in an "inside" language. For example, a woman using the German discourse particle *doch* in Hebrew discourse "appropriately captures the intention she wishes to convey during this particular speech act" (Matras 2020: 93–94). While inserting German *doch* may be a matter of "convenience", it is precisely this "convenience" that merits attention: the speaker is utilizing an element of her multilingual repertoire that appropriately captures the intention she wishes to convey during this particular discursive act. This she does despite the fact that the language of the immediate context is Hebrew, and possibly backed by the fact that all the participants in the interaction know German. While at a basic level such an occurrence is a commonplace component of code-switching, in the arguments developed here the discourse elements of speaker volition, performance, and shared understanding are pertinent. Further, as explained more in the chapter, ideologies about the outside language come to the forefront.

In previous work (Peterson 2017), I advanced the notion of licensing in relation to pragmatic borrowing from English into Finnish. In this work, licensing is proposed, along with positive politeness and semantic bleaching, as explanatory factors for pragmatic borrowing. In this chapter, the notion of licensing is further explicated, expanded to a wider range of discourse situations. It is clear that at least in some contexts licensing relies on a bilingual mode, and it is most effective when all interlocutors share the same or at least overlapping linguistic repertoires – as with the example of a speaker inserting German discourse particles into Hebrew discourse. This type of use points toward volition, and choices made on the part of the speaker, which in turn points toward performativity, which Eckert (2019: 752) characterizes as "the engine of social practice, coordinating social and individual change". In this sense, performativity is distinguished from discourse in that it actively and overtly drives forward social meaning as well as individual identity.

Performative use of English in a foreign language context is most likely a strategy to project a certain kind of identity and style within a given setting, for example engagement with a perceived or potential audience. Performative use of English could exist at the level of language choice, if the participants choose to use English as opposed to another shared linguistic option that might be available to them, for example the use of "Scandinavian", the name given to the pan-Nordic use of language that (ideally) is mutually intelligible across the Nordic countries. Performative use of English is also in effect when speakers code-switch or use borrowings from English in their discourse in another language. For example, when a student uses an expression such as "This ain't Seaworld, its [sic] as real as it gets!!" (Wide and Peterson 2015) in a stretch of Swedish discourse, and the turn in English has no obvious propositional contribution, the intention is difficult to interpret as anything other than performative. This example is an apt illustration of what Fiedler (2018: 116) characterizes as the "pragmatic-functional reasons for the use of words and phrases influenced by English [. . .] to add flavour to the message, to sound modern, trendy, cool and educated, and to be part of a globalizing world".

In this chapter, I continue the treatment of licensing from English with regard to foreign language settings. Drawing on previous work, and with application to the information presented here, I advance the following definition of licensing, especially as it relates to English in the contemporary global setting: licensing allows a speaker to engage in linguistic behavior that is not seen as native (or possibly even appropriate) in the recipient culture or language. The use of English-sourced items or discourse licenses linguistic behavior that speakers would not be willing or able to engage in through their native language(s), due to issues such as pragmatic weight and appropriate styles (Peterson 2017). In short, the use of English licenses speakers to behave in a way that their other languages do not.

2.2 Contact with English

English has taken on a special de facto status in many settings around the world where it has no official status and where it is introduced to the overall population as a foreign language. In Finland, like other countries in Europe, English has been the main foreign language taught in public schools for some 70 years. Coupled with other external factors such as English being the major language in overall global communication and economics, some scholars surmise that English has even become something like an unofficial third language in Finland (Leppänen 2008) in addition to Finnish and Swedish – both national languages in Finland. As would be expected from relatively prolonged language contact, the national languages in Finland demonstrate ample evidence of interaction with English at all levels. In recent years, the formal learning of English in the classroom has been augmented by the strong presence of the language in the private sphere through popular culture. This type of language contact is an example of unidirectional contact, which sets it apart from other historical forms of (mutual) language contact. What this means in effect is that English influences Finnish and Swedish, but the reverse is not true, or at least not anywhere near the same extent. This type of borrowing scenario has been referred to as remote, weak, non-contiguous, and, in line with Bloomfield (1933), is most likely to result in cultural borrowings.

In an influential 2014 publication, Andersen introduced the term *pragmatic borrowing* to refer to language contact involving discursive/pragmatic features borrowed from English into recipient languages. While pragmatic borrowing is not limited to any certain type of language contact scenarios, the languages discussed by Andersen in his original contribution were all languages of Europe, referring particularly to the borrowing of interjections, discourse markers, expletives, vocatives, general extenders, tags, focus constructions, intonation, and paralinguistic phenomena from another language into such languages as Danish, Norwegian, Finnish, Swedish, German, and Italian (Andersen 2014: 17). It should be noted that these types of borrowings differ from domain specific lexical borrowings within the established areas of, for example, travel and tourism, information technology, mass media, high education, etc., in many ways. For one, pragmatic borrowings have the potential to penetrate an entire speech community, rather than being limited to specific domains of use. Furthermore, pragmatic borrowings seem to be in variation with heritage[1] forms in the receiving language, whereas domain

---

[1] *Heritage form* refers to a pre-existing form in a receiving language, for example the standard and historical Finnish form *kiitos* 'please/thank you'. This term is explained further in Peterson 2017, but, briefly: borrowings can and do become nativized, rendering terms such as *native* ambiguous.

specific lexicon is not (Andersen, Furiassi, and Mišić Ilić 2017; Peterson 2017). Furthermore, because they have the possibility to penetrate a speech community, pragmatic borrowings are not concomitant to bilingualism (Peterson 2017). They become entrenched into a speech community to the extent that even monolingual people, for example elderly Finnish people who do not know English, can still use and understand a borrowing such as *pliis* 'please' in Finnish. Subsequent work on pragmatic borrowing called for an expansion of the definition of pragmatic borrowing to account for not just what is borrowed in such a contact situation (i.e., pragmatic elements), but to account for the overtly pragmatic motivations for extensive borrowing from English, thereby enlarging its scope to include not only a wider range of linguistic features, but aspects beyond the lexical level.

With respect to pragmatic motivations for using English-sourced borrowings, an array of research has been written on the pragmatic and social meanings associated with not only the use of English in foreign language or second language settings, but also on the use of English-sourced elements in other languages. These accounts seem to congregate around an expected collection of notions and qualities: both English and English-sourced borrowings are noted to evoke associations and meanings of youth culture, global orientation, urbanicity, and modernity (Peterson 2017; see also Fiedler 2017), but also "language displays" such as signaling "[. . .] superior technology, chic and modern lifestyles, adventure, international and the sense of belonging to a 'global village'" (Martin 2011: 267).[2]

In previous work (Peterson 2017), I posited that established borrowings in Finnish such as *pliis* 'please' most likely enter into Finnish discourse through the occasional use of second-language insertions in the speech of bilinguals. Already at this stage, the insertions from English carry a stylistic effect of urbanicity, a global orientation, and, as I posited for *pliis* in Finnish, positive politeness, or in other words offering a socially-close option for using a lexical politeness marker in Finnish, something that is not accomplished with the heritage form *kiitos* 'please/ thank you', which is relatively formal. These overlapping layers of meaning in the borrowed form offer a fine example of the social and ideological effects of texts in discourse as presented by Fairclough (2003), and, especially, the process of meaning making in discourse. In his work, Fairclough makes frequent reference to what he considers the three parts of meaning making: the production of the text, the text itself, and how the text is received. With the use of English in various forms, as described in this chapter, we see an additional layer of meaning which

---

[2] A favorite characterization of English used in Finland comes from a former student: "The English voice is that of an international expert who dares to use humor and excites the reader with danger, while Finnish is commonly used as the language of the engineers" (Salo 2015).

is the symbolic or indexical property of English: the use of English, whether at the level of lexeme, code-switch, or as a conversational or discursive choice, is imbued with the perceived qualities discussed earlier (Blommaert 2010).

In this chapter, English elements are observed at different levels of discourse. While so far the information in this chapter has focused largely on the level of lexical borrowing, the notion of licensing from English in no way is limited to the lexical level. Beyond the level of discourse markers and lexical items, changes in heritage pragmatic routines have been observed, presumably due to the cultural influence of Anglo-American societies, a topic which is taken up further in Section 3.2.

At the level of conversational choice or as an ideological entity, English has a special status in today's world, and this status is full of conundrums. English is neutral; English is not neutral. English is global; English is local. English is impersonal; English is highly personal. Against the backdrop of the supposed neutrality and globality of English, Wee (2010) highlights that with English, its supposed neutrality is based on the ideology that it represents the language of no one and simultaneously the language of everyone. Yet although English has in some ways acquired neutral status, its spread and heritage are far from neutral, being firmly rooted in colonialism and economic exploitation – even today (see, e.g., Piller 2016; Peterson forthcoming). Another contradiction is that at the same time English is viewed as something ubiquitous and neutral, it is also an object of desire and even fetishization (Kelly-Holmes 2014), with the use of English itself allowing a point of view from another language which is constructed as the norm in the receiving community.

With relation to licensing through English, then, there are intertwining factors that set the stage for the seemingly unique possibility for English to enter into this realm in the current era. That is, for foreign language users of English, the language is imbued with characteristics and properties both real and imagined (Blommaert 2010), and these characteristics carry over into its use and appropriation into foreign language contexts and into the discourse of individual users. These characteristics take on a life of their own in the receiving language context, with emergent qualities that may or may not have to do with the pragmatic and social qualities of English and its components within native-speaker settings. In the remainder of this chapter, this interplay of factors is explored at four different discourse levels: the lexical level, at the level of code-switching and phraseology, at the level of language choice in conversation, and at the level of language ideologies about English. *Lexical level* refers to the borrowing of vocabulary items from English into Finnish. *Code-switching* and *phraseology* are distinguished from borrowing in that these stretches of discourse tend to be longer than one word and are likely to be used in the language of multilingual speakers as a unique contribution to a single conversation or unit of discourse. *Language choice* refers to the language decided upon as the medium of communication for a given unit of discourse, for example a conversation. For example, a group of speakers from different language backgrounds might agree to hold a discussion in English as a lingua franca. By *level of language ideologies* I make use of a concept introduced earlier in this chapter: entrenched beliefs about particular ways of using language.

3 Licensing through English

The concept of licensing was introduced in the previous section. In this section, the concept is put to task as an explanatory factor for examples drawn from various levels of discourse and interaction. Examples are drawn from previous and ongoing work, starting with the lexical level and moving on through code-switching and pragmatic routines to language choice in conversation and, finally, the licensing of language ideologies.

3.1 Lexical level

In Finland today, especially among the younger cohorts of the population (Leppänen et al. 2009) the linguistic reality is, in effect, tantamount to bilingualism: among the younger population in particular, there is great social pressure to be highly proficient in English in addition to the mother tongue, which is usually Finnish or Swedish. While the consequences of these expectations are still very much under investigation (but see Blommaert et al. 2012; Peterson forthcoming), for our purposes it is of more interest to focus on the linguistic outcomes of this phenomenon in terms of language variation and change with regard to Finnish and the Swedish spoken in Finland. As noted by Matras (2020: 93–94): "In speech communities in which the native language is always or nearly always spoken in a bilingual mode, since everyone is bilingual, the permanent license to integrate foreign grammatical operators can lead to long-term integration of such operators into the recipient language". That is: language contact between English and Finnish has led to extensive incorporation of English-sourced material into Finnish discourse.

As discussed in my own previous work (and that of others; see, e.g., Matras 2020), borrowings into a language often have their "seed" in code-switches from bilingual individuals. These switched elements then develop in the speaker's overall repertoire and have the possibility to be picked up by others in the community. Eventually, if the borrowed elements spread, they can even be used by non-bilinguals because the semantic, pragmatic, and social practices associated with the borrowed elements are embedded in the form and its routine use. Thus, the licensing associated with the form expands throughout an entire community.

In Section 2.2 of this chapter, the notion of pragmatic borrowing was introduced, and an overview of some of the work in this area was highlighted. In this section, developments drawn from this body of work are explored through the lens of licensing. Previous work on pragmatic borrowing (Peterson 2017) has posited that borrowing forms from English carries an undercurrent of pragmatic motivation, and this motivation stems in part from perceived qualities of English, as discussed in Section 2.2. With regard to the borrowing *pliis* 'please' in Finnish, for example, the first attested spoken use was in a 1940s film in an utterance from teenagers who were discussing American jazz (Paunonen and Paunonen 2000). We interpreted this discourse turn in the film to index social meanings in line with what English-sourced borrowings still index today: youth language, urbanicity, and a global orientation (Peterson and Vaattovaara 2014). The motivation to use an English form in such a context has clear links to the previous discussion of licensing: the introduction of an unambiguously English-sourced word adds social meaning to the conversational exchange that presumably would not be achieved from using strictly monolingual Finnish discourse.

In addition to the notion of licensing, semantic bleaching and positive politeness are two related phenomena which have been advanced as interacting to motivate and sustain the borrowing of English-sourced elements in Finnish (Peterson 2017). Semantic bleaching, of course, refers to the emotional weakening of taboo items, a process related to euphemism (Burridge 2012). In this case, the semantic weakness of the taboo items is a property of the fact that the taboo items in question come from a nonnative language, thereby offering emotional distance from the semantic and pragmatic load associated with such terms in a native language (Dewaele 2010). The notion of positive politeness is borrowed from the classic work by Brown and Levinson (1987), meaning in brief that discourse is used to achieve social closeness and solidarity. Positive politeness has been advanced as a particularly important contribution to everyday language change, as the vast majority of everyday discourse is, in fact, carried out among people who are socially close (Wheeler 1994). This information, coupled with the characteristics and indexes of English as a source language make for compelling reasons to consider English-sourced elements as carriers of positive politeness in Finnish discourse.

A prime example of licensing with reference to just one lexical form, *pliis*, comes from a comedy sketch which aired on Finnish television in 2014.³ The name of the sketch, *Viinapäivä* 'Booze Day' is a spoof on the cultural concept of *karkkipäivä* 'candy day'. For many Finnish households, it has become cultural practice to engage in the eating of candy on Saturdays, almost as a ritual. In the comedy sketch, two adult actors play the mother and father of a boy and a girl. The setting is a supermarket, and the family of four stands in front of an aisle stocked with beer and hard cider. In a childish display, the adult actors playing the mother and father throw a tantrum, repeatedly shouting that they want *viiniä* 'wine'. The childish display is added to by the fact that the actors repeat the refrain shown in (1):

(1) *Viiniä*   <u>pliis</u>   *viiniä*   <u>pliis!</u>
    wine-PART please wine-PART please
    'Wine please, wine please!'

This short sketch resonates for its intended audience, made clear by the fact that the YouTube video has been viewed 2.6 million times since the sketch aired in 2015. The crux of the humor is its upending of a cultural text in Finland, which is accomplished through the role reversal of parent and child. It is critical to note that a significant component of this stylization is the repeated use of the borrowing *pliis* 'please', which adds to the overall absurdity of the exchange in that *pliis* in such a discursive exchange would almost certainly be within the jurisdiction of the children, not the parents. Specifically, the use of the borrowing *pliis* is a significant part of what licenses the adults in the situation to take on a childish persona.

A particularly revealing example of licensing is that of the borrowing of taboo items from English in the form of swear words. Here we see a clear example of cultural loans, in that naturally Finnish, like all languages, already possesses a wealth of discursive options for swearing. In recent decades, however, as an output of the language contact between English and Finnish, Finnish discourse has begun to frequently feature swear word borrowings from English (like other languages; see, e.g., Beers Fägersten 2017).

The most comprehensive study of this phenomenon so far is an online survey that was answered by 445 Finnish speakers in 2018 (Vaattovaara and Peterson 2019). The survey tested a series of English-sourced/Finnish heritage swear word pairs: *shit/paska, fuck/vittu, damn/perkele*. Respondents to the survey listened to

---

3 This example comes from the joint work of Peterson, Hiltunen, and Vaattovaara (2021), and I gratefully acknowledge my co-authors' permission to use the example in this chapter.

audio samples containing the target forms in a discursive context, and they were asked to assess how "acceptable" the utterance was according to a Likert scale activity (among other tasks; see Vaattovaara and Peterson 2019). The results of the semantic pair *fuck/vittu* are especially interesting here, as this is the word pair that was considered the most potentially offensive, or in other words the most pragmatically strong. For this particular task on the survey, respondents heard the utterances *siis mitä vittua/siis what the fuck* 'so/like what the fuck' spoken by the same middle-aged man's voice, and they were asked to compare how ordinary/natural they considered the phrases according to a 6-point Likert scale, followed by optional open-ended commentary on the task. It is important to note that the English borrowing version of the target utterance was prefaced by the discourse marker *siis* 'so/like' in Finnish to position it as a Finnish, not an English utterance. In addition, the English borrowing version was uttered with Finnish intonation and pronunciation.

The resulting data show that, while the heritage Finnish phrase *siis mitä vittua* 'so what the fuck' was, not surprisingly, considered more common by the respondents than the English borrowing, the Finnish phrase evoked more and stronger reactions in terms of its pragmatic weight. Several respondents commented on what they perceived as a reduced pragmatic load in the English-sourced borrowing. For example, a woman between the age of 30–35 commented:

(2) *Jostain syytä [sic] "what the fuck" on ehkä pehmeämmän kuuloinen kuin "mitä vittua" omaan korvaan.*

[For some reason, *what the fuck* might sound softer than *mitä vittua* to me.][4]

Another respondent, a woman aged 40–49, accessed the intersectional properties of the use of the borrowed English phrase, commenting on the role of age and profession:

(3) *Tuntuu että haetaan sanaa, joka olisi riittävän vahva nuorille mutta ei kalahtaisi ikäihmisen tai opettajan tai vanhempien korvaan niin pahasti.*

[It feels like trying to find a word that would be strong enough for youth but not as terrible to the ears of the elderly or teachers or to parents.]

---

4 Translations from the original Finnish are courtesy of students at the University of Helsinki, who used the survey data for a course assignment.

Anecdotal evidence supports such an interpretation: school-aged children in Finland report that English swearwords often remain overlooked, while the equivalent terms in Finnish or Swedish do not go unnoticed by teachers. Through the vantage point of licensing, using English-sourced swear words in Finnish discourse offers obvious discourse strategies: speakers, including younger people, get to swear, but without the social or pragmatic risks that might accompany using Finnish swear words.

3.2 Code-switching and phraseology

As discussed previously in this chapter, the use of English-sourced items in Finnish discourse has been advanced as being motivated by a host of factors, including social meanings, pragmatic force, and licensing, the latter entailing elements of both semantic bleaching and positive politeness. In this section, the focal point switches to longer stretches of discourse, which are most accurately identified as code-switching in discourse, a phenomenon that with regard to English-sourced material often has a relationship to phraseology (see Fiedler 2017). Through the use of English-sourced stretches of discourse in an otherwise Finnish discourse setting, speakers "construct and broadcast a particular relationship between what is said and aspects of the conversational context" (Matras 2020: 114–115); in effect, they are likely to be offering up the styles and characteristics discussed in Section 2.2 of this chapter. The use of such strategies offers a juxtaposition to the discourse setting the speakers find themselves in. For our purposes, such switches are considered volitional.

In research describing the same kind of phenomenon in German, Fiedler (2017) notes that not just lexical items but "phraseological units like greetings, discourse markers, catchphrases and other types of pre-fabricated constructions" are borrowed from English, which has "significant pragmatic implications, because they are closely related to culturally influenced text patterns, discourse norms and speaker attitudes" (Fiedler 2017: 89). With this investigation, we observe communicative forms such as catchphrases, slogans and other multi-word items (Fiedler 2017: 90) in Finland Swedish, with additional examples from other languages.

In a previous study, Wide and Peterson (2015) explored a corpus of online forum discussions from the years 2006–2011, housed at the University of Turku in Finland. The forum discussions are from Swedish-language communities in Finland, namely students who were attending Swedish-medium universities in Finland and readers of Swedish language newspapers in Finland. Swedish is an official language in Finland, spoken by about 5.5 percent of the population, or by about 380,000 Finns. The standard written norms for Swedish in Finland come straight from Sweden, yet there is great variation in the varieties of spoken Swedish in Finland. This background makes the exploration of Finland Swedish computer-mediated communication especially interesting, as it is a written format but with spoken language characteristics (Wide and Peterson 2015).

In the Swedish computer-media data, which consisted of about 50,500 words, approximately one out of every 10 words was an English lexeme (although there were difficulties in determining if a word was English or not; see Gottlieb et al. 2018). We observed three main tendencies for the use of English in the data, all of which entailed the use of code-switching.[5]

The first tendency was to use an entire clause in English as part of a user's signature, for example:

(4) *"I'm not bad. I'm just drawn this way". – Jessica Rabbit*

(5) *Real life should just curl up in a hole and die.*

In examples (4) and (5), the English code-switches did not offer propositional content to the overall discourse in which the text was embedded, but were rather included as an apparent act of identity, appearing each time a student wrote a comment.

A second major strategy exhibited in the data was to use English code-switches to signal the end of a discursive act, apparently as a strategy to end a discussion or sign off from a forum. Examples here include those in (6)–(8).

(6) [name], *varsågod. I'm intrigued.* # '[name] please go ahead. I'm intrigued'.

(7) [name] *you're welcome* #

(8) *Och do the cause justify the means?* # 'And do the cause justify the means?'

---

5 In this chapter, I have chosen to use the term *code-switching* rather than *translanguaging*. In part, this is because a level of discourse/structure approach is taken in the flow of information in the chapter, from the lexical to language choice levels. An alternative and meaningful perspective to the speaker volition and creativity present in this chapter's data would be one of translanguaging and enregisterment (as presented, for example by Lüpke 2021). I am thankful to an external reviewer for this suggestion. Furthermore, in keeping with certain perspectives on the ontologies of code-switching and translanguaging, these two concepts are most accurately described as belonging to a continuum (Lüpke 2021; Treffers-Daller 2021).

Examples (6) and (7) were methods for inviting a new "speaker" to take the floor and to signal the end of the current turn. The example in (8) was a means of exiting a forum discussion, signaling that the person was signing off.

The examples shown here offer several insights into the role of English in such discourse, in particular with the notion of licensing. In all of the examples, the switch into English signals a shift in social meaning, if not in propositional meaning. Unlike the lexical borrowing examples offered in Section 3.1, the code-switched elements demonstrated here seem to be in large part entirely performance and style-based. However, it is interesting to note that the position and framing of the English-sourced switches serves in some instances as a means of organizing the discourse: the switch to English holds social meaning, but it can also signal, for example, the end of a turn or an invitation for someone else to take the floor.

In her detailed work on English phrases and cultural borrowings into German, Fiedler (2017: 92) notes that the borrowings tend not to be well-known English proverbs that convey a general truth or virtue, but rather maxims and catchphrases that "represent our modern and competitive life". She also reports a number of linguistic cultural borrowings, ranging from Father Christmas in Germany now saying "ho ho ho", to young people closing their phone conversations by saying *Ich liebe dich/Ich hab dich lieb*, 'I love you' (Fiedler 2017: 94). Similar observations have been made in other linguistic settings with regard to the latter example: Peterson (2017) reports on an exchange in Swedish (in Sweden) that ended with the speakers in question concluding their conversation by exchanging "Love you" in English. In Iceland, as well, Hilmisdóttir reports (personal communication, September 20, 2020) that it is not uncommon for parents to end their goodbye-discourse when dropping their children off at daycare by saying "Love you!" in English. Likewise, Icelandic young people reported in a survey that they use "Love you" as a common farewell routine (Hilmisdóttir 2020).

3.3 Language choice in conversation

At the level of language choice, licensing through English is probably best characterized as a negotiated decision, although the negotiation is not always overt. A language choice can be dictated through those in authority with respect to a certain domain of use. For example, in an English-language classroom, students are most likely expected to speak English with each other during the time they are in the class, but once they leave the classroom their language of discourse changes. In workplaces where English is the official working language, meetings are likely to be held in English, and so on. The use of English as a working language in some business settings may in many respects be viewed as "natural" or "neutral", but as noted by researchers such as Cogo (2016) and Lønsmann and Mortensen (2018), this apparent naturalness belies a complex reality and hierarchy, with supplementary communication, for example, often occurring in other languages (see also Kuteeva 2020).

For this exploration, it is of interest to examine discursive situations in which English was not the obvious de facto language choice, and yet it was lifted to the status of discourse medium all the same. Each of the three examples presented in this section have been described to me after the fact by individuals who participated in the discourse event. Therefore, situations presented here are best considered interview data consisting of reported speech. Each of these situations took place in face-to-face interaction using spoken language; it is clear that exchanges using written language or computer-mediated communication could have different motivations for using English and thus are excluded (for now) from analysis.

Example 1. English in the business setting; different L1s
A 55-year-old Finnish person who works as an engineer for a pan-European company reported that he met a Spanish colleague in Germany. During a conversation that occurred between just the two of them, the Finnish person informed the Spanish person that he could speak good Spanish, and attempted to switch the language of the conversation. The use of Spanish lasted for a few conversational turns before the Spanish person said that he preferred to speak in English, at which point the Spanish person took the responsibility to shift the conversation back into English. According to the Finnish person, this decision was based not on aptitude or other language internal factors, but rather a discomfort with using Spanish as a mutual language during a business discussion.

In this situation, we do not have the benefit of knowing the point of view of the other participant – the Spanish man who elected to change the discussion to English. For the Finnish participant, however, the switch left him feeling slighted, as if "his Spanish was not good enough to talk about microbiology". This situation is offered as an example of licensing through English because, even though other language codes were options, English was negotiated on and ultimately selected as the medium of discourse due in large part to the fact that the discourse occurred in a business setting. Therefore, it was the purpose of the exchange that warranted the use of English.

Example 2. English during a personal transaction; same L1
In the second example, a Finnish person (age 43) visited Denmark for a holiday, during which time he rented an apartment from a private owner. During their meeting at the apartment, their language of interaction was English. Their conver-

sation soon revealed that both participants were originally from Sweden, and thus shared a mother tongue: Swedish. However, rather than switching to their shared mother tongue, they continued to speak English for the duration of the exchange.

In this situation, as with the previous, there are numerous interrelated explanations to account for why the exchange occurred in English. Like the first situation, one factor could well be that it is potentially awkward to switch the language of a conversation – or a relationship, no matter how fleeting the relationship is – to another language (Grosjean, Li, and Bialystok 2013).

In this situation, English could be viewed as some sort of neutral territory (as discussed in Section 2.2), and furthermore a neutral choice for what was essentially a business transaction. However, in talking later with the Finnish person who was involved in the exchange, it became clear that the choice to remain with English as the medium of the exchange was not a neutral choice. The choice to use English – and fluent English, at that – was to establish and maintain credibility in the exchange. It was a way to signal expertise and worldliness; in a way, the fluent use of English could be considered a source of competition.

Example 3. English for social functions; related L1
A third example, also from the private realm, involves a 43-year-old immigrant to Finland who does not speak Finnish, but who, as a native speaker of Danish, is able to converse fluently in Swedish, Finland's other national language (Danish and Swedish being closely related languages). He explained that in various social settings, he often prefers to speak English with speakers of Finland-Swedish, because, in his opinion, the conversation was more open, smoother, and "easier".

The third situation described here is perhaps the most characteristic of the core meaning of *licensing* through English, as, in addition to achieving neutrality, it is also viewed as opening up the possibility to converse in a way that is not perceived as native or appropriate in a Nordic language. It is especially of note that the shift into English in this discourse setting took place in a private, non-transactional realm – in contrast to the two previous examples. This example of language choice counters, for example, observations made by Salö (2020) who, with data obtained from the academic realm, noted that "national space seems bound up with national languages, whereas the international space is bound up with English".

3.4 Language ideologies

A fourth area where licensing from English comes into evidence is with regard to ideologies about the perceived qualities of English. In short, it is not just borrowing of linguistic matter from English into Finnish after several decades of remote language contact, but also ideologies in the form of social evaluations about how English should be spoken and written. These ideologies mirror those which are held in environments where English is a majority native language, notably in Great Britain; there is little evidence that the regard for use of English has taken on local norms.

A key difference in the social and linguistic ideologies between Great Britain and Finland (and other Nordic countries, see Levisen 2014) is the commonly held belief that while there are dialectal differences in Finnish, there are not class-based differences.[6] That is: while in Great Britain, notably, there are established class-based distinctions with how English is spoken and perceived, similar views about class-based distinctions are not an overt part of the language ideology in Finland (see Mooney and Evans 2015; Keskinen, Skaptadóttir, and Toivanen 2019). This does not mean that distinctions relating to class do not exist (see Piippo, Vaattovaara, and Voutilainen 2016), it simply means they are not part of the overt ideologies in Finland.

When it comes to English in Finland, the ideologies appear quite different from those held of Finnish. It has been suggested that ideologies about English closely align with those from Great Britain, as if the class-based ideologies have been nativized concurrently with the deepened and widened use of English in Finland (see Peterson forthcoming). Views of equality (at least in terms of social class) about Finnish are not equally evident when it comes to the use of English in Finland. This apparent contradiction is treated in a recent chapter (Peterson forthcoming), where I explore the notion of endormativity of English in Finland, determining that, rather than becoming more localized or nativized with duration of use and depth of exposure, ideologies about English become more prescriptivist with proficiency. Further, these prescriptive standards are firmly rooted in native settings such as Britain. Whereas in previous decades it was sufficient to be proficient in English, now the threshold is higher, and the "best" speakers of English are considered those who speak with what is perceived as a high-class "British" English accent. This ideology was evident recently with a feature story in Finland's largest newspaper about a Member of Parliament who "dropped jaws" in Brussels because of her "high class" British pronunciation – which she says she learned from watching the television series Emmerdale (Peterson forthcoming; Niemi 2020).

It is difficult to ascertain if these ideologies about English are a byproduct of the language education system in Finland, which, despite efforts to improve the

---

6 Note that the discussion here does not extend to class-based differences between *languages* in Finland, which is an entirely different matter.

range of exposure to varieties of English, remains – for now – firmly entrenched in its presentation of and adherence to two main global varieties, with particular reverence for Southern Standard British English. Note that we see a similar trend in other Nordic countries, which are routinely ranked as the best "English-speaking" countries in Europe (Forsberg, Ribbås, and Gross 2020).

The licensing from English with this example, then, is evident at the metalinguistic level. *Licensing* allows a speaker to engage in linguistic behavior that is not seen as native (or possibly even appropriate) in the recipient culture or language.

4 Conclusions

This chapter has been an exploratory endeavor to investigate the notion of licensing. In this case, the use of licensing is with respect to just one language, English, in settings where English is used as a widespread foreign language – in effect, where many people are often effectively bilingual in English and their native language(s). Licensing through English becomes a relevant concept as more and more discourse settings and populations emerge from long-term exposure to English – and the cultural norms and social expectations entrenched in it (Piller 2016).

In this chapter, discourse from a number of levels has been offered as a means to explore the notion of licensing. With regard to lexical borrowing from English, it was demonstrated that English-sourced borrowings, namely those that qualify as pragmatic borrowings, offer a stylistic meaning above and beyond their semantic content – which, naturally, offers the most revealing explanation for why they are borrowed in the first place. At the level of code-switching and phraseology, English-based code-switches were found to offer strategies in discourse organization, but more importantly as performance and emotive strategies. At the level of the conversation, licensing through English was demonstrated to be a source of offering a comfort zone in the conversation, a means of signaling aptitude, and a means of accessing perceived Anglo-American discourse styles. Finally, at the level of language ideologies, the chapter demonstrated that the ideologies regarding the use of English in settings such as Finland are in line with those from countries with an overtly colonial and class-based social history, rather than with the ideologies of social equality that have been part of the Nordic sensibility (especially since in the 1960s; see Keskinen, Skaptadóttir, and Toivanen 2019; Levisen 2012). In terms of licensing from English, this latter example seems to hold that proficiency in English offers the opportunity to take on class-based views of language variation that either do not exist or are not acknowledged with regard to the national languages.

As with any discursive event, it is important to note that the strategies put forth in this chapter are inherently risky. That is, in achieving solidarity through shared norms and expectations with one group of speakers, an interlocutor risks alienating or excluding others. The discourse strategies described in this chapter, making use of English-sourced elements, are by no means neutral in the Finnish setting (see Peterson 2017).

In conclusion, it is worth mentioning that discourse analysts no doubt can readily equate the observations in this chapter with long-observed contributions to the field. Central notions such as dialogism and polyphony (Bakhtin 1981) immediately come to mind. Certainly, a further exploration of licensing (through English) would be aided with the addition of these perspectives. Even if the underlying processes and tendencies presented in this chapter are not entirely new, the fact that we now witness new similar discourse norms emerging simultaneously in multiple global settings certainly merits attention, especially in light of the supposed "neutrality" of English.

References

Andersen, Gisle. 2014. Pragmatic borrowing. *Journal of Pragmatics* 67. 17–33.
Andersen, Gisle, Cristiano Furiassi & Biljana Mišić Ilić. 2017. The pragmatic turn in studies of linguistic borrowing. *Journal of Pragmatics* 113. 71–76.
Bakhtin, Mikhail. 1981. *The dialogic imagination: Four essays by M. Bakhtin*. Michael Holquist (ed.). Caryl Emerson & Michael Holquist (transl.). Austin: University of Texas Press.
Beers Fägersten, Kristy. 2017. The role of swearing in creating an online persona: The case of YouTuber PewDiePie. *Discourse, Context & Media* 18. 1–10.
Blommaert, Jan. 2010. *The sociolinguistics of globalization*. Cambridge: Cambridge University Press.
Blommaert, Jan, Sirpa Leppänen, Päivi Pahta & Tiina Räisänen (eds.). 2012. *Dangerous multilingualism: Northern perspectives on order, purity and normality*. New York: Palgrave Macmillan.
Bloomfield, Leonard. 1933. *Language*. New York: Henry Holt & Co.
Brown, Penelope & Stephen C. Levinson. 1987. *Politeness: Some universals in language usage*. Cambridge: Cambridge University Press.
Burridge, Kate. 2012. Euphemism and language change: The sixth and seventh ages. *Lexis* 7. 65–92.
Cogo, Alessia. 2016. Visibility and absence: ideologies of 'diversity' in BELF. In Marie-Luise Pitzl & Ruth Osimk-Teasdale (eds.), *English as a lingua franca: Perspectives and prospects. Contributions in honour of Barbara Seidlhofer*, 39–48. Berlin: De Gruyter Mouton.
Dewaele, Jean-Marc. 2010. *Emotions in multiple languages*. New York: Palgrave Macmillan.

Eckert, Penelope. 2019. The limits of meaning: Social indexicality, variation, and the cline of interiority. *Language* 95 (4). 751–776.
Fairclough, Norman. 2003. *Analysing discourse: Textual analysis for social research*. London & New York: Routledge.
Fairclough, Norman. 2009 [1992]. *Discourse and social change*. Cambridge: Polity Press.
Fiedler, Sabine. 2017. Phraseological borrowing from English into German: Cultural and pragmatic implications. *Journal of Pragmatics* 113, 89–102.
Fiedler, Sabine. 2018. Linguistic and pragmatic influence of English: Does Esperanto resist it? *Journal of Pragmatics* 133. 166–178.
Forsberg, Julia, Maria Therese Ribbås & Johan Gross. 2020. Self-assessment and standard language ideologies: Bilingual adolescents in Sweden reflect on their language proficiencies. *Journal of Multilingual and Multicultural Development* 42 (2). 1–15.
Gottlieb, Henrik, Gisle Andersen, Ulrich Busse, Elżbieta Mańczak-Wohlfeld, Elizabeth Peterson & Virginia Pulcini. 2018. Introducing and developing GLAD: The Global Anglicism Database Network. *The ESSE Messenger* 27 (2). 4–19.
Grosjean, François, Ping Li & Ellen Bialystok. 2013. *The psycholinguistics of bilingualism*. Hoboken, NJ: Wiley-Blackwell.
Hekanaho, Laura. 2020. *Generic and nonbinary pronouns: Usage, acceptability and attitudes*. Helsinki: University of Helsinki dissertation.
Hilmisdóttir, Helga. 2020. *Bæææ skvís! Love ya! The research project Icelandic Youth Language*. https://www.islensktunglingamal.com/post/b%C3%A6%C3%A6%C3%A6-skv%C3%ADs-love-ya (accessed 12 October 2021).
Johnstone, Barbara. 2008 [2002]. *Discourse analysis*, 2nd edn. Malden, MA: Blackwell.
Kelly-Holmes, Helen. 2014. Linguistic fetish: The sociolinguistics of visual multilingualism. In David Machin (ed.), *Visual communication*, 135–152. Berlin: De Gruyter Mouton.
Keskinen, Suvi, Unnur Dís Skaptadóttir & Mari Toivanen (eds.). 2019. *Undoing homogeneity in the Nordic region: Migration, difference, and the politics of solidarity*. London & New York: Routledge.
Kuteeva, Maria. 2020. Revisiting the 'E' in EMI: Students' perceptions of standard English, lingua franca and translingual practices. *International Journal of Bilingual Education and Bilingualism* 23 (3), 287–300.
Leppänen, Sirpa (ed.). 2008. *Kolmas kotimainen: lähikuvia englannin käytöstä Suomessa* [The third domestic language: close-ups of the use of English in Finland]. Helsinki: Suomalaisen Kirjallisuuden Seura.
Leppänen, Sirpa, Anne Pitkänen-Huhta, Tarja Nikula, Samu Kytölä, Timo Törmäkangas, Kari Nissinen, Leila Kääntä, Tiina Virkkula, Mikko Laitinen, Päivi Pahta, Heidi Koskela, Salla Lähdesmäki & Henna Jousmäki. 2009. *Kansallinen kyselytutkimus englannin kielestä Suomessa: Käyttö, merkitys ja asenteet* [National survey on English in Finland: Use, meaning and attitudes]. Jyväskylä: University of Jyväskylä. http://urn.fi/URN:ISBN:978-951-39-3815-4 (accessed 3 November 2020).
Levisen, Carsten. 2014. The story of "Danish Happiness": Global discourse and local semantics. *International Journal of Language and Culture* 1 (2). 174–193.
Lippi-Green, Rosina. 2012 [1997]. *English with an accent: Language, ideology and discrimination in the United States*, 2nd edn. New York: Routledge.
Lønsmann, Dorte & Mortensen, Janus. 2018. Language policy and social change: A critical examination of the implementation of an English-only language policy in a Danish company. *Language in Society* 47 (3), 435–456.

Lüpke, Friederike. 2021. Standardization in highly multilingual contexts: The shifting interpretations, limited reach, and great symbolic power of ethnonationalist visions. In Wendy Ayres-Bennett & John Bellamy (eds.), *The Cambridge handbook of language standardization*, 139–169. Cambridge: Cambridge University Press.

Martin, Elizabeth. 2011. Multilingualism and web advertising: Addressing French-speaking consumers. *Journal of Multilingual and Multicultural Development* 32 (3). 263–284.

Matras, Yaron. 2020 [2009]. *Language contact*, 2nd edn. Cambridge: Cambridge University Press.

Milroy, James. 2001. Language ideologies and the consequences of standardization. *Journal of Sociolinguistics* 5 (4). 530–555.

Mooney, Annabelle & Betsy Evans (eds.). 2015. *Language, society and power: An introduction*, 4th edn. London & New York: Routledge.

Niemi, Onni. 2020. Katri Kulmunin ihastuttava brittienglanti loksautti leuat somessa – kysyimme kielentutkijoilta, olisiko hän ylä- vai alaluokkainen britti [Katri Kulmuni's charming British accent dropped jaws in social media – we asked linguists whether she would be an upper or lower class Brit]. *HS Nyt*, 23 January 2020. https://www.hs.fi/nyt/art-2000006381598.html (accessed 12 October 2021).

Paunonen, Heikki & Marjatta Paunonen. 2000. *Tsennaaks Stadii, bonjaaks slangii: Stadin slangin suursanakirja* [Helsinki slang dictionary]. Helsinki: WSOY.

Peterson, Elizabeth. Forthcoming. Colonialism by proxy? English language ideologies in Finland. In Josephine Hoegaerts, Tuire Liimatainen, Elizabeth Peterson & Laura Hekanaho (eds.), *Finnishness, whiteness and decolonization*. Helsinki: Helsinki University Press.

Peterson, Elizabeth. 2017. The nativization of pragmatic borrowings in remote language contact situations. *Journal of Pragmatics* 113. 116–126.

Peterson, Elizabeth & Johanna Vaattovaara. 2014. Kiitos and pliis: The relationship of native and borrowed politeness markers in Finnish. *Journal of Politeness Research* 10 (2). 247–269.

Peterson, Elizabeth, Turo Hiltunen & Johanna Vaattovaara. 2021. A place for pliis. In Elizabeth Peterson, Turo Hiltunen & Joseph Kern (eds.), *Discourse-pragmatic variation and change: Theory, innovations, contact*, 272–292. Cambridge: Cambridge University Press.

Piippo, Irina, Johanna Vaattovaara & Eero Voutilainen. 2016. *Kielen taju: vuorovaikutus, asenteet ja ideologiat* [Language awareness: interaction, attitudes, and ideologies]. Helsinki: Art House.

Piller, Ingrid. 2016. *Linguistic diversity and social justice: An introduction to applied sociolinguistics*. New York & Oxford: Oxford University Press.

Salö, Linus. 2020. The spatial logic of linguistic practice: Bourdieusian inroads into language and internationalization in academe. *Language in Society*. https://doi.org/10.1017/S0047404520000743.

Salo, Tuomas. 2015. *English for excitement, Finnish for modesty: English and Finnish in Cosmopolitan's beauty product advertisements*. Helsinki: University of Helsinki BA thesis.

Treffers-Daller, Jeanine. 2021. Code-switching and the "bend it like Beckham" principle: On creativity in language contact. Keynote speech delivered at Language Contact in Times of Globalization 5 Conference, University of Klagenfurt, Austria, 8–10 September.

Vaattovaara, Johanna & Elizabeth Peterson. 2019. Same old paska or new shit? On the stylistic boundaries and social meaning potentials of swearing loanwords in Finnish. *Ampersand* 6. https://doi.org/10.1016/j.amper.2019.100057 (accessed 3 November 2020).

Wee, Lionel. 2010. Neutrality in language policy. *Journal of Multilingual and Multicultural Development* 31 (4). 421–434.
Wheeler, Max. 1994. "Politeness", sociolinguistic theory and language change. *Folia linguistica historica* 15 (1–2). 149–174.
Wide, Camilla & Elizabeth Peterson. 2015. English pragmatic borrowings in Finland-Swedish web forum discussions. Paper presented in the panel "Linguistic and pragmatic outcomes of contact with English as foreign language" at the 14th International Pragmatics Conference, Antwerp, Belgium, 26–31 July.
Woolard, Kathryn A. 1998. Introduction. Language ideology as a field of inquiry. In Bambi Schieffelin, Kathryn A. Woolard & Paul V. Kroskrity (eds.), *Language ideologies. Practice and theory*, 20–84. New York & Oxford: Oxford University Press.

Jyrki Kalliokoski & Anne Mäntynen
Chapter 10
Language ideologies and the translation of scholarly texts

Abstract: The chapter deals with language ideologies in the process of translating scholarly texts from the perspective of discourse studies. Special attention is paid to the ways in which *language ideology* and *discourse* intertwine and overlap theoretically or methodologically. The chapter focuses on the dialogue between the translator and the editor on the choice and use of concepts, especially on what the translator's lexical choices, the editor's comments and the translator's reactions to these comments reveal about language ideologies. The data consist of a manuscript of the Finnish translation of one scholarly publication, the comments on the manuscript made by the editor and the translator, an interview with the translator, and other ethnographic data. The analysis shows that the participants' views on which concepts should be used in a particular discipline vary according to their memberships in various discourse communities and according to their linguistic expertise. This becomes evident in cases where "foreign" linguistic elements, discipline-specific terms, or biased or historically loaded expressions are discussed.

Keywords: language ideology, scientific translation, translation process, Finnish

1 Introduction

This chapter deals with the construction of language ideologies in the process of translating scholarly texts (here, from English into Finnish) from the perspective of discourse studies. Our goal is to show how the notions of language ideology and discourse can be adapted to the analysis of the translation process of discipline-specific concepts and terms. The primary actors in the process are the translator and the editor employed by a Finnish scholarly publisher. We focus on the editor's comments on lexical choices in the draft version of the translation and the translator's reactions to these comments. Our main questions are twofold: 1) what do the choices and the discussion about them reveal about language ideologies?, and 2) how do language ideologies manifest themselves in the translator's lexical choices, the editor's comments and the translator's reactions to those comments?

We use the concept of *language ideologies* to refer to a shared set of beliefs and conceptualizations of language and its use, function and value in relation to particular social and cultural contexts and practices (e.g., Silverstein 1985; Kroskrity 2004). In our view, language ideologies are a fundamental part of social and institutional practices. Furthermore, talking about language (i.e., metadiscourse) is not merely based on conceptions of language but always entails ideological positions that have consequences (Gal and Irvine 2019: 1). Following Gal and Irvine (2019: 13), language ideologies can be considered as regimes of value that are connected to power but which operate in everyday life and in ordinary practices, like the one we examine here. Language ideologies are also about differentiation in both linguistic and social processes, and they always imply some sort of contestation about language and its relation to social structures (see Gal and Irvine 2019: 13). The basic question in research on language ideologies is how language use and linguistic structures are linked to social and societal structures. Conceptually, language ideologies refer to shared and recognizable ideas about the meaning and value of language and linguistic resources in a specific context, including the social and cultural meanings attached to such resources. Scholars of discursive sociolinguistics and linguistic anthropology (e.g., Silverstein 2003; Blommaert 2005; Agha 2007) have shown that language is fundamentally *indexical*. That is, every linguistic choice is contextual, and each choice activates social and cultural meanings. The relationship between linguistic choices and practices and language ideologies is not straightforward, however; it is possible to see language ideologies as meta-practices that need not be explicated in the linguistic situations on which they have an effect (Visakko 2015a: 5). The study of metadiscourse about linguistic choices offers a window for exploring the relationship between these choices and language ideologies.

As for the concept of *discourse*, it is used here to refer both to language use as social action (*discourse*) and to recognizable, sometimes historically deep-rooted ways of using language, and other semiotic systems in particular types of situations and activities in particular time and places (*a discourse*) (Gee 2011: 34–35; Pietikäinen and Mäntynen 2019: 35). The former (*discourse*) describes the way we understand the process of translating as social action in a particular social, cultural and historical context where participants are working with certain texts as members of various discourse communities. The latter (*a discourse*) describes the rationale of using language in a particular topic-, discipline- and context-bound way (for example, using a certain political or disciplinary discourse, such as discourse of Marxist economics in a scholarly book in Finland). In this chapter, language ideologies are seen as socially construed through and by *discourse*, by using language in social action (i.e., discussing the choice and use of concepts in the process of translating). Thus, by analysing the discussion on linguistic choices and the discussion on differentiations (i.e., the metadiscourse about language), we analyse the ways in which linguistic choices and language ideologies are intertwined in a particular professional practice, namely, translation of scholarly books (see Woolard 1998: 9; Mäntynen et al. 2012: 333; Piippo 2012: 220–225).

The work of a translator includes conscious decisions about how to express the meanings of the original text in translation. The linguistic choices made by the actors involved in the translation process are guided by language ideologies and normative conceptions of language use. At the same time, in our data, the translator and the editor discuss the choice and use of concepts in relation to particular *discourses* and to particular regimes of value (i.e., language ideologies).

The object of our study is the translation of scholarly publications as an editorial process. The chapter proceeds as follows: First we give a short introduction to the research on norms of translation and to ethnographic approaches in translation studies. Next, we present a preliminary discussion on the relevance of language ideologies for the translation process and the actors involved in the translating, editing and publishing of translated scholarly texts. In Section 3, we present our methods and data. Section 4 consists of analysis of a draft version of a Finnish translation of a scholarly book originally published in English. This manuscript contains handwritten comments about lexical choices by the editor and the translator. These comments constitute a dialogue between the actors of the editing process, where competing and layered language ideologies are being negotiated. The analysis is divided into three themes: first, the actors' language-ideological stances vis-à-vis "foreign" versus "domestic" lexical choices in the draft translation; second, the negotiations concerning discipline-specific expressions and, third, the actors' dialogue about historically "loaded" expressions.

2 Theoretical perspectives and background

Our research is theoretically based on studies of language ideologies from a discourse studies perspective as well as research on descriptive translation studies, especially translational norms (Toury 2012: 81–85) and ethnography of translation (Buzelin 2007). Following Lillis (2013), our approach can also be labelled as sociolinguistics of writing and translating. When looking at the process of translating and editing instead of the product (the finished translation), it is possible to perceive how norms and language ideologies emerge and are constructed in action (Buzelin 2007: 50).

Language ideologies are not homogenous, and competing and conflicting ideologies exist simultaneously in a society. Views of the correctness and appropriateness of linguistic choices (for instance, regarding their labelling as "domestic" or "foreign") vary in different contexts (Mäntynen et al. 2012: 328–329, 331; see also Visakko 2015b: 39–42, 79–82). Language ideologies are formed in discourses, they are dynamic, and their meaning is constructed in interaction. Accordingly, we approach language ideologies from the perspective of discourse studies. Language ideologies manifest globally, on the macro-level of language use, as principles concerning linguistic and stylistic choices and practices of discourse communities. Locally, they become apparent in individual linguistic choices and evaluations concerning those choices. There is a link between language ideologies and power asymmetries; for instance, expertise or authority can be at stake (Mäntynen and Solin 2010; Mäntynen et al. 2012).

Somewhat similar ideas of what influences language and linguistic choices have been discussed in descriptive translation studies by using the concept of translational norms (Toury 2012; Chesterman [1997] 2016; Schäffner 1998). Toury (2012: 81–85) has identified three types of norms that affect translations throughout the process: *preliminary norms*, *initial norms* and *operational norms*. Preliminary norms include translation policy and the directness of translations (e.g., tolerance of indirect translations), whereas initial norms refer to the choice between adequacy and acceptability – and to the degree of orientation toward either the source or target language and culture. It is worth noting that according to Toury (2012: 80), choices reflecting initial norms are made repeatedly on the micro-level, even though they operate on the macro-level as well. Operational norms then regulate the actual decisions made during translation, both linguistic and textual (Toury 2012: 82), and they become manifest in the translator's and the editor's discussion on the translation. Toury (2012: 75–77) also points out two aspects that are relevant in the study of translational norms: to explore where and by whom norms are negotiated, and to realize the competing and changing nature of norms. Toury (2012: 75) also notes how rare it has been in translation studies to study these phenomena.

In the process of translating scholarly publications, different language ideologies are inevitably present and negotiated between the actors, who have different professional and personal backgrounds and histories, and partly overlapping intertextual and discourse knowledge. In these negotiations, the issue is, on the one hand, about conveying scholarly thinking – in this case, to Finnish readers – and, on the other hand, the internal professional language of the scholarly community and its concepts which provide access to the international academic discourse within the discipline (Mäntynen 2012: 387–388, 2013).

We adopt a dialogical perspective to language use (Bakhtin 1981) in our analysis of translation of concepts as a part of the process of translating and editing.

We see this process as cooperation between the members of a professional community, the translator and the editor, and as a project of a community, not as (simply) an individual achievement of the translator. Accordingly, translating and editing are processes of entextualization and recontextualization in which discourse is reproduced in a new context using another language (Bauman and Briggs 1990; Silverstein and Urban 1996; Vigouroux 2009). This process involves negotiation about intertextual links and gaps, and the values, tones and history they carry (Bakhtin 1986; Briggs and Bauman 1992: 146–149; see also Agha 2007: 146–157).

Translation of scholarly work is not regulated only by norms of translation but also by the (competing) language ideologies of all those communities in which the actors of the translation process – as well as the potential readers of the published translation – are members. As explained by Mäntynen (2013), a single actor can have different memberships in this process. Besides being experts in their own profession, editors and translators can be experts in both editing and publishing. Furthermore, translators of scholarly literature are often acknowledged experts of their academic discipline (Mäntynen 2013). Our ethnographic data clearly show that scholarly publishers are a part of discourse communities formed by the larger scientific communities of academic disciplines. The actors in the process of translating and publishing have views about what kind of language should be used within a specific academic discipline when publishing or reporting research findings. These views can vary, however, depending on what other memberships the actors have, or what other kinds of expertise they possess.

Even members of the same discourse community may have different views about the choice of language or about the appropriate concepts and terms to be used when discussing specific topics. The linguistic expertise of a professional translator may differ from that of an editor. The translator and/or the editor may have expertise in the particular field of the book to be translated, and whether they recognize an individual expression as a term or not has an effect on which discipline or field of specialization one takes as a point of departure when looking for a translation equivalent. They may have different conceptions about whether an expression is a term or not, depending on their connections to the discipline or a more specific research tradition within the discipline.

In the process of translating scholarly texts, different expertises are layered. The experts taking part in the process can have several professional identities, simultaneously belong to more than one discourse community, and have different, multidimensional (sometimes even contradictory) views about language and the significance of linguistic choices. It is precisely at this point where language ideologies become relevant in translation studies.

3 Data and method

The data of our study comprise several draft versions of the Finnish translation of one scholarly book and the comments in the manuscripts by the publishing editor and the translator. In addition to these, we have used an interview with the translator and ethnographic observations as data (see Mäntynen 2012). The target text is a modern classic in economic history by David Harvey, *Uusliberalismin lyhyt historia* (Harvey 2008), originally published in English as *A Brief History of Neoliberalism* (Harvey 2005). The data were gathered by Anne Mäntynen in cooperation with the publisher and the translator in 2007–2008.

The data were gathered ethnographically. In both linguistic and social sciences, ethnography has traditionally been seen as a method for gathering data in face-to-face, spoken (or multimodal) interaction (e.g., Gumperz and Hymes 1972; Hammersley and Atkinson 2007). In our study, ethnography is understood as a rich methodology rather than a specific method. Following this approach, written interaction and the production of written documents are seen as (human) action (Copland and Creese 2015; Lillis 2008: 362). Lillis (2008, 2013) distinguishes between two basic ethnographic methods in sociolinguistics of (academic) writing: long-term participation "in participants' academic writing worlds" and the use of different sorts of data. The goal of this approach is to move the research focus from the product to processes of meaning construction by bridging the gap between text and context (Lillis 2013: 13–15; see Briggs and Bauman 1992). Similar ideas have been presented in ethnographically inspired research on translation (see Buzelin 2007).

As mentioned above, the object of the analysis is the manuscript of a Finnish translation of a scholarly book, and the comments (markings) by the editor and the translator. The comments are multimodal, and we have paid attention to their appearance and other visual features, such as the use of arrows and circles and the colour of the markings. This is illustrated in Figure 10.1. In terms of the analysis, it is significant that the handwritten markings are directed at specific points in the manuscript by the use of arrows or circling, like in Fig. 10.1. Furthermore, the translator and the editor use different colours in their markings – red for the translator, black for the editor – so that it is possible to distinguish the markings by the two actors in a reliable manner.

The notes in the manuscript are very concise, both in their linguistic and physical form. Figure 10.1 serves to illustrate how little space there is for the written dialogue between the translator and the editor. The editor's comment is written between the lines and the translator's reaction under the text.

Our data include an ethnographic interview with the translator (see De Fina 2020), carried out as a thematic, semi-structured interview. Mäntynen also had conversations with other translators and editors working on translations of schol-

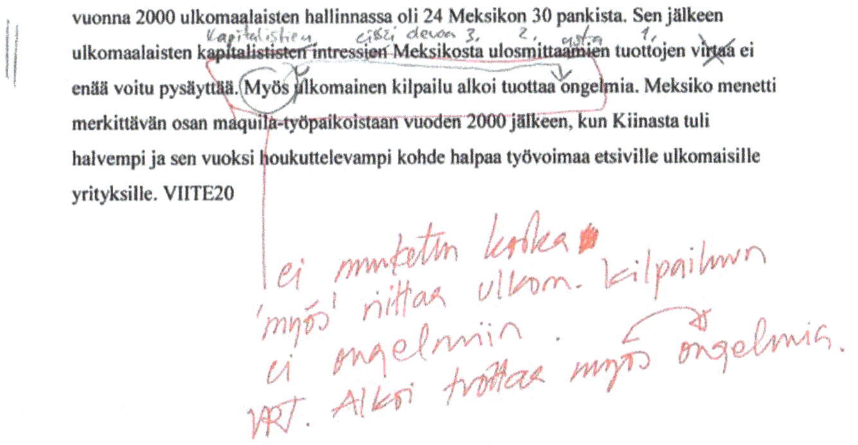
vuonna 2000 ulkomaalaisten hallinnassa oli 24 Meksikon 30 pankista. Sen jälkeen ulkomaalaisten kapitalististen intressien Meksikosta ulosmittaamien tuottojen virtaa ei enää voitu pysäyttää. Myös ulkomainen kilpailu alkoi tuottaa ongelmia. Meksiko menetti merkittävän osan maquila-työpaikoistaan vuoden 2000 jälkeen, kun Kiinasta tuli halvempi ja sen vuoksi houkuttelevampi kohde halpaa työvoimaa etsiville ulkomaisille yrityksille. VIITE20

ei muuteta kohtaa
'myös' riittää ulkom. kilpailuun
ei ongelmiin.
VRT. Alkoi tuottaa myös ongelmia.

Figure 10.1: The translator's comment (in red) on the correction suggested by the editor (in black).

arly texts. In the course of the project, we collected several e-mail messages and made field notes of the conversations with the relevant actors. The present study is a part of a larger project on the norms and ideologies of translation in late 19th- and early 21st-century Finland,[1] based on data from interviews, manuscripts and archives of publishing houses and other institutions. This ethnographic work has given us insight into the world of scholarly publishing, the context in which the translation of a scholarly book is made, and how linguistic choices are negotiated during the process of translation and editing.

4 Perspectives to language ideologies in the process of translating and editing

In this section, we present examples from the editing phase of the translation manuscript presented in the previous section. We approach the data from three perspectives, based on our observations about the dialogue between the actors in the editing process (i.e., the translator and the editor), as manifested in the notes in the manuscript. Furthermore, our observations based on the ethnographic interviews and field notes, as well as discourse concerning the translation of scholarly books into Finnish in various fora, have guided our choice of perspectives as well. The three perspectives regarding language ideologies are the

1 The project Norms and Ideologies of Translation was funded by the Kone Foundation.

following: 1) "foreign" vs. "domestic" elements (Section 4.1); 2) expressions that are specific to the academic discipline (Section 4.2); and 3) historically "loaded" expressions (Section 4.3). These three perspectives enable us to identify differences between the actors' stance towards lexical choices in the translation: what they consider appropriate, and on what grounds. Obviously, our three perspectives evoke the subjective – or, according to our interpretation, the ideological – aspect of linguistic choices; categories such as "foreign", discipline-specific or "loaded" do not have clear boundaries. In one interview, the translator mentions that a face-to-face discussion between the translator and the editor would be the usual practice and that the editing process under study is exceptional. In our case, however, the dialogue between the translator and the editor took place only in the notes they made in the manuscript. This may have increased the number of language-related comments and reasoning communicated in the notes.

4.1 Linguistic purism and the ideology of monolingualism

In this section, we discuss corrections and suggestions for changes in the manuscript where a choice between a loanword and an expression of Finnish origin is at stake. The relationship between domestic and foreign expressions is at the core of translation. This relationship has a clear connection to the concept of language ideology. Linguistic purism has been recognized as a widespread ideology in language planning (Thomas 1991), and purist views about "foreign influence" on local language have dominated discourse on language planning in Finland since the late 19th century as well. This ideology has manifested in the avoiding of foreign words and favouring of domestic expressions (Rintala 1998; Nordlund and Pallaskallio 2017; Mäntynen 2012).

Corrections directed at words of "foreign" origin comprise a recurring feature in our data. In addition to linguistic purism, we found a prevailing ideology of monolingualism throughout the translating and editing process. However, the ideology of linguistic purism is reversed from time to time in the editor's comments. Some negotiations about the use of foreign words originate from the editor's comments, suggesting a loanword instead of a more Finnish expression. In the end of this section, we give an example of this conflict between different language ideologies.

Favouring what is considered as domestic, Finnish expressions and rejecting international loans in translation is a typical manifestation of linguistic purism. In the dialogue between the translator and the editor, we detected the following recurring pattern: the translator has chosen a loanword with which the editor is not satisfied and suggests a domestic Finnish expression as an alternative. This dialogue may continue with the translator's reaction. In example (1), the translator uses *transnationaalinen* as the Finnish equivalent of the English *transnational*, whereas the editor suggests a Finnish explanatory paraphrase *kansalliset rajat ylittävä* ('crossing the national borders').

> (1) *Kansainväliset yhteydet ovat aina olleet tärkeitä, etenkin kolonialistisessa ja uuskolonialistisessa toiminnassa, mutta myös niissä* **transnationalistisissa** *[→kansalliset rajat ylittävissä][2] suhteissa, joiden juuret ulottuvat vähintään 1800-luvulle. Mutta nämä transnationaaliset [→kansalliset rajat ylittävät] yhteydet ovat selvästi sekä syvenneet että laajenneet uusliberalistisen globalisaation aikakaudella, ja on erittäin tärkeää ottaa ne tarkastelussa huomioon.* (MS, Chapter 1, pp. 29–30[3])
>
> The international links were always important, particularly through colonial and neocolonial activities, but also through **transnational** connections that go back to the nineteenth century if not before. But there has undoubtedly been a deepening as well as a widening of these **transnational** connections during the phase of neoliberal globalization, and it is vital that these connectivities be acknowledged. (Harvey 2005: 35[4])

The translator is not satisfied with the suggestion by the editor and offers a compromise as a solution:

> (1′) Translator's comment: *jättäisin miel. ainakin 1x transnat. indikoimaan mistä engl. käsitteestä suom. kumpuaa.* **Transnationaalisuus aika paljon puhuttu ihan tuossa lainamuodossakin** *... ja samalla saa tautologian tässä vähenemään. Toistaiseksi siis jälkimmäinen muuttamatta. Vaihda, jos saat* **anglismist allergiaa**. (MS, Chapter 1, p. 30)
>
> [I would like to leave *transnationaalinen* [adjective] at least once to indicate the original English concept from which it emanates. *Transnationaalisuus* [noun] is quite widely used as a loanword as well. This [solution] would also decrease tautology. So, for the time being, I will keep the latter one as it is. Change it if you are allergic to the Anglicism.]

Several linguistic norms and language ideologies can be discerned in the translator's comment. One of the guiding professional principles in the work of a translator of non-fiction and scholarly texts is that the translation should transmit the information contained in the original text as completely as possible. This principle is echoed in the translator's comment "I would like to leave *transnationaalinen* at least once to indicate the original English concept from which it emanates". The comment brings to light the importance of indexicalities in translation. Following

---

2 The editor's comments are placed in square brackets and indicated with an arrow in the examples. More extensive comments are presented after the examples. The translator's comments are indicated with a number and an apostrophe.
3 MS refers to the manuscript of the translation of Harvey's book.
4 Harvey 2005 refers to the original text: David Harvey, *A Brief History of Neoliberalism* (New York & Oxford: Oxford University Press, 2005).

Blommaert (2006: 164–165), translation is about translating indexicalities: since orders of indexicality are locally organized and repertoires are context-bound, the exportation of linguistic-communicative elements from one context to another creates problems of mobility. The translator's comment in (1) acknowledges this problem and argues for a solution. Regarding the translator's second remark, it is possible to interpret the frequency of the noun *transnationaalisuus* as an apology for the use of discipline-specific language: according to the translator, the loanword is widely used (in the discourse of social sciences); in other words, *transnational* is identified as a term. It is also worth noting that the translator refers to the stylistic ideal of avoiding tautology. This comment reflects the language ideology of rationalism promoting "clarity", manifested here by avoidance of tautology and unnecessary words (Bauman and Briggs 2003; on the Finnish, see Mäntynen 2003: 145–147).

The dialogue between the editor and the translator in (1) and (1′) includes playful aspects as well. The actors know each other and are able to joke about each other's language-ideological views (e.g., *Change if you are allergic to the Anglicism*). In the interview, the translator describes their reactions to the editor's corrections and perceives that they have been written "softly". In these instances of metapragmatic discussion about language (Lucy 1992; Silverstein 1992), language itself becomes the object of playful comments.

Irvine and Gal (2000) differentiate three semiotic processes underlying language ideologies: recursivity, iconicity and erasure. In the process of iconization, a feature indexing a certain social meaning is transformed from an index into an icon. By recursivity, Irvine and Gal refer to a semiotic process where a relation between a linguistic feature and its social meaning is projected onto some other relation. Both iconization and recursivity can be found in (1′) (see also Irvine 2001; Mäntynen et al. 2012: 330–331). First, the allergy metaphor in the translator's comment (*if you are allergic to the Anglicism*) refers to the assumed ideology of linguistic purism in the editor's correction. The translator implies that for the editor, the word *transnationaalinen* iconically represents the negative influence of foreign (impure) expressions in general. The translator's comment could, however, also be interpreted as reflecting the process of recursivity: allergy refers to a recurring affliction, which is here caused by the unnecessary use of expressions of English origin (instead of their domestic Finnish equivalents). The translator's reaction in (1′) implies that the word *transnationaalinen* rejected by the editor is one in the series of expressions which cause this metaphorical allergy.

As mentioned above, the negative attitude surrounding the use of expressions that are recognized as loanwords has a long-standing tradition in Finnish language planning. One further aspect of this tradition is the monolingual ideal: one language should be used at a time. In Finnish non-fiction literature, expressions in a foreign language (citations, code-switching, even names of institutions and organizations) are not favoured in the midst of a Finnish text. In (2) and (3), the editor suggests that the expressions in a foreign language should be translated.

(2) **Labour [→Työväenpuolue]** *oli 1930-luvulta lähtien rakentanut merkittäviä sillanpääasemia kunnallishallintoon.* (MS, Chapter 2, p. 18)

[T]he Labour Party had, ever since the 1930s, built significant redoubts of power in the arena of municipal governance. (Harvey 2005: 55)

(3) *Uusliberalismin kukoistus edellytti, että sosiaalisesti ankkuroidun liberalismin aikainen valtion ja kansakunnan välinen napanuora oli katkaistava. Se oli erityisen tärkeää niissä maissa, kuten Meksikossa ja Ranskassa, jotka saivat [→joissa vallitsi] korporatistisen muodon [→ korporativismi].* **Partido Revolucionario Institutional -puolueen [→Institutionaalisen vallankumouspuolueen]** *johdolla Meksikon hallinto oli pitkään perustunut ajatukseen valtion ja kansakunnan ykseydestä, mutta 1990-luvun uusliberalistiset ajatukset romuttivat tuon perinteen.* (MS, Chapter 3, pp. 22–23)

The umbilical cord that tied together state and nation under embedded liberalism had to be cut if neoliberalism was to flourish. This was particularly true for states, such as Mexico and France, that took a corporatist form. The Partido Revolucionario Institucional in Mexico had ruled on the theme of unity of state and nation, but that increasingly fell apart, even turning much of the nation against the state, as a result of neoliberal reforms during the 1990s. (Harvey 2005: 84–85)

However, the names of these political parties (and the parties they refer to) have a very different status in the minds of the potential readers of the Finnish translation. British Labour is a well-known institution in Finland. The translated name *Työväenpuolue* ('Workers' Party') is an established alternative to *Labour* in Finnish political and media discourse, whereas the Mexican party *Partido Revolucionario Institutional* is not widely known to the reading audience in Finland, neither in its Finnish translation nor in the Spanish original. Furthermore, the Spanish name is more transparent to English-speaking readers than Finnish-speaking ones. The editor's suggestion can be explained by a normative practice of preferring monolingualism in Finnish non-fiction literature. The fact that the original English text by Harvey uses the Spanish name of the party without an English translation supports this interpretation. The ideology favouring monolingualism is visible in the process of Finnish translation, not in the original text.

In (4), the translator has not translated the English expression *'looney lefties'*[5] (whereas the editor suggests that it should be translated. The editor offers the expression *kahjot vasurit* as a Finnish equivalent. The translator argues against this suggestion by appealing both to a subjective stylistic ideal (*tuntuu pöljältä*,

---

5 Inverted commas in the original.

'it feels stupid') and to the lack of logical translation equivalent (Rintala 1993; Mäntynen 2012: 382).

(4) *Edistykselliset Labour-[→työväenpuolue-enemmistöiset]valtuustot saivat Thatcherilta pilkkanimen* **"looney lefties"** *[→ **kahjot vasurit/vasemmistolaiset"**] (konservatiivinen lehdistö otti siitä kaiken irti [→ josta konservatiivinen lehdistö otti kaiken irti], ja hän ryhtyi ajamaan uusliberalistisia uudistuksia kunnallisverouudistuksen kautta [→kuntien rahoitukseen].*
(MS, Chapter 2, pp. 22–23)

Denigrating the progressive labour councils as 'looney lefties' (a phrase the Conservative-dominated press picked up with relish) she [Thatcher] then sought to impose neoliberal principles through a reform of municipal finance. (Harvey 2005: 60)

(4′) Translator's comment: *eikö voi jäädä engl? Tuntuu pöljältä, kun loogista suom. ei ole ja joutuu itse keksimään . . .* (MS, Chapter 2, pp. 22–23)

[couldn't it be left in English? It feels stupid when there is no logical Finnish translation and one just has to come up with something . . .]

In the manuscript, *"looney lefties"* appears in quotes because it is presented as an original expression used by Margaret Thatcher. From the point of view of authenticity, it would be reasonable to leave it untranslated. When comparing the translator's and the editor's suggestions, one can notice that the Finnish translation fails to preserve the alliteration of the original expression, and thus lacks (part of) the poetic effect of Thatcher's supposedly authentic expression.

Example 4 can also be looked at from the point of view of translation norms (Toury 2012). A dialogue about translating an individual expression is relevant from the point of view of operational norms, whereas the discussion of which language or languages should be used in the translation is connected with preliminary norms (Toury 2012: 82–84; see Section 2).

It is worth observing that neither the editor nor the translator suggests parallel use of two languages as a solution to the problem in (4): the original expression could have been placed in quotes, followed by a Finnish translation in brackets as an explanation. In our data, it appears that the ideology of monolingualism prevents this kind of solution, even in cases where parallel use of two languages would help understanding.

While examples 1–4 presented cases where loanwords were rejected in favour of original Finnish expressions, we will now discuss an example where this purist ideology is challenged by the editor. In light of our data, different language ideologies emerge locally during the process of translation and editing. The very same individuals engaged in a joint editing project can argue for linguistic choices that are based on conflicting language ideologies. Even a professional commentator of others' linguistic choices – in our case, the editor – does not have a consistent or static stance towards "Finnish" or "foreign" expressions. This is demonstrated in the following example:

> (5) *Kehittyvät maat eivät kuitenkaan ole ollenkaan vakuuttuneita siitä, että uusliberalistinen tie on se oikea, etenkään kun maat, jotka eivät olleet vapauttaneet pääomamarkkinoitaan (esimerkiksi Taiwan ja Kiina), selvisivät vuosien 1997–98* **rahoituskriisistä** *[→***finanssikriisistä***] huomattavasti vähemmin vaurioin kuin ne jotka olivat.* (MS Chapter 3, pp. 9–10)
>
> But developmental states are by no means convinced that the neoliberal path is the right one, particularly since those states (like Taiwan and China) that had not freed up their capital markets suffered far less in the **financial crisis** of 1997–8 than those that had.
> (Harvey 2005: 72)

In (5), the editor's preference to use loanwords as translation equivalents for concepts such as *finance* is in conflict with their comments in (1)–(3), where the editor promoted the use of domestic expressions as an alternative to loanwords. In example (5), the suggested corrections by the editor can be interpreted as a manifestation of the ideology of elevated speech (Irvine 2001); the use of loanwords implies professional academic competence in contrast to more mundane Finnish expressions. In example (5), a further explanation can be found in the discipline-bound norms of language use. In the discourse community of Finnish economists and historians, international loanwords are conventionalized and widely used to refer to concepts such as finance – or information or opposition (also discussed in our data) – and therefore the "foreign" and the "Finnish" words are not in free variation in this context. This interpretation gets support from the fact that the editor suggests that the Finnish word *rahoitus* should be replaced with the international word *finanssi* ('finance') throughout the manuscript. In the next section, we will discuss similar cases where the editor's comments can be explained by the language ideologies and professional linguistic practices of the discourse community of the academic discipline. All in all, the co-existing or conflicting language ideologies illustrated by examples (1)–(3), on the one hand, and example (5), on the other, witness the polycentricity of language-ideological systems and structures as described by Blommaert (2005: 75–77, 2010: 39–41). The actors of the translation process are simultaneously orientated towards several different norms and normative systems.

4.2 Discourse-specific expressions

In this section, we analyse cases where discipline-specific concepts and terms are being negotiated by the editor and the translator. A translator of a scholarly text has to be aware of the practices of speaking and writing in the particular branch of science in question, so that the translation finds its way to the target audience, and the concepts and terms used in the translation become a part of the language use of the discourse community. This is mentioned by all translators in the interviews. Furthermore, they appreciate expert readers and consider it important that the editor has the expertise of the discipline. In the present case, the translator talks about the contexts of translating scholarly literature and the significance of the scientific community and their own academic background in the following way (translated from Finnish):

> (6) Right, the readers know more about the thing than you. And in a way it's not very easy to find out [. . .] what has to be explained and what, for example, belongs to the way of speaking [. . .] what you are committed to when you choose a certain way of speaking and how you know what you got committed to.
>
> [. . .] Well, in a way controversial so that is this concept now this or that [. . .] I have a feeling that with my background I am able to operate with scholarly literature as a competent translator, because I have a general academic background. (Interview)

Sensitivity to language ideologies and norm systems regulating language use is part of the profession of a translator. The translator's comments in the excerpt above display how this professionalism includes balancing between different parties in an ongoing discipline-internal dialogue about concepts (*controversial* [concepts, things], *is this concept now this or that?*). The translator must become aware of the linguistic practices of the scientific communities and know how the work in translation is connected with ongoing discussions within the discipline. Scientific communities at large (researchers, students, other professionals in the field and lay enthusiasts) are normative as discourse communities, which also affects the translation of scholarly literature. In the Finnish context, this normativity becomes manifest in respect to the norms of the written standard language and language ideologies (purism, clarity, etc.) behind these norms. Another aspect of normativity is represented by the norms guiding the linguistic practices in science, both in general and for each discipline. Obviously, the norms shared by scholarly communities and disciplines partly overlap with the norms of the standard language.

When discussing the editor's and the translator's dialogue about the translation of the term *transnational* in example (1) (Section 4.1), we noticed that the translator defended their choice of the loanword *transnationaalinen* by implying that this concept was more established in the discourse community than its domestic Finnish equivalent; this was seen in the following note: "*Transnationaalisuus* on aika paljon puhuttu ihan tuossa lainamuodossakin [. . .]" ('*Transnationaalisuus* ['transnationalism'] is quite widely used as a loan word as well [. . .]'). In their comment, the translator uses the passive (impersonal) form of the verb *puhua* ('to speak'): *paljon puhuttu* ('widely used'). This grammatical choice leaves the agent unspecified. The linguistic form of the argument reveals that the choice is based on an intuition or subjective estimation about the prevalence of this term in the discourse of the discipline. For the time being, the Finnish translators of scholarly texts often have to rely on their intuition and subjective estimation, as there are no discipline-specific large corpora of scientific Finnish. The wiki-based Helsinki Term Bank for Arts and Sciences,[6] however, hosts discussions about the translation of terms. Furthermore, translators' academic and professional backgrounds (e.g., as researchers or members of scholarly communities), as well as and their skills in information retrieval, have an influence on how concepts are translated (see Vilokkinen 2017).

Examples (7) and (8) present a dialogue about the translation of the word *commodity* in the original text. The translator suggests the words *hyödyke* ('good'; 'commodity') and *tuotantotekijä* (this Finnish word is a compound: 'production' + 'factor') as equivalents for *commodity*. Both of these concepts are widely used in the Finnish economic discourse. The editor does not approve this choice but points out that the original text represents particularly the discourse of Marxist social and economic theory, and this should be reflected in the choice of the Finnish translation equivalents. According to the editor, *labour* is traditionally defined as *tavara* ('goods'; 'merchandise') in Finnish translations of Marxist texts.

(7) *Valtioiden tulee sen vuoksi yhdessä pyrkiä vähentämään pääomien vapaan liikkuvuuden esteitä ja avata niin tavaroiden kuin pääomien[kin] markkinoita maailmanlaajuiselle vaihdolle. Kiistanalaista on kuitenkin se, koskeeko tämä myös* **hyödykkeeksi** *[→tavaraksi] nähtyä työvoimaa.* (MS, Chapter 3, p. 3)

States should therefore collectively seek and negotiate the reduction of barriers to movement of capital across borders and the opening of markets (for both commodities and capital) to global exchange. Whether this applies to labour as a commodity is, however, controversial. (Harvey 2005: 66)

(7a') Editor's comment: *marxilaisille* **työvoima on tavara**

[to Marxists labour is goods/merchandise]

(8) *Puolueellisuutta synnyttää ennen kaikkea työvoiman ja ympäristön kohteleminen pelkkinä* **hyödykkeinä / tuotantotekijöinä** *[→***tavaroina***]. Konfliktitilanteessa tyypillinen uusliberalistinen valtio asettuu pikemmin puolustamaan yrityksille suotuisaa ilmapiiriä kuin työvoiman kollektiivisia oikeuksia (ja elämänlaatua) tai luonnon uusiutumiskykyä.* (MS, Chapter 3, pp. 7–8)

---

6 https://tieteentermipankki.fi/wiki/Termipankki:Etusivu/en.

> The biases arise in particular out of the treatment of labour and the environment as mere commodities. In the event of a conflict, the typical neoliberal state will tend to side with a good business climate as opposed to either the collective rights (and quality of life) of labour or the capacity of the environment to regenerate itself. (Harvey 2005: 70)

(8') Editor's comment: *Marxin yksi perusideoista on, että* **työvoima on tavara***!*

[One of the fundamental ideas of Marx is that labour is a commodity!]

The different views displayed in the translator's choices and the editor's comments can represent different reader positions. Examples (7) and (8) show how the choice of different alternatives for the translation equivalent is weighed in their notes, both from the perspective of the discourse of the discipline in general and from the point of view of established discourse and norms within each research tradition or school. Regarding the audience, this implies that the readership of classic works (and it is precisely the classics that are often translated) not only consists of representatives of a specific discipline or school but also experts in the field at large (representing other research traditions or theoretical orientations) and others who are interested in the discipline.

While the translator uses the words *hyödyke* and *tuotantotekijä* – terms from the discourse of economics in general – as translations for the concept *commodity*, the editor (ardently, by using an exclamation mark!) offers the word *tavara* as an alternative. In Standard Finnish, *tavara* has several meanings ('things', 'stuff', 'belongings', 'goods', among others). Some of these meanings would suit (at least metaphorically) the context of the translation. The editor points out that *tavara* carries a special meaning as a concept originating from the discourse of Marxist economic theory. The editor's expertise in economics, and in the discourse of Marxist economics in particular, enables them to present a contextually appropriate – and from the perspective of Standard Finnish, somewhat surprising – translation alternative. Our example shows that the actors must take into consideration the language ideologies and conventions of language use and interpretation of these different discourse communities. Furthermore, they have to be aware of the fact that the readership of the published translation can be heterogeneous, for example, in respect to whether the readers have access to discourse layers of the discipline, to the research tradition and to the semantic history of the concepts used in the texts produced within the discipline and research tradition (see Agha 2007: 146). Discourses are layered (Blommaert 2005) and texts belonging to both the same and different research traditions are in dialogue with each other; in the long run, the use of fundamental concepts is established in textual chains (Bakhtin 1986; Agha 2007). In examples 7 and 8, the word *tavara* creates an intertextual link to the Finnish translations of Marx, and further to his works as a whole, as well as to texts produced by his followers and critics. The intertextual link is based on the fact that *tavara* functions as an index for Marx and Marxism.

4.3 Historically loaded expressions

Concepts have a history. The interpretation of a single concept in a text is based on the reader's or the author's intertextual knowledge and experience about the discipline and its discourses (Bakhtin 1986). The examples in the previous section illustrate the intertextual asymmetry (Blommaert 2007: 8) between the actors of the process of translation and publication. The comments and corrections in their notes display how intertextual relations and references often get different interpretations, both in the same discourse community and between different communities. The meanings and connotations of concepts change over time. Our data show that while the use of concepts is regulated by the historical events with which they are connected, their use and interpretation, as part of the process of translating and editing, depend both on the date of the publication of the original text and the time of the translation process (and the time of the reception of the published translation). Blommaert (2007: 8) reminds that terms are not labelled sensitive or loaded by all users or in all social or historical contexts. He describes the variation of historically loaded interpretations of terms in respect to time, place and interpreters as follows: "The terms operate [...] at different scale-levels for the different groups, and at such levels the ideological load of these words changes from innocent and factual-descriptive to loaded and politically emblematic" (Blommaert 2007: 9).

Following the metaphor of scale presented by Blommaert (2007: 4), we noted interpretative jumping between scales relating to time, space and audience. A choice for a translation equivalent can turn out to be anachronic or it may carry useless or inappropriate connotations to contemporary readers. In the next example, the editor finds the translator's choices to be anachronistic or historically loaded.

(9) *Työvoiman järjestäytyneen toiminnan heikentäminen (kuten Britanniassa ja Yhdysvalloissa), ohittaminen (kuten Ruotsissa) tai väkivaltainen tukahduttaminen (kuten Chilessä) on uusliberalisaation välttämätön ehto. Vastaavasti uusliberalismi on usein ollut sidoksissa liike-elämän ja suuryritysten kasvavaan valtaan, autonomiaan ja* **yhtenäiseen luokkarintamaan** *[→ **kykyyn toimia luokkana**], joka on painostanut valtiovaltaa (kuten Yhdysvalloissa ja Ruotsissa).* (MS, Chapter 4, p. 30)

Weakening (as in Britain and the US), bypassing (as in Sweden), or violently destroying (as in Chile) the powers of organized labour is a necessary precondition for neoliberalization. By the same token, neoliberalization has frequently depended upon the increasing power, autonomy, and cohesion of business and corporations and their capacity as a class to put pressure on state power (as in the US and Sweden). (Harvey 2005: 116)

(9′) Editor's comment: *tämä on **SKP:n kieltä!***

[this is language of the SKP [Finnish Communist Party]!]

The editor's comment in (9') activates an interpretative frame that would likely be activated in the minds of many Finnish readers of the translation manuscript. The comment *SKP:n kieltä* ('SKP language') is based on the editor's intertextual knowledge and experience (see Blommaert 2007: 8–9). Finns who have lived most of their adult life in the 20th century or those who are acquainted with the history of the political and economic discourse of that time may find it easy to understand the motivation behind the editor's comments and possibly agree with them. But it is not difficult to imagine a 21st-century reader who would not see the link between the expression *luokkarintama* ('united front in class struggle') and a specific frame, such as the Finnish Communist Party. At the most, this expression may strike contemporary readers as an archaic or idiosyncratic rhetorical choice. The historical burden of concepts is visible only for those who know the history. It is precisely in cases like example (9) and in discussions between those involved in the process of translating and editing where the difficulty of translating concepts surfaces, particularly when it is not possible to clearly define the readership of the translation.

The editor's short exclamation *SKP:n kieltä!* implies that the "language of the Finnish Communist Party" is not appropriate in the translation of a scholarly text.[7] This implication becomes evident in the editor's suggestion for an alternative translation. The alternative is in fact closer to the expression used in Harvey's original text. The translator has chosen the expression *yhtenäinen luokkarintama* ('united class front'), whereas the original formulation in Harvey's book is *capacity as a class*. The editor does not use the translator's departure from the original wordings as an argument as such, but the tone of the translation alternative they suggest (*kykyyn toimia luokkana* 'ability to act as a class') is in line with the concepts used by the original author in both cases. The editor's comments on the politically and historically loaded concepts used by the translator echo the language ideology of rationalism, which aimed at purifying the language of science and government by rejecting its subjective, emotional and poetic functions (Bauman and Briggs 2003). The same comment appears later in the manuscript as a bare NP (*SKP-kieltä!* 'SKP language') followed by the translator's reaction: "*jaa☺ – tulee multa ihan luonnostaan . . .* " ('well☺ – *a natural reaction from me . . .* '). This reaction in fact carnivalizes the editor's normative approach and

---

[7] Notice how the same editor promoted the terminology of Marxist economic theory in examples (9) and (10).

offers an alternative, humorous mode for the dialogue. The translator's comment also illustrates the many layers of the editing process.

5 Conclusion

The concept of *language ideology* is a useful tool when studying the process of translation and the actors involved. Our analysis shows that by focusing on language ideologies, it is possible to reach a better understanding of the linguistic choices made in translations of scholarly books and of the motivations behind those choices with respect to the discourse practices of the disciplines and their discourse communities. The dialogue between the translator and the editor brings out two fundamental features of language ideologies: in a translation process, competing ideologies exist simultaneously, and different ideologies are linked with different, polycentric (Blommaert 2010) norm systems.

The simultaneous activation of different language ideologies in the translator's choices, the editor's suggested corrections, and the dialogue consisting of the comments by the two actors illustrate how a language user is constantly facing ideological choices. The translation of concepts that are used in a scholarly publication is a highly concrete situation of choices, which easily seems to provoke suggestions for corrections and comments from those involved in the process. The editor's reactions to translations of concepts expose the rich nuances of language use in dynamic and layered contexts. The corrections in which the editor suggests domestic expressions as alternatives to international loans have their motivation in the long tradition of Finnish language planning, where rejection of foreign influence in the spirit of linguistic purism has been a prevailing ideological feature. On the other hand, the editor also offers international concepts as a replacement for domestic ones. These suggestions can be explained by the editor's and the translator's different views about linguistic practices and the use of concepts within the academic discipline. In fact, these cases can be interpreted as representing a purism of a different kind. One further explanation for the alternation between international and domestic expressions in the same translated text can lie in the translator's effort to avoid tautology on the grounds of an aesthetic or rhetorical ideal. This issue of beautiful or rhetorically efficient language (see Herlin 2002) is also related to language ideologies.

Actors engaged in translating and editing do not necessarily share the same awareness of the history and temporal constraints of concepts or their links to specific research traditions or – as in our case – to (political) ideologies, which are manifested in their comments and reactions. All in all, our analysis shows that linguistic practices of academic discourse communities are reflected in the negotiations about translations of concepts used in scholarly texts, and furthermore, different actors have different views about the relevance of these practices with respect to individual expressions.

References

Agha, Asif. 2007. *Language and social relations*. Cambridge: Cambridge University Press.
Bakhtin, Mikhail M. 1981. *The dialogic imagination. Four essays*. Michael Holquist (ed.). Caryl Emerson & Michael Holquist (transl.). Austin: University of Texas Press.
Bakhtin, Mikhail M. 1986. *Speech genres and other late essays*. Caryl Emerson & Michael Holquist (eds.). Vern W. McGee (transl.). Austin: University of Texas Press.
Bauman, Richard & Charles L. Briggs. 1990. Poetics and performance as critical perspectives on language and social life. *Annual Review of Anthropology* 19. 59–88.
Bauman, Richard & Charles L. Briggs. 2003. *Voices of modernity. Language ideologies and the politics of inequality*. Cambridge: Cambridge University Press.
Blommaert, Jan. 2005. *Discourse. A critical introduction*. Cambridge: Cambridge University Press.
Blommaert, Jan. 2006. How legitimate is my voice? A rejoinder. *Target* 18 (1). 163–176.
Blommaert, Jan. 2007. Sociolinguistic scales. *Intercultural Pragmatics* 4 (1). 1–19.
Blommaert, Jan. 2010. *Sociolinguistics of globalization*. Cambridge: Cambridge University Press.
Briggs, Charles L. & Bauman, Richard. 1992. Genre, intertextuality, and social power. *Journal of Linguistic Anthropology* 2 (2). 131–172.
Buzelin, Hélène. 2007. Translation studies, ethnography and the production of knowledge. In Paul St-Pierre & Prafulla C. Kar (eds.), *In translation. Reflections, refractions, transformations*, 39–56. Amsterdam & Philadelphia: John Benjamins.
Chesterman, Andrew. 2016 [1997]. *Memes of translation. The spread of ideas in translation theory*, revised edn. Amsterdam & Philadelphia: John Benjamins.
Copland, Fiona & Angela Creese (with Frances Rock & Sara Shaw). 2015. *Linguistic ethnography. Collecting, analysing and presenting data*. London, Thousand Oaks, CA & New Delhi: Sage.
De Fina, Anna. 2020. The ethnographic interview. In Karin Tusting (ed.), *The Routledge handbook of linguistic ethnography*, 154–167. London & New York: Routledge.
Gal, Susan & Judith Irvine. 2019. *Signs of difference. Language and ideology in social life*. Cambridge: Cambridge University Press.
Gee, James P. 2011. *An introduction to discourse analysis. Theory and method*, 3rd edn. London & New York: Routledge.
Gumperz, John J. & Dell Hymes (eds.). 1972. *Directions in sociolinguistics. The ethnography of communication*. New York: Holt, Rinehart & Winston.
Hammersley, Martyn & Paul Atkinson. 2007. *Ethnography. Principles in practice*, 3rd edn. London & New York: Routledge.
Harvey, David. 2005. *A brief history of neoliberalism*. New York & Oxford: Oxford University Press.
Harvey, David. 2008. *Uusliberalismin lyhyt historia* [A brief history of neoliberalism]. Kaisa Koskinen (transl.). Tampere: Vastapaino.

Herlin, Ilona. 2002. Kauneus kielessä ja kielentutkimuksessa [Beauty in language and linguistics]. In Ilona Herlin, Jyrki Kalliokoski, Lari Kotilainen & Tiina Onikki-Rantajääskö (eds.), *Äidinkielen merkitykset*, 407–431. Helsinki: Suomalaisen Kirjallisuuden Seura.
Irvine, Judith T. 2001. "Style" as distinctiveness. The culture and ideology of linguistic differentiation. In Penelope Eckert & John R. Rickford (eds.), *Style and sociolinguistic variation*, 21–43. Cambridge: Cambridge University Press.
Irvine, Judith & Susan Gal. 2000. Language ideology and linguistic differentiation. In Paul V. Kroskrity (ed.), *Regimes of language. Ideologies, polities, and identities*, 35–83. Santa Fe, NM: School of American Research Press.
Kroskrity, Paul V. 2004. Language ideologies. In Alessandro Duranti (ed.), *A companion to linguistic anthropology*, 496–517. Malden, MA: Blackwell.
Lillis, Theresa. 2008. Ethnography as method, methodology, and "deep theorizing". Closing the gap between text and context in academic writing research. In *Written Communication* 25 (3). 353–388.
Lillis, Theresa. 2013. *The sociolinguistics of writing*. Edinburgh: Edinburgh University Press.
Lucy, John J. 1992. Reflexive language and the human disciplines. In John J. Lucy (ed.), *Reflexive language*, 9–32. Cambridge: Cambridge University Press.
Mäntynen, Anne. 2003. *Miten kielestä kerrotaan. Kielijuttujen retoriikkaa* [Talking about language. The rhetoric of language columns]. Helsinki: Suomalaisen Kirjallisuuden Seura.
Mäntynen, Anne. 2012. Kieli-ideologiat käytännössä. Sanajärjestyksen normittuminen tietokirjojen suomennostyössä [Language ideologies in practice. The construction of word-order norms in the translation process of non-fiction]. *Virittäjä* 116 (3). 378–409.
Mäntynen, Anne. 2013. Akateemisen tietokirjallisuuden suomennosprosessin erityispiirteitä [The translation process of academic works]. In Outi Paloposki & H. K. Riikonen (eds.), *Suomennetun tietokirjallisuuden historia 1800-luvulta 2000-luvulle*, 322. Helsinki: Suomalaisen Kirjallisuuden Seura.
Mäntynen, Anne, Mia Halonen, Sari Pietikäinen & Anna Solin. 2012. Kieli-ideologioiden teoriaa ja käytäntöä [Theory and practice in the analysis of language ideologies]. *Virittäjä* 116 (3). 325–348.
Mäntynen, Anne & Anna Solin. 2010. The local construction of language ideologies – A discourse studies perspective. Paper presented at NorDisco 2010: Nordic Interdisciplinary Conference on Discourse and Interaction, University of Aalborg, 17–19 November.
Nordlund, Taru & Ritva Pallaskallio. 2017. Competing norms and standards. Methodological triangulation in the study of language planning in nineteenth century Finland. In Tanja Säily, Arja Nurmi, Minna Palander-Collin & Anita Auer (eds.), *Exploring future paths in historical sociolinguistics*, 131–156. Amsterdam & Philadelphia: Benjamins.
Pietikäinen, Sari & Anne Mäntynen. 2019. *Uusi kurssi kohti diskurssia* [New course towards discourse]. Tampere: Vastapaino.
Piippo, Irina. 2012. *Viewing norms dialogically. An action-oriented approach to sociolinguistic metatheory*. Helsinki: University of Helsinki dissertation.
Rintala, Päivi. 1993. Suomen kirjakielen normeista [Finnish standard language norms]. *Sananjalka* 34. 47–67.
Rintala, Päivi. 1998. Kielikäsitys ja kielenohjailu [Perceptions of language and language planning]. *Sananjalka* 40. 47–65.
Schäffner, Christina. 1998. The concept of norms in translation studies. *Current Issues in Language & Society* 5 (1–2). 1–9.

Silverstein, Michael. 1985. Language and the culture of gender. At the intersection of structure, usage and ideology. In Elizabeth Mertz & Richard J. Parmentier (eds.), *Semiotic mediation*, 219–259. Orlando: Academic Press.

Silverstein, Michael. 1992. Metapragmatic discourse and metapragmatic function. In John J. Lucy (ed.), *Reflexive language*, 33–58. Cambridge: Cambridge University Press.

Silverstein, Michael. 2003. Indexical order and the dialectics of sociolinguistic life. *Language & Communication* 23 (3–4). 193–229.

Silverstein, Michael & Greg Urban. 1996. The natural history of discourse. In Michael Silverstein & Greg Urban (eds.), *Natural histories of discourse*, 1–17. Chicago, Illinois: The University of Chicago Press.

Thomas, George. 1991. *Linguistic purism*. London: Longman.

Toury, Gideon. 2012. *Descriptive translation studies – and beyond*. Amsterdam & Philadelphia: John Benjamins.

Vigouroux, Cecile B. 2009. The making of a scription. A case study on authority and authorship. *Text and Talk* 29 (5). 615–637.

Vilokkinen, Natasha. 2017. *Tiedontuojat. Opas tietokirjan suomentajalle* [Guide for non-fiction translators]. Tampere: Vastapaino.

Visakko, Tomi. 2015a. Promotionaalinen persoona semioottisena käyttäytymisenä. Verkon deitti-ilmoitukset lingvistisestä, semioottisesta ja antropologisesta näkökulmasta [Promotional persona as semiotic behavior. On-line advertisements from linguistic, semiotic and anthropological perspective]. *Virittäjä* 119 (3). https://journal.fi/virittaja/article/view/52731 (accessed 22 October 2020).

Visakko Tomi. 2015b. *Self-promotion as semiotic behavior. The mediation of personhood in light of Finnish online dating advertisements*. Helsinki: University of Helsinki dissertation.

Woolard, Kathryn A. 1998. Introduction. Language ideology as a field of inquiry. In Bambi B. Schieffelin, Kathryn A. Woolard & Paul V. Kroskrity (eds.), *Language ideologies. Practice and theory*, 3–47. New York & Oxford: Oxford University Press.

Eleanor Lutman-White & Jo Angouri
Chapter 11
Negotiating ideologies and the moral order in child protection social work

Abstract: Child protection social work is a quintessential moral domain of professional practice. This chapter is concerned with the ideologies associated with the moral order as enacted in child protection social work. We draw on audio-recorded interviews and focus groups conducted in England in which social workers and managers gave accounts of child protection social work, taking an Interactional Sociolinguistic perspective. In analysing these accounts, we show how social workers negotiate in situ and commodify the ideologies of child protection social work; a hierarchy of ideological positions emerges in a process through which the moral order is redefined interactionally in the encounter. Our findings highlight the intimate connection between ideology and the moral order in this particular context. They also provide a greater understanding of how child protection social work contexts for practice are (re)produced in and through interaction.

Keywords: social work, child protection, moral order, ideology, interactional sociolinguistics

1 Introduction

Child protection social work is a delicate and sensitive domain of activity as it involves vulnerable children and families. Moreover, it encompasses core social values and beliefs, such as those relating to protecting children from harm, and is a significant space for negotiating the roles and responsibilities of the state and the family for children's safety and wellbeing. Consequently, this domain of professional practice reflects and perpetuates dominant ideologies regarding moral rights, obligations and norms, making it a prime site for understanding the moral and social order.

In this chapter, we explore how professionals negotiate ideologies of child protection social work drawing on audio-recorded interviews and focus groups with social workers and managers from an English study of child protection social work. We take an Interactional Sociolinguistic (IS) approach and show the in-situ negotiation of dominant ideologies and the associated moral order, as it emerges in and through professionals' accounts in this setting. For the purposes of this chapter, ideologies are considered to be organising constructs that reflect commonly held views shared by professionals in one type of organisation and the corresponding sector. In our context this includes assumptions about the aims of child protection social work practice and the role of the core stakeholders; ideologies translate to expectations about the relationships between children, parents and the state. We consider that ideologies are negotiated, constructed, and resisted through the everyday talk and practice of work. We show, through the analysis of our data from interviews and focus groups with social workers and managers, that, although often considered elusive, they are very visible to the professionals in an institution and also carry a hierarchy.

We focus on the multiple ideologies that conceptualise the rights, roles and responsibilities of children, parents, families and the state in child protection social work. We pay special attention to the complex relationships between them when there are concerns about the care of children. The two main perspectives that conceptualise relationships between children, parents and the state when there are concerns about the welfare of children are a family support approach and a child protection approach (Verhallen, Hall, and Slembrouck 2019). Social workers operate in a profoundly moral realm (White and Wastell 2011) and ideologies relating to child protection social work embody moral elements as they involve the evaluation of the care of children, expectations about parenting behaviours, the attribution of responsibility and perceptions about the role of the state. Consequently, we also attend to the moral order of child protection social work as enacted in and through discourse. We understand the moral order as a system of accepted conventions, obligations and rights which yields criteria against which individual actions and interactions can be evaluated (van Langenhove 2017). The moral order provides a context for individual actions and interactions but is also re-enacted and perpetuated in everyday actions and interactions (van Langenhove 2017).

We understand discourse as an umbrella term encompassing different schools of thought and methodologies. Our own interest is in interaction analysis and we take a constructionist approach according to which social reality emerges in and through linguistic enactment, aligning with analysts of workplace interaction that focus on the situated here-and-how of interaction (Holmes and Stubbe [2003] 2015; Sarangi and Roberts 1999). We use the term discourse to refer to language in use (Gee [1999] 2014), and understand it as multimodal, including the verbal and non-verbal aspects of interaction. We take a perspective that understands discourse as connecting the situated encounter and the wider structural, social, cultural and organisational context. Consequently, discourse is the process through which ideology is acquired, expressed and perpetuated. Discourse theories are often categorised as micro-level, focusing on the situated here-and-now of interaction, and macro-level, attending to the wider understandings and narratives that provide ways of thinking, acting, doing and being in the world (Gee 2014). Different discourse theories engage with different parts of the micro-macro continuum. We position our work in the meso space of that analytical metaphor; we see the situated encounter as critical but also see the wider context that precedes the interaction as relevant. Our approach draws on the work of John Gumperz, often identified as the founding father of Interactional Sociolinguistics (IS). IS shares with Conversation Analysis (CA) a focus on the micro-moment, the situated encounter. Unlike CA however, IS positions the encounter within the local context where interactants are situated. As such, it is a particularly appropriate framework for looking into how professionals, in a given setting, negotiate and translate macro ideologies to tangible meanings relevant to their domain of activity.

Although IS is typically not used to discuss asymmetries in society and issues of power and politics, as argued elsewhere (Rampton 2010, 2016; Angouri 2018), this points to the way IS is used by scholars instead of the potential of the framework itself. Indeed, Gumperz's (1982) classic study on the breakdown in interaction between local staff and newly hired workers in a British airport cafeteria (often referred to as the gravy study), showed how differences in intonation patterns were associated with perceptions of appropriateness and im/politeness. The social evaluations associated with and enacted through language use and the political/ideological basis of sanctioning behaviours as in/appropriate provides a dynamic methodological and analytical framework for the study of sensitive contexts, such as the one we draw upon. Against this backdrop, we focus on the role of interaction in and through which accounts of child protection social work are constructed and ideologies of practice are negotiated. We aim to address a gap in the literature in relation to the ideologies of child protection social work which have predominantly been examined and theorised at the broader organisational, political and societal level. However, little is known about how the rights, roles and responsibilities of children, parents, families and the state and corresponding ideologies are constructed interactionally in social work practice. Focusing on situated interaction, we seek to contribute a greater understanding of how dominant ideologies emerge, circulate and become ideals enacted in situated practice. Within any child welfare system there will be tensions and contradictions between family support and child protection and also (in)congruities with other aspects of social work practice (Holt and Kelly 2018; Lonne et al. 2009; Parton 1997). Consequently, we pay particular attention to how these kinds of tensions and differences are negotiated at an interactional level.

We draw on data from an English study of child protection social work which included audio-recorded interviews and focus groups in which social workers and managers gave accounts of child protection social work. In these accounts they constructed child protection concerns about children, they positioned those that were involved and they also constructed the institutional response to these concerns. In analysing these accounts, we show how social workers negotiate the ideologies of child protection social work and the associated moral order in their talk, demonstrating an ordering of ideological positions and how the "order" in the moral order is manifested interactionally. We close the chapter with a model emerging from our data analysis and offer directions for future research.

2 Contemporary child protection systems and practices in England

As a general principle, the way that the state responds when families are experiencing difficulties and there are concerns about the welfare of children is related to values and conceptualisations regarding the rights, roles and responsibilities of children, parents, families and the state. Whilst these relationships between children, parents and the state are highly complex, when comparing systems internationally there are two prevailing ways of conceptualising them: an emphasis on family support and an emphasis on a tertiary model of child protection (Gilbert, Parton, and Skivenes 2011). These perspectives differ according to how child abuse and neglect are understood, how acceptable parenting practices are defined, how systems of protection are organised and the role of the state in protecting children and promoting their well-being (Gilbert, Parton, and Skivenes 2011; Parton 2014).

A family support or family service approach understands child abuse and neglect as arising from family conflict or dysfunction, with strong contributions from social and psychological difficulties including intersecting aspects of poverty, domestic violence, racism, parental substance misuse, disability and mental health problems (Bywaters et al. 2016; Gilbert, Parton, and Skivenes 2011). The state responds to families' problems by primarily offering supportive and preventative work (often with therapeutic underpinnings), focusing on parent-child relationships and the care of children (Parton 2017). At the other end of the continuum, in a child protection approach the state acts to identify and protect children who are at risk of or experiencing harm which is primarily attributable to parents' acts or omissions. It responds in an investigative way, relying on a legal framework that provides for authoritarian intervention (Parton 2014). Families' problems are framed in an individualistic way and the relationship between the state and the parents can be characterised as adversarial (Parton 2017). The reduction and prevention of harm to children is fundamental to both approaches, yet the way that the state responds, in a broadly supportive or interventionist way, differs between approaches.

In England, the appropriate balance between child protection and a family support approach has been a perpetual consideration (e.g., Department of Health 1995; Parton 1997). Historically there have been periods in which a child protection approach has prevailed and also periods in which a child-focused orientation has dominated, although the legal threshold for justifying statutory intervention, whether a child is suffering or is likely to suffer significant harm, has existed since the introduction of the Children Act 1989.[1] The current system in England in which social workers and other professionals operate has again become more child protection-focused (Parton and Williams 2017). It is predominantly focused on investigation and has a greater reliance on statutory interventions such as child protection plans and taking children into state care (Parton and Williams 2017). Reflecting a wider neo-liberal political ideology about the responsibilities of individual citizens, parents are held responsible for their children's wellbeing and future outcomes and parenting is instrumentalised (Holt and Kelly 2016). Parents are identified as culpable for situations that are frequently outside of their control, despite evidence of the social determinants that contribute to a likelihood of harm (e.g., Bywaters et al. 2018; Bywaters et al. 2016), factors that have intensified as a result of the Covid-19 pandemic (Legatum Institute 2020). Lack of attention to social and structural factors means that the impact of adversity on families, particularly in relation to neglect, and the impact of intersecting oppressions on women, minority ethnic groups and those with disabilities is under acknowledged (MacInnes et al. 2014; Platt 2009; Stone, Padley, and Hirsch 2019). Parents are expected to take action to change their situations, yet the services available to support them in doing this have been significantly diminished as a result of the UK government fiscal policy of austerity initiated in 2010 and cuts to public spending (Action for Children, National Children's Bureau, and The Children's Society 2016; National Children's Bureau 2012; Parton 2014), demonstrating that a family support approach is not prioritised. When operational thresholds for support are reached, children and families are often in crisis and the response is coercive and risk-led, resulting in increased statutory intervention (Bywaters et al. 2018; Hood et al. 2020; Tunstill and Willow 2017).

---

[1] For further information about the systems for protecting children in England please see HM Government (2018).

3 Ideology, language and the moral order

Dominant approaches, orientations and ideologies relating to protecting children and promoting their welfare, as outlined above, provide an understanding and theorisation of the issues at a broader organisational, political and societal level. However, ideologies are negotiated, perpetuated or challenged in situ. This approach foregrounds the crucial role of language and discourse in the emergence, circulation and enactment of these ideologies in situated encounters, something which has been given little attention in this particular professional context. Given the nature of child protection social work, we focus on a specific aspect of ideology: the moral order.

The study of ideology from a discursive perspective gives prominence to the role of language and social interaction in meaning making. It also makes relevant both the "brought along" context (Sarangi and Roberts 1999: 30) and what is locally constructed in the here and now, with different theoretical positions paying differential attention to the micro and macro contexts. There is a body of research taking a Critical Discourse Analysis approach which explores how ideologies are manifested in the here and now, with a focus on the role of discourse in the (re)production of power relationships and inequality in discourse. For example, analysts in this tradition have identified and studied political ideologies (e.g., Wodak 2015), gender (e.g., Lazar 2005), migration/immigration (e.g., Zhao, Rodriguez, and Monzó 2019), national identity (e.g., de Cillia, Reisigl, and Wodak 1999) and racism (e.g., Reisigl and Wodak 2001; van Dijk 2015) amongst others.

Within approaches that focus on the micro-level of interaction, attention has been paid to the ways in which professional practice ideologies are constructed in interaction. For example, in health care, conversation analytic studies have provided interactional evidence for the practical enactment (or not) of ideologies such as patient-centred care, patient choice and Shared Decision Making (e.g., Land, Parry, and Seymour 2017). In family therapy and family mediation, how the professional position of neutrality plays out in practice has been the focus of conversation analytic work (e.g., Greatbatch and Dingwall 1999; Patrika and Tseliou 2016).

The negotiation of ideologies which shape and are shaped in the interactional setting is intertwined with the moral order given that ideologies are frequently value-based (Tileaga 2006). Therefore, when ideologies are made relevant interactionally, the moral order, or understandings about what is "good" and "bad" and related rights, duties and responsibilities (van Langenhove 2017), is also invoked. Whilst there has been some focus on the practical accomplishment of morality in the interaction order in professional settings such as health visiting and family therapy (e.g., Heritage and Lindström 1998; Smithson et al. 2017), there has been little focus on this topic in child protection social work from a discursive perspective. Some attention has been given to the attribution of blame and responsibility in child protection (Hall, Sarangi, and Slembrouck 1997; Hall, Slembrouck, and Sarangi 2006). The moral order is particularly relevant to this context as this type of social work involves expectations about responsibilities, the evaluation of (in) actions, judgements about the best interests of the child and dilemmas about state intervention into private family lives.

This chapter focuses on this connection between ideologies and the moral order in the specific setting of child protection social work. We attend to how ideologies relating to child protection social work, enacted as ideals in talk, and the associated moral order are negotiated at an interactional level by social workers in their talk about their work. Talking about child protection work is doing professional practice in line with the position taken here. Extending studies that have examined the interactional accomplishment of morality in professional settings, our analysis unpacks this further and specifically shows how the "order" in the moral order is realised in the local interactional context. We show how contending ideals about child protection social work are navigated interactionally by social workers, demonstrating a consistency or regularity in the hierachy of ideals and consequently of the moral contingencies of child protection work. Analytically, we focus on the prioritisation of ideals and their (de)legitimation within the local interactional context, drawing also on wider social, professional and institutional ideologies and values. We discuss our methodological approach next.

4 Methodology

This chapter draws on data from a research project undertaken by the first author on child protection social work. The study involved fieldwork in two English local authorities. The subset of data which is the focus of this chapter comprises three focus groups and seven interviews with social workers and managers which were all audio-recorded and transcribed. Transcription is a representational and reflexive process (Bucholtz 2000). The data were transcribed verbatim with some interactional features included such as pauses and overlapping talk to facilitate an analysis that has at its core the construction and negotiation of meaning through social interaction.

As discussed, Interactional Sociolinguistics (IS) is the main analytic approach used to frame the analysis of the data as it brings together talk at the interactional level and the broader social and ideological meanings relevant to the professional context (Angouri 2018). In relation to the data drawn on in this chapter, the social workers' talk about their work with families in the interviews and focus groups was a key site for the negotiation of the ideals of child protection social work. It indexed wider social, professional and institutional values, ideologies about children and childhood, and expectations of parents including their roles and their behaviours. For the purposes of this analysis, ideals as enacted in talk reflect commonly held views and assumptions about the aims of child protection social work and constitute a resource for justifying or resisting existing ideologies within child protection social work practice. The analysis focuses on how dilemmas, conflicts and tensions between ideals about child protection social work are negotiated interactionally by social workers and consequently how the moral order is negotiated. We attend to how ideals are prioritised and (de)legitimised within the local interactional context. Drawing on research that considers how assessments are accomplished in talk and how behaviours and perspectives are problematised through contrast structures (Pomerantz 1984; Smith 1978), particular attention was paid to positive or negative evaluative elements of interactants' contributions, contrastive work and talk that emphasised the benefits or negatives of particular actions or situations.

5 Analysis

The focus of this chapter is how child protection social workers negotiate the ideals of child protection social work and the associated moral order. The analysis examines how social workers navigated any tensions and contradictions between the following four cross-cutting ideals constructed in and through interaction: protection from (risk of) harm, keeping children within their families, working in partnership with families and the appropriateness of the intervention to the circumstances. Within the ideal of "protection from (risk of) harm" the identification and management of risk dominates; the parents' care or behaviour is identified as problematic and the impact of neglect and other forms of abuse is a focus. Consequently, a need for action on the part of the institution is created. The ideal of "keeping children within their families" positions families as being best able to meet children's needs. This is in terms of identity, belonging and attachment according to which the family is constructed as a significant resource in which children are embedded. Institutions and social workers are positioned as performing an extensive supportive role. The related ideal of "working in partnership with families" recognizes the diverse social and individual factors that impact on parenting and promotes a collaborative, empowering and participatory relationship between families and social workers in order to reduce or prevent the abuse or neglect of children. Lastly, the ideal of "intervention as appropriate and necessary" favours family autonomy with state intervention only taking place in certain circumstances. Within this ideal, when state intervention is deemed necessary it must be appropriate to the needs of the family whilst being least intrusive.

The analysis will demonstrate an ordering of the ideals and consequently the moral order, showing how the ideal of protecting children from (risk of) harm dominated within social workers' accounts as a discursive and interactional accomplishment. The excerpts presented in the analysis each show how a particular ideal was indexed in the talk and each provides an example of how the ideal of protecting children from (risk of) harm was prioritised interactionally.

In the first extract, SW2 (social worker 2) constructs the ideal of protecting children from (risk of) harm as taking precedence over recognition that the parents are engaging well with professionals. She does this by explicitly rejecting the importance assigned to parental engagement by another social worker who spoke previously (not shown), illustrating the prioritisation of the ideal of protecting children from (risk of) harm.

Extract 1: (Transcription conventions are provided in Appendix 1)
Focus group 3.

```
1060    SW2    [. . .]
1061           I think you know those are the things that sometimes
1062           we don't think about in neglect sometimes we think
1063           about is the house clean is the house dirty you know
1064           have they actually bothered to tidy up today you
1065           know has the washing been done or is the washing not
1066           done you know is the garden organised is it- well
1067           it- d'you know what if the garden's a hazard the
1068           garden's a hazard (.) so either the children can't
1069           go in the garden (.) or if the garden th- if the
1070           children are allowed in the garden and the garden's
1071           a hazard well they're at risk of significant harm
1072           and literally for me it's that it's that
1073           straightforward and I don't get any more complicated
1074           than that around it you know if if a child if a
1075           child is in a situation whereby you know they they
1076           sleep on a a mattress on the floor that stinks to
1077           high heaven and you know results in them being
1078           bullied so badly at school that they start to self-
1079           harm well that puts them at risk of signif-
1080           significant harm
1081    SW1    Umm
1082    SW2    You know and that's for me where I'm at with those
1083           thresholds and I don't I- I don't for for me it's
```

```
1084                not about the engagement at all [I have to say you
1085     SW3                                        [umm
1086     SW2    know parents could be m- you know with the best will
1087            in the world we've got a case at the moment you know
1088            an- and these parents work really really well with
1089            us but can they keep the children safe no they
1090            ca::n't
1091     SW1    um
1092     SW2    They really ca:n't because the- g- they can't
1093            actually a because there's too many of them and b
1094            because they just can't cope and you know i- so are
1095            those children at risk of significant harm yes they
1096            are are mum and dad working with us yes they are
1097            it's not it's not different you know they- they're
1098            trying their best but actually at the moment their
1099            best is not good enough you [know
1100     SW3                                [sometimes
1101     SW2    And these children are getting injured
```

In this extract, SW2 indexes the ideal of protecting children from (risk of) harm through identifying risks to children, impact on children and problematising parental care, connecting risk and harm. She does this, for example, by discussing how the physical conditions of the home can pose risk to children (lines 1066–74). Letting children access a garden that contains hazards is equated to risk of significant harm. This echoes the centrality of significant harm within the legal framework (Children Act 1989) and the risk-averse practice cultures that are pervasive within contemporary child protection practice (Featherstone et al. 2018). Towards the end of the extract, SW2 refers to a specific family she is working with at the moment where the parents are unable to keep the children safe (lines 1087–92) and consequently "these children are getting injured" (line 1101). Again, the lack of safety of the children and the harm to them are explicitly highlighted as connected. In addition to specific references to harm to children, SW2 also discusses impact on children by providing an example of a sleeping environment that causes a child to smell and results in bullying at school and associated self-harm (lines 1074–80). This impact on the child is similarly regarded as equating to risk of significant harm reflecting the definition of significant harm enshrined in law (Children Act 1989). Consequently, through establishing risks to children and impact on them, children are positioned as vulnerable and at risk. This reflects a broader discourse of "child rescue" in which families are perceived as risky and children as vulnerable and in need of rescue, and which is evident in contemporary child welfare policy and political rhetoric (Featherstone, Morris, and White 2014).

In this extract, the parenting described, both in the general discussion at the beginning of the extract and the specific case example towards the end, is problematised. Through identifying parents' (in)actions or what they are unable to do and connecting these with risks to children through language that evaluates parents' abilities negatively, parenting is constructed as unsatisfactory. For example, when SW2 talks about the case that she is working with at the moment she directly attributes responsibility to the parents for the safety of their children and makes statements that explicitly allocate blame to parents when they are viewed as not meeting the safety needs of their children (lines 1086–90). The best efforts of the parents are evaluated as being "not good enough" (line 1099), invoking the moral order, and there is no discussion of the impact that poverty and other adversities might have on parenting. This absence of attention to structural factors that may contribute to poor parenting and a focus on individual blame is also evident in the dominant policy and political discourse (e.g., HM Government 2018). Whilst there is also discussion of the positive aspects of the parents' behaviour (line 1084, lines 1097–8), which offers a form of blame mitigation, overall parents are positioned as not fulfilling their responsibilities.

Through contrasting the ideal of protecting children from (risk of) harm with other aspects of working with families in child protection social work, this ideal is prioritised in the talk and consequently the order in the moral order is realised interactionally. SW2 constructs the ideal of protecting children from (risk of) harm as taking precedence over recognition of good parental engagement in her reflection on how she personally thinks the threshold for significant harm should be determined (lines 1082–4). Relevant here are the challenges for social workers in balancing their statutory responsibilities for protecting children with participatory practices which promote the rights of parents, aspects of practice which can conflict (Holt and Kelly 2016). Indeed, Healy (1998) suggests that there are limits to participation in child protection because of the specificities of child protection practice. The social worker states that parental engagement should not be taken into account when decisions are made about whether thresholds have been met (lines 1083–4), going on to give the example of the family she is working with where the parents are really well engaged with children's services but nonetheless the children are still experiencing harm (lines 1087–1101). Consequently, SW2 rejects parental engagement as a determining factor in whether a neglect case is serious enough to warrant child protection intervention and gives priority to the ideal of protecting children from (risk of) harm. Moreover, her view is not contested by the other participants. Therefore, interactionally, the views of SW2 and the ideal of protecting children from (risk of) harm, prevail. As a result, the ordering of the moral contingencies of child protection social work is also accomplished interactionally.

Extract 2 involves a discussion about court thresholds and how SW1 (social worker 1) perceives these to have changed since she was first a social worker (approximately 10 years ago). It illustrates the prioritisation of the ideal of protecting children from (risk of) harm that was a common feature within the data. The social worker's view that the impact of neglect on children should be recognised as significant and should be acted upon prevails over the approach of the courts who are stated as unwilling to remove children from harmful situations during proceedings.

Extract 2:
Focus group 3.

```
155   SW1   [. . .]
156         this point in time because whereas when I first
157         started to practice erm courts were more prepared to
158         [make that decision to remove those children from
159   SW2   [umm
160   SW1   that set of circumstances throughout the proceedings
161         they're no longer willing to do that now so it's
162         almost like the thresholds have- have moved and
163         people talk an awful lot now about well that's a
164         final hearing issue but as a social worker that's not
165         a final hearing issue for the children that I'm
166         working with that's a lived experience for those
167         children now today tomorrow for the next six months
168         sometimes eight months given the court timescales you
169         know >th- i-< they're still going to be living that
170         every single day you know but because people aren't
171         willing to see neglect as imminent risk of
172         [significant harm if a child can physically walk out
173   SW2   [umm umm umm
174   SW1   the door you know (.) that actually for me is is a
175         really dangerous situation that we've got ourselves
176         into erm because it's almost like erm ( )
177         something has to happen (.) and when you think
178         [. . .]
```

Through the social worker's prioritisation of the child's lived experiences and the identification of the potential for significant harm as a result of ongoing exposure to neglect, impact on the child is referenced which then indexes the ideal of protecting children from (risk of) harm. The social worker highlights the importance of the child's lived experiences of neglect (lines 166–7) and how these problematic lived experiences can endure for long periods of time during court proceedings (lines 167–8) when courts do not make the decision to remove children (lines 161).

This is a situation that, in this social worker's view, did not happen historically (lines 156–62). The social worker emphasises the perspective of the child in her descriptions of the enduring daily experiences of neglect for the child: "that's a lived experience for those children now today tomorrow and for the next six months sometimes eight months" (lines 166–8), highlighting the moral aspect of court decision making. The social worker's focus on the child's lived experience promotes child-centred practice, something which receives some emphasis in government guidance (HM Government 2018) but which social workers can struggle to enact in practice (Horwath and Tarr 2015). In lines 170–74 she talks about risk of significant harm and how there is a view that the often cumulative effects of neglect are not considered as placing the child at imminent risk of significant harm (Ayre 1998; Tanner and Turney 2003). Specifically relevant to the discussion in this extract, there is research evidence that suggests that cumulative concerns about child neglect are insufficient for court intervention, rather a specific incident is needed to prompt action in cases of neglect (Dickens 2007). The social worker alludes to this towards the end of the extract when she says: "something has to happen" (line 177) meaning that an incident would compel a court to take action.

This extract represents a common pattern in the data: the dominance of the ideal of protecting children from (risk of) harm through its consistent sequential and semantic prioritisation in relation to other perspectives and ideals. In this extract, the ideal of protecting children from (risk of) harm prevails as a result of the contrast between the perspective of the social worker and the problematic stated position of the courts reflecting the tensions and conflicts that can exist between social work and legal approaches (Dickens 2007). The social worker puts forward her own view that the impact of neglect on children should be recognised as significant and should be acted upon rather than delaying such decisions until the final hearing: "as a social worker that's not a final hearing issue" (lines 164–5). In contrast, through the descriptions of the child's daily lived experiences ("they're still going to be living that every single day", lines 169–70) and the invocation of the moral order, the approach of the courts is identified as problematic because they are stated to be no longer willing to remove children from harmful situations during the proceedings (line 161). The social worker describes the current situation as "dangerous" (line 175), again invoking the moral order. Thus, the ideal of protecting children from (risk of) harm is prioritised over the approach of the courts which illustrates the order within the moral order.

Extract 3 relates to the ideal of keeping children with their families. This extract also illustrates the ordering of ideals and the moral order because exceptions to the ideal of keeping children in the family are legitimised by the ideal of protecting children from (risk of) harm.

Extract 3:
Interview 6.

```
87   I    Okay (.) erm (.) and how did (.) erm (.) did mum
88        view the situation
89   SW   Erm (2.0) her (.) attitude towards the process I
90        think changed erm (.) in it reached a point where
91        it just became beyond her control I think and she
92        basically just completely buried her head in the
93        sand so just refused to erm engage with anybody she
94        had a wealth of support and again cause she was a
95        young mum she probably in all fairness was given
96        more opportunity than maybe we- you know she was
97        given a little bit more you know additional support
98        and extra time because of her age erm but she just
99        didn't engage with any of it so erm it was just a
100       case of like (.) sometimes she'd say yeah I know I
101       know I'm not doing what I should do like I need to
102       do there but putting it into action she just
103       couldn't do basically erm so yeah
```

In this extract, through contrastive work, the approach of children's services is juxtaposed against the response of the mother to the offered support. Consequently, the ideal of keeping children within their families is mobilised. Children's services are positioned as making every effort to support the family, trying to make it possible for the children to remain at home with the mother through the provision of support reflecting the recognition within policy that children are "best looked after within their families" (HM Government 2018: 8). The social worker states that the mother was offered a large amount of support and extra time to make changes (lines 93–4, lines 96–8). The mother's young age is given as a reason for the amount of support provided and the extra time given (lines 94–8). In contrast, the mother's behaviour is problematised; she is depicted as failing to engage with the support offered and as culpable for the situation. The mother is described as being overwhelmed with the situation becoming "beyond her control" (line 91), resulting in her refusal to engage with the support (lines 90–3). Furthermore, the social worker describes her as being aware of what she needed to do but unable to take action (lines 99–103), adding to the depiction of the mother as wholly responsible for the eventual removal of the children into care (this information was provided earlier in the interview), with children's services being absolved of responsibility. This illustrates how accounts given by social workers are used to justify professional and institutional action (Hall, Sarangi, and Slembrouck 1997).

Given that the children were removed from the family and placed in foster care, this extract also illustrates how the ideal of protecting children from (risk of) harm can function to legitimise exceptions to the ideal of keeping children in their families because the children were not being protected from harm despite extensive support being provided to the mother. The ideal of protecting children from (risk of) harm dominates because it can be used to account for exceptions to other ideals as evident in this extract. This demonstrates an ordering of ideals, showing how the dominant ideal is used as a device to (de)legitimise other ideals. This ordering of the ideals is representative of a moral order of positions within child protection social work.

The final extract is illustrative of the ideal of intervention needing to be appropriate and necessary. In this context, the need for intervention to be at the right level means that it should be commensurate with the extent of need and possible risk of harm. This extract demonstrates how the ideal of protecting children from (risk of) harm is used as a legitimating device for the ideal of intervention that is appropriate and necessary.

Extract 4:

Interview 4.

```
732   I    Okay erm (.) so you said erm (.) you find it have
733        found it m- more difficult to get a child off a plan
734        erm (.) have you got any examples of erm where you
735        were wanting the child to be off a plan and (.)
736        conference (.) perhaps were having a different
737        opinion
738   SW   Yeah (.) er quite a few erm I think it tends to come
739        from the other professionals being nervous (.) that
740        they're going to be the ones left holding holding
741        the baby as it were because they sort of saying well
742        you'll get them off a plan and then you're just
743        gonna disappear and we're gonna be the ones left and
744        they don't want that responsibility and they're
745        quite scared of it so what I find is they will often
746        say well yes things have changed but we need a
747        period of monitoring and it's like we can't use
748        child protection as the monitoring device that's not
749        what it's about it's oppressive you know it's quite
750        serious child protection and you need to understand
751        that and they'll say yeah but couldn't we just ( )
752        another six months just in case ( ) like no and
753        you used to hear that word just in case all the time
754   I    (     )
755   SW   and it would always be you know yes they have made
756        the changes but look at the history and I'd be like
757        yes I know but we're looking at now the here and now
```

```
758        this child is not at risk of suffering significant
759        harm they can't be on a plan you need to end it and
760        they'd be oh yes but (.) what if and it's [like well
761   I    [umm
762   SW   if that happens then we'll escalate it again
```

The social worker contrasts the cautious views of other professionals when it comes to decisions about whether a child should remain on a child protection plan with her own view that continuing a child protection plan when it is not needed is oppressive, underlining the social work commitment to anti-oppressive practice and social justice (Thompson [1992] 2016). This contrast work indexes the need for intervention to be at the right level and consequently the ideal of intervention being appropriate and necessary. Other professionals are positioned as having a preference for continuing a child protection plan "just in case" (lines 751–2) or as a monitoring device. The social worker states that other professionals can be anxious about taking responsibility for monitoring the situation once children's services are no longer involved (lines 739–45). This is identified as a reason for professionals wanting to continue child protection plans as a precaution. She also states that other professionals can reference the history of the case to argue that a child protection plan needs to continue (line 756). In contrast, the social worker references the need for intervention to be proportionate, drawing on the perspective of the service user to highlight the negatives of unnecessary child protection plans. This resonates with social work's concerns with recognising the impact of discrimination and oppression on service users (Thompson 2016). The social worker states that her contrasting view is that continuing child protection plans when they are no longer needed is oppressive (line 749), again emphasizing an anti-oppressive approach to practice (Thompson 2016). She is clear that "we can't use child protection as a monitoring device" because that is not what it is intended for (lines 747–8). Furthermore, to support her view, the social worker draws on the concept of significant harm, emphasising its importance in decision making. She states that if the child is no longer at risk of suffering significant harm currently, then a child protection plan is not needed (lines 758–9), a threshold which is outlined in law (Children Act 1989).

This referencing of the concept of significant harm connects the ideal of intervention that is appropriate and necessary with the ideal of protecting children from (risk of) harm, invoking the legal framework. Here the ideal of protecting children from (risk of) harm is used as a resource to construct the legitimacy of the ideal of intervention that is appropriate and necessary. Intervening at the level of child protection (i.e., keeping a child on a child protection plan) rather than at a lower level (such as child in need) is stated as only appropriate and necessary if the child is at risk of significant harm. Therefore, the ideal of protecting children from (risk of) harm is used as a legitimating device for the ideal of intervention that is appropriate and necessary, illustrating the common pattern in the data of the dominance of the ideal of protecting children from (risk of) harm. Illustrating how ideals are ordered interactionally displays the underlying moral order in child protection social work with an emphasis on the hierarchical features of this moral work.

6 Discussion

This chapter has explored the negotiation of ideologies about child protection social work and the associated moral order through examining illustrative examples of talk from interviews and focus groups with social workers. We focused on how ideologies about child protection work were enacted and indexed but also justified and resisted through spoken interaction. Through examining how social workers navigate any dilemmas, contradictions and tensions between co-existing ideals enacted in the talk, the analysis has shown that there was a consistency or regularity in the ordering of ideals. It details how one particular ideal, the ideal of protecting children from (risk of) harm, is preferenced interactionally. This ideal was sequentially and semantically prioritised over other ideals when more than one ideal or perspective was being talked about. It was also used to (de)legitimise other ideals; it was used to construct the legitimacy of the ideal of intervention that is appropriate and necessary and was used to legitimise exceptions to the ideal of keeping children within their families. The relationships between and ordering of the ideals are represented in Figure 11.1. The dominance of the ideal of protecting children from (risk of) harm is signaled through its appearance at the top of the figure, with the other subordinate ideals appearing lower in the hierarchy. Although the figure corresponds to our analysis and constitutes, evidently, a simplification, it also provides a framework for future research in this significant and underexplored area. Our findings extend other studies that have identified the possibility of multiple ideologies and positions in social work talk (Broadhurst 2012; Hall and Slembrouck 2011) by demonstrating how ideals are ordered and the mechanisms through which this takes place interactionally.

Many of the ideals enacted in the talk involve value-based ideologies and perspectives. Therefore, the analysis also illustrates the moral nature of the accounts of child protection social work which construct and position others and institutions according to value-based and moral expectancies (see also Dingwall, Eekelaar, and Murray [1983] 1995; Hall, Sarangi, and Slembrouck 1997). Specifically,

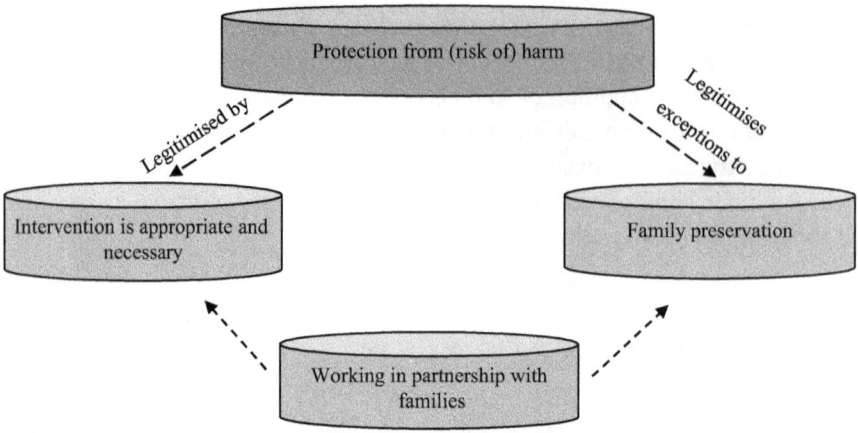

Figure 11.1: The ordering of ideals.

the analysis shows that the ordering of ideals interactionally also produces an ordering of the moral contingencies of child protection social work, revealing the "order" within the moral order and expanding on previous studies of the interactional accomplishment of morality in professional settings. The prioritisation of a particular way of understanding children, parents and the role of the state which is intimately connected with moral issues has been shown in the analysis. The dominant understanding is one in which vulnerable children need to be protected from risky parents by a state that acts in authoritarian ways that are justified as necessary. The illustration of how the order in the moral order is realised in the local interactional context adds to existing work on the moral order in professional settings and can be usefully further examined in allied professional contexts such as youth justice or children's disability social work services to shed light on the processes by which particular ideologies and moral understandings become dominant and are prioritised in the local interactional context.

The dominance of the ideal of protecting children from (risk of) harm at the micro-level reflects the wider context of the child welfare system in which the interactants operate and where a child protection approach dominates. The dominance of the ideal of protecting children from (risk of) harm means that the concept of risk is elevated which is reflected in the risk-averse practice cultures that permeate contemporary child protection practice (Featherstone et al. 2018; Morris et al. 2018). Therefore, through their talk in the interviews and focus groups the social workers (re)produce and maintain the institutional reality (Angouri 2018; Mäkitalo 2002; Sarangi and Roberts 1999), illustrating how institutional talk shapes and is shaped by the institutional context (Boden 1994). Our findings extend existing scholarship by providing a greater understanding of how child protection social work contexts for practice are (re)produced in and through interaction and by showing how IS is appropriate for an intersecting study of discourse and ideology. They also provide a greater understanding of why social workers may find it challenging to reconcile practices with the core values of social work that are obfuscated within the dominant individualised, risk-based approach. In closing, ideology, as an area and in relation to professional performance, has been addressed by discursive and sociolinguistic studies; however, there is little research connecting this to the societal moral order, particularly in sensitive contexts such as the one discussed here. We believe further research is timely and we hope our work has paved the way for future studies to follow.

Appendix 1 Transcription conventions

The transcription symbols used in this chapter are derived from the system developed by Gail Jefferson (see also Sidnell 2010).

[	A left square bracket marks the start of overlapping speech
negle-	A hyphen marks a cut-off word
said	Underlining indicates emphasis or stress of the word
so::	Colons show the degree of elongation of the previous sound
>fast< <slow>	"Less than" and "greater than" signs show markedly faster or slower speech
(.)	A short pause, untimed
(2.0)	Numbers in brackets show the length of pauses in seconds
()	Parentheses indicate indecipherable talk
[....]	Section of transcript omitted

References

Action for Children, National Children's Bureau & The Children's Society. 2016. *Losing in the long run: Trends in early intervention funding*. London: Action for Children, National Children's Bureau and The Children's Society.

Angouri, Jo. 2018. *Culture, discourse and the workplace*. London & New York: Routledge.

Ayre, Patrick. 1998. Significant harm: Making professional judgements. *Child Abuse Review* 7 (5). 330–342.

Boden, Deirdre. 1994. *The business of talk: Organizations in action*. Cambridge: Polity Press.

Broadhurst, Karen. 2012. Moral agency in everyday safeguarding work: Reclaiming hope in the 'small stories' of family support: Some lessons from John Dewey. *Families, Relationships and Societies* 1 (3). 293–309.

Bucholtz, Mary. 2000. The politics of transcription. *Journal of Pragmatics* 32 (10). 1439–1465.

Bywaters, Paul, Lisa Bunting, Gavin Davidson, Jennifer Hanratty, Will Mason, Claire McCartan & Nicole Steils. 2016. *The relationship between poverty, child abuse and neglect: An evidence review*. York: Joseph Rowntree Foundation.

Bywaters, Paul, Geraldine Brady, Lisa Bunting, Brigid Daniel, Brid Featherstone, Chantel Jones, Kate Morris, Jonathan Scourfield, Tim Sparks & Calum Webb. 2018. Inequalities in English child protection practice under austerity: A universal challenge? *Child & Family Social Work* 23 (1). 53–61.

Children Act. 1989. https://www.legislation.gov.uk/ukpga/1989/41/contents (accessed 20 October 2021).

de Cillia, Rudolf, Martin Reisigl & Ruth Wodak. 1999. The discursive construction of national identities. *Discourse & Society* 10 (2). 149–173.

Department of Health. 1995. *Child protection: Messages from research*. London: HMSO.

Dickens, Jonathan. 2007. Child neglect and the law: Catapults, thresholds and delay. *Child Abuse Review* 16 (2). 77–92.

Dingwall, Robert, John Eekelaar & Topsy Murray. 1995 [1983]. *The protection of children: State intervention and family life*, 2nd edn. Oxford: Blackwell.

Featherstone, Brid, Anna Gupta, Kate Morris & Sue White. 2018. *Protecting children: A social model*. Bristol: Policy Press.

Featherstone, Brid, Kate Morris & Sue White. 2014. *Re-imagining child protection: Towards humane social work with families*. Bristol: Policy Press.

Gee, James P. 2014 [1999]. *An introduction to discourse analysis: Theory and method*, 2nd edn. London & New York: Routledge.

Gilbert, Neil, Nigel Parton & Marit Skivenes (eds.). 2011. *Child protection systems: International trends and orientations*. Oxford & New York: Oxford University Press.

Greatbatch, David & Robert Dingwall. 1999. Professional neutralism in family mediation. In Srikant Sarangi & Celia Roberts (eds.), *Talk, work and institutional order: Discourse in medical, mediation and management settings*, 271–292. Berlin: De Gruyter Mouton.

Gumperz, John. 1982. *Discourse strategies*. Cambridge: Cambridge University Press.

Hall, Christopher, Srikant Sarangi & Stef Slembrouck. 1997. Moral construction and social work discourse. In Britt-Louise Gunnarsson, Per Linell & Bengt Nordberg (eds.), *The construction of professional discourse*, 265–291. London: Longman.

Hall, Christopher, Stef Slembrouck & Srikant Sarangi. 2006. *Language practices in social work: Categorisation and accountability in child welfare*. London & New York: Routledge.

Hall, Christopher & Stef Slembrouck. 2011. Categorisations of child 'in need' and child 'in need of protection' and implications for the formulation of 'deficit' parenting. In Christopher Candlin & Jonathan Crichton (eds.), *Discourses of deficit*, 63–80. Basingstoke: Palgrave Macmillan.

Healy, Karen. 1998. Participation and child protection: The importance of context. *The British Journal of Social Work* 28 (6). 897–914.

Heritage, John & Anna Lindström. 1998. Motherhood, medicine, and morality: Scenes from a medical encounter. *Research on Language and Social Interaction* 31 (3–4). 397–438.

HM Government. 2018. *Working together to safeguard children: A guide to inter-agency working to safeguard and promote the welfare of children*. London: The Stationery Office.

Holmes, Janet & Maria Stubbe. 2015 [2003]. *Power and politeness in the workplace: A sociolinguistic analysis of talk at work*, 2nd edn. London: Longman.

Holt, Kim & Nancy Kelly. 2016. Why parents matter: Exploring the impact of a hegemonic concern with the timetable for the child. *Child & Family Social Work* 21 (2). 156–165.

Holt, Kim & Nancy Kelly. 2018. Limits to partnership working: Developing relationship-based approaches with children and their families. *Journal of Social Welfare and Family Law* 40 (2). 147–163.

Hood, Rick, Sarah Gorin, Allie Goldacre, Wilson Muleya & Paul Bywaters. 2020. Exploring drivers of demand for child protection services in an English local authority. *Child & Family Social Work* 25 (3). 657–664.

Horwath, Jan & Sukey Tarr. 2015. Child visibility in cases of chronic neglect: Implications for social work practice. *The British Journal of Social Work* 45 (2). 1379–1394.

Land, Victoria, Ruth Parry & Jane Seymour. 2017. Communication practices that encourage and constrain shared decision making in health-care encounters: Systematic review of conversation analytic research. *Health Expectations* 20 (6). 1228–1247.

Lazar, Michelle (ed.). 2005. *Feminist critical discourse analysis: Gender, power and ideology in discourse*. Basingstoke: Palgrave Macmillan.

Legatum Institute. 2020. *Briefing: Poverty during the Covid-19 crisis*. London: Legatum Institute.

Lonne, Bob, Nigel Parton, Jane Thomson & Maria Harries. 2009. *Reforming child protection*. London & New York: Routledge.

MacInnes, Tom, Adam Tinson, Declan Gaffney, Goretti Horgan & Ben Baumberg. 2014. *Disability, long-term conditions and poverty: A report for the Joseph Rowntree Foundation*. London: New Policy Institute.

Mäkitalo, Asa. 2002. Talk in institutional context and institutional context in talk: Categories as situated practices. *Text – Interdisciplinary Journal for the Study of Discourse* 22 (1). 57–82.

Morris, Kate, Will Mason, Paul Bywaters, Brid Featherstone, Brigid Daniel, Geraldine Brady, Lisa Bunting, Jade Hooper, Nughmana Mirza, Jonathan Scourfield & Calum Webb. 2018. Social work, poverty, and child welfare interventions. *Child & Family Social Work* 23 (3). 364–372.

National Children's Bureau. 2012. *Beyond the cuts: Children's charities adapting to austerity*. London: National Children's Bureau.

Parton, Nigel (ed.) 1997. *Child protection and family support: Tensions, contradictions and possibilities*. London & New York: Routledge.

Parton, Nigel. 2014. *The politics of child protection: Contemporary developments and future directions*. Basingstoke: Palgrave Macmillan.

Parton, Nigel. 2017. Comparing child protection systems: Towards a global perspective. In Pat Dolan & Nick Frost (eds.), *The Routledge handbook of global child welfare*, 225–242. London & New York: Routledge.

Parton, Nigel & Sasha Williams. 2017. The contemporary refocusing of children's services in England. *Journal of Children's Services* 12 (2–3). 85–96.

Patrika, Pinelopi & Eleftheria Tseliou. 2016. Blame, responsibility and systemic neutrality: A discourse analysis methodology to the study of family therapy problem talk. *Journal of Family Therapy* 38 (4). 467–490.

Platt, Lucinda. 2009. *Ethnicity and child poverty*. London: Department for Work and Pensions.

Pomerantz, Anita. 1984. Agreeing and disagreeing with assessments: Some features of preferred/dispreferred turn shapes. In John Atkinson & John Heritage (eds.), *Structures of social action*, 57–101. Cambridge: Cambridge University Press.

Rampton, Ben. 2010. Linguistic ethnography, interactional sociolinguistics and the study of identities. In Caroline Coffin, Theresa Lillis & Kieran O'Halloran (eds.), *Applied linguistics methods: A reader*, 234–250. London & New York: Routledge.

Rampton, Ben. 2016. Foucault, Gumperz and governmentality: Interaction, power and subjectivity in the twenty-first century. In Nikolas Coupland (ed.), *Sociolinguistics: Theoretical debates*, 303–330. Cambridge: Cambridge University Press.

Reisigl, Martin & Ruth Wodak (eds.). 2001. *Discourse and discrimination. Rhetorics of racism and antisemitism*. London & New York: Routledge.

Sarangi, Srikant & Celia Roberts. 1999. The dynamics of interactional and institutional orders in work-related settings. In Srikant Sarangi & Celia Roberts (eds.), *Talk, work and institutional order: Discourse in medical, mediation and management settings*, 1–57. Berlin: De Gruyter Mouton.

Sidnell, Jack. 2010. *Conversation analysis: An introduction*. Chichester: Wiley-Blackwell.

Smith, Dorothy. 1978. 'K is mentally ill' the anatomy of a factual account. *Sociology* 12 (1). 23–53.

Smithson, Janet, Anne Barlow, Rosemary Hunter & Jan Ewing. 2017. The moral order in family mediation: Negotiating competing values. *Conflict Resolution Quarterly* 35 (2). 173–196.

Stone, Juliet, Matt Padley & Donald Hirsch. 2019. *Households below a minimum income standard: 2008/9–2016/7*. York: Joseph Rowntree Foundation.

Tanner, Karen & Danielle Turney. 2003. What do we know about child neglect?: A critical review of the literature and its application to social work practice. *Child and Family Social Work* 8 (1). 25–34.

Thompson, Neil. 2016 [1992]. *Anti-discriminatory practice: Equality, diversity and social justice*, 6th edn. London: Macmillan.

Tileaga, Cristian. 2006. Representing the 'other': A discursive analysis of prejudice and moral exclusion in talk about Romanies. *Journal of Community & Applied Social Psychology* 16 (1). 19–41.

Tunstill, Jane & Carolyne Willow. 2017. Professional social work and the defence of children's and their families' rights in a period of austerity: A case study. *Social Sciences and Social Work Review* 19 (1). 40–65.

Van Dijk, Teun A. 2015. Racism in the press. In Nancy Bonvillain (ed.), *Handbook of linguistic anthropology*, 384–392. London & New York: Routledge.

Van Langenhove, Luk. 2017. Varieties of moral orders and the duel structure of society: A perspective from positioning theory. *Frontiers in Sociology* 2 (9). https://doi.org/10.3389/fsoc.2017.00009 (accessed 22 December 2020).

Verhallen, Tessa, Christopher Hall & Stef Slembrouck. 2019. Family support and child protection approaches. Historicising perspectives on contemporary discourses of social work. *Qualitative Social Work* 18 (2). 286–301.

White, Sue & David Wastell. 2011. Theoretical vocabularies and moral negotiation in child welfare: The saga of Evie and Seb. In Christopher Candlin & Srikant Sarangi (eds.), *Handbook of communication in organisations and professions*, 259–276. Berlin: De Gruyter Mouton.

Wodak, Ruth. 2015. *The politics of fear: What right-wing populist discourses mean*. London: Sage.

Zhao, Meng, Jorge Rodriguez & Lilia D. Monzó. 2019. Media discourses that normalize colonial relations: A critical discourse analysis of (im)migrants and refugees. *Language, Discourse & Society* 7 (13). 127–142.

Raquel Lázaro Gutiérrez & Jesús Manuel Tejero González
Chapter 12
Challenging ideologies and fostering intercultural competence: The discourses of healthcare staff about linguistic and cultural barriers, interpreters, and mediators

Abstract: Ideologies are shared representations that are expressed and reproduced through discourse in the social practices of groups (Van Dijk 2006). Whereas ideologies are abstract and general social beliefs, attitudes are expressions and manifestations of the set of beliefs that shape a particular ideology in discourses, defined in terms of the topics that they address. Discourse is, thus, the object of our study, and our aim is to examine the discourses of healthcare staff about migration, translation, interpretation, and mediation, with a special focus on how racist attitudes prevail and how social macro-features such as culture, society, or politics influence the agents (healthcare staff) that participate in communicative encounters between healthcare service providers and immigrants. Using a content analysis methodology, we will analyse comments made by SESCAM (Healthcare Service of Castilla-La Mancha) workers in the discussion forums of an online training course on "Techniques and skills to overcome cultural and linguistic barriers". Knowing SESCAM workers' attitudes helps us target racist and xenophobic behaviours and misconceptions to reorient them. We hope that the results obtained from this study will help to improve the response of health organisations in minimising cultural barriers that hinder the accessibility of migrant populations to advance healthcare equity.

Keywords: attitudes, discourse, translation and interpreting, mediation, migration

1 Introduction

Since 2007, the Healthcare Service of Castilla-La Mancha (SESCAM), in collaboration with the University of Alcalá, has been providing training to its professionals on skills to overcome cultural and linguistic barriers in assisting migrant populations, covering contents such as the use of mediation and interpretation services in the care of patients of immigrant origin, attention to religious and cultural diversity, and the relationship between migration and physical and mental health.

This training, which is offered both onsite and online, has already been taken by more than 3000 professionals belonging to both clinical and non-clinical staff. Within this training, an online course is provided twice a year, which includes discussion forums as part of the teaching-learning methodologies. These foster discussions on course-related topics, namely migration, interculturality, translation, interpretation, and mediation. This chapter explores SESCAM workers' attitudes towards these topics through the analysis of comments on the discussion forums of the online courses offered from 2016 to 2019.

The chapter is structured in 8 sections. The first sections address the relationship between ideology and attitudes and how they are reflected in discourse, which is the object of our study, paying special attention to the context of this study, namely interculturality and multilingual communication in the healthcare setting. Then, the context and the methodology of the study are described, and the main research results are presented, followed by conclusions, limitations, and suggestions for further research.

2 Manifestation of ideologies in discourse

Van Dijk (2006) defines ideologies within a multidisciplinary framework that includes a discursive component (together with a social and a cognitive one). Hence, ideologies are shared representations that are expressed and reproduced in the social practices of groups. Social group members may acquire, confirm, change, or perpetuate ideologies through discourse. However, "ideologies are foundational social beliefs of a rather general and abstract nature" (Van Dijk 2006: 116), whereas attitudes are expressions and manifestations of the set of beliefs that shape a particular ideology in discourses, defined in terms of the topics that they address.

Ideologies are subject to change or even disintegration, although usually through a slow process that involves "many experiences and discourses" (Van Dijk 2006: 116), as both the process of developing and disintegrating ideologies is gradual. For the optimal provision of an institutional service, it may be useful, as it has been proven in our case, to tackle ideologies that might be considered racist, with the aim of reorienting them towards more inclusive and tolerant beliefs (and attitudes) that serve as a basis for universal healthcare assistance to patients of any background. The inconsistency of some of the social beliefs that promote prejudice towards migrant populations is an asset in the disintegration of racist ideology, especially when discussion is encouraged within a professional group made up of individuals from different ideological backgrounds.

Several scholars, such as Van Dijk (2006) and Baker (2006, 2020), have argued that discourse and language are more powerful than we may realise. Language is a weapon of manipulation, and it is used by media institutions to influence our minds (Kostakopoulou 2010). Media representations of migration impact ideas and beliefs that shape public discourse and opinions, including cases where people are not directly associated with or have not experienced encounters with migrant populations.

The set of ideas and beliefs has also been termed "frame", understood as the product of the selection and interpretation of issues and facts. In other words, frames are points of view from which reality is both understood and constructed (Baker 2006). They are recreated in discourse to shape narratives (Durham 1998). Narratives about immigrants include their depiction as lazy, people who steal jobs (Van Dijk 2006), passive victims, a threat to culture, security and welfare, a dehumanised group (Greussing and Boomgaarden 2017), and a homogeneous and problematic group (Baker 2020), amongst other attributions.

The difference between research approaches based on discourse and those based on narratives is that the latter focus on the stories (narratives) behind discourse. These stories contain characters, settings, outcomes, and a plot (Fairclough 1995), which complete the occurrence of discourse or linguistic patterns, even if most of them remain hidden and have to be deducted or inferred. In Baker's (2006: 12) words, "narratives are the stories we elaborate in order to make meaning of our lives and to both guide and justify our actions". This elaboration is collective, as once internalised, narratives are repeated and reconstructed (Harding 2012), resulting in a particular ideology. Furthermore, narratives can also be shaped and circulated by institutions or a group of people belonging to a particular institution, and are related to the notions of truth, knowledge, and power (Baker 2020; Foucault 1980). According to Foucault (1980), in our societies, there are regimes of truth, and discourses are accepted or sanctioned according to whether they are truthful or not. But who is entitled to carry out this task? This is usually in the hands of politicians, governments, institutions, powerful companies, etc. However, alternative discourses can also be produced by particular groups (also professional groups belonging to institutions, as in our case) or individuals.

This is the interplay in which our study is positioned. On the one hand, the aim of our online courses is to circulate a particular narrative that corrects and reorients both individual and collective narratives linked to racist ideologies to foster attitudes and abilities of healthcare staff that enable them to assist all kinds of populations from different backgrounds under the principle of universal assistance. On the other hand, the aim of our study is to examine the discourses of healthcare staff about migration, translation, interpretation, and mediation, with a special focus on how racist attitudes prevail and how social macro-features such as culture, society, or politics influence the agents (healthcare staff) that participate in communicative encounters between healthcare service providers and immigrant patients (Aguilar Solano 2015).

3 Interculturality and health care

As previously stated, the training programme that includes the online courses we are referring to aims to foster the intercultural competence of SESCAM staff members. Before delving into intercultural competence, it is necessary to review other key concepts that are related to (and usually confused with) it: multiculturalism, interculturality, and interculturalism. Our rationale behind this training is that all societies today are multicultural (Tylor [1987] already made this claim in the 1980s). However, there has been an evolution in the understanding of societies where people from different cultures coexist. In the traditional sociological literature on the phenomenon of migration (Bartolomé Pina et al. 1999; Pont Vidal 1994; Ruiz Alonso 2000; Torres Santomé 1997), *multiculturalism* has been understood as the simple juxtaposition of cultures. However, cultural integration is more accurately described as *interculturality,* identified with the interdependence between diverse cultures, capable of exchanging norms, values or models of behaviour in conditions of equality and participation (Aguilar Gil 2011).

Interculturality, in fact, refers to the communicative interaction that occurs between two or more human groups from different cultures (Austin Millán 2004).

Interculturalism goes one step further: it is based on the idea that all cultures are equivalent; there is no culture that can be considered superior to the others, and therefore, it is necessary to find ways to learn from each other to live together and ensure the full participation of all cultures in society and its institutions, since diversity is a source of wealth in an intercultural, pluralistic, and multicultural world (Parekh 2005). Following Yampara (2009), all cultures have positive values and negative or anti-values, and mutual respect requires willingness and ability to express our disagreements, to defend them in front of those with whom we disagree, to discern the difference between respectable and non-respectable disagreement, and to be willing to change our ideas by meeting them with well-reasoned criticism. Interculturalism is at the core of the performance of these actions: as Maalouf (1999: 20) points out, "the more an immigrant perceives that his or her culture of origin is respected, the more he or she will open up to the culture of the host country".

On the other hand, intercultural competence could be defined as the ability of individuals and institutions to respond respectfully and effectively to people of all cultures, classes, ethnic groups, and religious denominations in a way that recognises, affirms, and values cultural differences and similarities, as well as the value of individuals, families, and communities, and that protects and preserves their dignity. There are four key concepts directly related to intercultural competence that have to be addressed to fully achieve it: racism, discrimination, stereotypes, and prejudice (Montes Berges 2008). In Van Dijk's (2006: 96) words:

> [. . .] racism is a complex system of social inequality in which at least the following components are combined:
>
> a) ideologically based social representations of (and about) groups
>
> b) group members' mental models of concrete ethnic events
>
> c) everyday discriminatory discourse and other social practices
>
> d) institutional and organisational structures and activities
>
> e) power relations between dominant white and ethnic minority groups.

It should be noted here that, according to Van Dijk (2006), racism is a social system, whereas ideology is made up of sets of beliefs that organise the social system but are also produced by it. In this chapter, a racist ideology is that which exists in a racist social system: it is built around social representations and mental models, and developed and reproduced through the use of discriminatory discourse, social practices, and institutional activities.

Prejudice has been defined as a negative attitude towards a social group or towards a person perceived as a member of a particular social group (Ashmore 1970). Stereotypes would be the cognitive component of prejudice: those erroneous beliefs about people who belong to that group. Discrimination, in turn, is the behavioural component of prejudice. Unfortunately, many prejudices persist in our society, and translate into discriminatory behaviour. When these behaviours occur in the context of a public service, in addition to discrimination there is inequality and injustice in access to public services, or more specifically to healthcare, which violates the rights of the people who are the targets of discrimination.

For instance, in a study carried out during the first decade of this century on healthcare for the immigrant population in Spain (Jansá and García de Olalla 2004), the following results were found that deconstruct some of the most common stereotypes about migrants and healthcare:
– Mental health: Migration does not imply a greater risk of mental disorders, although adaptive disorders can occur as a consequence of the situations of

intense and prolonged stress to which these people are subjected (for instance, the so-called Ulysses Syndrome or Immigrant Syndrome of Chronic and Multiple Stress, which appears to be linked to the experience of migration).
- Sexually transmitted diseases: Despite the increase in the number of women and men of immigrant origin practicing prostitution, the sources cited in this study found that the rates of HIV infection among the native population and the immigrant population practicing prostitution were similar.
- Use of health services: Despite the popular belief that the immigrant population "abuses" health resources, the data indicate that hospital care for this group is less costly than for the native population, a fact possibly related to the age and previous health status of this group (Cots et al. 2002 cited in Jansá and García de Olalla 2004).

Although Jansá and García de Olalla (2004) were able to contest some common stereotypes about migrants, they are still very present in our mindsets and reflect racist ideologies, which constitute prejudice against social groups whose ethnic origin is different from one's own. Xenophobia, as opposed to racist ideologies, is a prejudice against groups that have cultural values different from ours. One of the tools to prevent and combat xenophobia is intercultural communication, a symbolic process in which people from different cultures create shared meanings. It occurs when there are significant cultural differences that lead to different interpretations and expectations about how to communicate competently.

4 The Interculturality Program of SESCAM

The Interculturality Program of SESCAM not only comprises training for staff members. When it began in 2007, it also included intercultural mediation, translation of documents, and telephone interpreting services. Due to the diversity in the understanding and provision of these services around the world (a sign of underprofessionalisation, as suggested by Lázaro Gutiérrez 2019), we consider it worth mentioning how intercultural mediation, translation, and telephone interpreting were provided. We understand intercultural mediation or social mediation in multiethnic or multicultural contexts as the modality of intervention of third parties in social situations of significant multiculturalism. It is oriented towards the achievement of the recognition of the other person or group and the reconciliation of the parties, communication and mutual understanding, learning and development of coexistence, regulation of conflicts, and ethnoculturally differentiated institutional adaptation (Six 1997; Raga Gimeno 2006; Ortí, Sánchez, and Sales 2008).

In the field of healthcare, linguistic and intercultural mediation facilitates communication between health professionals and immigrants. It is a support system to solve the possible conflicts that can arise from cultural and linguistic barriers, and it aims to facilitate information to patients and to achieve good mutual communication, adherence to treatment, and a good therapeutic relationship. In Spain, intercultural mediators and health interpreters coexist, and both figures are responsible for facilitating communication between service providers and users with limited command of the language of the host country. Interpretation and mediation are different but related interventions. Interpretation allows us to overcome language barriers by facilitating communication between two people (the health professional and the patient), while mediation aims to overcome cultural barriers, facilitating the management of conflicts related to different values, beliefs, customs, or habits of people coming from different cultural backgrounds (Valero Garcés and Lázaro Gutiérrez 2004; Lázaro Gutiérrez 2014). Theoretically, interpreters in the healthcare field limit themselves to transferring information while maintaining a neutral role and remaining faithful to the original text, whereas mediators deal with a greater and more diverse number of tasks, such as providing healthcare personnel with information on the cultural particularities of patients, guiding patients on how the healthcare system works and the services it offers, participating in health promotion activities, and even mediating in cases of conflicts that arise from cultural differences (Vargas Urpí 2013). Mediators, therefore, can intervene with their own voice (García-Beyaert and Serrano Pons 2009), and part of their job is to make sure that both parties meet their expectations (Sales Salvador 2014).

In practice, the differences between mediators and interpreters in the healthcare field are blurred, and it is common for these two professions to be mixed up (Lázaro Gutiérrez 2014), which may suggest a low degree of professionalisation or acceptance of these new professional figures in the society and communities in which they work. Regardless of the name they are given today, it is expected that the same person will be able to perform both tasks (interpretation and mediation) by adapting to the changing contexts of the healthcare field. As a result, we can find interpreters providing clarification on cultural aspects and mediators transferring messages from one language to another (although it should not be forgotten that intercultural mediators do not have to know more than one language and, as an example, we can bring up those who mediate between the Roma and non-Roma ethnic groups in Spain). Given these mixtures and the lack of definitions, some authors have proposed the term *mediador interlingüística e intercultural (MILIC)*, or 'interlinguistic and intercultural mediator' (CRIT 2014), to refer to this new professional figure. A fundamental aspect of the work of the intercultural mediators of SESCAM is, thus, to inform and advise immigrant patients about the functioning of the health system (procedures for obtaining a health card, educational accompaniment by the corresponding centre or hospital, etc.).

In addition to face-to-face intercultural mediation, SESCAM began offering telephone interpretation in 2009 in 54 languages. It was available 365 days a year, 24 hours a day, and accessible from any fixed or mobile phone terminal. The interpreters were university graduates, trained in interpretation and interculturality, and were bilingual, native speakers of one of the languages they interpreted. The importance of healthcare interpreting has been acknowledged in many European countries, including Spain (Faya Ornia 2016). There is a need to provide health services with a complementary interpretation resource to the intercultural mediation service to facilitate access to healthcare for the entire population with limited command of the languages of Spain under the same conditions as the rest of the population (Abril and Martin 2011).

In addition, the translation of written documents was integrated into SESCAM. There was the possibility of requesting a sight translation of a document from the company hired for the telephone interpretation. It had to be sent by fax or e-mail, and the sight translation of the document was rendered by telephone to the healthcare professional by an interpreter. In addition, through a collaboration agreement between the University of Alcalá and SESCAM, general information documents such as models of informed consent forms, information guides for pregnant women, or recommendations for the care of the newborn were also translated into several languages.

Unfortunately, the services of intercultural mediation, telephone interpreting, and translation of documents were suspended in 2011 for budgetary reasons. Since then, a significant number of SESCAM staff members have been fighting to obtain funds to reactivate them.

5 Object, aims, and methodology of the study

The interculturality program of SESCAM has since 2007 included the implementation of training courses for the development of intercultural skills both onsite and online. Their design follows the model of the Isir Network, created by the Andalusian School of Public Health (Serrano Falcón and Mañero Rodríguez 2011). These courses have been held year after year, twice a year, with an annual enrolment of 200 to 300 students. At least 3000 professionals (clinicians, nurses, assistants, and other administration and service staff members) have received training in intercultural competencies throughout these years. In 40 teaching hours, the course *Técnicas y habilidades para supercar barreras culturales y lingüísticas* [Techniques and skills to overcome cultural and linguistic barriers] includes a theoretical introduction to "health organisations competent in interculturality", notions of mediation and interpretation in the care of patients of immigrant origin, attention to religious diversity, a module on the specific characteristics of the care of the Roma population, vaccinations and infectious diseases in the population of immigrant origin in primary care, and the relationship between migration and mental health.

This course includes discussion forums as part of the teaching-learning methodologies. These foster discussion on course-related topics, namely migrations, interculturality, translation, interpretation, and mediation. Our main aim is to explore SESCAM workers' attitudes towards these topics through the analysis of discussion forum comments from the online courses offered from 2016 to 2019. We hope that the results obtained could help to improve the response of health organisations and public services in general to eliminate, or at least minimise, cultural barriers that hinder the accessibility of migrant populations to healthcare in conditions of equity with the rest of the population.

To achieve our aim, an analysis was carried out using content analysis techniques to examine the discourse in the comments made by the health professionals in the course's participation forum. We explore possible cognitive (thoughts) and emotional (feelings) components of the perception that the professionals have of their interaction with patients of immigrant origin. Content analysis is defined by Julien (2008: 120) as "the intellectual process of categorising qualitative textual data into clusters of similar entities, or conceptual categories, to identify consistent patterns and relationships between variables or themes". Content analysis can be either latent, when conducted in an inductive and qualitative way, or manifest, when carried out in a deductive and quantitative manner (Morse 1995). Through content analysis, researchers make sense of data, as they derive meaning from discourse or other artefacts. Using this method, it is possible to identify both conscious and unconscious messages, as the object of analysis is both what is made explicit and what is implied, taking into account the way in which it is expressed and the context that surrounds it.

The kind of content analysis that is performed in this study is latent, that is, qualitative and primarily inductive. Context is used to make sense of the words expressed by SESCAM workers to discover patterns or lines of thought (attitudes) and to later classify information into categories. Our data are extracted from the comments written in the forums of 8 editions of the course "Techniques and skills to overcome cultural and linguistic barriers", offered twice a year from 2016 to 2019 and followed by around 1000 students. The total amount of data is around 1 million words.

Our methodology is organised into two phases:
1. The main exploratory or inductive (Van Gorp 2010) phase involves reading a sample of comments (around one quarter of the whole data set) and classifying them into tentative categories and subcategories.
2. A second, deductive phase consists of the review of all the data, searching for new examples and confirming the pertinence of the classifications.

6 Main results and discussion of findings

The analysis of the comments written by SESCAM workers allows us to know about their feelings, perceptions, and attitudes towards immigration, interculturality, translation, interpretation, and mediation. The main categories obtained after the analysis will be offered and discussed in the following sections.

6.1 Myths and prejudice

The existence of myths, misconceptions, and stereotypes related to migrants and migrations has been the object of study of authors such as Cots et al. (2002), Jansá and García de Olalla (2004), and Greussing and Boomgaarden (2017). In our corpus, we find references both to the stereotypes reported by these authors (*immigrants use healthcare services more than natives, immigrants steal our jobs, immigrants receive more subsidies than natives, immigrants have more mental health conditions, immigrants suffer more from gender-based violence, they bring disease*, etc.) and to the fact that stereotypes exist and must be avoided. The following are examples of the stereotypes *immigrants use healthcare services more than natives* (1) and *immigrants steal our jobs* (2):

> (1) *De acuerdo también con la mayoría de las cosas, que se comentan por parte de todos los compañeros del curso, lo único que pienso, es que cuando emigramos nosotros nos tenemos que atener a unas culturas propias del país al que vamos y tenemos los derechos que nos dan; sin embargo aquí por parte de algunos inmigrantes tienen derecho a más servicios que los propios nativos, y ya no decimos cuando nos imponen sus propias culturas* (May 2018).
>
> [I also agree with most of the things, which have been commented by all the course mates, I just think that, when we emigrate we have to adapt to the cultures of the country we go to and we have the rights we are given; however, here, some immigrants have the right to more [healthcare] services than the natives themselves, not to mention when they impose their own cultures on us.]

(2) *La inmigración aporta positivamente diversidad cultural, aumento de consumo, más mano de obra, pero por desgracia también aporta aspectos negativos como la disminución salarial, competencia laboral, economía sumergida y aumento de la discriminación y xenofobia entre muchos aspectos* (May 2018).

[Immigration positively brings cultural diversity, increased consumption, more workforce, but unfortunately it also brings negative aspects such as lower wages, job competition, underground economy, and increased discrimination and xenophobia amongst many other things.]

There are even some comments that directly address and reverse common misconceptions, such as those stating that immigrants use healthcare services less than natives since they are usually healthy, young people, or those referring to greater access to subsidies by immigrants, as the following example shows.

(3) *Es muy habitual que la población autóctona crean que los inmigrantes se están beneficiando de mayor número de ayudas que la propia población de origen, para ello es habitual en los profesionales tener que hacerse los sordos y centrarse en la situación propiamente dicha de la persona demandante. En estos comentarios influye mucho el desconocimiento, falta de empatía y falta de humanidad pues no ven a la persona sino al inmigrante* (November 2016).

[It is very common that autochthonous populations believe that immigrants are profiting from a greater number of subsidies compared to the native population; to tackle this, it is common amongst professionals to have to turn a deaf ear and focus on the very situation of the demanding person. These comments are very much influenced by a lack of knowledge, lack of empathy and lack of humanity as they do not see the person but the immigrant.]

Immigrants are generally considered in the forums as a homogenous group. However, some comments appear to emphasise the need to not generalise but to acknowledge diversity, as seen in the following example:

(4) *Es evidente que la inmigración es un fenómeno muy complejo. Las características de los inmigrantes no pueden generalizarse, de la misma manera que los fines de la inmigración también son muy dispares. Sin embargo todos (o casi todos) tenemos la misma imagen del inmigrante no regularizado, con bajo nivel socioeconómico y/o escasa cualificación personal* (May 2018).

[It is obvious that immigration is a complex phenomenon. The characteristics of immigrants cannot be generalised, as the goals of immigration are also very diverse. However, we all (or almost all) have the same image of a non-regularised immigrant, with a low socio-economic level and/or low personal qualifications.]

The media have been identified as a promoter of the perpetuation of stereotypes (for instance, the nationality of criminals is mentioned when they are not

Spanish), and training and education in equality and values is suggested both for children at school and workers in their workplaces.

6.2 Empathy and sympathy

Not surprisingly, one of the most salient findings is the marked dichotomy between "we" and "they". With some exceptions, SESCAM staff is made up of workers of Spanish origin who have not lived anywhere but Spain. Although most of them show empathy towards immigrants, they have not migrated themselves. Some of them, aware of the apparent homogeneity of the group, ventured into telling personal stories, including relatives being married to immigrants, some years working abroad, relatives having to travel abroad to find a job, or even their own immigrant backgrounds, with scarce reaction within the forums.

Empathy and solidarity are expressed both as a wish and a personal duty, in that it is emphasised that "we should put ourselves in their shoes", whereas due to the emigration past (and present) of Spain, it is recalled that "we can all be immigrants", as can be seen in the following comment:

(5) *Habría que ponernos todos en la piel de unos padres que no le pueden dar de comer a sus hijos, o de los que saben que si quedan en su país los van a matar . . . para entender las causas por lo que las personas necesitan emigrar. Nosotros haríamos lo mismo* (June 2018).

[We should all put ourselves in the shoes of those parents who cannot feed their children, or of those who do not know whether they will be killed if they stay in their country . . . in order to understand the reasons why people need to migrate. We would do the same.]

However, the line between empathy and sympathy is very thin, and we can perceive the latter in comments that refer to the main difficulties immigrants encounter when entering the host society:

(6) *Yo comprendo perfectamente que puedan tener problemas psicológicos por su forma de vida, por su precariedad laboral, por sus dificultades de adaptación y por tener que soportar, en muchas ocasiones el rechazo y la discriminación de las personas con las que conviven* (May 2019).

[I perfectly understand that they may have psychological problems because of their way of life, their precarious working life, their adaptation difficulties and because they have to often endure rejection and discrimination from those they live with.]

(7) *Creo que ante situaciones nuevas es necesario adaptarse, o intentarlo al menos. En el caso de inmigrantes la adaptación no debe ser fácil (idioma a veces, cultura, costumbres . . .)* (October 2017).

[I think that when faced with new situations, it is necessary to adapt, or to try to, at least. In the case of immigrants, the adaptation does not seem easy (sometimes language, culture, habits . . .).]

Some of these thoughts are linked to the most common misconceptions about immigrants, which have already been compiled in other studies, such as Van Dijk (2006), Greussing and Boomgaarden (2017) or Baker (2020). As such, it can be argued that, in general, SESCAM, as an institution, still has a long way to achieving intercultural competence, as described by Omeir Green (2014):. A more dynamic vision of cultures needs to be fostered to avoid otherness and paternalism. Some voices already point to that objective, as the following example illustrates:

(8) *Yo también pienso como muchos de mis compañeros, que lo más importante es aportar nuestro grano de arena para que no haya esta distinción entre culturas, ya que con que haya una persona que trate a todos por igual, sean de la cultura y la raza que sean, es suficiente para que pueda servir de ejemplo a otros, e incluso sirva de modelo para seguir sus pasos* (November 2016).

[I also think like many of my mates do, that the most important thing is to do our bit in order to eliminate that distinction amongst cultures, as once there is one person who treats everybody equally, regardless of their culture or race, it is enough as an example for others, even as a model to follow his or her steps.]

6.3 Integration, equality, and conviviality

There are many references to the integration of immigrants in our data, some of them very negative. Integration is sometimes perceived as a duty of the immigrant, and it is linked to respect for the host society: "they must show respect, learn our culture and integrate ino our society". Although integration is sometimes presented as a unilateral effort and duty, there are also examples of shared responsibility:

(9) *Todos podemos y debemos poner de nuestra parte para que tanto inmigrantes, cómo otros grupos que puedan estar discriminados se integren en nuestra sociedad y procurar facilitarles las cosas. Evitar que esto suceda es tan sencillo cómo tratarnos con respeto y educación, porque ante todo, somos personas y para ello creo que es muy importante transmitir estos valores desde que somos pequeños. Vivimos en una sociedad multicultural, esto lo vemos desde el colegio donde los niños están acostumbrados a convivir con niños de muchos otros países y para ellos es natural y así tenemos que verlo todos. No hacer ninguna distinción* (November 2016).

[We all can and must try our best so that both immigrants and other groups which might be discriminated against are integrated into our society and try to make things easier for them. Avoiding this [being discriminated] from happening is as easy as treating each other with respect and politeness, because above all, we are persons and for it [integration] to happen, I think it is very important to transmit those values from a young age. We live in a multicultural society, we see this at school where children are used to interacting with children from many other countries, and for them it is natural, and we all have to see it that way. Without making distinctions.]

Dialogue and patience from both sides and mutual adaptation are emphasised as a must to achieve harmonious conviviality. Equality and equal treatment are also recurrent topics, although the focus sometimes is on not depriving the native populations of the same privilege or good treatment that immigrants may receive, as can be seen in the following example:

(10) *Estoy de acuerdo en que para disminuir la xenofobia y la intolerancia la clave está en la tolerancia y el respeto. Pero igual de importante es que el personal sanitario trate a todos los pacientes con igualdad y respeto y proporcionarle una atención personalizada; como que todos los pacientes sean conscientes de todos sus derechos y obligaciones, no solo los derechos* (June 2018).

[I agree in that in order to reduce xenophobia and intolerance, the key is tolerance and respect. But equally important to healthcare professionals is treating every patient equally and respectfully and providing personal assistance, so that all patients are aware of all their rights and obligations, not only their rights.]

6.4 Cultural diversity and intercultural mediation

Culture is both seen as a problem and as an asset. Cultures in contact pose misunderstandings and imply the need to adapt (to each other), as we can see in the following examples:

(11) *Que se asimilan características culturales de otras nacionalidades, religiosas, alimentarias, políticas etc., siendo esto positivo para la sociedad porque la enriquece siempre que no haya confrontación entre las diferentes culturas, pero a la vez que esto es positivo, se puede convertir en hechos negativos en algunos sectores de dicha sociedad, causando enfrentamientos por parte de algunos individuos que no aceptan otra forma de vida en su sociedad, que la que han tenido antes de la llegada masivas de inmigrantes* (June 2018).

[Other cultural, religious, food-related, political characteristics from other nationalities are assimilated, this being positive for the society because it is enriching as long as there is no confrontation amongst the different cultures, but while it is positive, it may be negative in some societal sectors, causing confrontation by some individuals who do not accept any other way of life in their society, apart from the one before the massive arrival of immigrants.]

(12) *También a los inmigrantes nosotros les parecemos "raros". Estoy de acuerdo en trabajar para aprovecharnos de su cultura y enriquecernos. Pero también las personas que vienen a nuestro país deben esforzarse por integrarse y participar de nuestra cultura* (June 2018).

[Immigrants also consider us "strange". I agree in working on it so that we can benefit from their culture and enrich ours. But people who come to our country must make an effort to integrate and participate in our culture.]

The title of the course already depicts culture as problematic as it aims at overcoming cultural barriers. A distinction is made between "our own" culture, "their" culture, and the "institutional" culture. The acknowledgement of the features of one's culture is the first step to recognising others' cultures. On the other hand, it is fascinating that a topic such as the institutional culture, that is, the way in which procedures are organised and behaviours are performed in a particular institution, such as SESCAM, is mentioned and considered by the forum participants. It implies that particular rules apply only inside the institution, for example, treating all patients equally even though members of staff may have other opinions and behaviours outside the workplace.

(13) *Yo creo que a veces, cuando presencias una "discusión" entre dos personas, si puedes observar el proceso con cierta atención, descubres cuándo el motivo del conflicto tiene que ver con su "forma de ser" (incompatibilidad de caracteres, decía Joaquín Sabina en una canción), pero también cuándo el origen no está en ellos, sino en los valores o creencias de una institución o cultura a la que pertenecen, a veces sin saberlo* (October 2016).

[I think that sometimes when you witness an "argument" between two people, if you are able to pay close attention, you will discover when the cause of conflict is related to their "ways" (mutual incompatibility, said Joaquín Sabina in a song), but also when the origin is not in themselves, but in the values and beliefs of an institution or the culture they belong to, sometimes without knowing it.]

Although cultural diversity is generally considered positive and enriching, it is also acknowledged that cultural differences may pose a problem, as seen in the following example:

(14) *Desde mi punto de vista, una de las partes positivas es acercarnos a sus culturas y modos de vida. Y la parte negativa es la mala adaptación por parte de algunas etnias (se están creando "guetos" en pueblos y ciudades y lo que ello conlleva)* (June 2018).

[From my point of view, a positive thing is that we get closer to their cultures and ways of life. And the negative part is the maladaptation of some ethnicities ("ghettos" are being created in villages and towns, with all its implications).]

In fact, culture is perceived as a greater barrier to accessing healthcare services when compared with language. To overcome these cultural difficulties, several tools are suggested, such as training in interculturality to foster cultural competence or the use of intercultural mediators, who are perceived as a one-directional tool aimed at solving cultural conflicts (the mediators teach the immigrant our culture and inform staff about cultural peculiarities of patients, so that the mediators can reorient the behaviours of the staff accordingly).

> (15) *Creo que en muchos aspectos es necesaria la figura de un mediador intercultural ya que por las costumbres, tradiciones, creencias, etc que tienen en sus países de origen no parece lógico que no acepten determinados tratamientos o fórmulas que les van a mejorar o van a hacer más llevadero el dolor, el sufrimiento físico o la enfermedad al provenir de una vida totalmente distinta a la nuestra y que nosotros tampoco comprendemos* (June 2016).
>
> [I think that in many aspects, the presence of an intercultural mediator is needed, because it does not seem logical that their habits, customs, beliefs etc. brought form their home countries (should) prevent them from accepting certain treatments or procedures that will improve their health or alleviate their pain, physical suffering or illness, because they come from a life that is totally different from ours and we do not understand.]

6.5 Language as a barrier

Although the barrier of language in access to healthcare is present in the comments of SESCAM workers, it is less prominent than culture. Participants emphasised the feelings of failure and despair when they do not manage to communicate and even have to let their patients go without being sure they have understood each other. It is also perceived that the lack of a common language or the lack of understanding due to language barriers is a source of mistrust, particularly on the part of immigrants. The following example illustrates this:

> (16) [...] *a veces te queda la sensación interna de que no has podido ayudarle porque no sabes muy bien lo que quieren. Si chapurrean un poco el español, al menos esa sensación disminuye mucho* (May 2018).
>
> [... sometimes you get the internal feeling that you have not been able to help him [the patient] because you do not know what they want. If they speak a bit of Spanish, at least that feeling gets a lot better.]

But what do we need to overcome linguistic barriers? Although some of the participants in the forums think that they can manage by speaking slowly and using gestures and empathy, others explain how they use other tools to communicate. Some patients bring their own interpreter, who can be a relative or a friend – sometimes a child. This is widely criticised, as the general belief is that ad hoc interpreters make mistakes and are not trustworthy. Regarding the use of children as interpreters, SESCAM workers' opinion is that they are not mature enough to carry out this task satisfactorily and that children working as interpreters constitute abuse, as the following examples show:

(17) *En mi lugar de trabajo tratamos con mucha población inmigrante y a veces tenemos que ayudarnos del familiar que entiende algo más de español, pero aun así te quedas con la sensación de que no te han entendido del todo* (October 2016).

[In my workplace, we deal with a sizeable immigrant population and sometimes we have to get help from a relative who knows a little more Spanish, but you still get the feeling that they have not understood you completely.]

(18) [. . .] *cuántas veces sin querer hacemos a la gente dar paseos de más por una falta de entendimiento por ambas partes, por más que te esfuerzas por explicar y apuntar las cosas se va la persona y te quedas dándole vueltas: ¿se habrá enterado?, o el traductor es un niño pequeño que debería estar en el colegio y está día tras día acompañando a sus compatriotas pero tampoco se sabe si lo que les ha explicado es lo correcto por las caras que ponen* [. . .] (May 2018).

[. . . so many times it happens that, without meaning it, we make people walk around unnecessarily because of a lack of understanding from both sides, no matter how you struggle to explain and note things down, the person leaves and you are left thinking and thinking: did he understand? Or the translator is a small child that should be in school and day after day, he is accompanying his fellow compatriots, but you never know if what he has explained is correct judging by their [the fellow compatriots'] facial expressions.]

Some comments are in favour of healthcare staff learning languages. Many feel confident about their command of English and are eager to use it, but it seems that they are not taking into account that English is not spoken by everybody, and their patients may not use it as well as they do. When it comes to the use of languages that the staff does not speak, they suggest finding the support of colleagues who do.

Other tools and resources used to overcome the linguistic barrier are mobile phones, and particularly the use of what they termed "Saint Google", which is not only able to translate words and sentences but also capable of voicing them. However, the use of their own resources is linked to a feeling of survival and the mourning of the loss of a professional telephone interpreting service. In their opinion, this service was lost not only because of budgetary matters, but also because they failed to use it as much as they should have due to time constraints, which prevented them from learning how to access it or use it.[1]

Multilingual guides are mentioned as a good tool to solve linguistic difficulties, although some also mention that they are not useful because using them

---

[1] The SESCAM telephone interpreting service was reactivated in December 2021.

takes time and communication loses fluency. The use of Universal Doctor Speaker, a piece of software that functions as an electronic communication guide, is also mentioned. In addition, those who had worked with intercultural mediators rated the experience very positively. However, among those who did not use any of those resources, confusion occurs, as they refer to Universal Doctor Speaker as assisted translation software or intercultural mediation as onsite interpreting.

The presence of translation, interpretation, and mediation services is generally considered essential, although others argue that if the effort is made to provide them, then immigrants should make the effort to learn our language, so that they are only needed during the first few months of their residency in the country. This is also supported by the idea that communication through an interpreter is slow and impersonal and is therefore not as efficient as direct communication without intermediaries. Some think that interpreters and mediators are not that useful, as there are many words (technical, jargon or slang) that they do not know. Indeed, interpreting and intercultural mediation are difficult tasks, making it impossible to reach perfect accuracy. However, onsite interpreters constitute the best solution to linguistic problems, but they are too expensive.

There is great confusion about what translation, interpretation or mediation are, and some workers refer to both translation and interpretation as translation. Some of them, when they want to refer to the complex process of rendering meaning, which involves not only the translation of words, but the use of inverted commas for the words "translation" or "translate". Some signal that they prefer mediators because telephone interpreters do not take culture into account, which expands on the finding that culture is more salient as a communication barrier when compared to language.

6.6 What are our needs?

Now that we are aware that linguistic and cultural barriers hinder the access of the migrant population to healthcare, how do we solve it? Apart from the classic use of translation, interpreting, and mediation services, SESCAM workers offered some interesting suggestions. Some recommend that the patient's family doctor act as the facilitator of linguistic and mediation services, with the responsibility of providing integral care that includes efficient communication.

> (19) *Pienso que cuando un paciente extranjero es derivado al especialista, es fundamental que el médico de atención primaria haga de filtro y si observa que ese paciente tiene dificultades para entender su enfermedad o su tratamiento le gestione directamente un mediador intercultural que le acompañe al especialista; o lo solicite a quien proceda, no sé si a Atención al Usuario* (June 2018).

[I think that when a foreign patient is referred to a consultant, it is essential that the GP acts as a sieve and if he detects that the patient has difficulties in understanding his condition or his treatment, he should immediately arrange for him an intercultural mediator to accompany him to the consultant; or he can apply for it to the corresponding person, perhaps at User Service.]

An intercultural mediator should be assigned to patients from their very first medical consultation, as it is done with social workers. Basic information documents, such as leaflets or guidelines, should always be translated into different languages so that they are at hand when needed. The same should apply to documents that need to be signed, such as informed consents, for which sight translation by a telephone interpreter is not considered sufficient:

(20) *En mi opinión, hay pequeñas acciones administrativas que también pueden facilitar mucho las tareas del personal sanitario o no que trabaja en el hospital y se enfrenta a este tipo de situaciones. Por ejemplo, ese consentimiento informado en alguno de los idiomas más comunes de las personas extranjeras que acuden a los centros, facilitaría mucho la toma de decisiones por parte de la paciente y el trabajo de la profesional que le atiende* (October 2017).

[In my opinion, there are simple administrative actions that can help medical and non-medical staff working at the hospital and are subjected to these kinds of situations. For instance, providing informed consent forms in one of the most common languages of the foreign people that come to the centres would make decision-making much easier for the patient and facilitate the professional's work.]

Ethics should also be considered at every stage in the integral assistance for migrant patients, both by healthcare providers and linguistic and cultural service providers. It would be ideal that the mediator and the interpreter were the same person and, if possible, the assistance they provide should be complemented by volunteers who accompany the patient for other matters that could include assisting them in buying food or clothes or helping them with administrative matters. It is agreed that both willingness and resources are needed and, when the resources exist, they have to be used efficiently (although some think that interpreters and mediators have never existed – they are an invention of politicians).

7 Conclusion

In this chapter, we have gone through SESCAM workers' attitudes about migration, communication, translation, interpreting, and mediation as presented in the forums of an online course titled "Techniques and skills to overcome cultural and linguistic barriers". As mentioned above, attitudes are expressions and manifestations of a set of beliefs that shape a particular ideology *in discourses, defined in terms of the topics that they address.*

The comments of the forums have allowed us to grasp different ideologies that range from those more tolerant towards migration to those that are marked by racism and xenophobia. Although most of the participants in the forums had an open mindset and were able to recognise and respect other cultures, some voices contributed to the most general misconceptions about migration: "immigrants receive more subsidies than natives", "they steal our jobs", "they abuse the (healthcare) system", etc. Regarding effective communication, SESCAM workers perceive culture as a greater barrier when compared to language. Most of them believe translation, interpretation, and mediation services are essential, and regret having them but not using them enough. This was due to the chronic and increasing lack of time among healthcare providers, which translated into solving problems with whatever was at hand, regardless of its efficacy or accuracy. For this reason, and because patients who do not speak Spanish (well) are a minority, *ad hoc* interpreters are still used (although they are considered to make mistakes); Google Translate is also popular.

Attitudes are manifestations of ideologies based on the principle that ideologies are subject to change and disintegration. One of the main aims of the course is to smooth out racist attitudes and prejudice against immigrants to foster the provision of public and universal healthcare assistance to patients of any background and fight inequality and injustice in access to public healthcare. Knowing SESCAM workers' attitudes helps us target those behaviours and misconceptions to reorient them. We hope that the results obtained from this study help improve the response of health organisations in minimising cultural barriers that hinder the accessibility of migrant populations to healthcare in conditions of equity with the rest of the population.

8 Limitations and further research

The main limitation of this study is the possibility that participants in the forums self-censored their comments. In Van Dijk's words (2006: 124), discourse is not always ideologically transparent and "given specific contextual conditions, speakers may of course hide or dissimulate their ideological opinions".

On the other hand, content analysis is an iterative process, and it is possible to discover new categories each time data are revisited. To validate the results, it is necessary that more researchers examine the data and check the categories we have suggested, which is something that will be approached in future studies.

References

Abril, María Isabel & Anne Martin. 2011. La barrera de la comunicación como obstáculo en el acceso a la salud de los inmigrantes. In Francisco Javier García Castaño & Nina Kressova (eds.), *Actas del I Congreso Internacional sobre Migraciones en Andalucía*, 1521–1534. Granada: Instituto de Migraciones.

Aguilar Gil, Marta. 2011. *La Educación intercultural como vía de integración social: opiniones y actitudes de la comunidad escolar ante el nuevo modelo educativo*. Salamanca: Universidad Pontificia de Salamanca dissertation.

Aguilar Solano, María. 2015. Non-professional volunteer interpreting as an institutionalized practice in healthcare: A study on interpreters' personal narratives. *Translation & Interpreting* 7 (3). 132–148.

Ashmore, Richard D. 1970. Prejudice: Causes and cures. In Barry E. Collins (ed.), *Social psychology: Social influence, attitude change, group processes, and prejudice*, 245–339. Reading, MA: Addison-Wesley.

Austin Millán, Tomás. 2004. *Comunicación intercultural. Antologías sobre la Cultura Popular Indígena*. México: Conaculta.

Baker, Mona. 2006. *Translation and conflict: A narrative account*. London & New York: Routledge.

Baker, Mona. 2020. Translation and solidarity in the century with no future: prefiguration vs. aspirational translation. *Palgrave Communications* 6. 1–16.

Bartolomé Pina, Margarita, Flor A. Cabrera Rodríguez, Julia Victoria Espín López, María Ángeles Marín Gracia & Mercedes Rodríguez Lajo. 1999. Diversidad y multiculturalidad. *Revista de Investigación Educativa*, 17 (2). 277–320.

Cots, Francesc, Xavier Castells, Carme Ollé, Rafael Manzanera, Jordi Varela & Oriol Vall. 2002. Perfil de la casuística hospitalaria de la población inmigrante de Barcelona. *Gaceta Sanitaria* 16. 376–84.

CRIT (eds.). 2014. *La práctica de la mediación interlingüística e intercultural en el ámbito sanitario*. Granada: Comares.

Durham, Frank D. 1998. News frames as social narratives: TWA flight 800. *Journal of Communication* 48 (4). 100–117.

Fairclough, Norman. 1995. *Critical discourse analysis*. London: Longman.

Faya Ornia, Goretti. 2016. La necesidad de servicios de traducción e interpretación en el sector sanitario. La situación en Londres, Düsseldorf y Madrid. *Entreculturas* 7–8. 543–574.

Foucault, Michel. 1980. Truth and power. Colin Gordon (transl.). In Colin Gordon (ed.), *Power/Knowledge: Selected interviews and other writings 1972–1977*, 109–133. New York: Random House.

García-Beyaert, Sofía & Jordi Serrano Pons. 2009. Recursos para superar las barreras lingüístico-culturales en los servicios de salud. In Joaquín Morera Montes, Alberto Alonso Barbarro & Helena Huerga Aramburu (eds.), *Manual de atención al inmigrante*, 53–66. Madrid & Barcelona: Ergon.

Greussing, Esther & Hajo G. Boomgaarden. 2017. Shifting the refugee narrative? An automated frame analysis of Europe's 2015 refugee crisis. *Journal of Ethnic and Migration Studies* 43 (11). 1749–1774.

Harding, Sue-Ann. 2012. "How do I apply narrative theory?": Socio-narrative theory in translation studies. *Target* 24 (2). 286–309.

Jansá, Josep M. & Patricia García de Olalla. 2004. Salud e inmigración: nuevas realidades y nuevos retos. *Gaceta sanitaria* 18. 207–213.

Julien, Heidi. 2008. Content analysis. In Lisa M. Given (ed.), *The Sage encyclopedia of qualitative research methods*, 120–121. Los Angeles: Sage.

Kostakopoulou, Dora. 2010. The anatomy of civic integration. *The Modern Law Review* 73 (6). 933–958.

Lázaro Gutiérrez, Raquel. 2014. Use and abuse of an interpreter. In Carmen Valero Garcés (ed.), *(RE)Considerando ética e ideología en situaciones de conflicto*, 214–221. Alcalá de Henares: Servicio de Publicaciones de la Universidad de Alcalá.

Lázaro Gutiérrez, Raquel. 2019. Occupation as part of our identity: A pilot study on translators' and interpreters' visual narratives. In Eugenia Dal Fovo & Paola Gentile (eds.), *Translation and interpreting. Convergence, contact and interaction*, 89–126. Bern: Peter Lang.

Maalouf, Amin. 1999. *Identidades asesinas*. Fernando Villaverde (transl.). Madrid: Alianza.

Montes Berges, Beatriz. 2008. Discriminación, prejuicio, estereotipos: conceptos fundamentales, historia de su estudio y el sexismo como nueva forma de prejuicio. *Iniciación a la Investigación* 3. 1–16.

Morse, Janice M. 1995. The significance of saturation. *Qualitative Research* 5 (2). 147–149.

Omeir Green, Cyril. 2014. Lección inaugural de la Maestría de Comunicación Intercultural, Bluefields, RAAS. *Revista Universitaria del Caribe* 10 (1). 29–32.

Ortí, Roberto, Enric Sánchez & Dora Sales. 2008. Interacción comunicativa en la atención sanitaria a inmigrantes: diagnóstico de necesidades (in)formativas para la mediación intercultural. In Beatriz Gallardo, Carlos Hernández & Verónica Moreno (eds.), *Lingüística clínica y neuropsicología cognitiva. Actas del Primer Congreso Nacional de Lingüística Clínica*, 114–139. Valencia: Universitat.

Parekh, Bhikhu. 2005. *Repensando el multiculturalismo*. Sandra Chaparro Martínez (transl.). Barcelona: Istmo.

Pont Vidal, Josep. 1994. Políticas municipales de extranjeros y multiculturalidad. *Papers. Revista de Sociología*, 43. 149–160.

Raga Gimeno, Francisco. 2006. Comunicación intercultural y mediación en el ámbito sanitario. *Revista española de lingüística aplicada* 1. 217–230.

Ruiz Alonso, Felipe. 2000. Emigración y multiculturalidad en la Unión Europea. *Sociedad y Utopía*, 16. 201–224.

Sales Salvador, Dora. 2014. La delgada línea roja de la imparcialidad. In CRIT (eds.), *La práctica de la mediación interlingüística e intercultural en el ámbito sanitario*, 55–90. Granada: Comares.

Serrano Falcón, Carolina & Carlos Mañero Rodríguez. 2011. El fenómeno de la inmigración sanitaria en Andalucía: el modelo granadino. In Francisco Javier García Castaño & Nina Kressova (eds.), *Actas del I Congreso Internacional sobre Migraciones en Andalucía*, 1467–1478. Granada: Instituto de Migraciones.

Six, Jean-François. 1997. *Dinámica de la mediación*. Pepa Larraz Genovés (transl.) Barcelona: Paidós.

Torres Santomé, Jurjo. 1997. Multiculturalidad y antidiscriminación. *Cuadernos de Pedagogía*, 264. 30–34.

Tylor, Edward B. 1987. *Antropología: introducción al estudio del hombre y de la civilización*. Antonio Machado y Álvarez (transl.). Barcelona: Alta Fulla.

Valero Garcés, Carmen & Raquel Lázaro Gutiérrez. 2004. Estudio empírico sobre la comunicación entre personal sanitario y pacientes inmigrantes. In Carles Serra & Josep Miquel Palaudàrias (eds.), *Actas del IV Congreso sobre la inmigración es España: ciudadanía y participación*, 1–4. Girona: Servicio de Publicaciones de la Universidad de Girona.

Van Dijk, Teun A. 2006. Ideology and discourse analysis. *Journal of Political Ideologies* 11 (2). 115–140.

Van Gorp, Baldwin. 2010. Strategies to take subjectivity out of framing analysis. In Paul D'Angelo & Jim Kuypers (eds.), *Doing news framing analysis: Empirical and theoretical perspectives*, 84–108. London & New York: Routledge.

Vargas Urpí, Mireia. 2013. ISP y / o mediación intercultural: la realidad de los profesionales que trabajan en el contexto catalán. *Cuadernos de Aldeeu* 25. 131–163.

Yampara, Simón. 2009. Interculturalidad: encubrimiento o descubrimiento de las matrices civilizatorio-culturales. *ISEES: Inclusión Social y Equidad en la Educación Superior* 4. 33–56.

Brett A. Diaz & Marika K. Hall
Chapter 13
Taking a corpus-based approach to investigating discourse and ideology in the language sciences

Abstract: This volume takes on discourse and ideology, concepts entrenched in many fields and subfields across language-focused study. This dispersion has led to the concepts becoming at times contested, conflated, and in other words, difficult to nail down precisely. In an attempt to better understand this tension, this chapter explores the use of ideology and discourse in the context of academia by looking at research articles that take them on as subjects. To do this, we draw from contemporary work in corpus-assisted discourse studies (Partington, Duguid, and Taylor 2013), collocation (Sinclair 1991), and empirical semantics (Sinclair 2004; Stubbs 1995, 2009), to capture the patterns of language use involving the nodes DISCOURSE and IDEOLOGY. Our findings reveal that each word has strong, consistent collocations that influence the meaning of the word in use. Each word's patterned meaning becomes identifiable through repeated, systematic use, especially when they function as modifiers, head nouns, and compound phrases. Further, these patterns partially explain the blurring of the two terms, as a result of the constructions the terms tend to appear in. We conclude by suggesting that the relation between discourse and ideology may be better depicted as a dialectical relation, rather than contested or in contention.

Keywords: discourse, ideology, language use, corpus-assisted discourse analysis, semantics, collocation

1 Introduction

In this chapter, we attempt to disambiguate how discourse and ideology are actually employed by academics through a corpus analysis. Corpus linguistics, or more specifically corpus-assisted discourse studies (Partington, Duguid, and Taylor 2013), provides a fruitful approach to examining "real life" language use on a large scale. It has increasingly been employed in qualitative works within discourse and critical discourse analytical studies (e.g., Baker 2006; Baker et al. 2008; Koteyko 2006), including, but not limited to news discourses (e.g., Baker et al. 2008; Bednarek and Caple 2014), legal and political discourses (e.g., Diaz and Hall 2020; Subtirelu 2013), as well as studies dealing with language policy and planning (e.g., Fitzsimmons-Doolan 2014). As such, corpus-assisted methods also lend themselves to examining ideologies – for example, in Diaz and Hall (2020), the authors demonstrate a means through which ideological structures can be identified in texts. More specifically, their analyses reveal ideological structures that underpin legal texts surrounding language policy and planning in the United States. For example, their analysis of collocates of "language" reveals that left-positioned words (those that preceded "language" in a stretch of words) included terms such as "American", "native", "English", and "foreign" which is indicative of hegemonic institutional and legal practices and ideologies categorizing individuals based on ethnolinguistic assumptions (cf. Subtirelu 2013; Vessey 2017).

Here, we are extending a similar approach to examining the use of discourse and ideology in order to further illuminate the actual usages of the concepts in the context of academia by looking at a corpus of research articles that feature them. We take an empirically based approach to the topic by employing corpus linguistic methods to identify, extract, and analyze instances of their use. We locate frequently used multi-word sequences, called collocations (discussed more fully in Section 3), that carry the meanings of the terms. More specifically, we are interested in how the collocates of the two node words (DISCOURSE and IDEOLOGY) cluster together, as the words that co-occur with them create meaning categories and insights into how the nodes are used and conceptualized. Moreover, frequent co-occurrences of certain words alongside ideology and discourse have the potential to convey implicit messages (Sinclair 1991; Baker et al. 2008; Hunston 2002). For example, as Baker, Gabrielatos, and McEnery (2012) found, the node "Muslim" co-occurred with terms such as "community", "world", and "extremist" in the British press (1998–2009). Although these are just a few examples of the noun collocates, a picture already emerges as to how "Muslim" is used in these particular news discourses (e.g., homogeneity and conflict, as the authors note). Although the authors are careful not to postulate as to how and to what extent readers internalize these, if one takes the position that reality is constructed through discourse (e.g., Potter 1996; Holborow 2015), then collocations at least have the potential of shaping how we understand, conceptualize, and employ particular words.

This approach is also conducive to disambiguating ideology and discourse, as their collocations may reveal subtle differences in their usage. In other words, even if discourse and ideology are thought to be somewhat interchangeable, or overlap in meaning, a collocation analysis may reveal that they are not actually used identically, and further, what the potential differences are. Thus, we are less interested in how or whether scholars are explicitly defining the concepts in their articles, but rather what is revealed by the actual phrasal-level use of the concepts in their local textual environs, in order to uncover the linguistic differences and similarities between the two that reveal their lexical semantics.

In the following sections, we first provide definitions for both discourse and ideology (Section 2), followed by a description of our corpus and methods (Section 3). In Section 4, we introduce the most frequent collocates for both nodes, as well as examples to illustrate how they appear in their actual context. We further discuss these findings in Section 5 and provide our concluding remarks in Section 6.

2 Discourse and ideology

As pointed out throughout this volume, many branches of academic research in linguistics and related fields utilize both discourse and ideology as conceptual frames or descriptors. However, they are sometimes used without a robust definition, which presupposes a shared knowledge among academics regarding what each concept means and/or presupposes (e.g., Mills 2004). Simultaneously, there is an extensive body of literature acknowledging the elusiveness of the concepts, as well as their overlapping usages, and a number of theoretical frameworks have been proposed (e.g., Fagerholm 2016; Hamilton 1987; Purvis and Hunt 1993; Van Dijk 1998). As such, it may be difficult for junior and senior scholars alike to navigate the discourses (pun intended) regarding discourse and ideology in academia.

As a starting point, it may be worth briefly examining how ideology and discourse are commonly defined, as well as their potential conflation. As Purvis and Hunt (1993: 491) note, "one of the distinctive features of contemporary post-Marxism is the displacement of the concept of ideology by that of discourse", capturing the practice of conflating the two concepts. This may be in part because ideology, for some, may have a negative connotation (Määttä 2022 [this volume]). For example, politicians may accuse their opponents of subscribing to a particular ideology, while maintaining that they themselves are free from ideological bias or view their own ideologies as positive and others' as negative (e.g., Lopes 2015; Van Dijk 2013). This may also be evident in contrasting "ideological" with "scientific" in academia, whereby the former may be utilized to undermine certain fields of inquiry in the humanities or social sciences, for example. In other words, ideologies can be construed to be in opposition to someone else's "knowledge" or "truth", which may be too loaded for some scholars, prompting the use of the perhaps more neutrally viewed discourse.

Of course, this practice is also dependent on how the concepts are understood, which may determine the ways in which they are employed. For example, some simply define discourse as language use, or language that exceeds the sentence level (e.g., Koteyko 2006) with the purpose of examining specific linguistic features, which may then relate to broader social issues. For others, though, discourse itself constitutes social practice (Schiffrin 1994; Fairclough [1995] 2010), including relations of communication between people, events, or objects (Fairclough 2010), with the recognition by scholars such as Scollon (2001) that although discourse and social action are linked, those links are not always discernable. Discourse can also be understood with or without underlying assumptions regarding power and power relations (e.g., Foucault 1972, 1977, 1982; Van Dijk 1998), or as Gee (1999) would refer to them: "small-d" (language use) and "big D" (language use + social and material aspects). When these other social aspects, and power, are thought to (at least in part) constitute discourse, this is where ideology may become intertwined with it. Similarly, while ideology might simply be understood as beliefs or attitudes, there are a number of elements in the definitions across scholars that distinguish one ideology from another in terms of power relations, cognition, identity, and the means through which it is distributed, or in what ways it can be expressed, to name a few (e.g., Fairclough 2010; Hamilton 1987; Holborow 2007; Wodak 2002; Woolard 1998; Van Dijk 2013; Vološinov 1973). One, if not the only means of distribution and expression of ideologies, however, is discourse (especially if discourse is thought to extend to social and material aspects as well).

If discourse were simply understood as language use and ideology as beliefs, the distinction could be relatively straightforward. However, if discourse is thought to be part of cognition as the site in which reality is constructed and represented (e.g., Van Dijk 2006a; Edwards 1996), then teasing apart language use from beliefs could become more difficult. To this point, people's thought and social experience are entwined, and they navigate the world through discourse. Cognition in this way is related to both social activity (discourse, language use) and a larger frame of understanding (beliefs, ideology). This interweaving then could be one site of inconsistency, because both discourse and ideology would constitute core elements of social reality, constructed through the language we see and hear. In a Foucauldian (e.g., Foucault 1972) sense, for example, discourses shape the ways in which individuals construct a worldview – both in its material and immaterial senses – but also how we interact with others through actions that are socially constructed and preferred/dispreferred. Thus, ideologies are produced and reproduced in and through social practice. This creates a notable overlap where both discourse and ideology can be understood as being forms, components, and constitutive of social practice (cf. Fairclough 2010; Määttä 2014; Potter et al. 1990; Van Dijk 2006b).

3 Corpus of academic articles

Our data (Table 13.1) come from research articles published in major English-language journals whose articles include analyses featuring discourse and ideology, and have digitally accessible articles available dating back to at least 1990.[1] Once we had identified journals that fit the criteria, we searched for articles that included either discourse, ideology, or both as subject terms, keywords, in the title, or abstract (in the absence of keywords). We then confirmed that all of the articles dealt with these topics by reading the abstracts for the selected items. These methods produced a total of 869 articles published between 1990 and 2019 from 4 journals: *Discourse & Society (DS)*, *Language & Communication (LC)*, *Language in Society (LS)*, and *Multilingua (ML)*. Some journals, such as *Discourse & Communication*, were excluded as they either were not established until after 1990, or we were unable to obtain digital access. As such, it is important to note that the scope of the corpus is limited in its breadth in terms of the number of journals and articles, as well as the language used in the texts. In the following discussion, we will mark examples with the abbreviation for each journal (DS, LC, LS, and ML), alongside the year it was published (e.g., DS2000 for *Discourse & Society*, 2000).

Table 13.1: Total corpus figures.

Measure	Count	
Articles	869	
Words	8,629,472	
Word types	126,050	
	Discourse	**Ideology**
Collocate[1] Types	2,839	586
Collocate Tokens	125,990	16,560

[1]Collocate measured as: Frequency ≥5, Span ±3, MI + Log-likelihood ≥3.0, Range ≥5.

We used AntConc[2] (Anthony 2020) to view and analyze our corpus, and generated the top 50 collocations of each term, followed by concordance analysis for their semantic preference. AntConc takes spates of text that include certain terms,

---

[1] Originally, this last criterium was established to account for potential differences in the usages of the terms over time – however, this did not arise as a salient issue.
[2] A freeware corpus analysis toolkit for concordance and text analysis.

or in our case collocations, and aligns them vertically, one instance stacked on another, called concordances (Figure 13.1). We did not use lemmatized texts, instead restricting our searches to the specific forms DISCOURSE and IDEOLOGY. AntConc allowed us to evaluate collocations of DISCOURSE or IDEOLOGY quickly, and in context, to compare with other uses. Collocation, in brief, is the habitual co-occurrence of two or more words together (Firth 1957; Sinclair 1991), which are identified by statistical methods, e.g., mutual information (MI) score (Cheng, Greaves, and Warren 2006; Church and Hanks 1990; Stubbs 1995; Xiao and McEnery 2006). We defined collocations as words co-occurring with either DISCOURSE or IDEOLOGY a minimum of 5 times, within a span of 3 spaces from the referent word, an MI + Log-likelihood score of 3.0 or greater and occurring in at least 5 different articles. Collocates will be presented in capitals for the analysis, and italicized in excerpts, to differentiate them from more general uses or descriptive uses, e.g., DISCOURSE, the node collocate, will be stylized to separate it from discourse, the subject of an article.

materiality and advantage that is sought/achieved. discourse is thus ideological in that it not only (a) construes and
revealing and representative of the ugandan aids discourse, of its ideological dilemmas and conflicts. condoms ar
e square is considered the strategic principle of all ideological and political discourse, to the point that the core mea
nasize good/bad things of us/them) one finds in all ideological discourse (van dijk, 1998, 2003). since social–politica
ift. cavanaugh 2004 also describes nostalgia as an ideological-affective discourse of language shift among bergam
:...' (berkson, 1920: 39). in the 'americanism as an ideological process' (conservative) discourse, language was the
ak, 1997) because it incorporates the historical and ideological contexts of discourse used by participants. our case i
are a valuable starting point to study cognitive and ideological determinants of discourse. thanks to the ubiquity of
as a valuable starting point to study cognitive and ideological determinants of discourse (hart, 2010; koller, 2005).
ways involves ideologies, ideological attitudes and ideological discourse structures (see the special double issue of

Figure 13.1: Example of concordance lines.

We then conducted concordance analysis for each collocation in its local text, in order to assess their semantic categories, or their semantic preference. A collocation's semantic preference is a way of understanding what the text is about, what it means, by reading not just the collocation but the surrounding text or talk. That preference is understood in light of a number of linguistic forms, including its words, syntactic organization, and morphology, as they come together in regular, syntagmatic constructions (Sinclair 2004). In our data, we use tables to present the collocate, its syntactic position (left or right of the node word), and its MI score. All three are minimally necessary to establish a preference analysis: each collocation, with collocates in patterned positions, appearing at better-than-chance rates. Thus, meaning is conveyed not by individual words but phrases, used in frequent, consistent patterns. In our study, preference analysis consisted of reading each line containing a collocation, to evaluate the way that collocation is used, to see not just that a collocation appeared, but what sorts of topics were being addressed consistently by those terms, and their lexicogrammatical forms. This allowed us to inductively understand the conditions under which those terms would be called upon, and eventually find common characteristics in each context, revealing the semantics underlying the language use. To better understand semantic preference, Stubbs (2009: 124) gives us the example of *budge*. *Budge* collocates frequently with negations positioned immediately to the left: *won't budge*; *don't budge*. An expanded analysis revealed that these collocations happen with sturdy objects, such as doors, and locks. Thus, the semantic preference of *budge* is to occur (1) with left-positioned negations, and (2) with a small subset of words that, when they appear together, confer a meaning of something like to be sturdy or not to give way.

In the following analysis, we demonstrate how discourse and ideology appear in the data. Although some usages presented here may seem quite intuitive, it is nevertheless important to establish that those intuitions actually materialize in practice as to avoid relying on assumptions. Furthermore, through demonstrating the different ways of looking and thinking about the corpus results we hope to provide a fertile starting point for further examinations of discourse data utilizing corpus methods. We will organize our report around semantic groupings of DISCOURSE and IDEOLOGY as they appear in the texts: as academic-genre and technical uses (4.1); as categories of discourse and ideology (4.2); overlapping collocations (4.3); as distinct concepts with specific syntactic formats (4.4). Within each section, as stated above, we provide a list of the most frequent collocates for each grouping, and further illustrate their immediate co-texts through examples. It is important to note that these examples are merely intended to illuminate and expand on the statistical data to show how syntactic positions, lexical items, and morphology contribute to the meaning, rather than the examples individually constituting the analysis.

4 Semantic groupings of discourse and ideology

4.1 Academic and technical uses of discourse and ideology

Perhaps the most intuitive semantic grouping, considering the corpus, forms around academic and technical uses of DISCOURSE and IDEOLOGY, and as such, it provides a very accessible starting point. We claim that it is intuitive, as within the practice of academic writing and research journal articles, we would certainly expect a rich and consistent set of technical and metadiscursive terms (Tables 2 and 3) concerned with, for example, methodological issues (e.g., discourse analysis). This is especially true for discourse, which we have selected to discuss first.

Thus, to begin, as seen in Table 13.2 below, DISCOURSE has semantic functions as a concept in and of itself but is also a technical term with such collocates as MARKERS, ANALYSTS, CONTEXT, and PARTICIPANTS, which tend to be positioned to the right of DISCOURSE. These sorts of technical or metadiscursive terms are methodological, and the sorts of technical aspects of studying discourse. The terms and collocates included below are functionally constrained to the genres and professional language use of which they are a part, and this semantic group differentiates itself from the object of analysis or the subject under study, which is better captured in Section 4.2 below, where discourse specifies areas of content.

Table 13.2: Collocates of academic and technical uses of *discourse*.

Collocate	Slot[1]	Frequency	MI Score
approach	R	351	5.55
markers	R	327	6.80
historical	R	269	5.42
analysts	R	255	7.03
study	L	230	3.73
context	M	194	3.40
research	M	150	3.16
marker	R	150	6.34
based	R	133	3.45
analytic	R	131	6.37
using	L	129	3.77
theory	M	114	4.24
participants	R	113	3.05
genre	R	109	4.61

[1] Slot refers to the habitual position of the collocate relative to the referent word: to the right (R), left (L), or mixed positioning (M), meaning the word appeared in similar frequencies R or L.

On the one hand, collocates in this group make up the signs of scholarship expected in research articles. They tend to appear in analytical reports, data descriptions, and methods sections of the articles. In a sense, these are the observed constituents of discourse that the authors reveal. At a purely metadiscursive level, APPROACH, HISTORICAL (primarily in the form of DISCOURSE-HISTORICAL), STUDY, RESEARCH, BASED, and THEORY are components of the genre of research articles. In other words, DISCOURSE in this group is marked by the genre, and rhetorical moves made by members of this community when explaining their theoretical and methodological orientations. However, it also tells us that discourse is a focal point of inquiry, rather than a feature of something else, such as social ideas or social groups. To provide a couple of examples:

(1) a *discourse-based* rhetorical approach reveals (LC2017)

(2) we conduct our analysis within the framework of the *discourse-historical approach* (DHA) in *critical discourse analysis* (CDA) (DS2012)

A case that deviates from this pattern includes BASED without hyphenation (i.e., discourse-based):

(3) they form part of a particular kind of racist discourse, a *discourse based on fear* – fear of loss of livelihood, and loss of cultural identity, fear of the unknown and unknowable 'other' (DS1995)

Here, DISCOURSE BASED refers to a fear that is attached to discourse, rather than being strictly tied to academic/methodological/conceptual usages. Importantly, thus, as we point out in our previous sections, it is important that the researcher examine the contexts in which these collocates appear as to avoid overgeneralizations or conjectures.

As with discourse, IDEOLOGY is also associated with technical, academic, and metadiscursive language (Table 13.3). However, it is markedly more limited, as there were only three terms that emerged in the analysis: ANALYSIS (left), EXPRESSED (right), and CRITIQUE (left).

Table 13.3: Collocates of academic and technical uses of *ideology*.

Collocate	Slot	Frequency	MI Score
analysis	L	45	3.14
expressed	R	15	4.60
critique	L	15	5.59

The most frequent collocate, ANALYSIS, always occurs as ideology being analyzed (i.e., an analysis of ideology) or in lists, such as in keywords (e.g., IDEOLOGY, critical discourse ANALYSIS . . .) implying that ideology is indeed something to be analyzed. However, while ideology is the point of interest, it is typically accessed through a means of, e.g., critical discourse analysis. This, of course, is also quite intuitive when ideology is considered a belief, necessitating an access point, such as discourse.

As for the remaining two collocations, CRITIQUE, in our corpus, is commonly used either as IDEOLOGY CRITIQUE, or CRITIQUE OF IDEOLOGY, both of which attach themselves primarily to Marxist thought (as apparent from, e.g., citations or explicit mentions of Marxism in the vicinity of CRITIQUE + IDEOLOGY). Finally, EXPRESSED refers to the location or manifestation of ideology, again attaching discourse (*text* in the example below) to ideology as an access point:

(4) whether one's ideology is *expressed* directly in the text or not (DS2004)

To some degree, this reveals that ideology has a meaning that sets it apart from discourse in the way it is used to perform genre conventions. Our findings points to discourse being wrapped up in a variety of academic language that goes beyond its investigation as a subject, such as also reflecting methods and approaches, while ideology does not share these characteristics. It seems that people do not express their ideology or that they are engaging in an ideological project, while they are more transparently participating in (per se, academic) discourse. Thus, while discourse can have markers (Table 13.2), ideology is not discussed in this way – i.e., scholars are not engaging in examining ideological markers in texts. Rather, in order to study ideologies, one must access them indirectly through appointed indicators (e.g., textual features [discourse]). As such, in an academic and technical sense, discourse and ideology are sometimes related but not interchangeable, as the former provides an access point to the latter.

4.2 Categories of discourse and ideology

Perhaps the most interesting group that materialized in our analysis was predominantly left-positioned types, or categories, of DISCOURSE (Table 13.4) and IDEOLOGY (Table 13.5) in (e.g., MEDIA DISCOURSE or POLITICAL IDEOLOGY). As we shall see again with collocates in Section 4.4.1 where DISCOURSE is left-positioned, the position of the collocate has a distinct, identifiable effect on what discourse means. The exception to left-positioned categorial collocates is TYPES which tends to appear to the right of DISCOURSE. This collocate nonetheless reifies the categorical aspect of the discourse under study: [*DISCOURSE*] *TYPES*. It is worth recalling here that these collocations, as tokens of a certain form in language use, are prone to some variation while the core form remains. In this case, typically left-positioned collocates are discursive emanations of particular social groups, or avenues of power. This then is the substance of discourse.

These left-positioned collocates, such as POLITICAL and INSTITUTIONAL, for example, describe the subject matters of discourse that are being scrutinized, and thus what types of discourse they care categorized into. There is quite a range of subjects present in the collected articles of our corpus, but the role of categorizing with left-positioned collocates is consistent. The consistency of left-positioned categories demonstrates that discourse is typically accompanied by the area associated with it (e.g., PUBLIC, MEDIA, PARLIAMENTARY, ACADEMIC), or the purpose of its contents (e.g., POLITICAL, RACIST, INSTITUTIONAL, RACIAL), showing discourse to also be a matter of activity, as much as a subject of its own.

Table 13.4: Collocates as categories of *discourse*.

Collocate	Slot	Frequency	MI Score
political	L	1343	5.44
critical	L	1328	7.13
public	L	611	5.08
media	L	483	5.02
news	L	353	4.67
racist	L	208	5.27
new	L	192	3.10
power	L	190	3.65
dominant	L	182	5.02
institutional	L	179	5.02
types	R	173	4.84
forms	L	146	3.71
order	L	144	3.33
french	L	137	4.25
racial	L	129	4.57
ideological	L	129	3.65
level	L	126	3.69
parliamentary	L	120	6.49
discriminatory	L	103	6.57
academic	L	102	5.13

Each category above represents some descriptive content about discourse. They appear typically as adjectives, and show that as a subject, discourse tends to be discussed in the context of politics, power, and social issues more broadly. Furthermore, the appearance of modifiers CRITICAL and POWER alongside DISCOURSE point to the prevalence of critical discourse analysis/studies being utilized widely.

In all, however, 15 of the top 50 most common collocates for discourse deal directly with some political or social type of discourse, such as in Excerpt 5 below:

(5) in Catalan *political discourse*, Islam is the only religion that is referred to in negative contexts (DS2017)

Importantly, these results show that discourse is often a feature of something, some visible element of that topic, rather than standing on its own. Discourse, then, becomes a ground for something that scholars are investigating, providing objects of analysis. In Excerpt 5, for example, what is being investigated in POLITICAL DISCOURSE is not discourse in itself, but how and in which contexts certain things are discussed (here, religion). Furthermore, some scholars investigate these broader themes through a micro-lens. In other texts in the corpus, for example, linguistic features or language use are examined in conjunction with, e.g., attitudes and ideologies embodied or furthered through discourse.

Thus, discourse has a tightly bundled semantic usage where a left-slotted collocate tends to accompany it, outlining it as a type of social activity in certain social conditions. The most frequent co-selection of DISCOURSE is with POLITICAL, indicating that when scholars in these journals are investigating any discourse, it is very likely to be within some political sphere. A glance at other common words of this type indicates that even if discourse is not exclusively political (e.g., governmental), it is INSTITUTIONAL or DISCRIMINATORY, both of which are core elements of critically oriented social analysis of groups and their inclusive-exclusive action (Excerpts 6 and 7):

(6) the questions asked by institutional representatives in *institutional discourse* can perform ideological work (LS1999)

(7) justification of intergroup hostility is a typical feature of *discriminatory discourse* which is produced to maintain inequality and injustice (DS2018)

This leads us to two observations about DISCOURSE in the academic realm. One, political contexts are the most common area of inquiry with regards to discourse. This does not mean that DISCOURSE is not used in other contexts or subject areas, but in and amongst the articles we examined, it is by far the most frequently attended to category of discourse. Secondly, and by extension of the former point, DISCOURSE is not exclusively political, but its overwhelming semantic feature is to be involved with institutional and social structures. It is unlikely that this meaning is isolated to these articles, or representative of only one era of scholarship on discourse. Rather, its common usage with social structures shows that, when scholars are talking about discourse, it is understood as a premise that it is part of some social structure or institution. This implies that while studies examining discourse may include analyses of language use in the form of linguistic features or practices, discourse is not understood solely as language use in a neutral sense. Interestingly, institutional, social, and political structures involve, for example, attitudes, beliefs, and power relations – or ideologies – but the term ideology is not always explicitly invoked or defined. This perhaps implies that ideology could indeed be switched out for other terms. In other words, if DISCOURSE is modified by something that is already thought to be inherently ideological, then IDEOLOGY need not necessarily be invoked explicitly.

Nonetheless, we also see IDEOLOGICAL as a collocate of DISCOURSE, as exemplified in Excerpts 8 and 9 below:

(8) frequent use of *ideological discourse* structures, aiming at producing a positive image of 'us' (DS2008)

(9) performance plays a critical role in the joint construction of linguistic as well as other ideologies, while the relative stability of *ideological discourse* plays a role in determining the form that performances take (LS2004)

Interestingly, in Excerpt 9, IDEOLOGICAL does not simply modify DISCOURSE, but DISCOURSE STRUCTURES. The same author also uses IDEOLOGICAL DISCOURSE PATTERNS in another instance in a similar vein. An examination of the context in which Excerpt 10 occurred also revealed that the statement occurred immediately after a sentence referring to STRUCTURES:

(10) we thus see a unifying force in language, one that encourages the reiteration of certain ideological positions, partly because of their inseparable relation to pre-patterned, performable *linguistic structures* and partly because of an ideological context that accepts the truth of those positions (LS2004)

Thus, while LINGUISTIC STRUCTURES here is separated from the immediate context in which IDEOLOGICAL DISCOURSE occurred, the author has defined ideological discourse as pertaining to the marriage between ideology and linguistic structures previously. IDEOLOGICAL DISCOURSE, then, seems to be used as a means of combining ideology (e.g., beliefs, common sense, knowledge) with specific linguistic features or structures.

The IDEOLOGY collocation group again shows that there is a tendency for left-positioned descriptors to lay out IDEOLOGY as belonging to certain categories or being a manifestation of social group politics (Table 13.5).

Table 13.5: Collocates of *ideology* as *categories*.

Collocate	Slot	Frequency	MI Score
language	L	873	6.42
dominant	L	111	6.98
linguistic	L	90	4.53
political	L	88	4.17
social	R	74	3.22
racial	L	55	6.01
gender	L	54	5.05
racist	L	51	5.91
modern	L	34	5.86
nationalist	L	32	7.27
underlying	L	31	6.68
liberal	L	23	6.15
cultural	L	23	3.40
nation	L	21	4.18
own	L	20	3.04
marxist	L	19	8.25
national	L	18	3.07
monolingual	L	17	6.52
local	L	17	3.48
western	L	15	4.33
general	M	15	3.16

One exception to the social group politics has to do with super-structure: LANGUAGE, LINGUISTIC, and MODERN which outline that IDEOLOGY in those contexts is specifically about language, and current (i.e., different from past ideologies). It also bears mentioning that, like DISCOURSE ANALYSIS, the high frequency of LANGUAGE with IDEOLOGY is at least partially related to its place as a common notion in a number of disciplinary fields. Table 13.5 shows that the word IDEOLOGY tends to follow DOMINANT, POLITICAL, SOCIAL, RACIAL AND RACIST, GENDER, NATIONALIST, CULTURAL, LOCAL, NATIONAL, WESTERN, and COMMON, which divides ideologies according to different social, ethnic, cultural, linguistic, and national boundaries, in some ways very similarly to DISCOURSE. Due to this overlap, we will examine these similarities further in the following section.

4.3 Overlapping collocations of ideology and discourse

Indeed, if we examine the categories of discourse, we see that five of the exact same terms are often associated with both discourse and ideology (Table 13.6).

Table 13.6: Overlapping Collocates of *ideology* and *discourse* as *categories*.

Collocate	Slot	MI Score	
		Ideology	Discourse
dominant	L	6.98	5.02
political	L	4.17	5.44
social	R	3.22	3.24
racial	L	6.01	4.57
racist	L	5.91	5.27

Due to this overlap, it is pertinent to examine these shared collocates in context. Perhaps tellingly, SOCIAL when attached to IDEOLOGY is often used in terms of social identification, identity, injustice, and domination, for example, whereas when attached to DISCOURSE it is more prevalently social practice, relations, actors, and constructions. Although there is certainly a similarity, it seems discourse is thought to be social more in terms of interpersonal relations, while ideology is social in terms of how a person identifies, or in the ways tinged by social injustice or domination. To look at more specific examples, below we have selected excerpts from the corpus that demonstrate how DOMINANT, POLITICAL, and RACIST are used as modifiers of both DISCOURSE and IDEOLOGY.

Excerpt 11 demonstrates the functional differences between an ideology and discourse, by showing two things: that discourse is a function of the language or communication used, and that it often belongs to something. The excerpt references a corpus that produced collocates that grounded the discourse analysis of the excerpted article. This is then contrasted with Excerpt 12, which shows ideology is something that is constructed through discourse:

(11) in the French corpus, collocate analyses point to a *dominant discourse* of belonging that equates the in-group with the French-speaking majority and yet presents it as forming a rather open 'society' that is inclusive of cultural and ethnic diversity (DS2011)

(12) the monolingualising tendencies of state, social, media and economic institutions produce and reproduce this *dominant ideology* of homogeneity (ML2002)

Importantly, the DOMINANT DISCOURSE being scrutinized seems to do things, has agency, and is used to accomplish some goal. In this case, discourse accomplishes the feat of positioning a certain population as a group, and further that they are associated with certain liberal characteristics. As the excerpts show, a dominant discourse must nonetheless be about something else. The discourse is not itself the point, but rather an expression of the in-group, or expressed about the in-group. That the DISCOURSE is DOMINANT comes from this in-group and describes the power of the group. Dominant ideology, however, as demonstrated in Excerpt 12, refers specifically to something that shapes reality – i.e., relating to the creation of worldviews rather than group dynamics.

An examination of examples of political discourse and political ideology reveals a similar pattern, where ideology is constructed specifically as something that occurs in the human mind (e.g., as a basis of the formation of common sense), and discourse as an interactive strategy:

(13) Chilton's analysis of Reagan's 1986 state of the union address includes observations on the intertextuality of the text, specifically the mixing of religious and *political discourse*, as a positive politeness strategy (DS1992)

(14) in fact, most articles repeated conservative arguments without mentioning their conservative background thus effectively naturalizing conservative *political ideology* into common sense (DS1996)

Thus, with discourse we see an emphasis on *how people speak* and as such, social interaction, whereas with ideology we see it relating to the inner workings of the human mind – or more explicitly, what might be characterized as the basis of common sense.

Finally, we can focus in on the differences between racist discourse and racist ideology:

(15) confronted with a *racist discourse*, a black person could be positioned as marginal and may be motivated to confront it by claiming it is typical of pervasive white racism (DS1996)

(16) I hope to gradually chip away at the layers of discourse to reveal the construction of a *racist ideology* embedded within the structure of newspaper discourse (DS2000)

In Excerpt 15, RACIST DISCOURSE is positioned as something that is done or committed against another. As such, discourse can be used to do harm, or to confront, and as such, weaponized. Interestingly, in Excerpt 16 we see RACIST IDEOLOGY co-occurring with LAYERS OF DISCOURSE, and NEWSPAPER DISCOURSE, metaphorically EMBEDDED in discourse. In this case, racist ideology is not mobilized against another, but rather it resides in the discourses that are used as weapons. The excerpt reveals that ideology is a core, conceptual subject, an ideology which is based on race. The author in this excerpt is precise in their differentiation of the discourse from the ideology.

Excerpt 16 highlights the conceptual boundaries between DISCOURSE and IDEOLOGY even when they (1) have shared terms, and (2) appear tightly bundled in a single sentence. The proximity of DISCOURSE and IDEOLOGY is quite helpful in summarizing the foregoing section in general. As we have seen, left-positioned categories apply to both DISCOURSE and IDEOLOGY, and have direct effects on the substance of what each word means. Discourse tends to be involved in activities and require agents that carry it out. In contrast, ideology often stands as its own subject, and represents categories of belief or world view. In both cases, the words are enmeshed with social orders, groups, and organizations, which find their expression either in analysis of their discourse behaviors, or analysis of ideological constructs.

4.4 Distinct concepts

To further discuss the differences between discourse and ideology, in this section, we specifically tackle them as distinct concepts.

4.4.1 Discourse as modifier

One semantic group forms when DISCOURSE appears to the left of collocates, such as DISCOURSE STRATEGIES (Table 13.7), which does not happen for IDEOLOGY. This category tends to represent the usage of DISCOURSE as a focal subject, where its left position designates another noun as belonging in the discourse sphere (DISCOURSE + X, where DISCOURSE modifies X).

Perhaps unsurprisingly, the most frequent collocation for DISCOURSE in the data is ANALYSIS, the disciplinary head of several disciplines (e.g., discourse analysis and critical discourse analysis). STUDIES follows this and again indicates discourse as a discipline. In other cases, we have STRATEGIES, PRACTICES, STRATEGY, STRUCTURE, and FEATURES. These are activities and properties that are not necessarily related to discourse as an action, or even communication. Yet the frequent association of discourse with these terms aligns them over time.

Table 13.7: Collocates of *discourse* as a modifier.

Collocate	Slot	Frequency	MI Score
analysis	R	2656	6.35
social	M	476	3.24
studies	R	421	5.54
strategies	R	304	4.93
used	M	213	3.00
practices	R	143	3.50
strategy	R	140	4.29
structure	R	137	4.28
practice	R	126	3.90
structures	R	117	4.70
features	M	114	3.90

Thus, for example, PRACTICES becomes associated with the analysis of discourse as an activity, and STRATEGIES implying an activity, where discourse can be manipulated to suit some goal. To illustrate:

(17) we explore how the New York Times aims to influence its target audience with certain discourse patterns or *discourse strategies* (LC2012)

In the above excerpt, thus, there is an implication that DISCOURSE STRATEGIES (or patterns) are something that can be fabricated to advance an agenda.

What is interesting about this group is that a number of the collocates appear in both singular and plural forms. At first glance this might seem redundant, but in fact the difference between the two forms is that in all cases in this corpus, plural forms represent concepts and subjects. These plural nouns have more to do with discourse as a field: these are objects of inquiry that discourse researchers are interested in, and they represent conceptual topics. People, societies, groups, etcetera have DISCOURSE STRATEGIES that they use. This is similar to DISCOURSE PRACTICES:

(18) black *discourse practices* influence how black people read and respond to the social world (DS2007)

By contrast, singular uses here are used to explain particular instances of discursive events:

(19) advertisers embark on the *discourse practice* of self-advertising equally strategically, producing versions of themselves for selective consumption (DS1996)

Therefore, when used in the singular form, there is a single practice that is usually being scrutinized, and it is this single activity that is the focus. This highlights discourse as a multi-leveled event: it is potentially conceptual and material, but clearly disambiguated by the form of the collocates. One case in this group worth mentioning in brief is SOCIAL. This collocate appears in a wide range of settings. Although it appears mostly to the right of DISCOURSE, it appears in a variety of exact sequences. The two words are related as elements of social reality, and commonly appear together to describe, e.g., [DISCOURSE AND] [THE SOCIAL], [SOCIAL PRACTICES], [SOCIAL ACTIVITY] (e.g., "discourse as social practice" or "discourse and social practice"). So, in these cases, DISCOURSE acts as a modifier, compounding with SOCIAL to constrain the PRACTICES or the ACTIVITY as a category. This particular collocate demonstrates the need for qualitative analysis, and recognition that these patterns are tendencies but not static or bounded sets. Rather, they have shared semantic power together, in evidence by their habitual co-appearance.

4.4.2 Ideology as a distinct concept

Ideology also differs from discourse in the way that it is an independent concept that can relate to other concepts on its own, rather than constraining and bringing them into its orbit. The meaning of ideology is, in these collocations, distinguished by the structure in which it appears. These groupings are often distinguished by OF for right-positioned collocates, or AND for left-positioned collocates (Table 13.8). For example, IDEOLOGY IN NEWS shows that news can be discussed as expressing ideology, while POWER AND IDEOLOGY shows that power and ideology are intertwined but distinct.

Each of these collocates, whether left- or right-positioned with IDEOLOGY, represents a distinct, conceptual, or subject area that is operationalized through IDEOLOGY. These semantic borders are borne by the linguistic structural pattern. Taking NEWS again, we can consider the differences between NEWS IDEOLOGY, IDEOLOGY IN NEWS, and NEWS AND IDEOLOGY. In one case, we find that there is an ideology within a specific area, but that the area itself is not the object of analysis. The collocation IDEOLOGY IN NEWS is the dominant form. NEWS IDEOLOGY appears at a much lower rate. In both cases, NEWS is a particular area in which IDEOLOGY can be identified. Yet by contrast we do not find IDEOLOGICAL

NEWS, which would communicate something more akin to a form of news, the singular concept, adjectivally modified. The inclusion of a connective such as *of*, *in*, or *and* differentiates ideology itself from those concepts, whereas we saw in Section 4.1 that left-positioned adjectival modifiers hold ideology to the concept it is being used to describe (e.g., RACIST IDEOLOGY).

Table 13.8: Collocates connecting *ideology* to distinct concepts.

Collocate	Slot	Frequency	MI Score
discourse	L	243	4.64
power	L	74	4.96
news	R	49	4.49
analysis	L	45	3.14
identity	R	40	3.75
practice	R	37	4.80
media	R	33	3.82
role	L	24	3.55
theory	L	23	4.60
based	R	22	3.52
politics	L	21	4.85
society	R	20	3.49
culture	L	20	3.87
critical	L	19	3.67
system	L	17	3.82
history	R	17	3.90
concept	L	17	4.25
associated	R	17	4.05
american	R	17	3.49
chinese	L	16	3.71
racism	L	15	3.86
common	M	15	3.31
authenticity	R	15	6.46
white	R	14	3.57

Strikingly, DISCOURSE appears with IDEOLOGY at the highest frequency, and ANALYSIS is also relatively frequent. However, overwhelmingly, ANALYSIS is attached grammatically to DISCOURSE rather than IDEOLOGY (e.g., a critical discourse analysis of ideologies), to the analysis in the article (e.g., in my analysis, "ideology"), or to something other than ideology directly (e.g., discourse, speech, or text):

(20) what the critical linguists and later on the critical discourse analysts did was develop a linguistic framework of *analysis* to analyze ideology and power 'behind' and 'over' such grammatical constructions (ML 2006)

Furthermore, in most cases, DISCOURSE appears in the corpus as DISCOURSE AND IDEOLOGY, or separated by a comma in list-form (i.e., DISCOURSE, IDEOLOGY, AND . . .) indicating that the two are overwhelmingly treated as separate concepts. In our corpus, we only identified one exception to this (Excerpt 21). In this example, the author is taking a cognitive approach to ideology (Van Dijk 1995), whereby discourse is viewed as a vehicle for the transmission of ideologies, and these are shaped by and further shape society. However, it is used in a very general sense without an identification of a specific type of discourse, discourse features, or social groups who participate in its transmission.

(21) thus, uncovering a *discourse ideology* shows how society shapes this discourse; it discloses what the texts mean and not only what they say (explicitly or implicitly) (DS2002)

IDEOLOGY and DISCOURSE are intricately intertwined, but through examining actual usage we are able to uncover the sometimes subtle ways they are distinguished and distinguishable.

5 Distinguishing between ideology and discourse

This volume takes on the sometimes conflated meanings of discourse and ideology in scholarly work, as well as seeks to provide an overview of how the two are used. Our corpus query, on the one hand, confirms that the two concepts are deeply entwined, but on the other hand, there are significant linguistically-grounded differences in the way they are deployed by authors. The consistent syntagmatic usage of each word demonstrates that discourse is related to the practices and material expression of social groups and culture, while ideology tends to be associated with groups and cultures themselves, a sort of substantial component of the group identity. However, this close connection and subtle semantic separation often leads to the very conflation that can be difficult to cut through.

As our data shows, DISCOURSE is often modified by terms already ideological in nature, such as POLITICAL. Thus, the discourse prism is known through different ideological surfaces as one of its key features. This weaves ideology into the nature of discourse itself. Furthermore, the confusion looms larger when discourse appears as the object of inquiry. When scholars scrutinize discourse, for example a DOMINANT DISCOURSE, they tend to then characterize that discourse as a manifestation of the ideology or social group itself, as if the discourse and the ideology are one and the same. As in excerpt 12 above, it is the DOMINANT DISCOURSE that has agency, and is the vessel of an ideological in-group. The result is that, at least in terms of co-text, discourse comes to stand for the ideology itself, because actual reference to ideology is reduced or elided out. Therefore, it would seem that ideology and discourse are conflated, or ideology becomes displaced by discourse as Purvis and Hunt (1993) point out. This, we find, is partially true in the sense that ideology is not always invoked, but we argue more specifically that it is the "modifier + DISCOURSE" that more easily becomes conflated with ideology (e.g., RACIST/NATIONALIST/POLITICAL + DISCOURSE). In this sense, the distinction that Gee (1999) makes in terms of "small-d" and "big D" discourses can also be understood as *modifier + DISCOURSE = Discourse*, whereas linguistic features and language use without reference to social and political aspects = discourse.

This phenomenon is apparent from the comparatively few uses of IDEOLOGY as a key term, when compared to the frequency of DISCOURSE. Of course, part of this is also a result of the usage of theoretical approaches, such as discourse analysis, critical discourse analysis, and the more broad discourse studies which would add to the frequency of the usage of discourse in the corpus – however, as our examples demonstrate, this does not account for the entirety of the difference. When IDEOLOGY is explicitly used, it appears as a subject that coheres with specific areas under scrutiny (e.g., DOMINANT, POLITICAL, RACIST, etcetera). Therefore, ideology becomes an undercurrent to the scholarly work on discourse, which is the expression thereof. Furthermore, taken together, this relates both discourse and ideology back to forms of social practice (cf. Fairclough 2010; Schiffrin 1994; Van Dijk 2006b).

As already pointed out in the introduction to this volume, ideology and discourse can be conceived of as theoretical concepts, analytical tools, or sometimes both. Yet, scholars may vary in what kinds of data they are working with as starting points – i.e., is the data thought to be ideological from the start, or are ideologies identified within the data set through discourse analysis? The data, of course, is often conceived of as discourse, whether spoken, textual, material, or consisting of actions. This quite accurately captures what we found in our data as well – a difference in the usage of discourse and ideology centered on whether the author specifically wanted to focus on discourse, as specific features, or ways of using language, rather than to identify features that were thought to be specifically ideological. Naturally, there was also some overlap, where both were utilized. It is hard to overlook the reasoning, messaging, and rhetorical purpose of discourse, no matter how cleanly one wishes to keep the two concepts separate.

Thus, while discourse and ideology are both utilized in studies examining interactions, texts, speech, and actions within and across social groups, DISCOURSE is used at a much higher rate to accomplish specific tasks, such as identifying linguistic features that reveal something about social order or structures, for example. This practice then becomes entwined with ideology through either explicitly using the term IDEOLOGY, or through modifiers of DISCOURSE that identify an area (e.g., POLITICAL, DOMINANT, NATIONAL, and RACIST) that might be intuitively considered as relating to ideology, which then seems to make the explicit use of the term ideology unnecessary.

6 Concluding comments

This volume addresses discourse and ideology, and the sometimes difficult task of teasing these concepts apart. Yet our analyses demonstrate that authors over the years have been rather canny about the issue, whether by design or serendipity. The linguistic form constraints on these terms are clear. In discourse, authors featured in the corpus have developed a scrutable concept that expresses social activities, organizational expression, and cultural meaning. In short, discourse is a vehicle of ideology. Ideology, on the other hand, has a conceptually distinct meaning, with inherent dimensions: it is the substance of social structures, organizations, and belief expressions. To wit, we cannot know ideology without its discourse, and discourse is empty when bereft of ideology to express. Individually they are worth scrutinizing, but only together do we uncover beliefs people hold, expressions of power in society, and the contingencies of our social realities.

Ultimately, our corpus has demonstrated that discourse and ideology have been used differently in the literature, but understanding the linguistically-mediated connection between the two is key to differentiating them. This tightly-coupled relationship prompted us to consider that, perhaps, conflation is not the issue. Perhaps it would be intellectually profitable to change how we position the relationship from conflation, to seeing the two concepts as needing each other. We propose this reframing with the hopes that it might alleviate some of the confusion scholars, senior and junior alike, may experience. In its place is a dialectic that emphasizes unique aspects of the two concepts, and underscores the influence of each concept on the other. Discourse and ideology as dialectic is an on-going relationship, the analysis of which has different goals that coalesce around specific, social questions. In short, if discourse and ideology need each other, they must have durable boundaries that can be drawn on and more clearly delineated, and thus exposed in scholarship, analysis, and classrooms alike.

References

Anthony, Laurence. 2020. *AntConc*. Tokyo: Waseda University. http://www.laurenceanthony.net/software (accessed 13 October 2020).

Baker, Paul. 2006. *Using corpora in discourse analysis*. London: Continuum.

Baker, Paul, Costas Gabrielatos, Majid Khosravinik, Michał Krzyżanowski, Tony Mcenery & Ruth Wodak. 2008. A useful methodological synergy? Combining critical discourse analysis and corpus linguistics to examine discourses of refugees and asylum seekers in the UK press. *Discourse & Society* 19. 273–306.

Baker, Paul, Costas Gabrielatos & Tony McEnery. 2012. Sketching Muslims: A corpus driven analysis of representations around the word 'Muslim' in the British press 1998–2009. *Applied Linguistics* 34 (3). 255–278.

Bednarek, Monika & Helen Caple. 2014. Why do news values matter? Towards a new methodological framework for analysing news discourse in critical discourse analysis and beyond. *Discourse & Society* 25 (2). 135–58.

Cheng, Winnie, Chris Greaves & Martin Warren. 2006. From n-gram to skipgram to concgram. *International Journal of Corpus Linguistics* 11 (4). 411–433.

Church, Kenneth Ward & Patrick Hanks. 1990. Word association norms, mutual information, and lexicography. *Computational Linguistics* 16 (1). 22–29.

Diaz, Brett A. & Marika K. Hall. 2020. A corpus-driven exploration of U.S. language planning and language ideology from 2013 to 2018. *Journal of Language and Politics* 19 (6). 915–936.

Edwards, Derek. 1996. *Discourse and cognition*. London, Thousand Oaks, CA & New Delhi: Sage.

Fagerholm, Andreas. 2016. Ideology: A proposal for a conceptual typology. *Social Science Information* 55 (2). 137–160.

Fairclough, Norman. 2010 [1995]. *Critical discourse analysis: The critical study of language*, 2nd edn. New York: Longman.

Firth, John R. 1957. *Papers in linguistics 1934–1951*. London, New York & Toronto: Oxford University Press.

Fitzsimmons-Doolan, Shannon. 2014. Using lexical variables to identify language ideologies in a policy corpus. *Corpora* 9 (1). 57–82.

Foucault, Michel. 1972. *The archaeology of knowledge*. Alan M. Sheridan Smith (transl.). New York: Pantheon Books.

Foucault, Michel. 1977. *Discipline and punish: The birth of the prison*. Alan M. Sheridan Smith (transl.). New York: Pantheon Books.

Foucault, Michel. 1982. The subject and power. Leslie Sawyer (transl.). *Critical Inquiry* 8 (4). 777–795.

Gee, James P. 1999. *An introduction to discourse analysis: Theory and method*. London & New York: Routledge.

Hamilton, Malcolm B. 1987. The elements of the concept of ideology. *Political Studies* 35 (1). 18–38.

Holborow, Marnie. 2007. Language, ideology and neoliberalism. *Journal of Language and Politics* 6 (1). 51–73.

Holborow, Marnie. 2015. *Language and neoliberalism*. London & New York: Routledge.

Hunston, Susan. 2002. *Corpora in Applied Linguistics*. Cambridge: Cambridge University Press.

Koteyko, Nelya. 2006. Corpus linguistics and the study of meaning in discourse. *Linguistics Journal* 1 (2). 132–157.

Lopes, Antonio. 2015. *Is there an end of ideologies?: Exploring constructs of ideology and discourse in Marxist and post-Marxist theories*. Newcastle upon Tyne: Cambridge Scholars Publishing.

Mills, Sara. 2004. *Discourse*, 2nd edn. London & New York: Routledge.

Määttä, Simo K. 2022. Discourse and ideology in French thought until Foucault and Pêcheux. In Simo K. Määttä & Marika K. Hall (eds.), *Mapping ideology in discourse studies*, 21–43. Berlin: De Gruyter Mouton.

Määttä, Simo. 2014. Discourse and ideology: Why do we need both? In Laura Callahan (ed.), *Spanish and Portuguese across time, place, and borders. Essays in honor of Milton M. Azevedo*, 63–77. New York: MacMillan.

Partington, Alan, Alison Duguid & Charlotte Taylor. 2013. *Patterns and meanings in discourse: Theory and practice in corpus-assisted discourse studies (CADS)*. Amsterdam & Philadelphia: John Benjamins.

Potter, Jonathan. 1996. *Representing reality: Discourse, rhetoric and social construction*. London, Thousand Oaks, CA & New Delhi: Sage.

Potter, Jonathan, Margaret Wetherell, Rosalind Gill & Derek Edwards. 1990. Discourse: Noun, verb or social practice? *Philosophical Psychology* 3. 205–217.

Purvis, Trevor & Alan Hunt. 1993. Discourse, ideology, discourse, ideology, discourse, ideology . . . *The British Journal of Sociology* 44 (3). 473–499.

Schiffrin, Deborah. 1994. *Approaches to discourse*. Oxford: Blackwell.

Scollon, Ron. 2001. *Mediated discourse analysis: The nexus of practice*. London & New York: Routledge.

Sinclair, John. 1991. *Corpus, concordance, collocation*. Oxford: Oxford University Press.

Sinclair, John. 2004. *Trust the text: Language, corpus and discourse*. London & New York: Routledge.

Stubbs, Michael. 1995. Collocations and semantic profiles: On the cause of the trouble with quantitative studies. *Functions of Language* 2 (1). 23–55.

Stubbs, Michael. 2009. The search for units of meaning: Sinclair on empirical semantics. *Applied Linguistics* 30 (1). 115–137.

Subtirelu, Nicholas Close. 2013. 'English . . . it's part of our blood': Ideologies of language and nation in United States Congressional discourse. *Journal of Sociolinguistics* 17 (1). 37–65.

Van Dijk, Teun A. 1995. Discourse semantics and ideology. *Discourse & Society* 6 (2). 243–289.

Van Dijk, Teun A. 1998. *Ideology: A multidisciplinary approach*. London, Thousand Oaks, CA & New Delhi: Sage.

Van Dijk, Teun A. 2006a. Discourse, context and cognition. *Discourse Studies* 8 (1). 159–177.

Van Dijk, Teun A. 2006b. Ideology and discourse analysis. *Journal of Political Ideologies* 11 (2). 115–140.

Van Dijk, Teun A. 2013. Ideology and discourse. In Michael Freeden, Lyman Sargent & Marc Stears (eds.), *The Oxford handbook of political ideologies*, 175–196. New York & Oxford: Oxford University Press.

Vessey, Rachelle. 2017. Corpus approaches to language ideology. *Applied Linguistics* 38 (3). 277–296.

Vološinov, Valentin Nikolajevitš. 1973. *Marxism and the philosophy of language*. Ladislav Matejka & I. R. Titunik (transl.). New York: Seminar Press.

Wodak, Ruth. 2002. Aspects of critical discourse analysis. *Zeitschrift für Angewandte Linguistik* 36. 5–31.
Woolard, Kathryn A. 1998. Introduction: Language ideology as a field of inquiry. In Bambi Schieffelin, Kathryn A. Woolard & Paul Kroskrity (eds.), *Language ideologies: Practice and theory*, 3–47. New York & Oxford: Oxford University Press.
Xiao, Richard & Tony McEnery. 2006. Collocation, semantic prosody, and near synonymy: A cross-linguistic perspective. *Applied Linguistics* 27 (1). 103–129.

Christina Higgins
Chapter 14
Afterword
Locating discourse and ideology

1 Preamble

As a North American scholar who specializes in discourse analysis and sociolinguistics, I appreciate the invitation by Simo Määttä and Marika Hall to reflect on this collection of contemporary scholarship that examines the relationships between discourse and ideology. As this volume makes clear, there are some rather long-standing traditions for the study of discourse and ideology that are tied to geography, language, and intellectual lineage. Like all theoretical concepts, discourse and ideology have situated historical ontologies and epistemologies that are challenging to decipher to any newcomer who grapples with them. In reading the volume, my own experience as a U.S.-trained scholar makes it starkly clear how situated and perspectival this research can be in terms of one's academic socialization, geographic location, and disciplinary orientation. Thus, I feel it is important to locate myself metadiscursively in order to comment on the volume as a whole. I am certain that a reflection by a scholar located in France or Brazil or Kenya would have a rather different take, and in taking a reflexive approach here, I encourage other scholars who take part in the commentary genre to more often address their positionality as they do this kind of intellectual work. In some scholarly traditions, the discursive label that might be affixed to this reflexivity is "self-indulgence", or "navel-gazing", but I favor the more optimistic label of "situated reflexivity" instead. In a time when scholars are invited to recognize the over-representation of intellectual knowledge produced by scholars in WEIRD (western, educated, industrialized, rich, democratic) contexts (Henrich, Heine, and Norenzayan 2010; Clancy and Davis 2019) as produced by academics who are mostly located in the global north, I find it especially important to reveal more about our dispositions, identities, and genealogies as scholars.

I come to this reflection chapter as a white, female, U.S.-born scholar of multilingualism in the field of applied linguistics. My conceptualization of applied linguistics is that it refers to language research that has relevance for real-world contexts. In my own scholarly work, I investigate a range of social questions about multilingualism by studying discourse, most often as it takes place in naturally-occurring conversations. Initially, I focused my research on multilingualism in Tanzania and then turned to concentrate on discourse in Hawaiʻi, where

I currently reside. These two contexts are embedded in post-colonial discourses and ideologies regarding language, politics, culture, and economic relations. In my scholarly circles, I have encountered the investigation of ideology mainly through studies of language ideology, whereas research on discourse has largely been tied to the study of language use in the form of spoken interaction, and to a lesser degree, the production and reception of written texts. My intellectual training and scholarship drew attention to what the editors in this volume refer to as "functional" approaches to discourse, as outlined by sociolinguists such as John Gumperz and Jan Blommaert, whose interests in contextualization and language ideologies have encouraged me to explore the links between language use and the ideologies attached to languages in multilingual practices. I was also partly influenced by ethnomethodology and conversation analysis and the insistence on emically-grounded interpretations of data, as evidenced in conversation and interaction. In my work, I have studied workplace conversation, public health communication, and beliefs about marginalized languages by drawing on an eclectic approach comprised of ethnography, social theory, and microlevel discourse analysis. My academic socialization encouraged an emphasis on language use as the first realm to investigate, followed by attention to the larger sets of beliefs, cultural practices, and institutional norms that shape the language use. From my observations, this emphasis still holds true today in most North American academic contexts where language and linguistics are a central disciplinary focus, at least in terms of how new scholars are trained and socialized into the field of discourse studies. The same is true for how discourse and its links to ideology is represented in contemporary textbooks, which tend to foreground discourse in the form of talk and text before linking it to ideological discussions (e.g., Paltridge 2012; Jones 2012). In my training and continued experience, scholarly examination of ideology and deep discussions of foundational scholars associated with this term are often found in other disciplinary homes outside of applied linguistics, such as literature, sociology, education, and political science.

Based on my experiences in "the field", exposure to foundational texts on ideology and discourse from philosophical and theoretical traditions are uncommon unless undertaken by individuals. Early on, I was usually only exposed to the seminal works of major scholars such as Foucault, Bourdieu, and Bakhtin through secondary reading and in small, self-governed reading groups in graduate school and beyond. I strived to analyze the microlevel of language with reference to social theory, often drawn from these critical and/or post-structuralist theorists who wrote about the nature of language, power, and social life. Oftentimes, discussions of discourse invoked Bourdieu's writings about distinction, cultural capital and habitus, Foucault's treatment of subjectivity, knowledge and power, and Bakhtin's work on legitimacy, heteroglossia and double-voicing.

My interest in multilingual practices in East Africa led me to deeply engage with Bakhtin (1981, 1984) early in my career, as his writings about multivocality were a rich resource for making sense of how people used English, Swahili, and other languages in their everyday lives in ways that were not well explained by existing dominant analytical frameworks about multilingualism. Throughout my career, I have felt the most comfortable in my analysis of discourse/ideology by starting with a careful examination of discourse using the tools of interactional sociolinguistics, conversation analysis, and narrative analysis. I have always strived to make sense of discourse data with reference to social theory, and to make connections between what Gee (2004) would refer to as the small "d" discourses of interaction and the big "D" Discourses of practice, schemas, and common senses that circulate, shape, and are shaped by the discourses being examined. Nonetheless, I don't think I'm alone in noting a difficulty in sometimes fully grasping much of the dense scholarship produced by these social theorists writing about the nature of language, discourse, and ideology.

2 Themes in this collection

Now that I have made what I consider to be important caveats regarding my own positionality on discourse and ideology, I attempt to comment on some of the themes and contributions in this collection of chapters. This is indeed a timely book. At this moment in which the global COVID-19 pandemic lingers on, we are all surrounded by texts and communication practices that show how discourse and ideology operate. Of course, ideological debates about public health, vaccines, and personal freedom are not the only discursively and ideologically divisive issues of the day. A glance at the headlines in mainstream news sources in the U.S. points to an alarming example: "Texas school administrator told teachers to include Holocaust books with 'opposing' views when explaining new state law". The article notes that after the story went viral, the superintendent of the Texas school district apologized, and publicly stated, "there are not two sides of the Holocaust", noting that the teaching of "historical facts" does not require multiple perspectives. Still, when teaching "current events", teachers in Texas are now required to offer readings and perspectives from "opposing viewpoints" (Killough 2021). This news item emerged as a result of new legislation in Texas and elsewhere in the U.S. that has restricted how teachers engage with their students in teaching and learning about racism, due to a backlash in some communities towards the use of anti-racist books and curriculum in schools. More broadly, the legislation can be understood as a counter-discourse to social movements in the

U.S. that have shined a light on police brutality towards Black and Brown people. This example illustrates how the discursive construction of history as "facts" and current events as requiring "opposing viewpoints" is interlinked with ideological debates around racism in the U.S. It also draws attention to the role of white Americans in responding to social movements that encourage critical awareness of race and power relations in both historical and contemporary contexts.

Similarly, this edited volume engages in the examination of discourse and ideology in a range of contexts where divisive rhetoric on race, belonging, liberty, gender, societal change, and nationality are often in the foreground. Several chapters attend to the role of discourse in perpetuating and disrupting national ideologies that negatively portray immigrants in Spain and Belgium (Lázaro Gutiérrez and Tejero González, Verschueren), and another explores discourse and subjectivity among Tunisians who defy authoritarian regimes in their own country through social protest discourses and performances (Guellouz). National identity and resistance are also examined with attention to parochial and patrimonial mindsets in an examination of discourses resisting multiculturalism and the #metoo movement in France (Louar). In today's world, these discourses are easy to find in most contexts, as ideologies of "the nation" in relation to ethnolinguistic identities and cultural dispositions are increasingly articulated and contested through discourse in public spaces.

Beyond these divisive rhetorical practices on polarizing ideologies, the book also pays attention to ideological concerns that are more centrally about language in terms of linguistic practices and language ideologies, yet which are also entangled with nationhood, identity, and power relations. Here, the authors tackle the role of language subordination vis-à-vis standardized language varieties in the francophone minority region of Acadia in Eastern Canada (Vernet), the role of ideologies about audience and histories of indexicalities in translation into Finnish (Mäntynen and Kalliokoski), the practice of "licensing" through English, whereby Nordic speakers of English engage in frequent pragmatic borrowing of English, thereby tapping into its ideological framings and indices (Peterson), and a corpus analysis of the terms "discourse" and "ideology" in English-medium academic texts as a means to understand how these terms are constructed through their semantic collocations (Diaz and Hall).

The remaining chapters are case studies on the relationship between discourse and ideology by applied linguists, social work researchers, healthcare researchers, discourse analysts, literary scholars, and translation specialists who examine ideologies about social practices in state institutional contexts. Of course, these are also bound up in ideologies of the nation-state and its role and responsibilities to all residents, as these contributions examine the discourses emerging from contexts where migrant and low-income families struggle within state systems. Lutman-White and Angouri analyze focus group conversations and interviews among social workers and managers in England to show how they articulate the ideologies of child protection social work and its associated moral order in their talk. They examine how the institutional support for families has changed in recent years, leading to the emergence of a dominant discourse that centers on child-protection, rather than helping families stay together or providing families with the resources they need to succeed. Lázaro Gutiérrez and Tejero González report on work they have done in a healthcare training setting in Spain, where they analyze discourses of Spanish healthcare staff made about migrants in the context of training about diversity and intercultural healthcare. In analyzing written comments made in online forums, the authors explore how the staff express ideologies about migrants with regard to discourses that posit us/them boundaries, which articulate insurmountable cultural differences, and which position language as a barrier to healthcare.

As a scholar who uses discourse analytical frameworks alongside social theory, I am always intrigued by how other scholars frame their studies in terms of theory and method, and how they ground their findings. The volume begins with a series of chapters that shows the continued linkage of discourse/ideology studies with French scholarly traditions, and with the French language. Määttä provides a succinct overview of the relations between ideology and discourse in French scholarship, which in turn nicely segues to the next set of chapters. His chapter provides a needed history of these terms as a prelude to the volume as a whole. Next, Vernet's study of language diversity in Acadia, a French-speaking region of Canada, examines language ideology through the ways that contact languages like Chiac are both discursively valorized and subordinated with reference to standardized French in the same institutional spaces at a university. Vernet's analysis departs from French discourse analysis traditions by employing ethnographic methods. He illustrates how the syllabi and teachers' discussion about language standards proscribing Acadian varieties of French were the discursive sites where rules and conditions about language were located. The next two chapters return to French discourse analytic traditions by examining ideological practices in relation to subjectivity, power, liberation, and performance. Here, the authors do not explicitly discuss their research methods, but rather provide rich examples to unpack with reference to the theoretical relationship between ideology, discourse, and transformative social meanings. Guellouz examines discourse and performativity in Tunisia by taking on the challenging subject matter of immolation as transformative, performative act. The role of discourse as language use is arguably minimal here, whereas the discussion of the nature of discourse and its material effects on subjectivities is extensive. In her analysis, she describes how an immolation done in protest of the Tunisian government and the utterance *dégage* ('leave') created new sets of subjectivities by offering new discursive materialities. The analyst's interpretation is the main resource here. Through the discursive effects of repeating *dégage,* she argues that ideologies of protest enter into public space, thereby changing the space through discourse. Similarly, Louar's study of language troubles in France that examine Macron's rhetoric denying multiculturalism and public discourse on the irrelevance of the #metoo movement is focused on the theoretical arguments and illustrations of concepts. In both chapters, the analysis of the meanings of these discourses are presented without recourse to perspectives apart from the authors'. This is of course a normative style of research for this genre of scholarship on discourse and ideology, but it is notable for its distinction with the rest of the contributions in the book.

In other cases, methods are briefly explained with the goal of getting to the question of the nature of discourse and ideology more directly. This is the case with Verschueren, who draws attention to the importance of examining the rhetorical nature of discourses of the "new normal" in newspapers in Belgium as sites where ideologies about immigration, integration, and secularism are produced and formed into an "anti-multiculturalism" discourse. Similarly, Lázaro Gutiérrez and Tejero González briefly describe a large corpus of texts produced through healthcare worker training, but few details are provided regarding the content analysis that is mentioned before illustrating key aspects of ideologies and attitudes towards serving migrants in the healthcare context.

Other chapters point to methods that are used in the service of examining discourse and ideology which indicate a more empirical bent, including interactional sociolinguistics (Lutman-White and Angouri), ethnography (Mäntynen and Kalliokoski; Vernet), survey methods (Peterson) and corpus linguistics (Diaz and Hall). This shows that discourse and ideology can benefit from methods that explore the contextualized nature of discourse with reference to its "brought about" and "brought along" contexts (Giddens 1976), for they acknowledge that the context and form in which discourses are articulated are central to understanding their ideological expression. These chapters all stand in great contrast with the methods of the French discourse chapters that come early in the book as they point to an interest in researching discourse and ideology in a systematic, grounded manner. This raises the question of whether there is a shared set of epistemological approaches to the study of discourse, or even if current approaches to discourse studies are so methodologically disparate that they might merit different disciplinary identities, rather than different schools of thought or sub-disciplinary traditions.

While most of the authors do not discuss their methodology in detail, Miller's chapter is a standout as a reflexive enterprise that considers how scholars' data collection in the form of interview questions asked and analytical tools tend to be at odds with their epistemological alignments with the non-essentialist nature of discourse and ideology. Her chapter acknowledges the mismatch between approaching data with an intent to code and categorize while foregrounding the performative and fluid nature of discursive practices as they relate to identity. She takes a critical eye to her own research, noting how she focused on certain features of participants in her studies in order to answer research questions that she crafted with attention to the participants' linguistic and newcomer status. Miller's chapter is a reminder about the importance of reflexivity in discourse research. Research is itself part of the discursive process, whereby researchers engage in the disciplining of discourse and do so from their (relatively) powerful positions in society as intellectuals with access to certain forms of cultural capital.

3 The nature of discourse and ideology

So, what is the nature of discourse and ideology, as identified in this volume? Most contributors identify a strongly intertwined relationship between the two concepts. Collectively, the authors identify discourse as the use of language as articulated in social practices, whereas ideology refers to beliefs, mental models, and sense-making practices that are shared by a group or society. Van Dijk's chapter is important here, as it reiterates his view of discourse as a vehicle for ideology, a meaning that is expressed similarly in most chapters. For him, mental models are at the interface of societal beliefs and individuals' discourse practices, and these mental models are mediated by context, such as the professional or personal identities of the speakers and their relations with others. In this way, Lutman-White and Angouri's chapter shows how a certain moral order about child welfare is part of the shared social cognition of social workers as they articulate their sense-making in focus groups and interviews. While a discourse of family preservation is a possible mental model that could be a dominant discourse in their ideological positioning, the social workers' discourse is marked by more attention to the risks that children are exposed to, and hence, a discourse of child protection emerges as the dominant narrative that they share, and as a rationale for the institutional practice of separating children from their parents. This narrative is simultaneously shaped by the social workers' institutional realities, which the authors argue have made it more likely for low-income parents to struggle to meet their children's needs without support due to austerity cuts.

Verschueren's chapter draws our attention to the ways in which discourses that are aligned with arguably regressive ideologies emerge in places we might least expect, such as progressive or "left" media houses. His discussion of an anti-discourse in Belgium toward multiculturalism shows how ideologies about immigration and societal diversity have been rearticulated in political discourse by "mainstream" national leaders in Europe and in texts such as newspaper editorials. He analyzes an editorial in a liberal newspaper that expounds upon the development of Arabic schools in Brussels, pointing out that they will offer an alternative site for learning language to Koranic schools, which are portrayed as problematic due to their association with orthodoxy and the constraints they put on girls in terms of wearing headscarves. Through the editorial, a common sense is presented in which certain forms of language maintenance are recommended as long as they are highly secular. The text produces an anti-discourse toward religious practices and a utopic discourse toward secular societies, which are imagined to be populated by groups who have superficial ethnolinguistic differences and a shared common core of the same values. In analyzing this text, Verschueren shows us how discourses about multiculturalism which strive to be frank and supportive of some aspects of diversity are in fact part of the spread of increasingly exclusionary ideologies about diversity.

Finally, Mäntynen and Kalliokoski's chapter on the ideological debates in translation offers some vivid examples of how mental models are not always shared, and how that gap is made visible in discourse. They describe an editor's recommendation for the word *tavara* ('goods') in Finnish as the better choice for translating English *commodity* instead of a translator's choice, a compound of *hyödyke* and *tuotantotekijä* ('production' + 'factor'). According to the editor, Finnish academic convention informs this choice due to Marxist associations with this word and the definition of *commodity* as 'tavara' in Marxist thinking. This indexicality was not as relevant from the translator's point of view, however. This shows the ties between discourse and ideology in the act of translating, and reveals the gaps in mental models and also the natural histories of discourse for certain discourse-ideological links.

3.1 Discourse as a site for social change?

A question that this book raises is whether and to what degree this examination of discourse and ideology can be tied to applied or more public take-up of these discussions. As a scholar with an interest in applied linguistics and citizen sociolinguistics (e.g., Svendsen 2018), I often wonder how the analysis of discourse might be put to use in different ways, either in more public circulation, as in the case of sharing some of these insights with wider audiences through popular press houses, or in the case of participatory research involving institutions and stakeholders who are enmeshed in discourses and ideologies and who might benefit from a reflective approach to this. It is of course already a lot of work to analyze discourse and its relationship to ideology, and scholars have long made important contributions through describing how social and ideological shifts have taken place in and through discourse (e.g., Fairclough, Cortese, and Ardizzone 2007). Nonetheless, after we have a clear understanding of how discourse and ideology are working together, I find it very important to ask: What real-world purposes can this analysis serve?

The chapters here that explore institutional practices in particular raise the question of what studies of discourse and ideology might be helpful for and who might benefit. Lázaro Gutiérrez and Tejero González offer a clear context in which the analysis of ideologies towards migrants could lead to useful knowledge about how the Spanish healthcare system is doing in terms of serving the public. For them, discourse is a site not only for identifying ideologies but also potentially for social change. While employee training might be a challenging context in which to radically reshape prejudicial ideologies and dispositions toward migrant patients, their findings invite consideration of what other sites might be well suited for discussions of these discourses. It seems likely that nursing and medical education would be likely suspects, in addition to workplace training for healthcare administrators. One can imagine a critical pedagogy of sorts in which the discourses from the online forums are used to invite discussion about the positioning of migrants in Spanish society and to develop a metadiscursive literacy about the discourses healthcare workers encounter in these contexts.

Lutman-White and Angouri's study on discourses of social workers offers another study with implications for professional practices and state policies regarding child protection and social work. Their analysis of discourses that favor child protection, and which seem to offer rationales for removing children from their families, reveal the power of the state institutions' increasingly austere levels of support for impoverished families. The result is that social workers' ways of talking about their work articulates a common sense in alignment with these forms of welfare. The question that arises here is, how might this be applied or put to use? Would the practice of social work involving children be informed for the better through some kind of metadiscursive awareness of these discourses/ideologies? Could metadiscourse about social work be a site for any level of professional transformation and change, even in a highly neoliberal state?

Another contribution that encourages consideration of the more applied role of discourse is Vernet's study on language ideologies in Acadia, which invites reflection on the apparent "linguistic schizophrenia" (Kachru 1977) in a university context where Acadian and Chiac are legitimized yet disallowed in the French-language institutional spaces of higher education, since mainstream/standardized French is preferred. It is possible to imagine events inviting public discussion of these circumstances among academics and the community alike to see what a metadiscourse about this might lead to. While the prescribed linguistic norms may persist, it would be interesting to see how explicitly addressing these practices might open up spaces for further legitimating "vernacular" languages. The practice of requiring students from this region to take two French courses as part of their studies is reminiscent of a prior language policy at my workplace, the University of Hawaiʻi at Mānoa, where many local students speak Pidgin (Hawaiʻi Creole). These students were required to take Speech courses from the 1930s through the 1970s in order to "correct" their Pidgin and replace it with English; if students failed to eradicate Pidgin from their spoken language, they were dismissed from the university (Tamura 1996). This policy ended when the ideologies of language rights and civil rights began circulating in Hawaiʻi, alongside the Hawaiian Renaissance, a movement that strived to revitalize the Hawaiian language and cultural practices such as hula that were once banned by missionaries. Performative and discursive practices tied to ethnic identity, local pride, and sovereignty helped to displace deficit discourses tied to Pidgin speakers and to Pidgin, which in turn led to institutional change: the Speech courses were no longer a gatekeeping device for higher education. I am curious if events that encourage more honest and open discussion of language ideologies in Acadia might speed up the process of linguistic awareness and even lead to institutional change.

Other contexts in this edited volume have more applied implications for professional practices, particularly in professional work in language and linguistics. Miller's chapter argues for scholars to make reflexivity an intrinsic part of their work in applied linguistics as they go about selecting and analyzing discourse data. In my view, this is especially important in the acts of socializing students into the field in our classrooms, at conferences, and in our textbooks. In addition, Mäntynen and Kalliokoski's chapter draws attention to the ideological complexity underlying the difficult work of translation. Again, metadiscursive dialogues about this complexity are necessary, not only in the professional work of translation, but in all language-related work. In my own work on multilingual practices, for example, I have often struggled to effectively gloss transcripts to convey all of the meanings that are embedded. My choices for translation are always partial, and the limitations of publishing conventions often make detailed explanations about these choices difficult to manage. My graduate students also regularly experience this challenge when translating from languages like Korean, Japanese, and Mandarin into English, but we do not have any translation scholars to get guidance from for such projects on a regular basis. Accessible guidance on translation in discourse-related work that shows how to manage the ideological-discursive relationship would surely be very welcome among a wide audience of language scholars (cf. Blommaert 2006).

4 Situating discourse and ideology on a broader scale

In closing, I return to the issue of location and the relevance of considering how situated the knowledge on discourse and ideology has been for research and thinking in sociolinguistics, discourse analysis, applied linguistics, critical discourse studies, and other language-related fields. Across the chapters, it is striking, though not surprising, that nearly all of the scholars are located in resource-rich locations in North America or Europe, and that almost all of the contexts of study focus on populations and language practices in these same contexts. Guellouz's paper on discourse and performativity in Tunisia is the only exception here. In most scholarship around the world, of course, this over-representation of the global north is normative, as the majority of academic publications are produced by scholars in these contexts, in English. Nonetheless, this raises the question of reflexivity with regard to the geographic locations of scholars and their exposure to different lines of intellectual discourses, and the possibilities of additional or other approaches to the theorization and study of ideology and discourse. In other words, what is this volume missing in terms of more geographically diverse approaches to discourse and ideology? This is a promising direction for future work, not only to deepen academic discussions of these weighty topics through diversity, but also to gauge how situated and constrained our frameworks for knowing might be.

In Hawaiʻi, ideology and discourse from a Native Hawaiian perspective, for example, would necessarily engage with concepts, authors, and intellectual lineages that have very little crossover with the references and constructs in this volume. Instead, concepts such as moʻokūʻauhau ('genealogy') and moʻolelo ('history/story') would likely be used to probe into Hawaiian worldviews, histories, and discursive struggles, and writings by seminal Hawaiian scholars such as David Malo (Malo 1903) and Native Hawaiian methodologies (Oliveira and Wright 2015) would frame the scholarship. In other contexts, insights into discourse and ideology as framed by Southern theory (Connell 2020; Santos 2014) invite us to acknowledge the limitations of current knowledge and to expand the canon by looking at discourse and ideology from different vantage points. It challenges the universalist relevance of particular social theories by critiquing the dominance of western thought in intellectual debates and scholarship. Southern theory pluralizes epistemological approaches by inviting more ways of knowing into intellectual spaces from previously underrepresented regions and intellectuals. The study of discourse and ideology can certainly be enriched – and ultimately, perhaps, even existentially challenged – by more ways of knowing from different corners of the world.

References

Bakhtin, Mikhail M. 1981. *The dialogic imagination*. Michael Holquist (ed.), Carol Emerson & Michael Holquist (transl.). Austin: University of Texas Press.

Bakhtin, Mikhail M. 1984. *Rabelais and his world*. Hélène Iswolsky (transl.). Bloomington: Indiana University Press.

Blommaert, Jan. 2006. How legitimate is my voice? A rejoinder. *Target* 18 (1). 63–76.

Clancy, Kathryn B. & Jenny L. Davis. 2019. Soylent is people, and WEIRD is white: Biological anthropology, whiteness, and the limits of the WEIRD. *Annual Review of Anthropology* 48 (1). 169–186.

Connell, Raewyn. 2020. *Southern theory: The global dynamics of knowledge in social science*. London & New York: Routledge.

Fairclough, Norman, Giuseppina Cortese & Patrizia Ardizzone (eds.). 2007. *Discourse and contemporary social change*. Berlin: Peter Lang.

Gee, James P. 2004. *An introduction to discourse analysis: Theory and method*. London & New York: Routledge.

Giddens, Anthony. 1976. *New rules of sociological method*. London: Hutchinson.

Henrich, Joseph, Steven J. Heine & Ara Norenzayan. 2010. Most people are not WEIRD. *Nature* 466 (7302). 29–29.

Jones, Rodney. 2012. *Discourse analysis*. London & New York: Routledge.

Kachru, Braj B. 1977. Linguistic schizophrenia and language census: A note on the Indian situation. *Linguistics* 186. 17–32.

Killough, Ashley. 2021. Texas school administrator told teachers to include Holocaust books with 'opposing' views when explaining new state law. https://www.cnn.com/2021/10/15/us/texas-schools-books-holocaust-state-law/index.html (accessed 15 October 2021).

Malo, David. 1903. *Hawaiian antiquities (Moʻolelo Hawaiʻi)*, Vol. 2. Honolulu: Hawaiian Gazette Company.

Oliveria, Katrina-Ann R. K. N. & Erin K. Wright (eds.). 2015. *Kanaka ʻŌiwi methodologies: Moʻolelo and metaphor*. Honolulu: University of Hawaiʻi Press.

Paltridge, Brian. 2012. *Discourse analysis: An introduction*. London: Bloomsbury Publishing.

Santos, Boaventura de Sousa. 2014. *Epistemologies of the South: Justice against epistemicide*. London & New York: Routledge.

Svendsen, Bente A. 2018. The dynamics of citizen sociolinguistics. *Journal of Sociolinguistics*, 22 (2). 137–160.

Tamura, Eileen H. 1996. Power, status, and Hawaiʻi Creole English: An example of linguistic intolerance in American history. *Pacific Historical Review* 65 (3). 431–454.

Index

Adorno, Theodor 4
agency 3, 16, 25, 58, 61, 71–72, 75, 82–83, 118, 126, 130–131, 152, 154, 193, 262, 268
Agha, Asif 180, 183, 194
Althusser, Louis 3, 5–7, 21, 25, 27–29, 33–35, 37, 58, 69–71, 82
analytical philosophy 5, 8, 28
Angermuller, Johannes 30, 33, 53, 103, 119
anthropology 5, 9, 138
applied linguistics 2, 8, 11, 13, 15, 119, 121, 123, 129, 273, 280, 282, 283
articulation 7, 72, 77, 81
assemblage 13, 67, 72, 130–132
attitudes 12–14, 34, 51, 56, 61, 89, 90, 98, 109, 137, 141–146, 148, 151, 153–154, 168, 188, 214, 223, 224–225, 227, 231–232, 241–242, 250, 258–259, 278
Austin, John L. 77, 81–82, 226

Bachelard, Gaston 3, 25, 92, 95
Baker, Mona 225, 235
Bakhtin, Mikhail 5, 28–29, 125, 128, 175, 182–183, 194–195, 274–275
Balibar, Étienne 25, 32
Barthes, Roland 7, 28–29
Bauman, Richard 74, 79–80, 138, 183–184, 188, 196
beliefs 3, 9–10, 12–14, 23–24, 38, 45, 55, 57–58, 61, 69, 91, 94, 97, 108, 112, 118, 140–141, 143–144, 146, 158, 164, 173, 180, 201, 223–225, 227–229, 237–238, 242, 250, 256, 259, 263, 269, 274, 279
Benveniste, Émile 29–30
bilingualism 47, 50, 56, 159, 160, 162, 164, 174, 230
biopolitics 75–76
biopower 36
Blommaert, Jan 9–10, 37, 53, 79, 137, 163, 164, 180, 188, 191, 194, 195–197, 274, 282
Bourdieu, Pierre 16, 37, 55, 58, 81, 82, 123, 274
Briggs, Charles 79–80, 122–123, 125–129, 183–184, 188, 196

Bucholtz, Mary 129, 207
Butler, Judith 71, 81, 125

Canagarajah, Suresh 129–130
children 14, 88, 109–112, 114, 166, 168, 170, 201–206, 208–218, 234, 236, 238, 279, 281
circulation 12, 53, 73, 82, 98–99, 123, 203, 206, 225, 275, 280
code-switching 159–160, 163–164, 168–170, 174, 188
cognition 13, 87, 90–92, 94, 96, 137–142, 144–145, 153, 224, 227, 231, 250, 267, 279
cognitive sciences 11, 13, 137–140, 142, 147
community 60, 74, 77, 90, 109, 110, 113, 119, 140, 158–159, 161, 163–165, 168, 179–180, 182–183, 191–195, 197–198, 227, 229, 248, 255, 275, 282
connotation 23–24, 37, 52, 56, 195, 249
conscience 3, 23, 99
consciousness 3, 7, 23–25, 67
context 2, 8–9, 11–12, 14–15, 21–22, 24, 32, 37, 45, 48, 53, 56–57, 73–77, 79–83, 92–93, 104, 108, 112, 114, 118–119, 128, 138–140, 142–145, 147, 149, 153, 158–160, 163, 165, 167–168, 180, 182–185, 188, 191–192, 194–195, 197, 201–203, 206–207, 215, 218–219, 224, 227–229, 231, 247–249, 252–255, 257–261, 273–274, 276, 277–279, 281,–283
contextualization cues 9, 79
conversation analysis 9, 119, 124, 127, 138–139, 203, 206, 274–275
critical discourse studies 1–3, 8, 10–11, 16, 35, 255, 257, 263, 266, 268, 283
critical linguistics 3, 8
critical sociolinguistics 10
critical theory 4, 8, 53
critique 1–4, 6–12, 16, 21–24, 35, 45, 53, 69, 73, 88, 91, 97, 99, 121, 124, 138, 146, 247, 257, 266, 274, 276, 279, 281, 283
cultural studies 3, 5–8, 37

De Saussure, Ferdinand 4–5, 7, 26
Deleuze, Gilles 36, 72, 83, 130
Derrida, Jacques 7, 28, 36, 81, 122
Destutt de Tracy, Antoine 22–24, 27
diglossia 60, 62
discrimination 2, 90, 93–94, 105–107, 154, 216, 227, 233–234
discursive formation 6, 31, 33–36, 38, 54
distortion 3, 8, 23–24, 26, 58
diversity 12, 45–46, 48–57, 59–61, 90, 92, 95, 99, 103, 105–106, 108, 115, 144, 150, 223, 226, 228, 231, 233, 236–237, 261, 277, 280, 283
domination 3, 7, 32, 34, 45–46, 48, 53, 57–58, 61, 69–71, 75, 81–82, 89, 104, 139, 145, 148, 153, 261

Eagleton, Terry 3, 23–24, 58, 68–69
Eckert, Penelope 10, 160
emancipation 4, 12, 16, 67, 69–72, 74–75, 77, 80–83, 88, 96, 98
emotions 90, 118, 143, 165, 196, 231
empowerment 16, 59, 97, 146
Engels, Friedrich 3, 24–26, 57, 58, 67
Enlightenment 4, 22, 93, 96
enregisterment 9
entextualization 79–80, 126, 128–129
episteme 87, 91, 99
epistemological break 3, 25, 28, 70
epistemology 1–3, 5, 12, 15–16, 25, 28, 38, 70, 87, 91–92, 94, 96, 98, 119–124, 130–131, 273, 278–279, 283
essentialization 46, 50–51, 60, 90, 98, 117, 119, 121, 125–126, 279
ethnicity 16, 93, 106–107, 143, 154, 205, 227–229, 237, 260–261, 282
ethnography 9, 45, 48, 119, 138, 148, 179, 181, 183, 184–185, 274, 278

Fairclough, Norman 8, 25, 53, 139, 158, 162, 225, 250, 268, 281
falsity 3, 23, 25, 57, 58, 111–112
Fanon, Frantz 94
feminism 1, 88, 119, 122, 141, 146–147
formalism 4, 5, 27, 30, 138

Foucault, Michel 3–8, 11, 21–22, 28, 30–38, 54–56, 61, 76, 87–88, 119, 124, 225, 250, 274
Freud, Sigmund 3, 25
functionalism 2–5, 9–10, 26–28

Gadet, Françoise 5, 28, 30
Gal, Susan 9, 27, 46, 180, 188
Gee, James P. 10, 117–118, 137, 180, 202–203, 250, 268, 275
gender 12, 16, 52, 71, 73, 87–92, 95–98, 107, 110, 113–114, 126, 148, 205–206, 228, 230, 232, 260, 273, 276
genealogy 15, 273, 283
governmentality 6, 36
Gramsci, Antonio 6–8, 24–25, 32
Guattari, Félix 36, 72, 83, 130
Gumperz, John J. 9–10, 184, 203, 274

habitus 16, 274
Hall, Stuart 3, 6–7, 25, 82, 87
Harris, Zellig 5, 27, 29, 33
Hart, Christopher 139, 146
hegemony 6, 24, 87, 94, 99, 248
Heller, Monica 10, 53–54, 59
historical body 16
Horkheimer, Max 4
Hymes, Dell 4, 26, 184

iconicity 123, 126–127, 188
ideas 5, 7–9, 21–25, 29–30, 32, 34, 57, 69, 99, 104, 115, 118, 131, 141, 159, 180, 182, 184, 194, 225–226, 255
identity 7, 9–10, 15–16, 25, 46, 47, 52, 56, 60–61, 90, 91, 93–94, 99, 107–108, 115, 118–119, 123–124, 137, 139, 145, 147, 153, 160, 169, 183, 206, 208, 250, 255, 261, 266–267, 273, 276, 278–279, 282
ideological discourse 13, 83, 93, 137, 139, 145–148, 153, 259
indexicality 14, 37, 74, 127, 163, 180, 187, 188, 208–209, 217, 276
ingroup 13, 143, 148, 149, 151, 153–154, 261–262, 268
interactional sociolinguistics 14, 201, 203–204, 206–209, 211, 217–219, 275, 278

interdiscursivity 6, 32, 35, 38, 82
interpellation 3, 12, 25, 34, 58, 69, 71, 81, 82–83
intertextuality 5–6, 29, 53, 182–183, 194–196, 262
Irvine, Judith 9, 46, 180, 188, 191

Jakobson, Roman 9, 28
Johnstone, Barbara 158

Kristeva, Julia 28–29
Kroskrity, Paul V. 10, 27, 180

Lacan, Jacques 5, 7, 27–29, 33, 35, 36, 37, 70, 119
Laclau, Ernesto 7–8
language contact 2, 11, 50, 56, 158–159, 161, 164, 166, 173
language ideology 9, 13–14, 27, 61, 103, 105, 109, 112, 158, 163–164, 172–174, 179–183, 185–188, 190–192, 194, 196–197, 274, 276–277, 281–282
language policy 89, 91, 98, 186, 188, 197, 248, 282
Lévi-Strauss, Claude 28–29, 36
linguistic anthropology 1, 3, 9, 90, 138, 158, 180

Maingueneau, Dominique 5, 6, 22, 27–28, 33, 36, 119
majority 13, 46–47, 105, 165, 173, 261, 283
Mannheim, Karl 3, 26, 145
Marxism 3, 5–6, 8, 24, 26–27, 30, 32–35, 37–38, 57–58, 69, 82, 107, 180, 193–194, 249, 256, 280
Marx, Karl 3, 23–26, 32, 35–36, 57, 58, 67, 69, 194, 195
materiality 6–7, 24–25, 32, 34–36, 54, 57–58, 61, 68, 71, 121, 123–124, 126, 128–130, 164, 168, 250, 265, 267–268, 277
materialization 24, 119, 126, 129, 256
meaning 3–4, 10, 13, 14, 23–24, 26–27, 31, 33, 35, 37, 47, 50, 54, 58, 60, 69–70, 72, 103–104, 108, 114, 118, 121–124, 128, 130–131, 138, 147, 149–150, 152, 158, 160, 162, 165, 168, 170, 172, 174, 180–182, 184, 188, 194–195, 203, 206–207, 213, 225, 228, 231, 239–240, 247–248, 252–254, 256, 258, 265, 267, 269, 277–279, 282
media 2, 25, 47–48, 54, 58, 60, 91, 93, 96, 98–99, 104, 115, 138, 140, 142–144, 149–150, 154, 161, 169, 189, 225, 233, 257, 261, 266, 279
mental models 13, 137, 142–146, 153, 154, 227, 279, 280
migration 11–14, 104, 105, 108, 109, 111, 124–126, 140–143, 150, 152–153, 172, 206, 223, 225–236, 238–242, 276–278, 280, 281
minority 12, 45–48, 50, 54, 57, 59, 105, 114, 205, 227, 242, 276
misogyny 16, 97
Mouffe, Chantal 7–8
multilingualism 2, 11, 108, 159, 163, 224, 273–275, 282
myth 28–29, 91, 98, 121, 232

narrative 91–93, 98, 119, 122–123, 148, 203, 225, 275, 279
nationalism 2, 11–12, 87, 91, 94–95, 97, 98–99, 105, 107, 115, 141–142, 152, 161, 172, 175, 187, 189, 206, 260, 276, 280
normativity 13, 31, 47, 48–49, 51–52, 56, 59–60, 87, 97–98, 105, 108, 113, 118, 120, 125, 131–132, 140–141, 150, 163, 168, 173–175, 181–183, 185, 187, 189–192, 194, 196–197, 201, 226, 274, 278, 282–283

objecthood 6, 29, 31–32, 54, 71, 123, 129–131, 250
objectivity 8, 16, 32, 35, 79, 119, 121, 141
ontology 2, 10, 119, 122, 130, 273
outgroup 13, 143, 148–150, 153
overdetermination 3, 6, 25

Pêcheux, Michel 5, 7, 21–22, 33–35, 37, 53, 58
Pennycook, Alastair 119, 131
performance 12, 67–70, 72–76, 79–80, 83, 90, 159, 170, 174, 219, 226, 259, 277

performativity 12, 53, 59, 61, 67–69, 72, 74–77, 80–83, 119, 125, 160, 277, 279, 282, 283
phenomenology 8, 36, 71
philology 5, 33
politeness 157, 160, 162, 165, 168, 203, 236, 262
politics 1–3, 7–12, 21–24, 33–34, 36, 47, 48, 58, 67–68, 70–72, 74–77, 79–80, 83, 87, 89–91, 93–99, 104–108, 115, 119, 129, 131, 137–140, 145, 149–150, 154, 180, 189, 196–197, 203, 205–206, 210–211, 223, 226, 236, 248, 257, 258, 259, 260, 261–262, 266, 268, 274, 280
poststructuralism 36, 118, 119, 274
power 3–8, 10–12, 16, 32, 36, 46–48, 53, 57–58, 60–61, 68, 70–71, 76, 79–83, 88, 96–97, 104–105, 115, 128–129, 139, 146, 153–154, 180, 182, 189, 195, 203, 206, 225, 227, 250, 256–257, 259, 262, 265–266, 269, 274, 276–277, 281
pragmatics 5–6, 8, 10–11, 24, 77, 79, 103, 111, 138, 144, 157–165, 167–168, 174, 276
psychoanalysis 5, 27, 29, 33–34, 35, 69, 70
psychology 123, 137–140, 142, 144, 148, 204, 234

race 12, 16, 71, 73, 89, 91, 93–95, 99, 123, 126, 227, 235, 257, 260–263, 266, 273, 276
racism 1, 14, 16, 92, 104–105, 107, 139, 141–147, 149, 153, 204, 206, 223–228, 242, 255, 257, 260–263, 266, 275
Rancière, Jacques 95, 99
reality 3–4, 8, 17, 23–26, 57, 60, 70, 76, 87, 92, 97–98, 106, 115, 119, 122–123, 127, 130, 163, 164, 171, 202, 218, 225, 247–248, 250, 262, 265, 273, 281
religion 1, 25, 59, 74, 93–95, 107, 109–114, 149, 223, 227, 231, 236, 248, 258, 262, 280
representation 6–7, 9, 14, 31, 34, 36–38, 56, 57, 69, 72, 76, 79, 87, 89, 121, 123–124, 126, 128–131, 138, 140–145, 148, 150, 153, 154, 163, 188, 193, 223, 224, 225, 227, 250, 273, 283
rhetoric 8, 96, 98, 111, 118, 138, 148, 151, 196, 197, 210, 254, 255, 268, 276, 278

Santos, Boaventura de Sousa 283
Schiffrin, Deborah 5, 27, 137–138, 250, 268
Scollon, Ron 16, 250
Silverstein, Michael 9, 68, 79, 180, 183, 188
social class 7–8, 16, 23–24, 34, 71, 73, 75, 81–83, 87, 158, 173–174, 195, 196, 227
social constructionism 119, 202
social psychology 13, 137–139, 142, 148
social structures 1, 12, 25, 45, 53, 58, 61, 180, 258–259, 269
social work 11, 14, 201–203, 206, 207, 208, 211, 213, 215–217, 219, 276, 281
sociolinguistics 1–3, 8–11, 45, 48, 59–60, 68, 158, 180–181, 184, 219, 273–275, 278, 280, 283
sociology 1, 4–5, 13, 24, 32, 57–58, 126, 137–139, 226, 274
Spivak, Gayatri 75
structuralism 4–5, 8, 26–30, 33, 34, 69–70, 82, 138, 274
subjecthood 3, 6, 12, 25, 29–31, 33–34, 36, 67–72, 74–76, 81–83, 122, 125, 128, 131
subjectivity 30, 34, 68–69, 71, 74–75, 81, 83, 99, 137–138, 142–143, 153, 186, 189, 193, 196, 274, 276, 277, 278
superdiversity 11
systemic-functional grammar 5, 8

théorie de l'énonciation 5, 30–33, 38, 54–56, 59, 61
Thompson, John B. 3, 58, 68–70, 104
translation 11, 14, 37–38, 73, 121–122, 127, 179, 181–198, 223–225, 228, 230–232, 239–242, 276, 280, 282

utopia 3–4, 13, 103, 106–108, 112, 145, 280

Van Dijk, Teun A. 8–9, 13, 17, 137, 139–140, 142, 144–146, 149, 152, 206, 223–225, 227, 235, 242, 249–250, 267–268, 279

variation 50, 56–57, 161, 164, 169, 175, 191, 195, 256
Verschueren, Jef 10, 12, 111, 118, 276, 278–280
voice 29, 37, 68, 78, 80, 99, 115, 124, 129, 131, 152, 154, 162, 167, 229, 235, 242
Vološinov, Valentin N. 24, 29, 32, 250

Wodak, Ruth 1, 8–9, 33, 53, 119, 149, 206, 250

Woolard, Kathryn A. 3, 9, 27, 58, 60, 158, 181, 250
worldview 3, 9, 23, 58, 250

xenophobia 14, 16, 107, 223, 228, 233, 236, 242

Žižek, Slavoj 91

www.ingramcontent.com/pod-product-compliance
Lightning Source LLC
Chambersburg PA
CBHW071736150426
43191CB00010B/1599